The Political Ecc

The Political Economy of Racism

The Persistence of Anti-Blackness in the United States

Michelle Holder and
Jeannette Wicks-Lim

polity

Copyright © Michelle Holder and Jeannette Wicks-Lim 2026

The right of Michelle Holder and Jeannette Wicks-Lim to be identified as Authors of this Work has been asserted in accordance with the UK Copyright, Designs and Patents Act 1988.

First published in 2026 by Polity Press Ltd.

Polity Press Ltd.
65 Bridge Street
Cambridge CB2 1UR, UK

Polity Press Ltd.
111 River Street
Hoboken, NJ 07030, USA

All rights reserved. Except for the quotation of short passages for the purpose of criticism and review, no part of this publication may be reproduced, stored in a retrieval system, or transmitted, in any form or by any means, electronic, mechanical, photocopying, recording, or otherwise, without the prior permission of the publisher.

ISBN-13: 978-1-5095-4708-1
ISBN-13: 978-1-5095-4709-8 (pb)

A catalogue record for this book is available from the British Library.

Library of Congress Control Number: 2025936700

Typeset in 10.5 on 12 pt Times New Roman
by Fakenham Prepress Solutions, Fakenham, Norfolk NR21 8NL
Printed and bound in Great Britain by Ashford Colour Ltd

The publisher has used its best endeavors to ensure that the URLs for external websites referred to in this book are correct and active at the time of going to press. However, the publisher has no responsibility for the websites and can make no guarantee that a site will remain live or that the content is or will remain appropriate.

Every effort has been made to trace all copyright holders, but if any have been overlooked the publisher will be pleased to include any necessary credits in any subsequent reprint or edition.

For further information on Polity, visit our website:
politybooks.com

To Rhonda Williams and William Spriggs, two brilliant and fearless economists who wrote about, spoke about, and actively resisted anti-Blackness. Both left the world better than they found it. Their immense contributions to the economics profession will reverberate throughout, and stand the test of, time. We are both extremely grateful for, and to, them.

Jeannette and Michelle

In loving memory of my father, whose care and support made my journey to writing this book possible.

Jeannette

I dedicate this book to my mother Daphne and my daughters Dream and Damaris – I love you all, infinitely.

Michelle

Contents

Figures	viii
Tables	x
Acknowledgments	xi

Part I How We Use Stratification Economics to Analyze Anti-Blackness in the United States — 1

1	Introduction	3
2	The Construction of Race and the Origins of Racism in the United States	30
3	Afro-Latinxs and Anti-Blackness	66
4	An Intersectional Approach to Stratification Economics	79

Part II Demonstrating How Anti-Blackness Stratifies the US Economy — 111

Primer to Part II		113
5	Education: Unequal Access, Unequal Outcomes	133
6	Unemployment, Occupational Crowding, Wage Inequality, and Anti-Blackness in the Labor Market	176
7	Wealth Attainment and Anti-Blackness: The Case of Black Women	197
8	The Criminal Legal System: Hardening the Racial Divide	219
9	Conclusion	256

Notes	262
References	297
Index	320

Figures

1.1	Black unemployment rate as percentage of White unemployment rate from 1972 to 2023	24
2.1	Timeline of US history: Major laws, state-sanctioned social practices, and economic institutions of explicit racial discrimination, 1600 to present	42
2.2	Trends in racial earnings gap among men: Black median annual earnings as a percentage of White median annual earnings, 1940–2014	46
2.3	Trends in percentage of survey respondents who believe that Black Americans' "lack of motivation" explains racial inequality, 1977–2018	52
2.4	Trends in percentage of survey respondents who agree that "discrimination" explains racial inequality, 1977–2018	53
2.5	Trends in attitudes toward government intervention to address racial inequality, by race	55
2.6	Trends in Americans' attitudes toward affirmative action policies in employment, 1986–2018	56
2.7	Asian population in the United States, 1860–2020	58
3.1	Reported primary ancestry of Afro-Latinxs in the US, 2011–2015	68
3.2	Proportion of select Latinx subgroup in the US who identify as Afro-Latinx, 2011–2015	77
4.1	Adjusted average hourly wage gaps relative to White men by race and gender, 1979–2015	84
4.2	Trends in unemployment rate by gender among workers age 20 years and older, 1972–2023	86
5.1	Trends in the share of US adult education attainment by race, 1940–2020	134

5.2	Trends in the percentage of Black students at majority-White schools in Southern states, 1954–2011	159
5.3	Segregation by race and poverty, 2011–2012	162
6.1	Unemployment rates by education level, 2022	182
6.2	Black and White annual unemployment rates, US 1972–2023	185
6.3	Black–White unemployment rate gap, US 1972–2023	186
6.4	Annual labor force participation rates of Black women and White women, 1972–2023	188
6.5	Estimated median annual earnings by race and gender, 2023	190
7.1	Median wealth in the US by race, ethnicity, and gender, 2019	204
7.2	Median weekly earnings in the US by gender and educational attainment, 2022	207
7.3	Percentage of adults 25+ years of age in the US who have completed a bachelor's degree or higher, 2021	207
7.4	Homeownership rates in the US by race, ethnicity and gender, heads of households, 2019	210
7.5	Average undergraduate and graduate cumulative federal loan amounts by race and gender, 2016/2017	213
8.1	Average incarceration rates per 100,000 population by region and race, 1850 and 1870	222
8.2	Trends in average incarceration rates per 100,000 population in Southern states by race, 1850–1980	225
8.3	Trends in average incarceration rates per 100,000 population in Northern states by race, 1850–1980	226
8.4A	Trends in prison incarceration rates, 1970–2022	227
8.4B	Trends in jail incarceration rates, 1970–2022	227
8.5A	Trends in prison incarceration rates by race, 1978–2022	228
8.5B	Trends in jail incarceration rates by race, 1985–2022	229
8.6	Trends in the proportion of voting-age population with a felony conviction, 1948–2010	232
8.7	Trends in prison incarceration rates by gender, 1970–2022	235
8.8	Trends in prison incarceration rates by gender and race/ethnicity, 1990–2022	236
8.9	Trends in annual government spending on policing and incarceration (2022$), FY 1971–2007	253

Tables

4.1	Occupational distribution by gender and average annual earnings in 1940	91
4.2	Occupational distribution of women by race, 1940	91
4.3	Occupational employment shares and wages among Black and White women, 2020	94
5.1	Economic outcomes in 2019 by educational attainment level	136
5.2	Economic outcomes in 2019 by educational attainment level and race	138
5.3	Economic outcomes in 2019 by educational attainment level, race, and gender	140
5.4	Percentage of Black students in 90–100% minority schools, select years from 1968 to 2018	160
5.5	Debt and default among BA graduates, by race: 12 years after college entry, 2004 entry cohort	165
5.6	Exit poll results of affirmative action bans in California and Michigan by race	172
7.1	Average annual childcare cost by race for single parents, 2019	212

Acknowledgments

This book is going into production a few months after Donald Trump's inauguration as the 47th president of the United States. In this short time, Trump's second term has hurled the United States into a frightful and repressive era.[1] One example particularly relevant for our book is his administration's determination to expunge from educational institutions work engaged in studying and/or addressing the problem of disparities between privileged and marginalized social groups, including racial groups.[2] The president's efforts hit at both people employed in Diversity, Equity, and Inclusion (DEI) programs and what his administration pejoratively calls "woke ideology." DEI programs are the institutional policies – such as in schools, businesses, and government agencies – that proliferated in response to the Black Lives Matter movement.[3] These programs are meant to go beyond increasing the "diversity" of perspectives operating within an institution by adding two additional priorities: achieving a measure of justice, or *equity*, for marginalized social groups that have experienced a long history of inequity, as well as fostering a climate of *inclusion* as a remedy to a long history of exclusion. Under the Trump administration, the mere mention of even one of these three words as part of any federal program risks the program's excision.[4] "Woke ideology" appears to refer to any analysis or discussion of racism, in particular.

In this environment, the educational institutions that we have been anticipating would be the primary forums through which we could share our book are vulnerable to the Trump administration's censorship. Consequently, we suspect that these institutions may not be willing and/or able to offer our book in their classrooms. Indeed, just about all higher education institutions appear vulnerable to the pressure to suppress any discussion of racism on their campuses given the acquiescence to Trump administration demands by super-endowed private institutions such as Columbia University, as well as elite public institutions such as University of Michigan.[5] And the Trump administration's attack on any critical analysis of racism and DEI efforts is happening everywhere: in education,[6] employment,[7] government,[8] public health,[9] the arts,[10] scientific research[11] (including in economics[12]), and more.[13] The tentacles of influence linked to federal authority and funds that reached across the country to promote racial equity in the wake of the 1960s Civil Rights Movement are now twisting around, and squeezing out, any discussion of diversity, equity, or inclusion.

We believe that this political conjuncture makes our book even more important to publish. This is for two basic reasons. First, our book documents the truth about racism and the racial hierarchy that operates in the United States, built primarily on a foundation of anti-Blackness. Presenting the facts of this truth is our way of doing, as W. E. B. Du Bois was wont to do: to "look America squarely in the face" and say, "This country of ours, despite all its better souls have done and dreamed, is yet a shameful land."[14] Second, this book is our attempt to fulfill the marching orders of the late, great, economist Rhonda Williams. Williams' directive – shared by Nina Banks in her 2021 National Economics Association (NEA) presidential address – was that "We have to publish to leave footprints. We have to publish so that others will have something to build on." Fellow economist Patrick Mason said of Williams' charge, "for Rhonda, research and journal publications weren't a selfish/careerist activity. It was her contribution to the struggle; we are all part of a collective enterprise."[15] We are publishing this book to leave footprints, so that anyone interested in our collective enterprise to eradicate racial oppression can build on our efforts. This propels us with excitement to get this book out. We want to share our book in spite of, and because of, the likely censorship that our type of scholarship will face in the coming years.

We are grateful for our network of colleagues in the NEA which buoys, motivates, and informs our work – the above is just one example of this. Along with Patrick, Nina, and Rhonda, we want to specifically thank William Darity Jr., Samuel Myers Jr., and Rhonda Sharpe, along with Lisa Saunders and William Spriggs, both of whom we lost while writing this book. We also want to put a spotlight on how we have benefitted from the numerous –and ongoing – conversations started at the annual Freedom and Justice summer conferences that the NEA co-sponsors along with the Association for Economic Research of Indigenous Peoples and the American Society of Hispanic Economists.

Acknowledgments

We would like to thank the University of Massachusetts School for Behavior and Social Sciences and the Political Economy Research Institute (PERI) of the University of Massachusetts for the multiple ways they supported the development of this book. These supports include providing Jeannette with the time, space, and resources to work on this book, as well as funding for our research assistant, UMass Economics doctoral candidate Daniella Medina. Daniella provided us with truly outstanding research, editorial, technical, *and* moral support. They contributed to our book in both small and large ways, in particular by authoring the textboxes that appear in each of the book chapters, excepting the conclusion. We'd also like to thank the City University of New York John Jay College Office for the Advancement of Research, as well as John Podesta and the Washington Center for Equitable Growth, for research and fellowship funding for Michelle which allowed her the time and space to write portions of this book.

We want to also thank Polity editor George Owers, whose enthusiasm for our book proposal gave us great encouragement; Polity editors Ellen MacDonald, Ian Malcolm, Evie Deavall, and Leigh Mueller, who treated us with generous amounts of both patience and guidance. We thank the anonymous reviewers of our book proposal and manuscript draft, as well as our colleague and friend Patrick Mason who gave us thoughtful feedback on our draft even while he was serving as the chair of the Economics Department at the University of Massachusetts Amherst. With the support of these reviewers, we were able to improve the quality of our book.

Michelle would like to thank, first and foremost, her (late) mother Daphne, her role model and chief cheerleader. Michelle would also like to thank Jeannette for inviting her to participate in this important project, as well as for graciously accommodating Michelle's scheduling needs throughout the years this book was written. Michelle would also like to thank daughters Dream and Damaris for their inspiration and patience as mom spent many hours writing; brothers Bert and Mike; niece and nephews Imani, Miles, and Ian; sister-in-law Nilda; cousins Yvonne, Desiree, and Gordon; godson Khaya Adams; and friends Adrian Techeira, Robert Jones Jr., Agnes Callamard, Julia Landau, Tony Medina, Helen Yosef Hailu, Joan Williams, Regina Eaton, Bobo Diallo, Rose Golden, Amy Adamczyk, Darrick Hamilton, Teresa Ghilarducci, Kate Bahn, Nina Banks, Stephanie Seguino, Jessica Gordon Nembhard, Alan Aja, Daniele Tavani, Rakeen Mabud, and Livia Summers – who lovingly cared for Dream and Damaris whenever needed; colleagues Elissa Braunstein, Heidi Hartmann, Jay Hamilton, Rita Taveras, Ian Seda, Daniel Stageman, Lygia Sabbag

Fares, and Gail Garfield. Finally, Michelle thanks John Jay College, City University of New York, for being her intellectual and professional home for the last 11 years, as well as President Karol Mason, Provost Allison Pease, Associate Provost Anthony Carpi, and Interim Dean of Faculty Angela Crossman.

Jeannette would like to personally thank Michelle for joining her on this book project. Michelle's knack for open communication, generous-hearted-yet-disciplined thinking, and wealth of knowledge made the project truly rewarding. Jeannette is ever indebted to her family – her family of origin and the family she created with her partner Ali – whose love and support made it possible for her to work on this book. Her family includes, along with partner Ali, her parents, Byung H. and Choon H. Lim, big sister Mee Mee (and partner Matt) and big brother David (and partner Rebecca), son Mason, daughter Summit, and in-laws Lee and Roy. Last, but not least, Jeannette thanks her long-time colleagues at PERI and at the University of Massachusetts Economics Department for their professional support and warm camaraderie. These include – in addition to the aforementioned Patrick Mason and Lisa Saunders – Peter Arno, Michael Ash, Lee Badgett, Shouvik Chakraborty, Nicole Dunham, Gerald Epstein, Judy Fogg, Mwangi wa Gĩthĩnji, Léonce Ndikumana, Robert Pollin, and Kim Weinstein.

PART I

HOW WE USE STRATIFICATION ECONOMICS TO ANALYZE ANTI-BLACKNESS IN THE UNITED STATES

1

Introduction

1.1. The Focus of Our Book

This book's goal is to provide a contemporary examination of racism, specifically anti-Black racism, in the United States through the lens of economics. This examination, however, eschews "mainstream" economic scholarship on the causes and persistence of racism. Instead, this volume will go beyond outdated, neoclassical economic theories of discrimination. We use as our starting point the following fact: "race" is socially constructed. Note that the concept of race is typically not a topic covered in depth in mainstream economic theory. Nevertheless, our book begins with the statement that the concept of race is only loosely linked to one's phenotype and has no meaningful biological basis. As such, inequality in economic outcomes by race, we argue, must be the product of racist practices and institutions, and cannot be ascribed to any inherent deficiencies in the Black[1] community of America.

In this volume we have chosen to focus specifically on anti-Black racism. We do this because the exceptionally persistent and pervasive qualities of anti-Black racism in US society suggest it has become a normalized characteristic and central organizing force in the economy. How and why does anti-Black racism contribute to the organization of the US economy? And what impact does this have on the livelihoods of American households, families, and workers? We attempt to answer these core questions by using empirical data to provide a clear picture of how race shapes the US economy and by providing the reader with a theoretical framework that can make sense of what the data show. We will also use examples from the experiences of other marginalized groups to illustrate qualities of anti-Black racism that are distinct from discrimination faced by other demographic groups as well as qualities that are shared in common. Our goal is to provide a deep, wide-ranging understanding of how anti-Black racism operates in the US economy, in order to stimulate dialogue about effective policies and political responses aimed at its reduction. To do this we use an interdisciplinary, political economy approach that combines insights from history, social psychology, African American/Black studies, women/gender studies, and sociology with economics. This means that we use historical, political, and social contexts – not just an economic context – to examine what determinate role racism has in wages and employment, working conditions and living standards, and economic security and freedom. Our approach emphasizes the experiences and actions of Black Americans, including Black women, and how they have shaped these economic conditions.

Our interdisciplinary political economy approach uses a specific theoretical framework: *stratification economics*. A central focus of stratification economics, pioneered by economists William A. Darity Jr., Rhonda Williams, and James Stewart, is the concept of social stratification, where social stratification refers to a hierarchy of social classes within a society. Stratification economics' core organizing theory is that group inequality is the result of how social groups rationally pursue their collective self-interest. That is, group inequality is the outcome of social groups competing and/or collaborating with other social groups to attain and maintain their relative position in a social hierarchy. We will introduce the key tenets of this approach. Later in the book, we will provide a primer that dives deeper into the features of stratification economics and explain how we use the approach to analyze racial inequality in the areas of education, the labor market, wealth, and the criminal legal system.

1.2. Stratification Economics as Our Main Theoretical Framework

Three important tenets from stratification economics will be particularly relevant for this volume. First, privileged groups have a material interest in maintaining sexism and racism – as well as other forms of oppression – because benefits accrue to advantaged groups as a whole. This is true even though a benefit to the privileged group as a whole does not always confer benefits to all individual members of said group evenly or at all times. Second, discrimination can, and does, persist in market-based economies, and only policy intervention, heavily influenced by collective action, can alter that in a sustainable way. At the same time, policy intervention can be difficult to accomplish if the privileged group dominates the political system. Third, American policies and practices have greatly benefited the level of intergenerational wealth transfers among White American families, generation after generation, while simultaneously disadvantaging Black American families over centuries. A stratification economist would also hold the following assumptions: a materially successful member of a subaltern group will not be shielded from discrimination, and within all demographic groups there are members who exhibit dysfunctional behavior, but it should not be assumed that such behavior can be ascribed to all members of the group.

Stratification economics combines: (1) sociology's focus on group identification and identity formation; (2) economics' assumptions that people behave rationally and according to their self-interest; and (3) social psychology's understanding of social beliefs, particularly about group identities. This approach seeks to explain how group identities influence the prevailing economic structures and outcomes, and how the economic system contributes to the production, and persistence, of group identity (Darity Jr., Hamilton, and Stewart, 2015).

Stratification economics contrasts sharply with the more conventional approach that is standard in American academia: neoclassical economics. Neoclassical economics focuses on how individuals operate in an economy to achieve individual – as opposed to collective – goals. In addition, neoclassical economics theorizes that the pressure of competitive markets requires employers to base their decision-making only on factors relevant to their firms' productivity. If employers do otherwise, the competitive markets will force them out of business. On this foundation, the neoclassical approach understands race-based economic inequality in the US as evidence of either: (1) a temporary disruption in markets which prevents them from operating as they should – such as an absence of adequate information; or (2) a reflection of racial inequality in non-market areas that influence individuals' productive capacities, such as culture or education.

This book will demonstrate that, within the economics discipline, stratification economics successfully describes and explains the US experience with regard to racial economic inequality. In particular, each of our chapters will show that: (1) racial economic inequality has persisted in the US economy over its more than four centuries of history; and (2) the intransigence of anti-Black racism can be explained by racist practices pursued by the dominant racial group – Whites – to attain and maintain their relative position in the social hierarchy, in both market and non-market areas.

A tenet of stratification economic theory which distinguishes it from other economic theories used to explain how groups become marginalized can be found in its proposed solution: this framework indicates the solution to eradicating individual and institutional practices that produce discriminatory outcomes is policy intervention. The significance of this cannot be understated. For example, *human capital theory*'s (HCT) explanation for differential outcomes based on race is that a group experiencing lower wages and higher unemployment, compared to another group with higher wages and lower unemployment, must on average possess lower human capital endowments – educational attainment, experience, training, etc. The solution according to HCT would be for the group experiencing less favorable outcomes to increase its average human capital endowments. However, as will be seen in chapter 6 on "Unemployment, Occupational Crowding, Wage Inequality, and Anti-Blackness in the Labor Market," this approach is insufficient in eliminating racially disparate outcomes in the American workforce. Additionally, throughout US history, White Americans have attempted to hoard educational resources necessary for human capital development in order to maintain an advantage in accessing higher wages and adequate employment (see chapter 5). Alternatively, affirmation of the power of policy intervention to erode racist and sexist practices and outcomes can be identified at many points in American history, such as the ratifications of the 13th and 19th amendments to the US Constitution, the Supreme Court decision in *Brown* v. *The Board of Education*, and the passage of the Civil Rights Act in 1964. As Darity Jr. has noted, the greatest decline in "measured" discrimination against Black Americans occurred during the period 1960–80, after the passage of the 1964 Civil Rights Act.[2] In chapter 7, we discuss Black women and the wealth gap, with stratification economic theory employed to highlight the critical role state-sanctioned anti-Black policies and practices have played in wealth disparities based on race in the US context, as well as the need for policy-based solutions.

Finally, our interdisciplinary political economy approach requires the examination of a wider range of topics than are typically covered in introductory economic textbooks. This book will include topics often overlooked by economics, such as: how economic forces helped develop the social concept "race"; the economic function of racist practices in the US criminal justice system; and the influences of the feminist movement, and racism in the feminist movement, on the economic rights of Black women and Black communities in general. Alongside such discussions, we will also cover more standard economic topics such as – noted earlier – racial inequality in wages, employment, wealth, and educational attainment.

1.3. On Using the Term "Political Economy" in This Book

The discipline of economics evolved from political economy. "Political economy" was the original term applied to the study of production, distribution, and consumption, and their relationships to customs and governance in nascent capitalist states. Political economy draws from a variety of fields, including sociology, political science, and philosophy. Adam Smith, widely considered the "father" of economics, and credited with being a founder of "classical political economy,"[3] studied moral philosophy in college. We chose to use the term "political economy" primarily because it more accurately describes our approach to explaining why anti-Black racism persists in the American economy. The "political economy" term encompasses elements that the term "economics" doesn't readily convey, such as the sociopolitical context within which societies make choices about what to produce, how to produce it, and how what's produced gets distributed, given scarcity.

1.4. How We Define, and Why We Examine, Anti-Black Racism

We define anti-Black racism as policies, practices, and behaviors intended to demean, marginalize, disempower, and disenfranchise Black people, as well as deliberate inactions by those with the ability to reduce and eradicate such policies, practices, and behaviors. By choosing to focus in this text on the implications of anti-Black racism for economic outcomes in the Black American community, we, the authors, assume anti-Black racism is alive and kicking in America. This assumption has an evidentiary basis – aside from whatever personal feelings and beliefs we possess, if one examines a number of economic, and other, indicators, it is clear that, in the aggregate, Black Americans experience the worst economic outcomes by demographic group, with the only exception being the Native American community. One could just about pick any major economic indicator used to gauge the well-being of the populace – poverty rates, wages, unemployment rates, wealth attainment, homeownership rates, etc. – and the position of the Black community with respect to that indicator is usually in the least desirable one, and always, with few exceptions, in a worse position relative to Whites. Of course, however, the impact of anti-Black beliefs, policies, and practices on the Black community in the US isn't relegated to markets and economic indicators alone. Research has shown that even Black women's hair apparently evokes anti-Black sentiment; a survey of 1,000 Black women aged 25 to 64 years old conducted by LinkedIn and Dove revealed that 66 percent of Black women changed their hair for a job interview for fear of not getting the position[4] (Michelle Holder, co-author of this book and a Black woman, confirms that she has done this). This issue is so prevalent that 23 states in the country have passed some version of the "C.R.O.W.N." (creating a respectful and open world for natural hair) Act which prohibits discrimination on the basis of race-based hairstyles.[5]

Throughout the centuries-old presence of Black people in America, arguments have been regularly advanced – on the basis of presumed moral, intellectual, physical, and cultural inferiority – that the overall position of African Americans in the US economy is one which is deserved. These arguments typically proceed along the lines of personal and collective responsibility of Black Americans – if Black people are poorer, earn lower wages, have higher unemployment rates, and have lower levels of wealth, that is because this demographic group is less productive and less industrious (for related discussion, see textboxes in "Primer to Part II" on the founders of the American Economic Association). In advancing such arguments, usually immigrant groups coming to the US in the second half of the twentieth century are held up as examples of what Black Americans could have achieved if only they, as a group, worked harder, were more interested in success, blamed racism less, completed college in comparable rates to White Americans – and the list goes on and on. This view puts forth the thesis that a "culture of poverty" must permeate the Black community in America;[6] Black people choose to engage in behaviors that negatively affect their earnings and wealth, and these behaviors are repeated generation after generation. Slavery cannot be blamed for these choices, the argument goes, because this ended over a century and a half ago. Nor can legal forms of racial discrimination and segregation in education explain these outcomes since major legal reforms, such as the 1954 US Supreme Court decision in *Brown* v. *Board* and the 1964 Civil Rights Act, made such practices illegal. What these arguments willfully omit and gloss over are how legal and other systems were carefully and intentionally designed over four centuries of European presence in North America to directly, and narrowly, benefit and advantage Whites in the US.

1.5. Different Forms of (Anti-Black) Racism

Racism, including anti-Black racism, can take different forms with different actors, with the commonality that all forms deleteriously impact Black people, given their race. People are most familiar with individual or personal prejudice, which is the negative belief of an individual or group of individuals about another group, given a characteristic that the latter group possesses.[7] These beliefs may lead individuals or groups of individuals to engage in interpersonal racism – actions or behavior that are hurtful or detrimental to (individuals in) the latter group. For example, federal hate crimes typically involve an extreme act of prejudice or bias against a member or members of a group by a member or members of another group, such as a heterosexual person directing homophobic slurs at a gay person,[8] or when Reverend Al Sharpton, founder of the National Action Network, was stabbed by a White man in Bensonhurst, Brooklyn in 1991, during a protest against racial violence and the murder of teenager Yusef Hawkins which took place in that neighborhood. Another form of prejudice is "laissez-faire" racism, where Whites concede that Blacks deserve equity but that inequitable outcomes are not the fault of racism or racist institutions.[9] Instead, laissez-faire racism involves the belief that inequitable outcomes are due to the behaviors and choices in the Black community, and thus policy intervention is unnecessary – Black responsibility and accountability are what's needed. Laissez-faire racism expresses an internalized belief in White racial superiority. We discuss laissez-faire racism at length in chapter 2, and we'd also like to note here this form of racism's similarity to the culture of poverty thesis discussed earlier in this chapter.

A Typology of Racism

Throughout the book, we discuss various forms of racism. Here, we spend some time to make sure we provide clear explanations of what we mean when we use each one, along with examples. Racism operates on multiple levels of social and economic life. *Internalized*, *Interpersonal*, and *Institutional* racism combine to produce and preserve racism on the *Structural* level.

Internalized Racism
Internalized Racism is defined as the personal acceptance of stereotypes and negative beliefs about one's own or another's culture

and behavior by racially marginalized people, which then become embedded in one's system of beliefs.[10] For Jamaican sociologist Stuart Hall, internalized racism describes "the 'subjection' of the victims of racism to the mystifications of the very racist ideology which imprisons and defines them" (Hall, 1986, p. 26).

> Because we exist within a world mapped by racial domination, we develop racialized dispositions – some conscious and some unconscious – that inform and direct our thoughts and behaviors in a relational way. (Desmond and Emirbayer, 2009, p. 345)

Racist images may be constructed by anyone who learns racism. However, it is racially marginalized people who experience internalized racism. White people, on the other hand, experience a related phenomenon that Robin DiAngelo (2018) would consider *internalized racial superiority* or *internalized White supremacy* – a personal sense of entitlement and superiority, which becomes embedded in a White person's system of beliefs. This informs their own racial biases and can manifest in defensive reactions when confronted with issues of race or racism – for example, denying the existence of racism or personal racial bias which helps maintain systemic racism and therefore perpetuates inequality. These internalized dispositions affect our interpersonal interactions in everyday life, within and between institutions.

A racially marginalized person does not experience internalized racism as a fact of their culture or biology. Rather, one is socialized to accept and internalize racial hierarchy and one's position within that hierarchy. As bell hooks said, when we consume media, we are often bombarded with images and representations that "reinforce and reinscribe white supremacy" (1992, p. 1). This causes Black, Indigenous, and People of Color (BIPOC) to see themselves through the gaze of the oppressor, which makes the decolonization of their minds and imaginations – and thus self-love, self-determination, and political struggle for liberation from racial oppression – difficult.

Examples of internalized racism include: believing – implicitly or explicitly – that whiteness is the norm or ideal; valuing white skin and/or features over dark skin and/or "ethnic" features that one perceives to be at odds with Eurocentric standards; self-loathing, shame, rejection of one's own identity and/or culture (sometimes resulting in self-mutilation); and hostility or prejudice expressed against members of one's own race or that of another racially marginalized group.

In *Black Skin, White Masks* (1967), Frantz Fanon explores the deep psychological trauma and struggles over identity experienced by Black people as a result of colonialism and the system of racialization it generated. In Fanon's own words, "the feeling of inferiority of the colonized is the correlative to the European's feeling of superiority. Let us have the courage to say it outright: It is the racist who creates his inferior" (1967, p. 93).

Interpersonal Racism
Interpersonal racism describes the conscious or subconscious influence of internalized racial bias in a person's interactions with and perceptions of other people, informed by stereotypes and misinformation attributed to race (Rodriguez-Knutsen, 2023). Because interpersonal racism occurs between individuals, one's racial beliefs create biases that nurture power dynamics in one's interactions with others, which results in disrespect, avoidance, suspicion, and dehumanization that reinforce systemic racial oppression (Cuyahoga Arts and Culture, 2019).

Interpersonal racism is shaped by media, cultural representations, and everyday interactions. Manifestations of interpersonal racism can be overt – for example, in the use of hate speech, racial slurs, exclusionary social practices, and acts of violence against individuals or racialized groups – and, perhaps more commonly, covert – for example, in daily practices, habits, and notions about others one perceives as common sense; for instance, "we may talk slowly to an Asian woman at the farmer's market, unconsciously assuming she speaks poor English; we may inform a Hispanic man at a corporate party that someone has spilled their punch, unconsciously assuming he is a janitor; we may ask to change seats if an Arab American man sits next to us on an airplane" (Desmond and Emirbayer, 2009). Actions like these can spring from intentional thought. However, these types of actions can also result from a kind of unconscious bias – a general sense of what is normative, practical knowledge.

Institutional Racism
Institutional racism is "systemic White domination of people of color, embedded and operating in corporations, universities, legal

systems, political bodies, cultural life, and other social collectives" (Desmond and Emirbayer, 2009). This form of racism operates through implicit/informal or explicit/formal rules, laws, and regulations within organizations, which are discriminatory against marginalized individuals and social groups (Rodriguez-Knutsen, 2023). Because different types of racism mutually reinforce one another in a broader terrain organized by White domination, the behavior of individuals within institutions is also informed by bias born from *internalized* ideas about race, which those individuals project onto other individuals or groups based on their perceived race or ethnicity in *interpersonal* interactions.

The deep-rooted historical practices of redlining and housing segregation in the US are prime examples of institutionalized racism. While redlining has come to refer to many kinds of historic race-based housing discrimination, the practice originated in the government homeownership programs of Roosevelt's New Deal in the 1930s (Jackson, 2021). These programs offered mortgages insured by the government as a kind of federal aid meant to counteract high rates of foreclosure as a result of the Great Depression. The Federal Housing Administration (FHA) and private lenders used color-coded maps to rank the credit worthiness of neighborhoods in cities across the country. By no coincidence, the neighborhoods where Black communities lived were outlined in red ink to indicate that they were deemed too risky for investment – that is, "not worthy of inclusion in homeownership and lending programs" (Jackson, 2021). As such, Black families were systematically denied homeownership opportunities, in the form of favorable mortgage terms and government-backed loans, available to White families. This worsened existing cycles of disinvestment in Black neighborhoods, inhibiting Black wealth accumulation and widening economic disparities that persist into the present.

In the US healthcare industry, doctors are more likely to exhibit preferences for White patients and reduce Black patients to negative stereotypes – for example, characterizations of Black patients as "difficult" or accusations of medical non-compliance. BIPOC patients, especially women, report receiving poorer medical care, and more frequently have their medical concerns minimized, dismissed, or ignored than White patients (Sabin et al., 2009). Within the criminal legal system, law enforcement officers are more likely to stop or detain **BIPOC** – especially Black men (see chapter 8) – compared to White civilians (Pierson et al., 2020). In addition, police officers are statistically more likely to shoot unarmed Black civilians than White ones; and, within the racialized system of mass incarceration, Black men receive longer sentences than White men for the same crimes (Dukes and Khan, 2017; United States Sentencing Commission, 2023).

Structural Racism
As the overarching matrix of relations that connect the aforementioned levels on which racism operates, *structural racism* is "the result of an interconnected collection of social norms, policies, institutions, identity strategies, and ideologies designed to preserve White supremacy" (Mason, 2023, p. 4). Although we are all used to hearing about interpersonal racism, structural racism has been a persistent feature of US political economy, culture, and society (Mason, 2023, p. 3). Structural racism thus involves the compounding and cumulative effects of an array of societal forces (history, culture, ideology) and interactions between institutions that systematically benefit White people and, relationally, deprive and enact violence against people of color.

Multigenerational anti-racist struggle to produce fundamental structural changes that abolish racism have been partially, but not fully, successful because, historically, we have made economic, cultural, scientific, institutional, and social choices that preserve racism. Moreover, racism has taken different forms in response to ever-changing conditions.

Written by Daniella Medina

Institutional racism, on the other hand, does not necessarily require continual intentional actions or behaviors from a privileged group that are detrimental to a subaltern group. Matthew Clair and Jeffrey S. Denis (2015) define institutional racism as the "particular and general instances of racial discrimination, inequality, exploitation, and domination in organizational or institutional contexts, such as the labor market or the nation-state." While institutional racism can be overt (e.g., a firm with a formal policy of excluding applicants of a particular race), it is more often evidenced by disparate impact, where organizations or societies distribute more resources to one group than another without overtly racist intent (e.g., a firm with an informal policy of excluding applicants from a low-income, minority neighborhood due to its reputation for gangs).[11] An example of institutional racism would be the New York City Police Department's "stop and frisk" practices in 2009: that year, 87 percent of individuals stopped and questioned for suspicion of criminal activity were Black or Latinx, while these two groups constituted only 51 percent of the NYC population and an estimated 80 percent of crime suspects based on descriptions from nearly a third of complaints filed in that city.[12]

Finally, structural racism is defined in the Cambridge dictionary as "rules, or official policies in a society that result in and support a continued unfair advantage to some people and unfair or harmful treatment of others based on race."[13] Structural racism is societally embedded, and thus doesn't necessarily need outright prejudice or discriminatory actions on the part of most members of the privileged class. Structural racism, therefore, is extremely difficult to eradicate, as this requires not only educating racist individuals about the harm of their beliefs to others and to the society at large, but also eradicating institutional racism in countless companies, organizations, and agencies, along with applicable legal and policy changes at the local, state, and federal levels.

Consider how residential racial segregation results from, among other factors, the combined impact of institutional racism in the mortgage lending practices of banks and marketing practices of realtors, the racial wealth gap, and interpersonal racism that make specific neighborhoods hostile to Black people and more welcoming to White people. Residential racial segregation, in turn, provides uneven access to high-quality housing stock; to stable, high-wage jobs; and to adequately resourced neighborhood schools which typically rely on local property taxes. The impact of uneven access to these advantages ripples out to other areas of life. For example, a student's ability to achieve their career goals depends, in part, on the educational resources available to them. Black students, disproportionately exposed to underfunded schools, face greater headwinds when trying to obtain the skills they need to enter higher education institutions that improve access to high-paying jobs. This barrier, and its racially disparate impact, is fortified by policies at higher education institutions which give preference to "legacy" applicants, reward achievements in activities only offered at elite schools – such as sailing or crew – or accept full-tuition-paying students at higher rates than those needing financial aid packages. These challenges in accessing educational resources – again, faced disproportionately by Black Americans – make it even harder for a worker to successfully acquire desirable employment, especially if prospective employers discriminate against their social status, credit scores, or the neighborhood in which they reside. Structural racism, in other words, refers to the whole picture: how the multiple channels through which interpersonal and institutional racism combine together to reproduce, reinforce, and magnify disadvantage.

Such structural racism is evidenced in the much higher poverty rate among Black Americans compared to White Americans – it is due to a variety of factors in the American economy, with racial discrimination playing a key role. According to US Census data, in 2022, 8.6 percent of persons identified as "white alone, not Hispanic" in the US were classified as poor (i.e., living below the federal poverty threshold), while 17.1 percent of "black alone"-identifying persons were poor.[14]

1.6. Why We Examine Anti-Blackness from an Economics Perspective

As economists, it seems obvious why we, the co-authors of this book, have chosen to examine the issue of anti-Blackness from an economics perspective. But there is also a nuanced response we can provide to such a query: we believe we *ought to and can* examine anti-Blackness from an economics perspective.

Scholarship about anti-Black practices, laws, and beliefs is not typically treated in the discipline of economics as it is in other disciplines. In our field, anti-Blackness falls under the umbrella term "discrimination," and discrimination is usually characterized as actions of individuals who indulge in "preferences" or "tastes" for biased behavior, with the role of institutions in facilitating and/ or perpetuating anti-Black outcomes invisible. In other fields such as sociology, law, and history, the role anti-Blackness has played in the evolution of American society is more explicitly addressed as deliberate behaviors, actions, and practices among individuals *and* institutions, with the intent being the disenfranchisement, marginalization, and subordination of the Black community in the *long term*. Within mainstream economics, the explanation for why individuals engage in discriminatory actions in market transactions is that they gain some satisfaction, or "utility," from the behavior in the *short term*, since "rational" individuals act with the intention to maximize their total utility. Thus, "institutions" can't be described as anti-Black within neoclassical economics, only "behaviors" and "individuals," and *time* is a non-factor. This is precisely why we have chosen to discuss anti-Blackness in the US within a political economy context, as this broader field pointedly includes among important actors in the economy not just individuals, companies, and the government, but institutional and *historical* frameworks and strategies. Indeed, this book is our contribution to the burgeoning field of stratification economics, a subfield of economics intended to bring a political economy approach to racism into the wider economics discipline.

1.7. Other Theoretical Frameworks that Influence Our Approach

The following appear in no particular historical order of importance, and the list is inexhaustive.

1.7.1. Marxist Theory

At the heart of Marxist theory is the idea of class struggle – there are owners of capital (land, buildings, equipment), that is, capitalists, and workers, and productivity of workers is siphoned off by owners who enrich themselves by remunerating workers with only a fraction of the value their productivity creates. Capitalists belong to the bourgeois class, and workers to the proletarian class. Early Marxian theoretical developments about the role of race and racism as organizing mechanisms within an economic system centered around ethnic and racial identities as being temporary kinds of "false consciousness," which would eventually be replaced by class consciousness.[15] However, the Black experience in America after emancipation, given Reconstruction, Jim Crow, and widespread discrimination, could not easily be characterized as false consciousness. The intentional political, economic, and educational disenfranchisement and marginalization of Black Americans by White society that persisted for another century markedly influenced American political and judicial systems, as well as other key interrelated institutions. This influence contributed to persistently higher rates of Black poverty, lower wages for Black workers, elevated Black unemployment, reduced levels of Black educational attainment, and lower Black homeownership rates compared to the corresponding White community. Marxian economic theory about racism had to evolve in order to provide explanations for the *persistence of racism* and not just the *existence of group identity*.

Strains of Marxian thought undertaking a more explicit treatment of race emerged to explain the way that racism is instrumentalized by the capitalist class. These perspectives argue that racism persists because it serves the interests of capitalists by dividing workers into conflicting groups. Consequentially, rather than uniting against exploitative capital, the proletariat becomes fragmented, engaging in internal conflict rather than collective action. In addition, some scholars, such as Samuel L. Myers Jr. and William J. Sabol (1987), have argued that racialized minority groups – specifically formerly incarcerated Black men in America – also benefit the progression of capitalism by serving as a source for the "reserve army of labor," a pool of unemployed or underemployed workers who can be drawn into capitalist production during economic expansions but easily expelled once their usefulness to capital has expired. Groups who form the reserve army of labor in the US are ones who are subaltern in the American labor market, and, along with formerly incarcerated Black men (but not formerly incarcerated White men), include other racialized minorities, women, teenage workers, and workers without a college degree. Ultimately, however, solutions within Marxian theory focus on ending exploitation of workers by dismantling the capitalist class, and not ending discrimination against racialized minorities, but the presumption is that racial discrimination can only come to an end once workers, regardless of race or ethnicity, unite. In the interim, some Marxist economists suggest that workers should continue to organize, as a solution to eliminate exploitation. Black political economists such as Jessica Gordon Nembhard have written about approaches Black people specifically can take to limit exposure to anti-Black racism in market activities, such as establishing Black cooperatives.[16]

1.7.2. Black Political Economy

Along with stratification economic theory, there are similar frameworks which would be useful in helping to understand why anti-Black behaviors and practices are still so prevalent in market and other activities in America, which stratification economics built upon. One such framework is the *Black political economy* (BPE) paradigm – in this construction, race is considered to be a "produced" form of property (i.e., an asset) possessed by groups, and individuals within those groups, and this property has income- and wealth-generating capabilities.[17] Since some collective identities possess (positive) economic value, members of groups with these identities seek to cultivate and protect highly valued identities, even if it means forgoing some income and/or wealth in the short run. BPE employs economic concepts such as externalities to explain how identities become organizing forces in an economy – identities produce positive externalities for those who identify with privileged groups, and negative externalities for those who don't. A major pillar of BPE is the notion that economic institutions can be viably organized while maintaining practices, and producing outcomes, that are anti-Black, which implies that racist behavior may not be irrational at all. This is in stark contrast to neoclassical economic theory, which suggests anti-Black employers are willing to pay a premium for workers of the same race in order to indulge in bigoted behavior, since marginalized workers would be hired by profit-driven non-racist employers at subpar wages. BPE not only attempts to explain how and why racism *exists*, but how and why it *persists* – mainstream economic theory falls short in illuminating why discrimination is such a stubborn feature of the American economy, since race is a characteristic of individuals without extrinsic value. BPE also recognizes the *dynamism* of anti-Black racism – it occurs, changes, and can be sustained, over *time*.

BPE should not be assumed to be synonymous with *Black Nationalism*. While both paradigms are concerned with Black self-determination, Black Nationalism considers *separation* of Black people from Whites, and the creation of institutions, economies, and nation states that have no dependence on White-controlled markets, as critical to Black self-determination,[18] as espoused by Marcus Garvey's "Back to Africa" movement. Alternatively, BPE seeks to explain persistent racism using authentic lived experiences of Black people that can then inform what actions and strategies are needed for Black freedom and liberation, which may not necessarily include complete separation from Whites. BPE has borrowed from Marxian economic theory even as it has also acknowledged the limits of a framework which centers class struggle, not race struggle, for informing the most effective strategies for Black self-determination.[19] Indeed, political scientist Caroline Hossein, who advocates for a *Black social economy* paradigm within *social and solidarity economy* (SSE) or *social economy* theories, argues that the goal of BPE is liberation and freedom of oppressed people everywhere, with BPE knowledge and practice rooted within the real lived experiences of Black people.[20] SSE advocates for an alternative economic system to capitalism, one which is "engaged in economic, social, and environmental activities to serve the collective and/or general interest, which are based on the principles of voluntary cooperation and mutual aid, democratic and/or participatory governance, autonomy and independence, and the primacy of people and social purpose over capital in the distribution and use of surpluses and/or profits as well as assets."[21]

1.7.3. Critical Race Theory and Intersectionality

Critical race theory (CRT) has recently garnered considerable, often negative, attention – attention that reflects confusion regarding its core tenets and objectives. Efforts to ban the inclusion of CRT in school curriculums have occurred across the US, some of which have been successful.[22] In these efforts, CRT has been mischaracterized as a one-dimensional theory solely about blaming White people – present as well as past – for racism, when in reality this theory focuses on how institutions operate within laws, policies, and practices that were designed and implemented to disempower African Americans while privileging White Americans.

Among its key tenets, CRT asserts that race is socially constructed and emphasizes the importance of "intersectionality"; Kimberlé Crenshaw used the framework of "intersectionality," which she conceptualized in 1989 to "address the marginalization of Black women within not only antidiscrimination law but also in feminist and anti-racist theory and politics,"[23] to examine domestic violence against women of color. Crenshaw argued that the experiences of women of color who have been subjected to rape and/or battery "are frequently the product of intersecting patterns of racism and sexism" (even as she acknowledged domestic violence also occurs to women in lesbian relationships).[24] Intersectional theory carefully notes that different forms of marginalization are not simply additive for someone who is a member of more than one group that experiences discrimination. Instead, forms of marginalization interact with and reinforce each other. While Crenshaw is credited with coining the term "intersectional," Black women had already been striving to codify what they knew to be true – that there are multiple and intersecting axes of oppression that women of color in the US encounter. The Combahee River Collective – named by activist Barbara Smith after one of Harriet Tubman's successful sojourns to liberate hundreds of enslaved people in South Carolina in 1863 – was a Black feminist lesbian organization active in the late 1970s in Boston, Massachusetts.[25] In their "Combahee River Collective Statement," members of the organization wrote:

> The major source of difficulty in our political work is that we are not just trying to fight oppression on one front or even two, but instead to address a whole range of oppressions. We do not have racial, sexual, heterosexual, or class privilege to rely upon, nor do we have even the minimal access to resources and power that groups who possess any one of these types of privilege have."[26]

In addition, in 1982 the Black feminist anthology *All the Women Are White, All the Blacks Are Men, but Some of Us Are Brave: Black Women's Studies* was published, edited by Akasha Gloria Hull, Patricia Bell-Scott, and Barbara Smith.[27] In this anthology Hull, Bell-Scott, and Smith capture the multiple dimensions of marginalization endured by Black women in America before the term "intersectional" gained traction in discourses and scholarship. We take up a more extensive discussion of intersectionality in chapter 4.

1.7.4. Feminist Economic Theory

Economists typically point to scarcity of resources as the central organizing problem of an economy, but *feminist economics* puts power relations between men and women as the central organizing problem – specifically, the subjugation of women in most economies. It also examines the topic of work – not just through the lens of wage work but also reproductive work, both paid and unpaid. There are different schools of thought within feminist economic theory, including "constructivist feminist economic theory" – which emphasizes how the social construction of gender influences the organization of economic activity – as well as "critical feminist theory," which places the material basis of women's subjugation, rather than the social construction of gender, at the center of how economic activity is organized. Critical feminist theory advocates for an alternative system to capitalism in which resources are widely and evenly allocated, and the patriarchy is dissolved.

1.7.5. Historical Womanist Theory

Black women can reasonably be focused on as a distinct demographic group experiencing both anti-Blackness and sexism in ways which are similar to, and different from, the ways Black men and White women, respectively, experience them. *Historical womanist theory* (HWT), which has roots in Marxist economic theory, posits that Black women are a "unique laboring class within the racialized patriarchal structure of the US"[28] in American capitalism, a system which thrives from a racialized, patriarchal approach to production, distribution, and consumption. While HWT does not assert anti-Blackness is targeted at women only, it does assert that Black women experience forms of marginalization that are different from those of Black men given their gender, and different from those of (primarily) White women given their race – similar to an intersectional approach – and that the most effective mechanisms for Black women to employ in achieving equity are to pursue consciousness-raising, visioning, and organizing.

1.8. Will Black Economic Well-Being Always Be Secondary to that of Whites in America?

As scholars who've spent a great deal of our professional lives researching, writing, and teaching about the evolution of anti-Black racism in America and its impact on the economic well-being of Black people and the larger American society, if we were to examine trends in some economic data, we might come to the conclusion that – at some point in the far-away future, centuries from now – the Black community will not be poorer, earn lower overall wages, have lower levels of college completion, lower levels of wealth, lower homeownership rates, higher unemployment rates, and higher mortality rates than Whites in the United States. Further, such an assumption could incorrectly conclude that capitalist economic production, left to its own devices, will eventually eradicate racism. Societal progress can be painfully slow and incremental, but large-scale societal change hasn't happened in this country's history due to laissez-faire capitalism – progressive social change happened due to agitation (Fannie Lou Hamer agitated for Black people's right to exercise the vote prior to the Civil Rights Act of 1964), collective organizing and action (The Brotherhood of Sleeping Car Porters, known in popular culture as the "Pullman Porters," was an all-Black union established in 1925 which secured better wages and work conditions from the Pullman Company after more than a decade of organizing), and even bloodshed (the Black Lives Matter movement, established in response to Trayvon Martin's murder in Florida in 2012, encountered many instances of violence, including after George Floyd's murder in 2020, during movement protests). But here are some key issues involved in trying to answer the question at the beginning of this section in this chapter: (1) Does our society need to endure more centuries of a subaltern status for the Black community in America? (2) Does anti-Black racism negatively impact economic growth? (3) What are effective strategies in positively moving the needle *more quickly* toward equitable economic outcomes for Black Americans? (4) Can the Black community continue to sustain the level of collective action needed to achieve more equitable outcomes, and how can it enlist more allies and cross-issue coalitions to maintain forward and positive momentum?

In response to the question at the beginning of this section – Will Black economic well-being always be secondary to that of Whites in

America? – our answer is no. The reason we research, write about, teach, and advocate for economic equity for Black people is that we believe it is possible. Indeed, this belief is a motivating factor for us to do the kind of work that we do. What we are chiefly concerned about is "How long?" How many more decades or centuries will it take for our society to finally eradicate Black marginalization?

As example of the issue of "how long" can be reflected in figure 1.1, where we depict what percent higher the annual Black unemployment rate has been compared to the White unemployment rate for the years 1972 (the first year for which the US Department of Labor's Bureau of Labor Statistics (BLS) began regularly publishing the monthly Black unemployment rate) to 2023. As can be seen in the chart, the relative gap in the unemployment rate between Black and White workers in the US has been slowly narrowing over time; the Black unemployment rate was regularly double the White unemployment rate for the years from 1972 to 2008, with the exception of 1975, but after 2008 – the year in which the first Black American president, Barack Obama, was elected to office in the US – it was no longer a rule of thumb that the Black unemployment rate was typically twice the White unemployment rate. However, given the pace at which the racial unemployment rate gap between Black and White workers has narrowed over the last 50 years, the data depicted in the chart suggest it could take another century from now for Black and White unemployment rates to achieve parity. Our contention, as the authors of this book, is that there are interventions which could increase the pace of change, and we identify various policy interventions throughout the chapters that follow. At the same time, the central purpose of this book is to reframe how we, as a nation, think about anti-Black racism. In particular, this book is our attempt to delegitimize the culture of poverty thesis as an explanation for racial inequality, and to replace it with historically and empirically grounded explanations of racial oppression. That is, we believe the following: (1) a White-identified social group pursued an early and deliberate strategy of anti-Black racism in the US to build and solidify a White-identified middle and wealthy class for centuries to come; (2) the features of American anti-Black racism were carefully constructed by the White-identified social group in legal, educational, political, and social systems and institutions for nearly 400 years, with the intention that economic outcomes for Black Americans would be largely secondary to those of White Americans; (3) Whites are not born racist toward African Americans, but from birth until death nearly everything White Americans are taught, are exposed to in the media, and experience in everyday life affirms and underscores a narrative of deficiency amongst Black people, in which the roles of the systems and institutions erected over centuries to ensure these outcomes are obscured and obfuscated. Blame is then more easily assigned to the victim, since the roles of systems and institutions, and the individuals responsible for conceiving and implementing practices and laws in these systems and institutions, are no longer as clearly identifiable as when they existed during the time of Jim Crow and segregation. We believe that this is critical to understand because, as long as the culture of poverty thesis persists in the American psyche, the effective policy interventions we advocate for will not achieve the popular support that a democratic political system requires for their adoption and effective implementation.

1.9. Structure of the Book

We have organized the material in this book in two main parts: Part I lays out how we see anti-Blackness in the US evolving and persisting, using the frameworks of stratification economics and intersectionality. In this part, we discuss the purposes anti-Black practices served in building the American economy; why they have endured; and how anti-Black practices, policies, and beliefs have manifested and impacted a specific Black demographic – Afro Latinxs. We end Part I with a chapter outlining why it is critically important to apply an intersectional lens to a stratification economics framework in order to achieve a fuller understanding of the impact of anti-Blackness on the Black community in America.

In Part II of this book, we examine how anti-Blackness is evidenced in America's educational system, labor market, and criminal legal system, with stratification economics and intersectionality as our theoretical foundations. We also include a chapter on how and why the racial wealth divide in the US has remained stubbornly wide, with a specific focus on Black women. Finally, in order to help our readers understand the differences in applying stratification or mainstream economic theory to explain the durability of anti-Blackness in major areas of the American economy, we include a Primer at the start of Part II.

1.10. Note on Capitalizing Black and White

The decision on whether to capitalize "black" and "white" in this book is one of the few that we, as co-authors, along with our research assistant Daniella Medina, struggled to come to consensus on. We discussed this

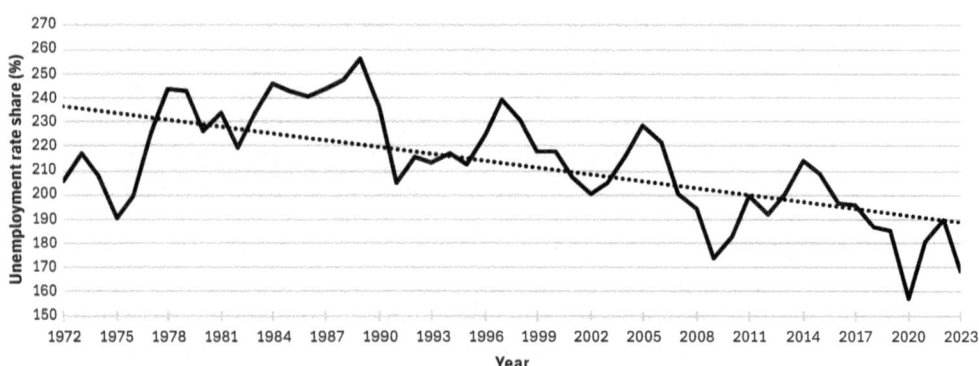

Figure 1.1 Black unemployment rate as percentage of White unemployment rate from 1972 to 2023.
Data source: US Department of Labor, BLS Current Population Survey.

issue right up until the final weeks of drafting our manuscript. As part of our process, Daniella presented us with their assessment of the current state of debate on the question. Note that Daniella's written assessment is reflected, and interwoven, throughout this section.

Their research on the contours of this debate reflected back to us, more or less, the basic contours of our ongoing conversations: (1) that no consensus exists, even among people who have considered the issue seriously and who are committed to the project of reducing racial oppression in the US; (2) that reasonable arguments exist for each of the options we have contemplated; and finally, (3) that these choices matter, and "produce a new consensus and create new facts of language. Words and capital letters are public property" (Appiah, 2020).

Our main challenge came down to choosing between two conventions: capitalizing Black and not white, OR capitalizing both Black and White. Each convention, to varying degrees, reflected our three primary concerns: (1) to honor the cultural and political identity of the Black community in the US; (2) to invalidate the notion of White supremacy; and (3) to draw attention to the social advantages that White Americans access through their racial identity. Below, we outline the primary considerations that ultimately informed our decision.

1.10.1. The Role of Language in Racial Designations

Racial designations are always evolving. While the labels we use contribute to the formation and persistence of racial identities, the identity labels that prevail are inseparable from social norms. Moreover, one's categorization in a normative racial schema isn't determined solely by the person being racialized. For instance, being Black involves identifying as Black *and*, arguably, being identified as Black. As such, the label "Black" plays a significant role in generating both Black identity and other relationally racialized and context-dependent social identities, which cannot be reduced to labels.

Language reform is complex. Often the domain of experts, widespread changes in racial designations under the banner of anti-racism do not exactly result from grassroot democratic processes. Rather, language reform is strongly influenced by academics, linguists, and those who hold political power, whose typographical decisions become linguistic conventions. The endorsement of the term "African American" by influential Black Americans such as Jesse Jackson, for instance, became conventional in the late 1980s despite resistance from Black Nationalists and Caribbean-descended Africans (Appiah, 2020; Wilkerson, 1989). Black Nationalists rejected what they perceived as an attempt to assimilate into mainstream, White-dominated American culture and preferred the reclamation of the term Black. Caribbean-descended Africans argued that the term "African American" fails to acknowledge the existence of Afro-Caribbeans in America. Nevertheless, mainstream media adopted the term and it gained widespread acceptance (Appiah, 2020; Walker, 2022).

Linguistic changes are a critical part of broader efforts to reshape social attitudes and norms and inspire ongoing dialogue about race and identity. This is exemplified by the Black Nationalist reclamation of the term Black (e.g., Black Power, Black Is Beautiful) in the 1960s. Used historically in the United States as a "negative foil" to White people – the opposite of that normatively considered "good" and "pure" – Black was an identity chosen to connote self-determination and an oppositional social distinction from the violence of White supremacy (Walker, 2022). Even then, the grassroot adoption of "Black" fueled intergenerational conflict within the Civil Rights Movement, and, complexly, became the conventional identifier in academia by the end of the decade with the institution of Black Studies at historically White universities.

1.10.2. The Decision to Capitalize Black

The decision to capitalize Black in this volume was an easy one. This convention prioritizes honoring the shared and unique cultural identity of Black Americans – a particular racialized group with a distinct history of racial oppression and struggle for liberation (Nguyen and Pendleton, 2020). The cohesion of this community's social identity reflects, in part, the political resistance put forth by Black Americans to their oppression by White Americans. Black journalist Lori Tharp (2014) articulates how the political resilience and ambition of the Black community requires Black to be treated as a proper noun:

> This is about identity and respect. With a mere slash of a copyeditor's pen, my culture is reduced to a color. It seems silly to have to spell it out, that black with a lower case "b" is a color, whereas Black with a capital "B" refers to a group of people whose ancestors were born in Africa, were brought to the United States against their will, spilled their blood, sweat and tears to build this nation into a world power and along the way managed to create glorious works of art, passionate music, scientific discoveries, a marvelous cuisine, and untold literary masterpieces.

In the English language, capitalization typically denotes proper nouns and names, reflecting human interests or actions, while lowercase entities are seen as "natural kinds," representing inherent features of the world (Appiah, 2020). As such, capitalization signifies that racial designations are human-made constructs (psychological and social) and not conditions of nature (biology), highlighting the "artificiality of race" (Du Bois, 1973; Haslanger, 2012).

By the logic of this linguistic convention, capitalization is thus compatible with the tenets of stratification economics that guide this volume. Capitalizing Black signifies that the term refers to a social condition – one with a particular history of subjugation by, and resistance to, White supremacy that gives rise to a collective identity (Appiah, 2020; Darity Jr., Mason, and Stewart, 2006).[29]

1.10.3. On Whiteness

Whiteness did not manifest as a coherent, objective, and stable social category. As we will discuss further in chapter 2, the ideologies, norms, practices, and systems of knowledge that constitute whiteness and the social groups racialized as White arose in the US within a system of racial domination devised to maintain the White ruling class of colonial Virginia (Allen, 1997). Whiteness conferred access to, and disproportionate control over, institutions and resources. Further, in the early twentieth century, Madison Grant's *The Passing of the Great Races* (1916) documents concerns among proponents of the growing Eugenics movement over preserving the racial purity of "true Americans." With the arrival of the "wrong sorts of Europeans" (e.g., Jewish and Southern European immigrants), Grant articulates the fear of Semitic and Mediterranean immigrants diluting Nordic whiteness and producing a "hybrid race of people as worthless and futile as the good-for-nothing mongrels of Central America and Southeastern Europe" (Appiah, 2020). Over time, such Europeans became White through a sociohistorical process. In particular, White became increasingly defined in relation to Black, rather than in terms of Northern vs. Southern European heritage. Thus, one must pay attention to the relationship between the identity labels "Black" and "White." Failure to do so misses the history of racialized violence that helped build the US. Additionally, ignoring this history naturalizes the machinations of racism, treating race as a neutral, objective feature of the world that does not need to be analyzed by political economists.

1.10.4. On Whether to Capitalize White

This decision was much more difficult. The only consensus we could discern within the current debate is a desire to avoid conventions that encourage us to forget that both Black and White are historically created racial identities.

1.10.4.1. Capitalizing Black and Not White

Some scholars who capitalize "Black" and not "white" do so in order to signify that "Black" represents a unified cultural identity in ways that "white" does not; Black feminist legal scholar Kimberlé Crenshaw puts it this way: "I capitalize 'Black' because Black people, like Asians, Latinos, and other 'minorities,' constitute a specific cultural group and, as such, require denotation as a proper noun. By the same token, I do not capitalize 'white,' which is not a proper noun, since whites do not constitute a specific cultural group" (1991, p. 1244).

Two prominent journalists have weighed in on the issue. For Ta-Nehisi Coates, the choice not to capitalize white decenters whiteness and white identity as normative and dominant in Western society. Likewise, for Nikole Hannah-Jones, not capitalizing white challenges the normalization of whiteness as the compulsory and natural kind of human and the dominant racial identity.

In addition, this convention may be chosen to invalidate white supremacist conceptions of a "White people." Like Crenshaw, Black economist Glenn Loury expresses the belief that capitalizing white leads to the idea that whites are a "coherent, unified people, an idea that has its roots ... in white identity politics of the most virulent kind."[30] Capitalizing White, in other words, feels akin to giving an affirmative nod to a kind of Jim Crow-era White identity (or, in more contemporary terms, a "Make America Great Again"-type White identity). Capitalizing White may inadvertently promote a notion of racial supremacy, an idea that flies in the face of what is acceptable in the social mainstream. Seeing White capitalized can – and does for us – feel jarring. On that basis, many reject this linguistic choice. Anne Price, current co-president of the Maven Collaborative, took this a step further in her 2019 blog that described her feelings on the matter: "We strongly believe that leaving white in lowercase represents a righting of a longstanding wrong and a demand for dignity and racial equity." And, until these wrongs are righted, "we cannot embrace equal treatment in our language."[31]

1.10.4.2. Capitalizing Both Black and White

This convention prioritizes making the point that race is relationally constructed. That is, racial categories are mutually constitutive, such that one cannot exist without the other. For this reason, racial categories should be represented equivalently.

By English typographical norms, keeping white in the lower case risks implying the notion that membership in the white racial group is a type of neutral, natural, or normal state – that is, a non-racialized status. This is in contrast to Black group membership, which the convention recognizes as socially constructed. The neutral status implies that the white racial identity has no effect, no consequence on members of the racial white group. This, in turn, obscures the social advantages that result through the social disadvantages conferred on members of the Black racial group. The Center for the Study of Social Policy articulates their explanation of why they began to capitalize both Black and White in 2020:

> To not name "White" as a race is, in fact, an anti-Black act which frames Whiteness as both neutral and the standard ... we believe that it is important to call attention to White as a race as a way to understand and give voice to how Whiteness functions in our social and political institutions and our communities. Moreover, the detachment of "White" as a proper noun allows White people to sit out of conversations about race and removes accountability from White people's and White institutions' involvement in racism. (Nguyen and Pendleton, 2020)

In a 1993 interview with Charlie Rose, Pulitzer Prize-winning author Toni Morrison put a finer point on this view with her incisive observation of how racism serves to provide White people with a sense of self-worth and identity:

> the racist white person ... is also a race, [their race] is also constructed, it's also made, and it also has some kind of serviceability. But when you take it away, if I take your [referring to a white person] race away, and there you are all strung out, and all you got is your little self. And what is that, what are you without racism? Are you any good? Are you still strong? Are you still smart? You still like yourself? I mean these are the questions ... If you can only be tall because somebody's on their knees, then you have a serious problem. And my feeling is that white people have a very, very serious problem.

Finally, normalizing being "white" has the effect of abnormalizing – pathologizing – being Black. It is this asymmetry in our nation's understanding of race and racism that we believe undergirds contemporary support for the culture of poverty-type diagnosis of racial inequality that our book project is written to upend.

1.10.5. Our Decision

After extensive discussions amongst the three of us, in which a majority of our small team initially leaned toward capitalizing Black and not white, and team members expressed our desire to be particularly sensitive to a member who identifies as Black, we came to the decision to capitalize both Black and White. As we noted earlier, the decision to capitalize Black was easy – we all agreed it should be conveyed in writing as a proper noun for reasons previously outlined. Where we initially disagreed was whether to capitalize white. Emotions weighed heavily in our early feelings on the matter, but we wanted to be thoughtful in our decision, and not be influenced solely by emotion. We decided we didn't want to convey to our readers, with our capitalization choice, that we assume the label "white" with a lower-case "w" was neutral, natural, and normative, and "Black" with a capital "B" was a deviation from the norm.

Thus, after some raw conversations about how some of us choose to identify or not, the smoke cleared and we decided unanimously to capitalize both "Black" and "White" throughout this book, except in this section, and except, of course, where original quotes, or book/article titles, etc., may not have.

2

The Construction of Race and the Origins of Racism in the United States

2.1. Introduction

As we discussed in chapter 1, stratification economics investigates *how* social groups rationally pursue their collective self-interest within hierarchical societies. We will use this chapter to explore how race became the US' archetypal weapon in the struggle between social groups to shape and occupy the upper rungs of the country's social hierarchy. That is, we will examine the construction, and continuous reconstruction, of the social concept of race, and racism's role in allocating relative group positions in the US social hierarchy.

Before delving further, we establish a foundational principle for this book: the understanding that race is a social construct. A large body of scholarship, particularly within sociology, confirms this principle.[1] Sociologists Lawrence Bobo, Camille Charles, Maria Krysan, and Alicia Simmons (2012) provide this definition of race as a social construction:

> Race, or, more generally, ethnoracial distinctions, is historically contingent and varies in exact configuration and salience over time. Such a base of social identity intersects with and is often importantly conditioned by other markers of social difference such as gender, age, class, and sexuality. Although distinctions seen as racial typically invoke consideration of physical and biological markers like skin tone and color, hair texture, eye shape, and possibly other features, none of these lends race its social meaning or significance. (p. 2)

A major objective of stratification economics is to understand and explain the material motivations from which racist ideologies emerge – i.e., racist ideologies that fasten "social meaning or significance" to race as a means of social stratification. Therefore, this chapter's main task is investigating the material incentives created by the social hierarchies that developed within the US. We start with colonial America and explore how, over time, collective identities formed and inspired collective action to maintain economic inequalities between social groups. In other words, we examine how historical context and the US social hierarchy produced race – its particular meanings and significance.

2.2. Constructing the Social Significance of Race

2.2.1. Colonial America Invents an Exceptional Race[2]

From the outset of the English colonial project in the early seventeenth century, race existed as a social category, although its meaning differs from today's modern-day usage.[3] Historian Jacqueline Jones documents how race referred to a mix of "racial, religious, linguistic, and ethnic characteristics" (1998, p. 37). Thus, race grouped individuals by national and cultural identities, using combinations of ascriptive features (e.g., skin tone) as well as behavioral choices (e.g., religion, language). Racial differentiation indicated the greater social dissimilarity between those from the different continents – i.e., Africa, Europe, and the New Worlds with which ascriptive differences coincided. In fact, members of White ethnic groups primarily identified themselves in terms of their ethnicity, rather than using the term "White."[4] At the same time, non-English White ethnics could – by adopting English, accepting the Anglican Church, and avowing loyalty to the English Crown – become "English." The difference ascribed to Africans, in contrast, barred them from fully assimilating into the English culture. Still, members of the colonies with African heritage, while always perceived as different because of their skin color, "were not always irredeemable aliens in the English eyes," says Jones (1998, p. 37).

Below we trace the historical process in which the institution of slavery came to predominate as a labor source in the colonies, and how "race," primarily distinguished by skin color, came to demarcate an "irredeemable," essential human difference. As we will describe below, the English colonists' increasing dependence on enslaving people to make their commercial enterprises profitable transformed the concept of race. In particular, English colonists developed a concept of race that divided people into categories of those who are fully human and those who are less-than-fully human. In other words, skin color no longer indicated a *degree* of difference between the African ethnic groups, on the one hand, and the English and other European ethnic groups on the other. Instead, skin color began to indicate a *type* of difference. This conception of race served dual purposes for the English colonists: it morally justified enslaving people, and it provided a rubric around which to build a legal and political infrastructure to make slavery operational.

On the Construction of Whiteness

In a 1998 PBS interview, American journalist Charlie Rose reminded Nobel Prize-winning novelist Toni Morrison of a question she was once asked by President Lyndon B. Johnson's former press secretary Bill Moyers. Moyers asked, "Can you imagine writing a novel that's not centered on race?" to which Morrison replied, "Absolutely." When Rose pressed her as to whether she will, Morrison said the following:

> That's what he [Moyers] asked me. I think, you see, I answered the question he didn't pose. You know, Tolstoy writes about race all the time. So does Zola, so does James Joyce. Now, if anybody can go up to an imaginary James Joyce and say, "You write about race all the time. It's central to your novels. When are you going to write about –" what? Because, you see, the person who asks that question doesn't understand that *he or she is also raced.*

To be White is all too often considered a non-racialized identity. As Toni Morrison crucially reminds us, *White people are racialized too.* So, when did Europeans start referring to themselves as White?

Americans did not manifest whiteness as a fully formed, objective, and stable social category. As we discuss in the Introduction, the ruling class of colonial Virginia developed the concept of "whiteness" to support a system of racial domination.[5] Anglo-European Americans further developed their ideas about the White race in reaction to the arrival of Jewish and Southern European immigrants to the emerging nation. Anglo-Europeans did not consider the new immigrants White and perceived them as a threat to American (Anglo-European) racial purity. Lawyer and anthropologist Madison Grant (1916) claimed that the dilution of Nordic "true" whiteness by procreation with the Semitic and Mediterranean races would produce a "worthless," "subhuman," "hybrid" race of people.

Benjamin Franklin offered his own catalogue of the world population by skin color in 1751, in which even Germans are regarded as insufficiently White in relation to English Anglo-Saxons: "All Africa is black or tawny; Asia chiefly tawny ... And in Europe, the Spaniards, Italians, French, Russians, and Swedes are generally of what we call a swarthy complexion; as are the Germans also, the Saxons only excepted who, with the English, make the principal body of white people on the face of the earth." Further, Franklin (1961 [1751]) expressed concern over the changing racial composition of the American population due to immigration, voicing a preference for purely "White" citizenry – a preference he considered "natural to Mankind."[6]

In *Black Reconstruction in America* (1935a), sociologist and historian W. E. B. Du Bois introduced the concept of the "psychological wage" of whiteness – the sense of superiority and social capital that accrues to White workers as a kind of wage premium over Black workers. The period of Reconstruction that followed the American Civil War saw massive immigration and industrialization. During this period, the psychological wage of whiteness served to create divisions among the working class to prevent solidarity among workers and maintain social and economic control.

In *The Wages of Whiteness* (1991), historian David Roediger traces the development of the concept of whiteness among European working-class people in the nineteenth-century Antebellum South (1812–61). White identity, he argues, was constructed in relational opposition to Blackness to instill a sense of racial superiority and unity among White workers, despite stark class divisions among Whites. Because White workers in the United States emerged in the context of a slaveholding republic, members of the White working class came to define themselves in terms of what they were *not* – Black and/or enslaved.[7] In particular, Irish immigrants endured extreme prejudice alongside that experienced by enslaved and wage-earning Black workers. Though it was certainly not clear to Irish workers that they were White, Irish immigrants ultimately worked to differentiate themselves from Black Americans to prove their whiteness and thus their Americanness (Ignatiev, 1995; Kolchin, 2009; Roediger, 1991). The Irish, who were once not considered White, were only able to *become White* – and thus improve their social standing and escape racial marginalization – by adopting racist attitudes and behaviors toward Black people. This served to reinforce racial divisions within the working class (Ignatiev, 1995).

For critical race theorist Cheryl Harris (1993), whiteness arises as a legally constructed form of property that confers both tangible and intangible benefits upon those welcomed into it. Whiteness, says Harris, developed with and through relational systems of domination of Black and Native peoples, "out of which were created racially contingent forms of property and property rights" through systemic dispossession and expropriation of land and bodily autonomy (Harris, 1993, p. 1709).

The common contemporary view among historians, biologists, and anthropologists recognizes race as a construct (Kolchin, 2009).[8] Whiteness is not a fact of nature, but something we've *kept alive*. Whiteness continues to be constructed through media and cultural representations in which White people are depicted as a default and normative kind of humanity (Dyer, 1997). It has been created and reified through historical, legal, social, cultural, ideological, psychological, scientific, and economic processes to sustain racial hierarchies and systemic inequality.

Written by Daniella Medina

2.2.2. The Demand for a Tractable Labor Supply

The process begins in the seventeenth century with the colonization by England of what is now known as North America – a commercial venture of resource acquisition for money-making purposes. The earliest English settlements include the Jamestown and Chesapeake colonies of Virginia – Virginia is the namesake of the for-profit company that funded the colonization efforts.[9] To develop the commercial potential – i.e., the profit-making capacity – of the New World, colonists needed access to an extraordinary amount of labor, more than could be supplied by colonists' household members. As historian Jacqueline Jones explains, "the market demand from Europe [for agricultural products from the colonies] quickly convinced Chesapeake planters that success in the commercial-colonial sweepstakes – with a well-ordered society based on a profitable export economy as the prize – would depend on their ability to control a large number of workers" (1998, p. 26). A cheap, tractable labor supply, in other words, was the linchpin to producing profitable exports.

2.2.2.1. Indentured Servitude

Colonial officials and landowners depended on a hierarchical social structure that would provide them with the requisite large supply of tractable labor. Initially, Georgia, Maryland, and the Chesapeake mostly relied on English indentured servants. Three factors figured prominently in this choice. First, the English colonists had to be vigilant against possible attack by non-English outsiders, e.g., Indigenous people or colonists from other nations with competing colonization projects. That is, the English colonists relied on a common national identity to promote a level of social cohesion sufficient to support collective action in protecting their settlements from the non-English, bolstering the security of their settlements. Second, the timing of early colonization coincided with political and social upheaval in England. Crumbling social institutions, war, overpopulation, poor harvests, and economic depression in England created a large supply of young English ready to migrate to North America. Third, a form of bonded-labor – "servant-in-husbandry" – already existed in England and could be tapped into by colonists for use in the colonies. In other words, the English indentured servant labor supply was historically contingent.

The English colonists, however, attempted to command their servants to do an amount of intensely miserable work that was unsustainable given the level of control permitted by the indentured servant system. The severe conditions under which these indentured servants labored, including the amount of labor expected of them, motivated the use of violence for labor discipline, as well as violent resistance by workers. Masters manipulated contracts to make fraudulent claims against their servants and extend contract tenures, effectively converting them to open-ended contracts that enabled masters to exploit their servants longer and thereby reap greater profits. Court cases disputing the terms of the contracts hobbled the court system. Social tensions rose, as masters began to fear retribution from their former servants: once indentured servants satisfied their contractual obligations, the former servants would be free and shared similar status with their masters. The corruption, combined with lethal working conditions that led to high runaway rates and intense social conflict, produced a level of social chaos that threatened the viability of the colonies. According to Jones, "Within a few decades of settlement, the shortcomings of the White indentured servants were well known" (1998, p. 77). In other words, the social stratification imported from England failed to meet the labor requirements of the colonists' commercial aspirations.

Colonists tried – mostly unsuccessfully – to force Indigenous people into the low stratum of bound labor. One significant reason for this failure is that Indigenous individuals benefited from the protection of an existing political and military infrastructure within colonial America to represent their interests. Trade with the Indigenous communities, including labor exchanges, had to be negotiated diplomatically, and transgressions by colonists risked retaliation. Additionally, regional knowledge among Indigenous individuals increased their chances of successfully escaping indentured servitude. Finally, vulnerability to colonists' disease, as well as the relatively small numbers of potential workers, also limited the practicality of trying to secure labor from Indigenous communities.

2.2.2.2. African Slavery and People of African Descent

The purchase of African slaves in colonial America occurred as early as 1619, according to historian Lerone Bennett Jr. (Hannah-Jones, 2021b, p. xix). Before the widespread use of slavery in the early colonies, people of African heritage occupied a range of positions: slave, servant, as well as overseer, landowner, slaveowner, and master (of servants). Some were English-speaking, some were Christians, and some (landowners) had legal standing in court. During this period, interracial communities were common: Black, White, and Indigenous people worked and lived together, socializing outside of work. Interracial intimate relationships existed among individuals who shared the same social status. At the same time, Black people in the English colonies existed in a somewhat ambiguous social class. As noted above, whereas non-English Europeans could become English if they spoke English, swore loyalty to England, and converted to Christianity, African people could not. Jones (1998) explains: "In the seventeenth century, the ethnocentric English planters of the Chesapeake interpreted a dark skin not necessarily as a badge of racial inferiority, but rather that this particular group of people bore close watching; to the extent that blacks could never become English they would remain a potential threat to the security of the colonies" (p. 39).

As the drawbacks of the indentured servitude system mounted, the political, social, and economic developments in England reduced the supply of indentured European servants. In place of indentured servants, the colonists built up a stratum of enslaved people. An expanding slave trade increasingly met the colonists' labor demands, spreading widely across the American colonies after the mid seventeenth century, and replacing the dissolving indentured servant system. The English colonists had, by now, accumulated knowledge about what was necessary to control bound labor, and the degree of coercion required to extract the labor they needed for their commercial enterprises. Colonists used brute force to control enslaved Africans, in combination with social isolation, and the enslaved effectively had no legal protections. As historian Eric Williams remarks, "the experience with white servitude had been invaluable … [it] was the historic base upon which Negro slavery was constructed" (2021 [1944], p. 19).[10]

Tying legal status to skin color augmented the degree of control slaveowners had over the people they enslaved. This is because only a small number of free Blacks resided in the English colonies, making enslaved Africans relatively easy to distinguish from other residents. As the practice of enslaving people expanded, the colonies developed a robust legal rubric that more tightly linked civil rights to race, with the rights of all Blacks – including free Blacks – increasingly circumscribed relative to those of Whites.

These legal controls included, among others, the implementation of laws restricting interracial marriage, the transfer of slave status to all offspring of female slaves regardless of the father's status, and the prohibition of Black men – free or enslaved – from bearing arms (Jones, 1998, pp. 76–80). Sociologist and Africana studies and legal scholar Dorothy Roberts describes the wide-ranging nature of these laws and their ultimately stratifying effect as "a set of measures designed to codify the superior status of White people and the subordination of Black people." We quote her observations at length here:

> The law gave white indentured laborers "freedom dues" – a payment in cash, land or supplies received when they completed their contract term – while enslaved Black people were entitled to no freedom at all. The legislature enacted a set of "slave codes," which declared that an enslaver who killed a person he enslaved while "correcting" the victim would not be prosecuted for a felony. The same statute, by contrast, prohibited masters from inflicting "immoderate correction" on white indentured laborers and allowed those laborers to file complaints against masters

who violated this restriction. The codes also prohibited Black or mulatto individuals from holding public office, testifying in courts, or otherwise swearing under oath. *This legal distinction in status based on race alone turned racial classification into a caste system. Through these laws, colonial landowners constructed race as a system of power in which anyone categorized as Black could be dominated by anyone categorized as white.* (emphasis added; Roberts, 2021, p. 51)

Racist ideologies – that is, theories about the racial inferiority of Black people and racial superiority of White people – emerged from these evolving economic and legal conditions, embellishing the social significance of "race." In other words, as the English colonists' use of enslaved labor increased, so too did the social meanings linked to the ascriptive characteristic of skin color, codified by social and legal advantages linked to "white" skin and disadvantages to "black" skin.

The status of slave in the social hierarchy of the English colonies, the uniquely African source of enslaved people, the distinctly darker skin of Africans, and the ethnocentric culture of the English colonies conjoined to effect a black "race." Jones puts it this way: "By resisting the total assimilation of black people into their own culture, and by singling them out for enslavement, White people in effect invented the black 'race' that is, the idea that blacks were a group irredeemably set apart" (1988, p. 94).

The ability to view African people as irredeemably set apart, in turn, supported the institution of slavery. As Eric Williams explains, "Racial differences made it easier to justify and rationalize Negro slavery, to exact the mechanical obedience of a plough-ox or a cart-horse, to demand that resignation and that complete moral and intellectual subjection which alone make slave labor possible" (2021 [1944], p. 19). The concept of race attributed full humanity as an exclusive characteristic of Whites, and in relation, a condition of sub-humanity to Blacks.

In summary, English colonists used racial categories to rationalize and operationalize a stratified society that relied on slavery. The reason for instituting the distinctive social institution – African slavery – was economic. The profitability of colonists' commercial enterprises demanded a class structure that facilitated the severe exploitation of a large labor force. The ability of the African slave trade to fulfill this need, combined with the fact that other labor institutions failed to do so, promoted the enslavement of Africans in the English colonies. Over time, the colonists developed a legal and social infrastructure that singled out enslaved Africans as a distinct group of laborers to be perpetually unfree. That is, a confluence of historically specific factors together determined the English colonists' enslavement of Africans in order to solve their labor problem. In the process, Africans became a black "race," essentially different from the other "race," i.e., Whites. It is in this way that race arises as the effect of a specific class structure embedded in a specific historical context.

2.3. Maintaining the Social Significance of Race

In this section, we show how the operation of *explicit* racial discrimination through most of US history has produced a durable racial hierarchy. Starting in the seventeenth century with the colonial settlements from which the US emerged, to the mid-1960s peak of the Civil Rights Movement, access to political and economic resources were unambiguously defined by race. Today, the same pattern of racial inequality in the basic economic dimensions of American life that existed prior to the mid-1960s persist. This pattern indicates that policy interventions to address racism in the US have fallen well short of what is needed to jettison the racial hierarchy. We will then discuss how a contemporary form of racism – *laissez-faire racism* – supports the current level of racial inequality with racial stereotypes, a dismissal of the US' racist history, and a resistance to vigorous policy interventions. This form of racism, combined with the persisting pattern of racial inequality, maintains the significant social meaning of race in the US.

2.3.1. The Making of a Durable Racial Hierarchy

We present a timeline in figure 2.1 to visually depict how legal, political, and social institutions explicitly used racial categories to distribute economic and political resources in significant ways over the near-entirety of the nation's 400-year history. The timeline marks the periods during which prominent forms of state-sanctioned, explicitly racist institutions operated. We list each of these below, followed by a brief description.

For about a quarter of a millennium – from 1619 to 1865 – slavery existed as a severe form of legally sanctioned racial oppression. Over the next 100 years (1865–1968), the nation's legal, political, and social institutions unambiguously used race to distribute economic, political, and social goods. These practices had the cumulative effect of amassing, monopolizing, and creating an institutional basis for the economic and political power of a group socially defined by the physical marker of "white" skin color. Only since 1968 has explicit racial discrimination been made generally illegal – i.e., just over 50 years as of the writing of this book. In other words, for 90 percent of US history, the nation has operated with a state-sanctioned social hierarchy explicitly structured by racial categories, creating and re-creating the social meanings of race.

- **1619–1865: Slavery.** For nearly a quarter of a millennium, enslaving people operated largely legally in the US. In the Northern states, slavery remained legal until roughly 1850.[11] In 1865, the 13th amendment ended slavery in Southern states, except as a form of criminal punishment.[12]
- **1865–1867: The Black Codes.** Southern states put in place "Black Codes" – laws to more easily and frequently criminalize the daily activity of Black residents, and thereby re-enslave them as punishment.[13]
- **1873–1930: The Nadir.** The Nadir is roughly the period between the effective end of Reconstruction (circa 1873) and the 1930s. These years earn the moniker – the Nadir – as a low point of civil rights for Black Americans in the US due to the high frequency and severity of massacres, lynching, and terror campaigns conducted with impunity by White supremacist organizations, White rioters, and White vigilantes against Black Americans.[14]
- **1877–1964: The Jim Crow Era.** The 87-year period of legally codified racial segregation, primarily – but not exclusively – in Southern states. The most prominent Jim Crow laws mandated racially segregated public accommodations, restricting Black people to inferior (or no) facilities, and giving White people exclusive access to superior (or any) facilities.[15] Social conventions about how Black Americans should conduct themselves when interacting with White Americans, severely enforced through racial violence by White Americans – such as through lynching – scaffolded these laws.
- **1890–1965: Black Southern Men Disenfranchised.** White Southern legislatures passed new voting rules and practices aimed at preventing Black men from voting after they gained this right through the passage of the 14th and 15th amendments (in 1868 and 1869, respectively). By 1890, these new laws and practices effectively disenfranchised Black men in the South (see chapter 4).
- **1930–1965: Black Southern Women Disenfranchised.** By 1930, White Southern legislatures adopted new laws and practices to disenfranchise Black women who gained the right to vote in 1920, through the passage of the 19th amendment.

- **1964–1968: The Civil Rights Movement.** This political movement eliminated major areas of legalized race-based discrimination:
  - The Civil Rights Act of 1964 made Jim Crow laws illegal and protects individuals from racial discrimination in other activities, such as attending public school, applying for employment or government programs.[16]
  - The Voting Rights Act of 1965 returned the franchise to Black Americans in the South.[17]
  - The Civil Rights Act of 1968 (Fair Housing Act) ended legally sanctioned racial discrimination in the housing market.[18]

Figure 2.1 makes clear how explicit anti-Black racism has dominated US history. The successful abolition of each set of racist institutions by Black political organizers and their allies – such as slavery or the Black Codes or Jim Crow laws – has been met with White political organizers' efforts to establish a new, if different, set of institutions aimed to re-establish the existing racial hierarchy. Later, in chapter 8, we discuss developments of *implicitly* racist practices, particularly within the criminal legal system and its massive expansion of incarceration, that developed in response to the Civil Rights Movement.

2.3.2. Whiteness: A Monopoly of Social Advantages

Next, we connect the racial economic inequality that existed throughout most of US history to the present day. We do this to demonstrate how race continues to be reconstructed in contemporary times. That is, we will show how racial groups continue to be a primary way for allocating political, economic, and social advantages, even after the dismantling of the legal infrastructure that gave race its original meaning.

To do this, we use economists William Darity Jr. and Rhonda Williams' conceptualization of how the normal operations of the US economy produce economic and political advantages, and the role of the US' racial history in determining who is best able to access these advantages. Darity Jr. and Williams (1985) start with a Marxist theorization of competition within capitalism – capitalism being the dominant economic system in the US since the dissolution of slavery.[19]

As explained by Darity Jr. and Williams, competition within a capitalist economic system is an ongoing, dynamic process as capitalists perpetually seek out ways to gain advantages in the market in which they are competing. This process tends to produce monopolies – i.e., a situation where one firm dominates and controls the supply of a good or service and thereby earns most of the profit from that market. Darity

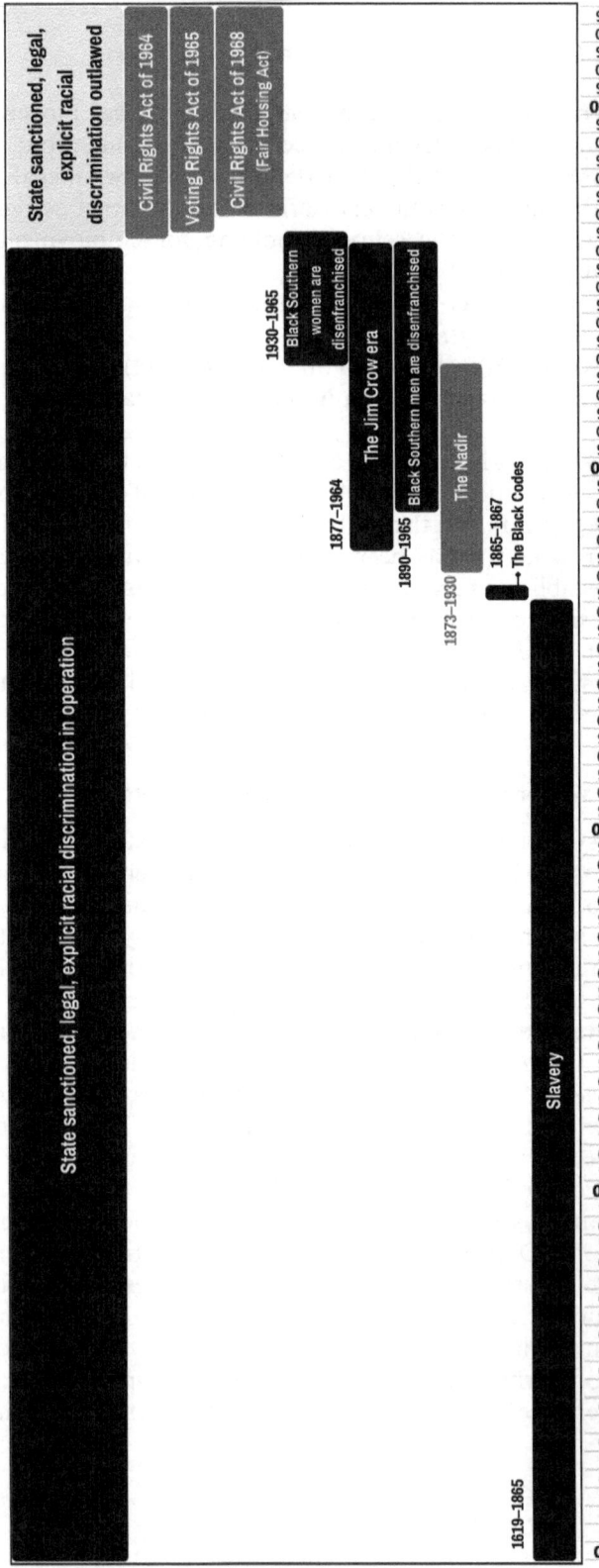

Figure 2.1 Timeline of US history: Major laws, state-sanctioned social practices, and economic institutions of explicit racial discrimination, 1600 to present.

Jr. and Williams explain that through this competitive process, winners in the first round of competition tend to "consolidate and concentrate" to maintain their superior position and use their combined winnings to fend off competitors and exclude losers. The Marxist view of monopolies, in other words, is that they emerge from the competitive forces within capitalism, and their monopoly position is durable.[20] This contrasts with mainstream – or neoclassical – economics which emphasizes how competition undercuts monopolies, as rival firms compete vigorously to get access to the monopolist's markets and profits. In this view, monopolies tend to be fragile and transitory.

Darity Jr. and Williams focus on competition not just between businesses, or owners of businesses, as in conventional economics, but also between workers. Darity Jr. and Williams explain how they extend this Marxist concept of monopoly competition to the labor market – where the majority of US adults access their income[21] – saying:

> Workers also can concentrate and consolidate, particularly by ethnicity and race. Via the control of training, evaluation, information, and the definition of jobs, winners in early rounds of labor market competition can insulate themselves from the most recent recruits to the wage labor force ... Marxist competition conceives of a world that tends toward monopoly. Specific ethnic and racial groups could gain control and dominance of particular occupation categories ... Culture is the magnet that provides the basis for concentration for labor powers. (1985, p. 260)

That is, ethnicity and race identification serve as weapons in the competitive fight to monopolize – obtain and maintain – favored positions in the social hierarchy.[22]

As we described above, in the beginning of US history, individuals trying to secure desirable social positions developed the social construct "race" to organize and coordinate their efforts (e.g., White people as enslavers of Black people). Colonists continuously elaborated on, and thereby reified, racial categories to maintain and legitimize the existing social hierarchy. Simultaneously, the operation of the social hierarchy maintains and legitimizes the concept of race. As the brief survey of US racist practices above illustrates, White racial solidarity proved to be an effective tool for monopolizing powerful social positions and desirable economic resources for White people.

An important consequence of explicitly racist policies is that White workers were the "winners in early rounds of labor market competition"[23] and were well positioned to maintain control over access to favored positions, such as preferred jobs, thus avoiding the lowest stratum of the working class – the unemployed. In other words, once a group is successful in dominating a particular niche in the social hierarchy, Darity Jr. argues, "they begin a long process of defending their turf from other groups they perceive as contestants. Thus, they become defenders of hierarchy ..."[24]

Consider, for example, how racial inequality evolved during and after the mid-1960s, when the Civil Rights Movement succeeded in abrogating explicitly racist laws with passage of the Civil Rights Acts of 1964, 1965 (Voting Rights Act), and 1968 (Fair Housing Act). These political achievements weakened White Americans' monopoly on higher-status occupations,[25] access to educational resources,[26] and, importantly, elected office.[27] To defend their favored position in the social hierarchy, White Americans had to create and implement new social institutions to replace the ones outlawed by the Civil Rights Acts.[28] This is the main thesis of legal scholar Michelle Alexander's 2012 book *The New Jim Crow*. Her scholarship, along with the work of other legal scholars such as Dorothy Roberts, historians Heather Thompson and Elizabeth Hinton, and economist Ellora Derencourt, traces how White political leaders pushed for a massive expansion of the criminal legal system to protect the basic features of the racial hierarchy from these seismic political shifts (see chapter 8). We also show, in other chapters, how the dominant racial group – White Americans – reacted to these challenges to their privileged position in the racial hierarchy with racial animus and racist resource-hoarding (see, for example, chapter 5 on education).

2.3.3. Evidence of Race's Enduring Social Significance

In fact, fundamental features of the US economy continue to reflect a White-dominated racialized social hierarchy. Trend data show that the degree of racial inequality along key economic dimensions has remained remarkably consistent between the period of US history when transparently racist policies operated (pre-1968) and contemporary times. These dimensions include racial disparities in employment, income, and wealth. In later chapters, we will explore these features, and others, in depth. Indeed, this book's core objective is to describe and explain the myriad of channels through which social groups compete over preferred positions in the social hierarchy. This is what it means to employ a stratification economics analytic framework: analyzing racial economic inequality as the product of rational actors finding ways to gain access to and hold on to resources, including by constructing social identities that can support collective action to gain advantage (or cause disadvantages) in this turf war.[29] Our goal in this chapter is to make clear the *historical* lineage of contemporary forms of racial inequality by presenting trend data that connect present-day conditions to the situation that existed under Jim Crow laws.

2.3.3.1. Unemployment

Research by economist Steven Shulman documents the remarkably stable relationship between the unemployment rates of Black and White workers. His 1991 study "Why Is the Black Unemployment Rate Always Twice as High as the White Unemployment Rate?" examines unemployment trends from 1954 to 1981, spanning the years before and after the passage and implementation of the 1964, 1965, and 1968 Civil Rights Acts.[30] One of Shulman's key observations is that, throughout this entire period, the Black unemployment rate is consistently twice that of the White unemployment rate, with no observable decline after 1968. In other words, despite the momentous political gains in civil rights during the mid-1960s, racial disparities in who experiences unemployment remained unaffected. As we saw in figure 1.1 in chapter 1, when we extend this analysis to 2023, it is clear that the patterns Shulman observed for the years 1954–81 continued into the twenty-first century. In other words, for at least a half-century, the Black unemployment rate has been double the White unemployment rate. It is only within the last two decades – beginning around 2008 – that this ratio has fallen below 2 for a period of multiple years.

2.3.3.2. Earnings and Income

The earnings picture is slightly more nuanced. The achievements of the Civil Rights Movement during the 1950s and 1960s appear to have narrowed the racial gap in pay rates – that is, compensation while working. However, the persistent racial gap in employment – including both unemployment and dropping out of the labor force – offsets these gains. That is, the greater rates of unemployment or lower rates of labor force participation among Black workers diminishes the benefits of gaining closer parity with White workers in pay rates. We illustrate this trend in figure 2.2.[31]

Figure 2.2 shows trends in two different measures from Patrick Bayer and Kerwin Kofi Charles' 2018 study, "Divergent Paths: A New Perspective on Earnings Differences Between Black and White

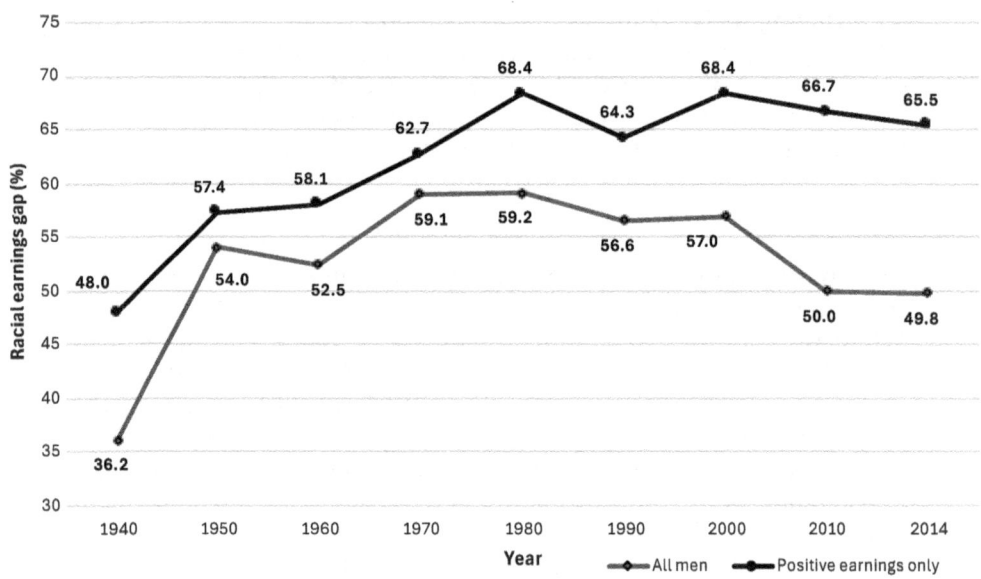

Figure 2.2 Trends in racial earnings gap among men: Black median annual earnings as a percentage of White median annual earnings, 1940–2014.
Source: Bayer and Charles (2018), Appendix Table 2, "Real earnings of non-Hispanic Black and White men – summary statistics."

Men Since 1940."[32] Their study examines the long-term trend in racial earnings inequality among men and takes into account the experience of both workers and nonworkers. The black line tracks the racial gap in median earnings based only on men of prime working age (25–64 years) with positive earnings (i.e., at least some earnings). Specifically, the data series provides the median annual earnings among Black men with positive earnings as a percent of that among White men with positive earnings. The measure rises when racial earnings inequality declines, with 100 percent indicating perfect equality. We focus on men because of the significantly different patterns of labor force participation among White and Black women, with White women being much less active in the workforce than Black women through the 1990s.[33]

We see a dramatic improvement in this racial earnings gap from 1940 to 1950. Several major historical developments of the time undoubtedly are responsible: (1) the re-emerging political activity advocating for civil rights after the Nadir; (2) the migration of an estimated 2 million Black Americans from the South to escape anti-Black violence and take up newly expanding employment in the Midwest and North;[34] and (3) the macroeconomic jolt from World War II.[35] Thereafter, the racial earnings gap continues to improve until 1980, with the percent of Black to White men's earnings rising from 57 percent to 68 percent. The racial earnings gap then stagnates, with the percent of Black to White men's earnings falling slightly to 66 percent by 2014. Overall then, *among those workers who are employed*, Black workers' relative position in the labor market has clearly improved over time – mostly between 1940 and 1980.

However, the grey line in figure 2.2 traces out a different story. This data series shows the median annual earnings among *all* Black men of prime working age (25–54 years old) as a percent of that among *all* White men of prime working age, including now men with zero earnings (i.e., unemployed men and men who have dropped out of the labor force). This trend line shows, again, the sharp gain in relative earnings for Black workers from 1940 to 1950. However, following that leap, Black workers' progress slowed. From 1950 – well before the passage of the Civil Rights Acts – to 2014, we see the racial earnings gap hover around 55 percent, sometimes lower and sometimes higher. In fact, the racial earnings gap in 2014 is wider than what existed in 1950.[36] In other words, the racial earnings gap in the present day remains just as wide as what existed when it was legal to employ explicitly racist policies in housing, employment, education, and elsewhere.

2.3.3.3. Wealth

Wealth is different from income. Income is the flow of money that a household receives over time to meet their everyday needs for food, clothing, shelter, and so on. This income typically comes from paychecks household members bring home from their jobs. Wealth, in contrast, is the stock of economic resources that a household is able to accumulate over time, such as in a savings account.[37] The quintessential analogy used in economic textbooks to distinguish income from wealth is the bathtub.[38] *Income* is the water flowing into a bathtub, *consumption* is the water flowing down the drain, and the water that accumulates in the bathtub is *wealth*. If a household consumes all its income, they accumulate no wealth. However, if the drain is slow (consumption is low) and the water pressure at the spigot is high (income level is high), then the household will accumulate wealth.

Textbooks typically do not discuss the following important elements of this analogy: (1) if someone pours a bucket of water into the tub (e.g., an inheritance or in vivo transfer), then the household's wealth rises; (2) if someone removes a bucket of water from the tub (e.g., theft, property destruction), the household's wealth falls; and (3) households *earn income* from their wealth (e.g., interest on a savings account or bonds, equity on a house that appreciates in value, dividends from stock). Having wealth itself can generate income, and become more wealth: *wealth begets wealth*.[39] In the bathtub analogy, the bathtub water spontaneously generates more water. In chapter 7, we take an in-depth look at factors that contribute to, or limit, wealth accumulation among Black women.

Due to all these features, wealth captures the combined economic fall-out of how racism operates in the US economy. This includes reducing income of Black households relative to White households; the now centuries-long legacy of state-sanctioned theft from, and violence against, Black communities; the bequeathing and transfer of accumulated wealth within White households; and the self-generating feature of wealth in a capitalist economic system. In these ways, the racial wealth gap sediments, over time, the economic consequences of all other dimensions of racial inequality in the US economy.[40] As such, the severity of racial inequality is unsurprising. Economists Moritz Kuhn, Moritz Schularick, and Ulrike Steins (2020) document how in 2016, the median Black household had *less than 15 percent* of the wealth of the median White household. Kuhn et al. (2020) also trace out the trend in racial wealth inequality between 1947 and 2016 and find that the racial wealth gap basically persists at this level over the entire period. In other words, the racial wealth gap is as wide today as it was prior to the 1960s Civil Rights Acts.

In sum, contemporary social practices have maintained the same pattern of racial inequality in the basic economic dimensions of American society – in employment, earnings, income and wealth – put in place during the years when explicitly racist policies governed wide swathes of everyday life. In the next section, we show how the continued success of White Americans in monopolizing favored status in the social hierarchy motivates and reinforces the use of racial categories, continuously reifying the social concept of race. In other words, the social concept of race is continuously reproduced by economic and political inequality.

2.3.4. Laissez-faire Racism: Contemporary Constructions of Race

In the above review of US history – particularly from the early seventeenth to the mid twentieth centuries – racial solidarity plays a critical role in securing White Americans' dominance over favored positions in the social hierarchy. This racial solidarity enabled the creation of the social and political institutions – i.e., norms, political rights, government policies – that gave White Americans greater access to valuable economic resources such as land, housing, schools, healthcare, jobs, financial capital, and so on. A White supremacist ideology fortified this racial solidarity by adding social meaning and value to the racial hierarchy, rationalizing its operation, particularly with theories about biological differences between the races (e.g., Black people are particularly well suited for physical labor[41]).

The success of the Civil Rights Movement during the 1950s and 1960s in abolishing explicitly racist laws and social institutions also drove explicitly racist views largely out of the mainstream and into disrepute. For example, in 1944, the majority (55 percent) of White respondents to a National Opinion Research Center (NORC) survey held the position that Whites should receive preference over Blacks in access to jobs, rather than an equal chance.[42] By 1972, only 3 percent of Whites responded affirmatively to this position (Schuman, Steeh, Bobo, and Krysan, 1997, pp. 104–11; also see Bobo, Kluegel, and Smith, 1997, p. 23). Despite these changing social norms and the elimination of explicitly racist laws and social institutions, how is it that the fundamental gaps in racial inequality that we reviewed above not only persist, but persist to the same degree? What can explain White Americans' continued ability to monopolize the advantaged positions in the social hierarchy?

Sociologists Lawrence Bobo, James Kluegel, and Ryan Smith (1997) show with survey data how the explicitly White supremacist ideology ("Jim Crow" racism) that was mainstream, particularly in the South, prior to the 1960s, has been replaced by a new set of implicitly racist views. These newer views continue to foster racial solidarity among White Americans and, importantly, prevent the adoption of economic and social policies that would undo the racial hierarchy initially constructed by explicitly racist views over most of US history.

In particular, as we will show below, contemporary views on race among many White Americans define a White racial group identity centered around the belief that White Americans deserve their present-day monopoly over favored social positions (i.e., internalized racial superiority). This belief is implied by their view that individual attributes of Black Americans predominantly explain their disadvantaged social position. Critically, these views fail to consider how White Americans initially came to occupy favored positions in the social hierarchy. What follows from this belief is White solidarity in resisting any significant policy interventions to change the existing social hierarchy. Bobo et al. have termed this racial ideology "laissez-faire racism," and characterize it thus: "This new ideology concedes basic citizenship rights to African Americans; however, it takes as legitimate extant patterns of Black–White socioeconomic inequality and residential segregation, viewing these conditions, as it does, not as the deliberate products of racial discrimination, but as outcomes of a free-market, race-neutral state apparatus and the freely taken actions of African Americans themselves" (1997, p. 38).[43]

The main features of laissez-faire racism include the following.[44]

(1) The persistence of anti-Black stereotypes. Anti-Black stereotypes translate into various forms of direct discrimination in labor, housing, and credit markets. Expressing these beliefs through discriminatory action is no longer systematically enforced by the state, nor is it generally socially acceptable when expressed explicitly. Instead, laissez-faire racism relies on discriminating on the basis of anti-Black stereotypes of behavior and attitudes that are obliquely identified with race; "de facto" racism replaces "de jure" racism. Bobo et al. describe the operation of de facto racism this way: "Rather than relying on state-enforced inequality as during the Jim Crow era ... modern racial inequality relies on the market and informal racial bias to re-create, and in some instances sharply worsen, structured racial inequality" (1997, p. 17).

(2) The belief that racial economic inequality results from Black people's individual choices. This view decouples racial economic inequality from past or current racial discrimination and racist policies. Instead, racial economic inequality is viewed as the consequence of personal deficiencies among Black individuals. As a result, only social policies to reform individual deficiencies are considered effective, and social policies intended to counter structural sources of persistent racial inequalities are viewed as ineffective.

(3) Resistance to public policy remedies. The first two elements of laissez-faire racism – anti-Black stereotypes and the belief that unequal outcomes are due to individual choices rather than structural barriers – combine to justify the existing level of racial inequality and the dominance of the favored positions in the social hierarchy by Whites. As Bobo et al. (1997) explain, "These social conditions continue to prompt many White Americans to feel both morally offended and apprehensive about losing something tangible if strong efforts are made to improve the living conditions of African Americans" (p. 41). Public policies to reduce racial inequality, as a result, are criticized as being unnecessary at best, and at worst, unfair.

Overall, the racial ideology of laissez-faire racism promotes solidarity among White Americans organized around two ideas: (1) that White Americans are entitled to the higher-status positions in which they predominate in the social hierarchy and, conversely, Black Americans are not; and (2) that the adoption of economic and social policies that would undo the existing racial hierarchy are unnecessary and/or unfair.

Recent research has produced empirical evidence of the persistent operation of anti-Black stereotypes – what we are calling de facto racism – through audit studies.[45] Researchers Michael Fix and Raymond Struyk describe the basic method of audit studies this way:

> Two individuals (auditors or testers) are matched for all relevant personal characteristics other than the one that is presumed to lead to discrimination, e.g. race, ethnicity, gender. They then apply for a job, a housing unit, or a mortgage, or begin to negotiate for a good or service. The results they achieve and the treatment they receive in the transaction are closely observed, documented, and analyzed to determine if the outcomes reveal patterns of differential treatment on the basis of the trait studied and/or protected by anti-discrimination laws. (cited in Bertrand and Duflo, 2016, p. 8)

These studies conclude that discrimination occurs if the protected group receives worse results or treatment.

One example includes economists Marianne Bertrand and Sendhil Mullainathan's 2004 study, "Are Emily and Brendan More Employable than Lakisha and Jamal?" Their field experiment:

> [sent] fictitious résumés in response to help-wanted ads in Boston and Chicago newspapers. To manipulate perceived race, they randomly assigned very white-sounding names (such as Emily Walsh or Greg Baker) to half the résumés and very African-American-sounding names (such as Lakisha Washington or Jamal Jones) to the other half. In total, they responded to over 1,300 employment ads in the sales, administrative support, clerical, and customer services job categories and sent out nearly 5,000 résumés. They find that white names receive 50 percent

more call-backs for interviews. (Bertrand and Duflo, 2016, pp. 12–13)

Sociologist S. Michael Gaddis (2019) sums up the empirical findings to date of such audit studies of racial and ethnic-based discrimination, "The literature suggests that racial–ethnic discrimination is prevalent across multiple and diverse contexts, knows no geographic bounds, and has been widespread for decades" (p. 446).

Survey data from the NORC GSS correspond with the existence of stereotypes that motivate this discriminatory behavior. Figure 2.3 shows responses, by race, to the question of whether individual attributes among Black Americans – a "lack of motivation or willpower" – can explain the economic disadvantages Black Americans experience. Between 1977 and the late 1990s, more than half of White Americans

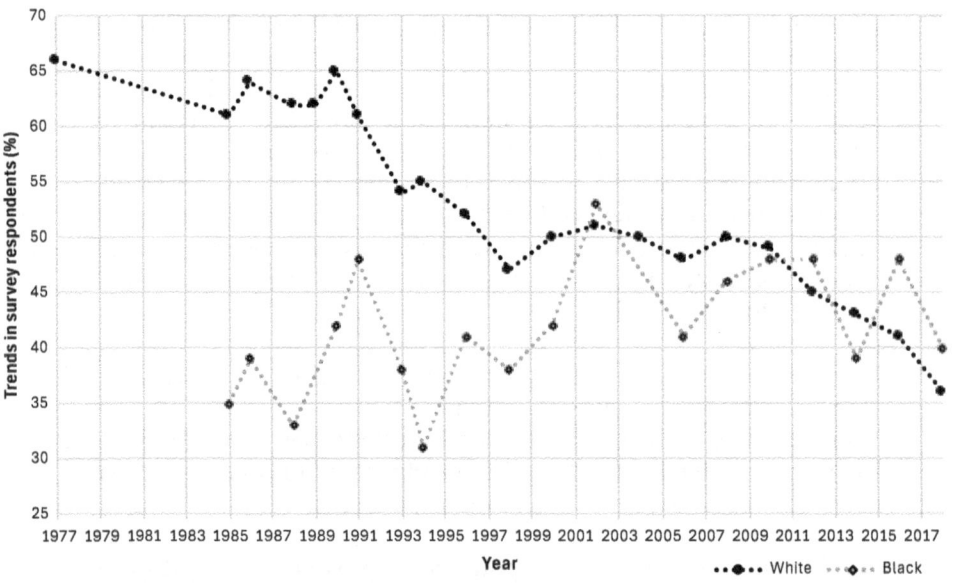

Note: Preceded by the statement, "On average, (Negroes/blacks/African Americans) have worse jobs, income and housing than white people," survey respondents were asked "Do you think these differences are ... because most African Americans just don't have the motivation or willpower to pull themselves up out of poverty?" Figure depicts percent who responded "Yes."

Figure 2.3 Trends in percentage of survey respondents who believe that Black Americans' "lack of motivation" explains racial inequality, 1977–2018.
Data source: Davern et al. (n.d.), General Social Survey (GSS) 1977–2018 data file accessed from GSS Data Explorer.

agree. It is clear that this is a racially informed view as more than half of Black Americans, in contrast, *disagree* with the statement over the same time period (data for Black Americans are not available until 1985). Not until 2010 does the percentage of White Americans who attribute "lack of motivation" as the cause of racial inequality fall consistently below 50%, similar to Black Americans.

The majority of White Americans hold the view that structural factors, such as discrimination, are not the cause of inequality (see figure 2.4). This is consistent with the first element of laissez-faire racism – a belief in racial stereotypes – as well as the second element, a belief that individual choices drive race-based outcomes. Between 1977 and 2014, about 40 percent or less of White Americans agreed with the idea that discrimination was a primary factor in explaining racial inequality in jobs, income, and housing. Put another way, among White Americans, support for the structural factor, discrimination, as a driver of racial inequality is 15 to 30 percentage points less than White Americans' support for the individual-based factor "lack of

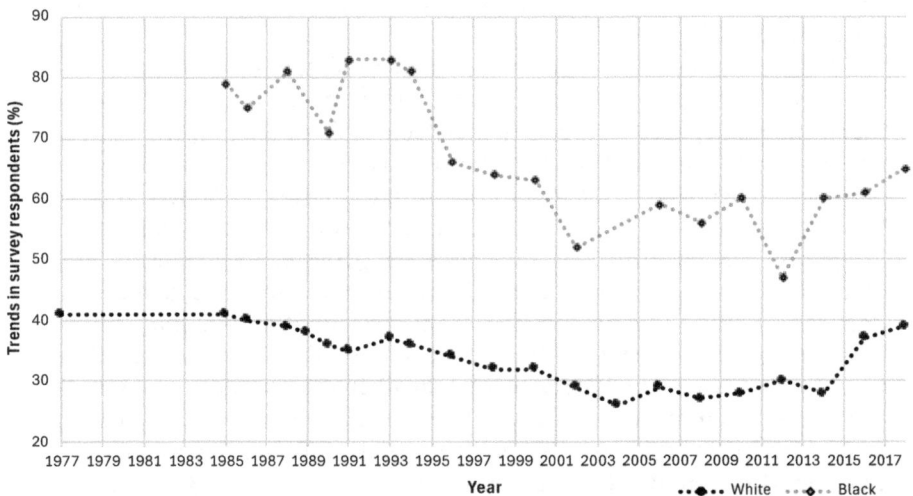

Note: Preceded by the statement, "On average, (Negroes/blacks/African Americans) have worse jobs, income and housing than white people," survey respondents were asked: "Do you think these differences are ... mainly due to discrimination?" Figure depicts the percent who responded "Yes."

Figure 2.4 Trends in percentage of survey respondents who agree that "discrimination" explains racial inequality, 1977–2018.

Data source: Davern et al. (n.d.), General Social Survey (GSS) 1977–2018 data file accessed from GSS Data Explorer.

willpower." Here again, the racial difference in beliefs is clear: for most of the last three decades (the period for which we have data), about 60% or more of Black Americans point to discrimination as a driver of racial inequality.

In another nationally representative public opinion survey (Gallup Poll), the vast majority – about 80% – of White respondents indicated by 1978 that Black Americans "have as good a chance as white people in your community to get any kind of job for which they are qualified." This compares to 51 percent in 1963.[46] Effectively, 30% of White respondents jettisoned discrimination as a causal factor for employment discrimination between 1963 and 1978, even while Black unemployment remained twice as high as the rate of White unemployment over this same time period (see Shulman, 1991, and figure 1.1 above). Moreover, roughly 80% of White respondents have consistently held the view that Black Americans received fair treatment regarding employment opportunities between 1978 and 2013. The views among Black Americans are starkly different. In 1963, 23% of Black Americans felt that they had as good a chance at obtaining a job for which they had qualifications. This increases substantially to 38% in 1978, but basically remains at this level with few exceptions through 2020.[47]

Finally, survey data provide evidence of the third element of laissez-faire racism – that public policy should not be used to reduce racial inequality (see figure 2.5). Between 1973 and 2014, the NORC survey results show that roughly two-thirds to three-quarters of White Americans feel that government spending is either "about right" or "too much" on "improving the conditions of Blacks." This again, is against the backdrop of measures of persistent racial economic inequality, basically unchanged in magnitude, over the same four decades. Echoing this perspective, from 1975 to 2018, the majority of White respondents feel that "the government has no special obligation to help improve their [Black Americans'] living standards." Only in 2018 does this figure dip slightly below the 50% mark. The view among Black Americans diverges sharply from that of White Americans: less than one-third of Black Americans feel that government spending on improving their conditions is adequate across the entire 1973–2018 period, and roughly 20% or less feel that the government has no special obligation to redress the impact of discrimination on their living standards.

Consistent with these sentiments, survey data indicate a high level of opposition among White Americans to public policies to redress discrimination, such as affirmative action (see figure 2.6). The

A. *Percent who Agree that Government is Spending About the Right Amount or Too Much to Improve Conditions of Blacks, 1973–2018*

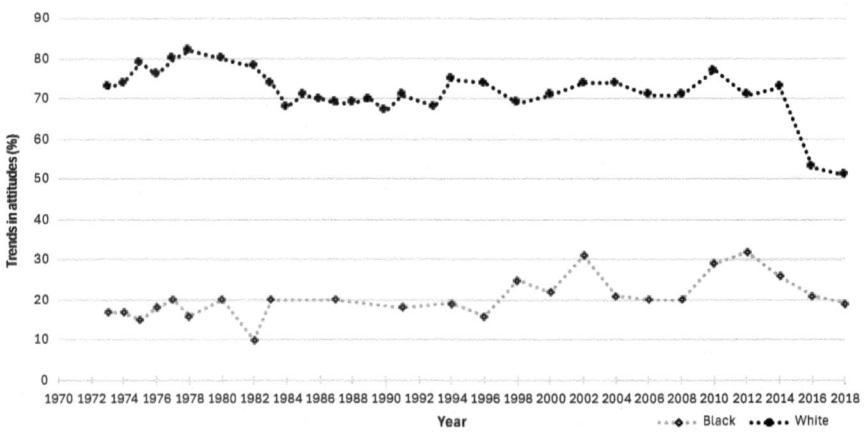

Note: The survey question "Spending on Blacks (NORC)" asks: "We are faced with many problems in this country, none of which can be solved easily or inexpensively. I'm going to name some of these problems, and for each one I'd like you to tell me whether you think we're spending too much money on it, too little money, or about the right amount ... Improving the conditions of blacks. Are we spending too much, too little, or about the right amount on improving the conditions of blacks?"

B. *Percent who Say that Government Has No Special Obligation to Help Blacks Improve their Living Standards, 1975–2018*

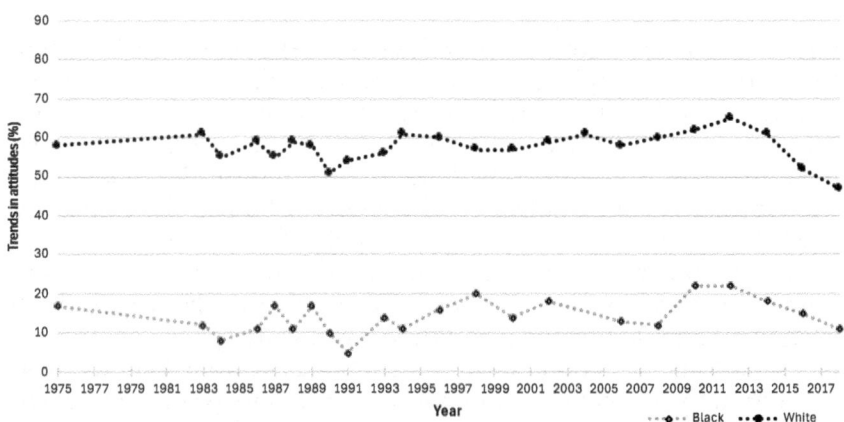

Note: The survey question "Help Blacks (NORC)" asks: "Some people think that (Negroes/blacks/African Americans) have been discriminated against for so long that the government has a special obligation to help improve their living standards. Others believe that the government should not be giving special treatment to (Negroes/blacks/African Americans). Where would you place yourself on this scale, or haven't you made up your mind on this?"

Figure 2.5 Trends in attitudes toward government intervention to address racial inequality, by race.
Source: Krysan and Moberg (2021).

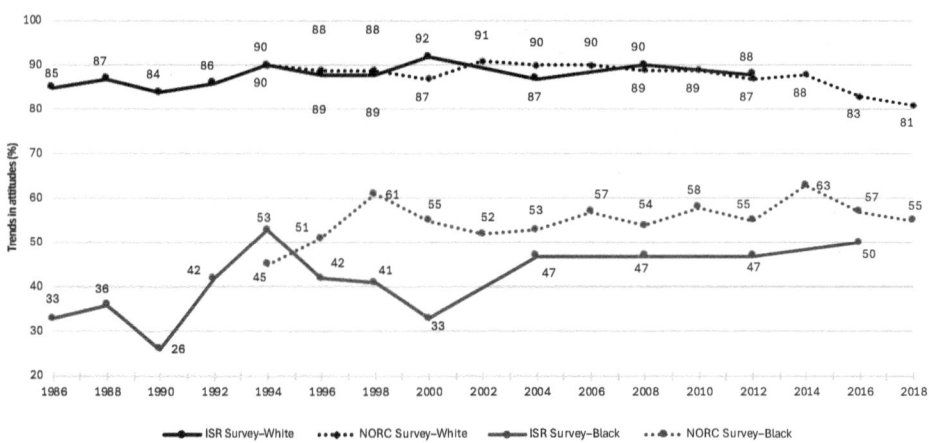

Figure 2.6 Trends in Americans' attitudes toward affirmative action policies in employment, 1986–2018.
Source: Krysan and Moberg (2021).

objective of affirmative action policies is to examine whether White Americans, for example, hold a monopoly on higher-status positions in a firm or other institution and to proactively implement policies to break up any apparent monopolies. As a result, the general public often associate words such as "quotas" or "reverse discrimination" with affirmative action policies.[48] The NORC GSS and the University of Michigan's Institute for Social Research (ISR) surveys ask about preferential treatment for Black Americans in the area of hiring and promotion in employment. Figure 2.6 shows that the large majority – between 80 and 90 percent – of White Americans oppose or strongly oppose affirmative action policies in employment from 1986 to 2014. Opposition to affirmative action policies is much weaker among Black Americans, with about one-third opposing such policies prior to 1990, rising to about one-half through 2018.

Bobo and his colleagues' assessment on this last point continues to hold as of the writing of this book in 2024, despite significant shifts in American views on racial inequality in recent years. In 2014, support for the view among White Americans that Black Americans' "lack of will" is a primary driver of Black economic disadvantages dropped significantly below 50% for the first time, to 43%, and continued to fall thereafter. Additionally, the percent of White Americans who identified "discrimination" as a primary explanatory factor of Black economic disadvantage exceeded "lack of will" for the first time in 2018 (39% vs. 36%, respectively). Even White Americans' view on whether government spending to aid Black Americans "is about right or too much" dropped an unprecedented 20 percentage points between 2014 and 2016. These dramatic changes in views on individual and structural factors among White Americans coincide with the swell of political organizing within the Black Lives Matter movement; a rash of highly publicized murders of Black Americans, including by police; and the presidential election of Donald Trump, a public figure known for holding thinly veiled racist views.[49] At the same time, interventionist policies such as affirmative action remain opposed by the great majority – at least 80% – of White respondents. Moreover, the view that government spending to aid Black Americans is about right or too much remains the majority opinion among White respondents.

2.4. Elements of a Multiracial Analysis

Our focus on the Black–White dimension of the racial hierarchy is due to its foundational role in the US social hierarchy. As we noted earlier (see figure 2.1), the near-entirety of this nation's roughly 400-year history operated with a social hierarchy explicitly structured with Black people filling its bottom rung. Of course, the competition between social groups for economic and political resources – i.e., favored positions in the social hierarchy – constructs social meanings for more than just Black and White racial categories. Describing this process would produce sufficient material for another book in its own right. Here, we offer a few observations about common features across the construction of racial categories.

2.4.1. Generalizing the Analytical Framework

As we have already elaborated on extensively above, our stratification economics approach focuses on the analytical category of social groups. This approach analyzes how advantaged social groups in an existing social hierarchy deploy political and economic resources to create or monopolize favored positions. And, likewise, social groups in unfavorable positions use the resources they can access to improve their position or eliminate unequal positions. These processes create the social meanings of race. To generalize our analytical framework to include other ethnoracial groups beyond Black and White Americans, we consider the following questions about how such groups interact with, and/or integrate into, US society.

(1) At the time of the group's entry into US society, what were the existing economic and political conditions of the receiving group(s)?
(2) What patterns of discrimination did the ethnoracial group face?
(3) What resources did the ethnoracial group bring with them upon entry to US society?[50]

In this section, we consider briefly the situation of Asians to demonstrate how answering these three questions is incisive for understanding the construction of the racial category "Asian" as well as "Black."[51]

2.4.1.1. The Asian Case

We begin with some context for our discussion of the racialization of Asian Americans. Figure 2.7 presents US Census data on the size and composition of the Asian community in the United States from 1860 to 2020.[52] Among the most notable dimensions of this community is its relative smallness as a share of the US population, particularly over the

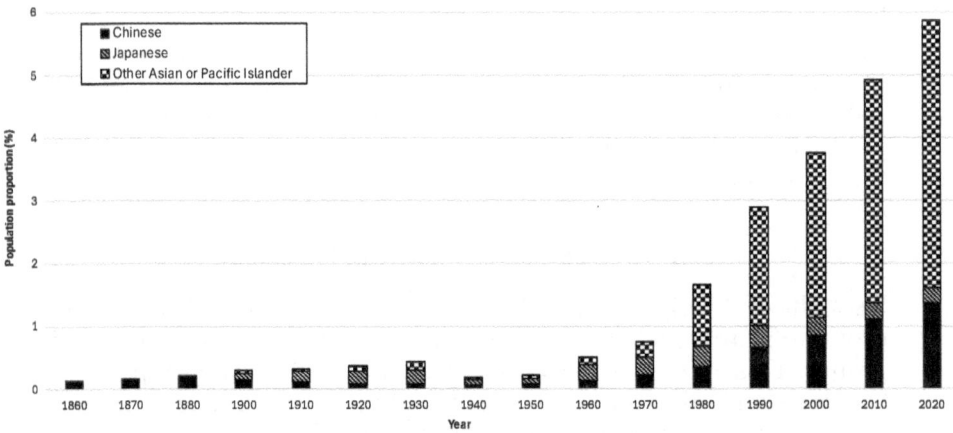

Figure 2.7 Asian population in the United States, 1860–2020
Data source: Ruggles et al. (2025), IPUMS USA: Version 16.0 [data set]. Minneapolis, MN: IPUMS.

century between 1860 and 1960. During this period, US immigration policy actively limited the size of the Asian community to a sliver – to 0.5 percent or less – of the US population. Over the next 60 years from 1960 to 2020, changes to immigration policy allowed this share to grow more than tenfold, to 5.9 percent in 2020.

American immigration policy not only actively curtailed the size of the Asian community in the US but also determined its composition in terms of origin countries and economic class. These immigrants came to the US, in part, to take advantage of growing employment opportunities, particularly in mining gold and building railroads in the West, but also in agricultural and garment factory work.[53] Anti-Chinese sentiment along the West Coast, particularly strong among the American workers competing with Chinese workers, pushed lawmakers to pass the Chinese Exclusion Act of 1882.[54] The Act restricted Chinese immigration on the basis of economic position, excluding Chinese laborers and their wives from entering the United States. Specifically, "the words 'Chinese laborers', wherever used in this act shall be construed to mean both skilled and unskilled laborers and Chinese employed in mining – but not teachers, students, merchants, or tourists."[55]

After 1882, the number of people emigrating from Japan to the US began to rise, pulled to the continent by the labor demand left unmet by the limited number of Chinese immigrants. Japanese immigrants experienced the same fate as the Chinese: anti-Japanese sentiment motivated lawmakers to pass the "Gentleman's Agreement" in 1907, which blocked the immigration of Japanese laborers specifically. President Roosevelt expressed his goal to "keep the movement of the citizens of each country into the other restricted as far as possible to students, travelers, businessmen, and the like ... what was necessary was to prevent all immigration of Japanese laboring men – that is, of the Coolie class – into the United States."[56]

Subsequent laws – the Asiatic Barred Zone Act of 1917 and the Immigration Act of 1924 – created a near-ban on Asian immigrants entering the US until 1965. As a result, by 1940, Asian residents in the US dipped below 0.2 percent of the US population – the lowest share since 1870.

The Immigration Act of 1965 (a.k.a. the Hart–Cellar Act) removed discriminatory immigration caps on non-European countries.[57] The new rules set preferences for highly educated workers, as well as those with family members already in the US. In other words, immigrants' ability to enter the country hinged significantly on their class status. This was especially true for immigrants from non-European countries who rarely had an already-established family foothold in the US. Between 1970 and 1980, Asians, as a percent of the US population, surged and this figure has continued to rise since. Finally, most of this growth was among Asian groups other than Japanese and Chinese. By 2022, about 70 percent of Asians in the US identified their origin country as somewhere other than China or Japan. This figure in 1960 was about 20 percent.

With that backdrop, we now consider how the racial category "Asian" developed, given the economic and political resources that Asian immigrants brought with them, as well as the economic and political conditions they faced when they arrived in the US. Take, for example, political scientist Claire Kim's description of how the defining racial characteristics of Asians evolved out of the political economic conditions of the mid-nineteenth-century US (Kim, 1999). Intense political upheaval in America at this time threatened the political viability of the labor practice of enslaving people. Chinese migrant workers – as members of a non-White race – had the potential to resolve this labor question for White landowners and businessmen. The not-whiteness of the Chinese made high levels of Chinese labor exploitation socially acceptable and politically viable: these Chinese workers did not have any claim to US citizenship.[58] In addition, designating Chinese workers as separate and different from enslaved Black people enabled White employers to dodge the politically contentious issue of slavery. We quote at length here Kim's description of how the social meaning of the racial category "Asian" evolved as part and parcel of the Black–White political contest of the times – a process she dubs "racial triangulation":

> Although Chinese immigrant labor promised to solve this dilemma [the need for cheap and plentiful labor], it raised the specter of a second form of slavery that would create yet another permanent class of degraded non-Whites. Racial triangulation reconciled the urgent need for labor with the imperative of continuing White dominance. By positioning Asian immigrants as superior to Blacks yet permanently foreign and unassimilable with Whites, racial triangulation processes fashioned a labor force that would fulfill a temporary economic purpose without making any enduring claims upon the polity. (1999, p. 109)

Kim then quotes a White Southerner with this blunt formulation of Chinese laborers' role: "Give us five million Chinese laborers in the valley of the Mississippi and we can furnish the world with cotton and teach the negro his proper place" (1999, p. 112). This trend, however, was short-lived. Kim describes how Southern plantation owners found it difficult to procure a sufficient supply of Chinese immigrant workers. Then, by 1877, political gains by Southern Democrats enabled Southern planters to reverse many of the Reconstruction-period reforms and re-establish an approximation of the labor conditions of slavery. This political reversal eliminated the demand for Chinese laborers. At about the same time, the Chinese Exclusion Act of 1882 also limited this labor supply.

Kim further notes that this political turn of events reduced the need to control the activity of Asians via discriminatory laws and practices, setting the conditions for a greater divergence in the social meaning attributed to the racial groups "Asians" and "Blacks." For example, Chinese workers, no longer *needed* as a "degraded non-White" labor force, faced fewer barriers to carving out a different economic position within the Southern economies. These workers achieved their foothold in a kind of intermediate position between Black and White Southerners, owning and operating grocery stores, for example. Kim, citing the research of historian James Loewen (1971) and scholar Jeannine Rhee (1994), describes how these Chinese also made efforts to distance themselves from the disadvantaged position of Black people while associating with Whites and their advantaged social position. Their efforts included discouraging intermarriage with Black people, giving their children "White-sounding" names, and participating in and supporting White social institutions (e.g., White churches).[59]

While Asians existed in a type of "intermediate" position in the social hierarchy between White and Black Americans, the racial designation "Asian" had an additional social meaning. "Asian" had a fundamentally un-American quality – a stigmatized un-assimilability into the American community that marked Asians as treacherous and untrustworthy. This view of Asians as un-assimilable served as justification for curtailing their political rights, subjecting them to what Kim terms "civic ostracism," and helped to pass anti-Asian immigration laws. As noted above, the combination of anti-Asian laws, including the Chinese Exclusion Act of 1882 and Immigration Act of 1924, effectively ended Asian immigration to the US at the close of the 1920s.[60]

Finally, passage of the 1965 Hart–Cellar Act that prioritized highly educated immigrants who could meet specific labor shortages in the US gave rise to a high share of the Asian immigrants coming in with professional or technical training, such as health professionals.[61] For example, for the 10 years after the passage of the Hart–Cellar Act, between 15 and 30 percent of Asian immigrants had professional or technical training. This compares to less than 13 percent across all immigrants over this same period.[62] As a result, many of these Asian immigrants came to the US with the skills needed to fill existing openings in relatively high-status occupations. This distinctive feature of US immigration policy forecast relative economic success for Asian Americans. In 2019, Asian-headed households had a median income of about $98,200, as compared to $68,700 across all US households.[63]

This Asian immigration story is illustrative of a pattern that Darity Jr. observes in his survey of the class trajectory of various immigrant groups to the US: that the economic class of immigrants play a determinant role in the economic position they achieve in the country they migrate to. Darity Jr. (1989) finds that: "Where ethnicity and class status overlap, a major conclusion can be drawn. Historically, the relative position of ethnic groups disproportionately represented in particular class positions remains remarkably stable as they migrate from one country or region to a new one. The ethnic success stories in the United States merely confirm this generalization" (p. 355). In other words, the relative economic success of Asian Americans can be linked to the resources that Asian immigrants brought with them starting in the mid-1960s: a large share of Asian immigrants were themselves already relatively economically successful in their home countries (i.e., highly educated).[64] And, at the same time, the US limited Asian immigrants specifically to those who could fulfill existing employment opportunities – i.e., meet labor shortages. The economic success of these Asian immigrants and their descendants has, in part, contributed to the characterization of Asians as a "model minority." For Asians and Asian Americans, the social meaning of race includes two dimensions: Asians are perceived as, on the one hand, a relatively economically advantaged minority – that is, "not Black" – and, on the other hand, fundamentally un-American – that is, "not White."

2.4.2. Racial Groups Are Mutually Constitutive

We want to offer one final observation on the question of how race is constructed, now broadened to consider multiple racial categories: the construction of each racial group is constitutive of all other racial groups. That is, the social meaning of the racial category Asian evolved from establishing political economic advantages and disadvantages for the group *relative to other social groups*. To borrow a term from Kim, the social meanings attributed to each racial group normalize the social hierarchy, the "normative blueprint" of who should get what political and economic resources. What Asians *should* get necessarily involves considerations of how this compares to what Blacks should get, and also what Whites should get, and so on. Kim's analysis of Chinese workers' role in the American economy during the mid nineteenth century illustrates: Chinese workers distinguished the "whiteness" of Whites, by supplying labor that was extra-exploitable by White employers – that is, workers that employers could exploit more than White workers. Chinese workers also helped define the "Blackness" of Blacks, by providing an extra-exploitable workforce to compete with the formerly enslaved Black workers and remind Black workers of their "proper place."

Fast forward to the twentieth century, and into the twenty-first: the racial triangulation of Asians and Asian Americans continues in the contemporary debate around affirmative action policies in higher education admissions.[65] That is, Asians' and Asian Americans' racial positioning, in what Kim refers to as "the field of racial positions," is defined in reference to the racial positioning of Blacks and Whites both. Today, to be Asian is to be socially valued as a "model" minority, viewed as such due to the group's relative economic success, particularly in relation to Black Americans. At the same time, Asians are a "minority" nonetheless, as the cultural essence of Asian Americans holds them to be forever-foreigners, un-assimilable to US values (Kim, 1999).

For this reason, Kim quotes well-known *Washington Post* columnist George Will's commentary on affirmative action policies during the 1980s in her article on racial triangulation. As Kim notes, the column came out as then-President Reagan was promoting the view that affirmative action policies increased diversity by using anti-Asian racial quotas. Will echoes this view in his 1989 column titled "Prejudice Against Excellence," lambasting affirmative action policies saying, "Affirmative action discriminated against Asian Americans by restricting the social rewards to competition on the basis of merit ... [I]t is lunacy to punish Asian Americans – the nation's model minority – for their passion to excel."[66]

Will's column has the effect of simultaneously: (1) attributing merit (i.e., excellence) to White Americans' monopoly on the upper echelons of US society by implying that competition on the basis of merit is the status quo, and that affirmative action interferes with it; (2) essentializing Asian-ness as including a "passion to excel," for which they are being discriminated against; and (3) essentializing a "lack of passion to excel" among non-Asian minorities, such as Black Americans, against whom affirmative action policies apparently are *not* discriminating. Will's commentary builds social meaning to racial categories by characterizing different groups' cultural traits relative to each other – which, in turn, map their racial positions in the social hierarchy.

2.5. Conclusion

We began this chapter with a description of how a state-enforced, explicit, and biologically defined racism developed within the political economy of colonial America. Explicitly racist laws persisted for 350 years of the country's roughly 400 years of development. Throughout this history, Black Americans and their allies rebelled against this racial oppression and made significant civil rights gains, peaking in the 1960s with the dismantling of the racialized legal infrastructure, as well as the social legitimacy of what sociologists Bobo et al. (1997) dubbed "Jim Crow racism."

We then observed how the high degree of racial inequality in the basic economic dimensions of American society – in employment, earnings and income, and wealth – remained preserved after the 1960s despite these major changes in contemporary legal and social practices. We underscore how the continued ability of White Americans to monopolize privileged positions depends on a new type of racism, a "laissez-faire" racism. Laissez-faire racism eschews discrimination as a causal factor for racial inequality and objects to public policy interventions intended to remedy discriminatory outcomes. The racialized structure of the social hierarchy – safeguarded by laissez-faire racism – continues to motivate and reinforce the social meanings of racial categories, continuously reifying the social concept of race.

Laissez-faire racism requires a collective and profound disregard of the political and economic environment developed over 350 years of US history by explicitly racist laws and institutions, and adopts a putatively colorblind outlook. This outlook ignores the roots, and continued offshoots, of racism-based inequalities, and the need for anti-racist laws and institutions to eliminate them. This ideology helps explain why Black Americans' attempts to break up White Americans' monopoly over favored positions in the social hierarchy through government interventions, such as affirmative action, appear as illegitimate incursions to be opposed by White Americans. In this way, laissez-faire racism provides a powerful ideological foundation to promote White racial solidarity and resistance against any radical changes to the racialized social hierarchy. As a result, race continues to serve as a major stratifying concept for US society.

This book focuses on Black–White race relations because it is the tension within these relations that dominates much of the political turbulence that defines the nation's history. At the same time, we show, if briefly, in the final section of this chapter, how the analytic framework we use to understand the political economy of anti-Black racism – stratification economics – can also be used to understand the political economy of racism with regard to other ethnoracial groups. In the chapter that follows, we illustrate how anti-Blackness impacts the combined racial and ethnic Afro-Latinx identity. We will look to other books to do justice to the analytical project of applying a fuller stratification economics approach to the construction of ethnoracial groups beyond the categories of Black and White.

3
Afro-Latinxs and Anti-Blackness

3.1. Introduction

This chapter will explore the potency of anti-Blackness for a demographic group whose identity includes not only race but also ethnicity – Afro-Latinxs, a group that forms a nexus between the Latinx community and the Black population in the United States. Two goals in examining this group in this chapter are to show how externally experienced anti-Blackness can be manifested within intragroup dynamics, as well as how a group whose identity is not solely Black is nevertheless impacted in very similar ways to Black-only identified individuals by anti-Black policies, practices, and behaviors. Existing economic research on Afro-Latinxs in the US shows that this group appears to share more in common socio-economically with Black Americans than with other major Latinx groups, particularly White-identified Latinxs, with respect to several key economic indicators. Why is this, and what role does anti-Blackness play in the common experiences between Afro-Latinxs and Black Americans? One clue may be research which shows that darker skin tones are associated with economic penalties for the Latinxs in the United States.[1]

African Americans and Afro-Latinxs have higher rates of unemployment and poverty compared to Latinxs in general, including White-identifying Latinxs.[2] Data also show that Afro-Latinxs and Black Americans have similar levels of wealth and household income.[3] However, Afro-Latinxs have a higher average educational attainment level when compared to the Latinx as well as Black communities, but this does not result in predicted returns for income or labor force status.[4] This disconnect between educational attainment and economic outcomes is especially noteworthy for the US Afro-Latinx demographic, and affirms literature that challenges prevailing economic theory that posits education as the primary avenue for achieving economic mobility.[5] As a related note, in chapter 5 we outline how educational opportunities have historically been hoarded by White Americans in order to legitimize their claim to greater economic rewards in the labor market.

Throughout this book, we use terms like the "Black community," "Black Americans," "African Americans," and "Blacks." In all instances in which we use the term "Black," it's likely the case that most readers assume we are talking solely about African Americans or Black people from the Caribbean or the African continent. However, under the umbrella term "Black" we include Latinx individuals of African ancestry. At the same time, it is the case that not all Latinxs of African ancestry acknowledge their Blackness – research shows that some dark-skinned Latinxs, if asked, will identify as White.[6] The construction of race, and how this translates to racial self-identification, are far from simple.

Stratification economic theory can help us understand the experiences of Afro-Latinxs in the US in the following ways: (1) because Afro-Latinxs often possess African phenotypical attributes, they are perceived, and therefore treated, as any other member of the Black community, the "non-dominant" group whose identity doesn't accrue value; and (2) because material benefits don't accrue as a result of being a member of the non-dominant group, there are members of the Afro-Latinx community who will deny their Blackness.

3.2. Afro-Latinxs and Externally Experienced Anti-Blackness

Contemporary scholarship on Afro-Latinxs shows the economic experiences of this demographic in the US more closely mimic the economic experiences of Black Americans than they do Latinxs in general. These common experiences not only encompass things such as poverty, unemployment, and income levels, but also extend to issues such as criminal legal system involvement: in a 2018 report by the ACLU-Florida on arrests and sentencing in Miami-Dade county, Afro-Latinx men had the worst outcomes at each point, from arrest to conviction and sentencing, compared to non-Hispanic White men, White-identifying Latinx men, and even non-Hispanic Black men.[7] These findings are consistent with a body of literature regarding the American pattern of a higher incarceration rate for Black men – as compared to White[8] – which we also discuss at length in chapter 8.

Why don't economic indicators for US Afro-Latinxs more closely resemble those for the American Latinx community in general? The Black-identified part of the Latinx community is subject to anti-Black beliefs, practices, and policies which we have delineated in the other chapters of this book. That is, the myriad ways through which anti-Blackness appears in the US economy produces an economically stratified Latinx community. In this section, we explore the sources of Black identity within the Latinx community.

Research conducted using US Census Bureau data from the American Community Survey (ACS) for the period 2011–15 points to one potential factor: it showed that African American was the most cited primary ancestry among Afro-Latinxs, followed closely by Puerto Rico[9] – see figure 3.1. If ancestral analysis is restricted only to Afro-Latinxs born in the US or its territories, then nearly a third of respondents report African American ancestry. Many Afro-Latinxs, therefore, identify with Black Americans due to the presence of a Black/African American parent or grandparent. Along with those Afro-Latinxs who have an African American parent, there are other

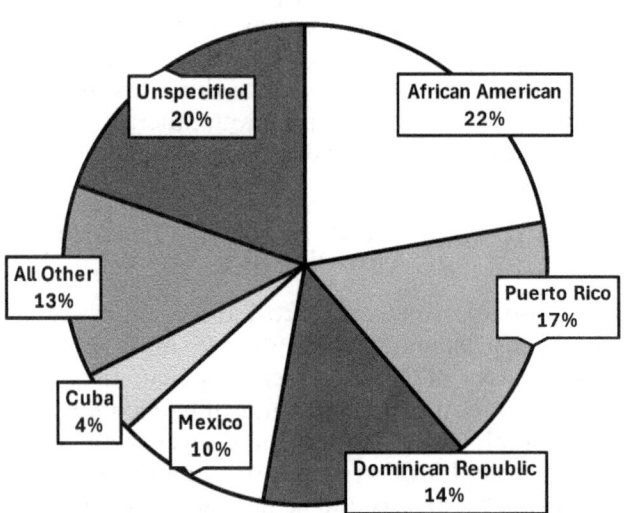

Figure 3.1 Reported primary ancestry of Afro-Latinxs in the US, 2011–2015

Data source: Author analysis of 2011–15 American Community Survey 5-year data obtained from Steven Ruggles, Katie Genadek, Ronald Goeken, Josiah Grover, and Matthew Sobek, Integrated Public Use Microdata Series, version 6.0 [data set]. Minneapolis, University of Minnesota, 2015. http://doi.org/10.18128/D010.V6.0.

contributing factors to the commonalities between Black Americans and US Afro-Latinxs.

In examining the issue of ancestral origins, although Afro-Latinx survey respondents reported more than 20 different nations of origin in ACS data for 2011–15, just a few countries and territories dominate this group's ancestral distribution, including Puerto Rico as the second most cited area of ancestry, followed by the Dominican Republic, Mexico, and Cuba.[10] The region which, therefore, predominates in the ancestral origins of Afro-Latinxs in the US is primarily the Caribbean, where large Black populations exist.[11]

Another explanation for the economic similarities between Afro-Latinxs in the US and African Americans may be marital patterns. Marital patterns reinforce the source of a shared Black identity, as can the economic effects of racism that both Afro-Latinxs and African Americans experience in the US. Recent research on Latinx intermarriage in the US shows race-based patterns operating within the group.[12] For example, in their study of Latinx intermarriage, Qian, Lichter, and Tumin found non-White Puerto Ricans "may follow the color line and marry Blacks more often than self-identified White Puerto Ricans, especially if the former are segregated from non-Hispanic Whites in neighborhoods or occupational niches."[13]

Shared cultural influences due to shared proximity may also play a pivotal role in how closely American Afro-Latinxs and Black Americans are aligned. On the one hand, African American culture has developed over four centuries. It is, thus, well defined, with identifiable elements extending back to not only the slave experience in the US but also West African culture. On the other hand, American Latinxs are a more heterogeneous group, with influences from many different countries and regions. For Puerto Ricans and Dominicans specifically, close proximity to Black Americans during different stages of migration likely had a racialized effect. Research indicates, for example, that there is a correlation between longevity in the US and racial identity falling along the "Black or White" framework.[14]

Afro-Latinxs who self-identify as Black may also choose their identity based on shared anti-Black experiences. Identity formation is complex and can be intergenerational. At different points in their lives, Afro-Latinxs (or their children) may "choose Blackness,"[15] which affirms unity with Black Americans and may occur whether they previously sought community with the latter group or not. Some social scientists have espoused the faulty view that anglophone

Caribbean and African-continent immigrants appear to possess a work ethic missing among Black Americans, and therefore conclude racism cannot be an important determinant in economic disparities.[16] This view negates, among other things, the important role of Black American culture in affirming and uplifting the identities of those within Black demographic groups, such as Afro-Latinxs.[17]

Whether due to possessing African phenotypical attributes given Caribbean ancestry or African American ancestry, which makes one vulnerable to anti-Black bias, or "choosing Blackness" given cultural affinities or shared experiences of Black marginalization in the US, data evidence clearly indicates that, among the Latinx community in America, Afro-Latinxs experience poorer economic outcomes – lower homeownership rates,[18] higher poverty rates, higher unemployment rates, lower median wages – than Latinxs overall. The Latinx community is economically stratified along racial lines in America due to the impact of anti-Black beliefs, policies, and actions on this demographic.

Philosopher Denise Ferreira Da Silva on Race and Coloniality

They seem to me people of such innocence that, if we understood them and they understood us, they would become Christian soon; for they do not have nor understand any faith, it seems to me; and, therefore, if the banished, who will remain here, learn well their language and understand them, I have no doubt, according to the holy desire of Your Highness, they will become Christian and believe in Holy Faith, . . . for it is sure this is a good and humble people, which will absorb anything given to them; and Our Lord gave them good bodies and good faces, as to good men, and he, who brought us here, I believe, was not without a cause.
Pedro Vaz de Caminha, *Carta a El Rei Dom Manuel* (1500)

These are the words used by the official chronicler of the fleet expedition of Pedro Álvares Cabral, Portuguese nobleman Pedro Vaz de Caminha, in a letter penned to King Manuel I of Portugal to describe early encounters with the Indigenous Tupinambá people upon arrival in the lands now known as Brazil.

While it was Spain that laid the initial groundwork for the colonization of the so-called New World beginning in the 1490s, it was Portugal that catalyzed the early expansion of Europe beyond established boundaries (Hart, 2003). Cabral's voyage in 1500 marks a significant event in the history of colonization. It was on this voyage that Caminha officially records Portugal's claim over Brazil, a territory that would later emerge as a key colony for the Portuguese.

Caminha's statement is reminiscent of those made by Christopher Columbus, who also used *innocence* to characterize the Indigenous people of a soon-to-be colonized America. For Afro-Brazilian contemporary philosopher Denise Ferreira da Silva, the portrayal of the Indigenous Tupinambá as "people of such innocence" represents a form of colonial ideology; such descriptions serve to justify European colonization and domination over Indigenous people by depicting them as childlike, primitive, and in need of European guidance.

In *Toward a Global Idea of Race* (2007), Ferreira da Silva locates in these descriptions of a European colonizer's first encounters with Black and Indigenous "others" the emergence of the idea of *affectability* in European thought – a moment that would come to define racialization.

These moments reveal the roots of Western philosophy's idea of self-determination, as the colonizer sees himself as being ruled only by *interior* motives – and thus capable of self-determination – in relation to Black and Indigenous others who are susceptible to *exterior* affectability: a people who "absorb anything given to them," who need to be brought into the right way of being by the religiously sovereign (Christian), "rational," White European – a people destined to be ruled by forces external to them. Race arises here as a signifier that marks some of us as affectable and others as self-determined.

Herein lies the flaw at the root of the idea of self-determination in modern thinking. Ferreira da Silva crucially reminds us that we all encounter forces outside of us constantly – therefore, we are *all* exteriorly affectable. There is no such thing as a sovereign, self-determined human and there is no human other fit to be controlled, completely and defenselessly at the whim of the exterior world.

Written by Daniella Medina

3.3. Latinxs and Anti-Blackness

Anti-Blackness can take many different forms, but one permutation of it is when members of groups with African ancestry don't acknowledge this ancestry. For example, recognition of the African presence in Latin America and the Spanish-speaking Caribbean by the countries and territories in this part of the world has had a complex and challenging history. Estimates suggest that an estimated 25 percent of the population in Latin America has African ancestry.[19] However, the notion of "mestizaje" complicates our understanding of the presence of Black-identified persons within Latinx populations. "Mestizaje" refers to people from Latin America and the Spanish-speaking Caribbean considered to be of "mixed" – Indigenous, European, and African – ancestry. Due to the promotion of the designation "mestizaje" by public policy in Latin America and the Spanish-speaking Caribbean, many individuals who would have once self-identified as Black came to abandon the designation in favor of "mestizaje" (Wade, 2010; Whitten and Torres, 1998). Moreover, sociologist Clara E. Rodriguez has written about the idea of Latinxs as "rainbow people."[20] However, the late, great Afro-Latina scholar and anti-Black racism activist Miriam Jiménez Román helped clarify why the concept of mestizaje poses difficulties for understanding the challenges of Latinxs with African ancestry:

> Latin@s may well be the only social group in the world who so emphatically insist on their ethno-racial mixture. But even as mestizo, or mixed identity – expressed variably as raza, "rainbow people," or "mutts" – is a commonplace collective designation, Latin@s are also understood to be "of any race." This apparent contradiction can be traced to the convergence of two seemingly distinct racial formations. On the one hand, the national ideologies of our countries of origin emphasize racial mixture and equate it with racial democracy – even as whiteness continues to be privileged, and indigenous and African ancestry are viewed as something to be overcome or ignored. On the other hand, in the United States Latin@s have been allocated an ambiguous racial middle ground that makes invisible those too dark to conform to the mestizo ideal, while simultaneously distancing them from other communities of color, particularly African Americans.[21]

Jiménez Román's quote alludes to the perception that Latinxs as a group occupy an ethnic space that is neither Black nor White – they are "mestizos." Mestizaje is the result of centuries of racial mixing among diverse populations, with the result being a "post-racial" environment. This "post-racial" space was, in fact, constructed through explicitly racialized policies.

The history of the US is rife with different approaches to classify race biologically, although race is not biological, from the eugenics movement to the so-called "one-drop rule" – during slavery, after emancipation, and through the Jim Crow period, if someone had at least one grandparent who was Black that person was considered Black, and labeled an "octoroon." American classifications of race and ethnicity seem ever evolving. Notably though, the first population census in the US, which took place in 1790,[22] did not ask questions about race or ethnicity. Rather, respondents were classified as "free white," "all other free," or "slave." However, the term "White" wasn't typically used by "New World" colonists in the sixteenth century – the terms "Christians" or "Englishmen" instead were the preferred nomenclature of the time.[23] Bacon's Rebellion in 1676 would mark a turning point in racial classification in the New World; indentured European servants and enslaved Africans in Virginia banded together to resist the ruling colonial elite.[24] Because of this uprising, it became imperative for the colonial elite and the wealthy planter class to stratify colonists, indentured European servants, and the enslaved, and the terms "White" and "Black" were thereafter associated with Europeans and Africans, respectively, to cement racial stratification. For more on this, see chapter 2.

Racial classifications other than White began to appear on decennial censuses by the middle of the nineteenth century, but a category didn't exist at that time for persons of Hispanic/Latinx ancestry. The category "Mexican" was added in the early twentieth century, but was subsequently folded into "White" classification; a stand-alone "Hispanic" category didn't appear until the 1970 census.[25]

Racial self-identification data point to some of the contested ground racial and ethnic classifications occupy. The US Census Bureau's American Community survey (ACS) data for the years 2011–15 indicate that about 31% of Latinxs classified themselves as "some other race" or "two or more races," while 66% classified themselves as White; only 2% of Latinxs indicated their race as Black.[26] In examining 2015 census data from the ACS about characteristics of the over 55 million Latinx people in the US (as of the 2020 decennial census in the US, that number increased to 60 million), approximately 64% of Latinx individuals identified Mexican as their ancestry, 9% identified as Puerto Rican, nearly 4% identified as Cuban, and just over 3% identified as Dominican.²⁷ Race and ancestry census data for Latinxs appear to suggest that, as of 2015, nearly half of Latinxs with Mexican ancestry in the US were identifying their race as White. While White self-identification is not limited to US Latinxs of Mexican origin, such self-identification is counterintuitive given the African as well as indigenous presence in the Caribbean, Latin America, and Mexico.²⁸

As noted previously, according to a 2018 report from the World Bank on Afro-Latinxs in Latin America, an estimated one in four Latin Americans has African ancestry. One might expect the percentage of Latinxs with African ancestry to be higher for Caribbean countries that were directly impacted by the transatlantic slave trade, and a survey conducted by the Pew Research Center in 2014 indeed found that Latinxs with Caribbean ancestry were more likely to identify as Afro-Latino or Afro-Caribbean than Latinxs without Caribbean ancestry.²⁹ The following question therefore naturally arises – why is the percentage of Latinxs in the US who identify as Black so low if there is a sizable African presence in Latin America, and if an estimated 16% of US Latinxs, as already noted (9% Puerto Rican ancestry; 4% and 3%, respectively, Cuban and Dominican ancestry), have origins in the Caribbean? It may be due to a resistance to identify racially, but this is not evident to the same degree among Latinxs who identify as White. It may also be due to a desire to distance oneself from a demographic group, Black Americans, with the least desirable economic outcomes when compared to Whites. Finally, it may be due to internalized anti-Black sentiments given the treatment of Afro-Latinxs in ancestral countries and territories.

Pew Research Center data from 2014, as noted in the preceding paragraph, seems to contradict US Census data which indicate that a sizable percentage of Latinxs in the US identify as White. The Center conducted a "National Survey of Latinos" from September to October in 2014 and found that 25% of Latinxs in the US identify as having African ancestry or being Afro-Latino or Afro-Caribbean.³⁰ Counterintuitively, however, and more in line with what census data suggests, when respondents from the same survey who identified as Afro-Latinx were asked a *different* question about their race, only 18% identified as Black, *while 39% identified as White alone or in combination*. Race and African ancestry may not necessarily be considered categorically similar for US Afro-Latinxs. The difficulty in accurately capturing the size and status of the Afro-Latinx community by a survey is illustrated by this Pew research, which shows contradictory self-identification patterns depending on the question posed.

Challenging the idea that the Latinx community considers itself a racial melting pot, economists Darity Jr., Jason Dietrich, and Darrick Hamilton, utilizing 1980 and 1990 census data, showed that a majority of Latinxs in the US identified as White, with the authors calling this a "flight toward Whiteness" within the US Latinx population.[31] These scholars clearly push back against the idea that Latinxs in America see themselves as rainbow people.

The phenomenon of Latinxs preferring a White, other, or mixed (but not Black) identity – given pervasive and quotidian coloristic, anti-Black treatment – presents a data challenge; how can the experiences and statuses of Afro-Latinxs be accurately captured if Latinxs in the US, including those with African ancestry or who come from the Spanish-speaking Caribbean, exhibit a preference for identifying as White? Echoing previously noted findings by Darity Jr., Dietrich, and Hamilton (2010), a study by economist Patrick Mason (2004) found that wage discrimination occurred for Latinxs across different ancestry groups, even for those identifying as White but who are dark-complexioned. Other methodologies have sought to capture complex racial formation, both quantitative and qualitative. For instance, surveys that ask both respondents and observers to evaluate respondents' skin hue (dark, medium, light), with a scale being provided to the observer, have illustrated the breadth of anti-Blackness in the American Latinx community. Nancy López et al.'s (2017) mixed-method (i.e., combining quantitative and qualitative research strategies) approach has been able to uncover internalized anti-Black sentiments by asking people not just how they self-identify, but how they believe others would identify them, which the researchers term "street race-gender." These approaches highlight the differences between how individuals self-identify vs. their social classification, with the latter being a more reliable predictor of economic outcomes.

Latinxs in the United States obviously don't have a monolithic identity. In addition, the construction of race is different among Latinxs compared to how it is interpreted in the US. For example, race is largely socially constructed along genealogical and ancestral lines in America, while race amongst Latinxs is based largely on phenotype and ancestry.[32] Nevertheless, anti-Black sentiments can be exhibited in both kinds of racial constructs.

3.4. Black Latinas and Anti-Blackness

If Afro-Latinxs can be considered a distinct subgroup of both Black and Latinxs populations, then Black/Afro-Latinas could also be considered a distinct part of the Afro-Latinx community. Popular assumptions about who Afro-Latinas are, and what their productive capacities are, have been highly stereotyped. For instance, Quiñones Rivera (2006) noted that in Puerto Rico, Afro-Latinas, or "Negras," are characterized as women engaged in low-wage, or even criminal, activities – selling food at roadsides or sex work – who live primarily in poor Black communities such as Loiza.

Marta I. Cruz-Janzen gives an account of what it is like being Afro-Latina in Puerto Rico and the United States:

> Latinegras are women who cannot escape the many layers of racism, sexism, and inhumanity that have marked their existence. Painters, poets, singers and writers have exalted their beauty, loyalty, and strength, but centuries of open assaults and rapes have turned them into concubines, prostitutes, and undesirable mothers, daughters, sisters and wives ... I am a Latinegra, born to a world that denies my humanity as a Black person, a woman, and a Latina; born to a world where other Latinos reject me and deny my existence even though I share their heritage.[33]

Representations of Afro-Latinas reflect perceptions of what the larger Latinx community assumes this group aspires to – in order to succeed, "Blackness" must be jettisoned. Dr. Marta Moreno Vega, founder in 1976 of the Caribbean Cultural Center African Diaspora Institute, noted in 2006 that the major problem feeding the sexism and racism which Afro-Latinas endure is poverty, which undermines individual and collective agency. Dr. Moreno Vega writes: "Poverty. Absolutely. Look at the South Bronx, Bed-Stuy, Brazil's favelas, Colombia's slums.... Most of what you'll find are people of African descent."[34]

The number of terms used to refer to Black or dark-complected Latinas – *grifa*, *jabá*, mulata, negra, *prieta*, *triğuena*,[35] morena, etc. – some of them considered to be derogatory, indicate that these women are often "color-stratified" by society. Angela Jorge (2010) noted that many of these terms are meant to convey skin-tone gradations, with the degree of degradation of a term associated with the degree of skin-tone darkness. It's also not just skin tone, but also hair texture, which can speak to one's African ancestry, and "taming" the latter is a foregone expectation if you are Afro-Latina. If one visits just about any hair salon in a Dominican-American neighborhood, the services typically offered are "press 'n' curls," "blowouts," and "perms," in order to straighten – i.e., get the curl and kink out of – the hair of (predominantly) women likely to have African ancestry.

3.5. Conclusion

Anti-Black attitudes and beliefs are so deeply woven into the American social and cultural landscape that even for a demographic who isn't solely Black, Afro-Latinxs, racialized outcomes are nearly a foregone conclusion. Although many Afro-Latinxs proudly "choose Blackness" while also being proud of their Latinx heritage, research shows that not all US Afro-Latinxs equate their African ancestry with being racially Black. Indeed, research shows that the Afro-Latinxs most likely to identify as Black in the US are of Panamanian descent (the mother of one of the authors of this book, Michelle Holder, was an Afro-Panamanian): 34% of Panamanians identify as Afro-Latinx in America, compared to only 11% of Dominicans, 6% of Puerto Ricans, and 3% of Cubans[36] – see figure 3.2 (note that percentages are rounded in the text). Why does a country in Central America have more than double the representation of Afro-Latinxs amongst its population in the US compared to the Dominican Republic, Puerto Rico, and Cuba, countries and territories whose populations arguably have a significant Afro-descended demographic due to the slave trade? With respect to Panama, the presence of the Black population in that country is due to descendants of a primarily West African enslaved population in that region, as well as the migration of men from Caribbean countries for

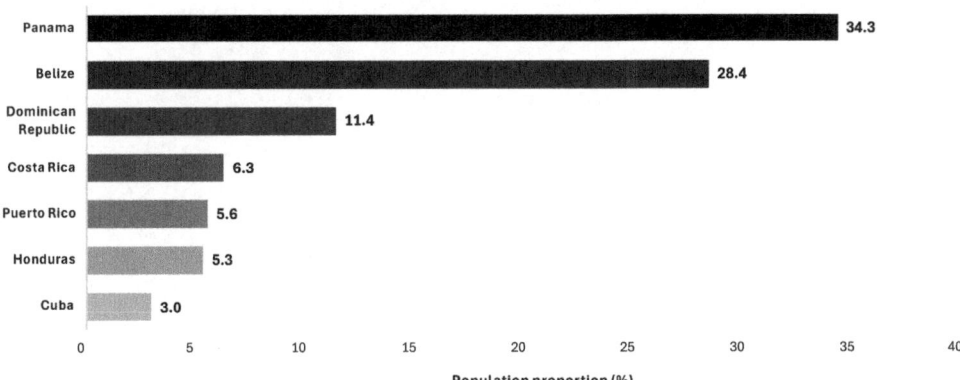

Figure 3.2 Proportion of select Latinx subgroups in the US who identify as Afro-Latinx, 2011–2015.

Note that the data in this chart are only for Latinxs in the US who are citizens.

Data source: Author analysis of 2011–15 American Community Survey 5-year data obtained from Ruggles et al., Integrated Public Use Microdata Series, version 6.0 [data set]. Minneapolis, University of Minnesota, 2015. http://doi.org/10.18128/D010.V6.0.

work on the Panama Canal at the turn of the twentieth century. But this does not, of course, explain why the percentages of self-identified Afro-Latinxs aren't higher among those in the US with ancestry in the Spanish-speaking Caribbean.

The American Afro-Latinx community has the potential to be not only a potent force for change regarding issues disparately affecting this group as outlined in this chapter, but also a community which can keep alive African cultural traditions and practices embedded in many Latinx communities (for example, the religious practice of Santería, which draws on West African beliefs as well as Catholicism). There are many local and regional Afro-Latinx organizations dedicated to the preservation of this community's culture in the US and the advocacy of policies that would be beneficial for this demographic, but such efforts, particularly regarding policy advocacy, at the national level need to be shored up. According to stratification economic theory, social change mainly happens through policy intervention, and history has demonstrated that policy change can happen with effective national movements. National-level organizations can ensure the presence, voices, and unique contributions of Afro-Latinxs in the US are acknowledged and valued in a visible way, as well as advocate at the federal level for needed policy changes that would be beneficial for this community.

4
An Intersectional Approach to Stratification Economics

4.1. Introduction

In chapter 1, we introduced the main analytical framework that we use in this book, stratification economics. In particular, we discussed how stratification economics investigates the ways in which social groups rationally pursue their collective self-interest, and how social groups compete and/or collaborate with other social groups to attain and maintain better relative positions in a social hierarchy. Stratification economics departs from the traditional economic approach to racism by identifying the material motivation behind racist ideologies, and the role of this material motivation in encouraging collective action to create and maintain economic inequalities between social groups. Importantly, these economic inequalities do not reflect each group's productive capabilities.

In chapter 2, we examined the history of social and economic conditions that produced the notion of race, and cultivated race as a principal organizing concept for the social hierarchy in the US. That is, chapter 2 described the development of social practices and institutions – especially those reified in law – that constructed race as a principal attribute with which to define social groups and the rules governing social interactions between those groups. Importantly, these social rules, enforced with violence, defined the channels through which White Americans could oppress Black and other non-White Americans. Chapter 3 examined how race and ethnicity interrelate for the Afro-Latinx community.

In this chapter, we will discuss in more detail the third main analytical tool that we will apply in this book: this is the framework of *intersectionality* that we introduced in chapter 1. Recall that Black feminists developed the intersectional approach to reflect how discrimination and marginalization differ depending on race, class, ethnicity, gender, sexual orientation, ancestry, and so on, in their analysis of oppression. More specifically, feminist sociologist Kathy Davis (2008) describes intersectionality theory as an examination of "the interaction between gender, race and other categories of difference in individual lives, social practices, institutional arrangements, and cultural ideologies and the outcomes of these interactions in terms of power" (p. 68). Davis' definition highlights how an intersectional approach pays careful attention to the way various forms of exclusion and bias *interact* to create distinctive and new forms of oppression. Her definition also acknowledges the importance of historical context – the importance of how the prevailing set of political, economic, and social arrangements shape expressions of dominance, resistance, and subordination.

Finally, we find Patricia Hill Collins' (1990) concept of a "matrix of domination" helpful in thinking about how to take an intersectional approach. The matrix of domination concept reminds us to think about how different forms of oppression and power have a matrix-like relationship: social groups accrue varying amounts of "penalty" and "privilege" within systems of domination by race, gender, capital, and so on; when these social groups intersect, these penalties and privileges are experienced simultaneously. Collins (1990) explains, "In this system, for example, white women are penalized by their gender but privileged by their race. Depending on the context, an individual may be an oppressor, a member of an oppressed group, or simultaneously oppressor and oppressed" (p. 223).

We use an intersectional approach within the stratification economics framework to understand racism in the US. In particular, we focus on how the intersection of racial and gender identities significantly defines individuals' access to political and economic resources and strategies for obtaining a favorable position in the social hierarchy. This chapter will demonstrate how an intersectional analysis permits greater insight into the channels through which social groups attempt to preserve or change the social hierarchy, to exert oppression or achieve liberation.

The Combahee River Collective

"As Black women we see Black feminism as the logical political movement to combat the manifold and simultaneous oppressions that all women of color face."
Excerpt from the "Combahee River Collective Statement," 1977

The spirit of intersectionality theory was alive well before the term was formally introduced by Crenshaw within the context of critical legal studies (1989). The Combahee River Collective was a Black feminist lesbian collective that met between 1974 and 1980 in Boston, Massachusetts. The Collective was named after the Combahee River Raid, an act of resistance planned and executed by abolitionist and former slave Harriet Tubman during the American Civil War. Tubman, of course, is also known for her leadership in the operations of the Underground Railroad, the network of abolitionists – Black and White, free and enslaved – that guided enslaved people to freedom. In one of the first military operations devised and led by a woman, Tubman, along with fellow abolitionists, collaborated with Union Army Colonel James Montgomery to disrupt Confederate supply lines along the Combahee River in South Carolina and free more than 700 enslaved persons in June of 1863. The Collective's name was chosen in recognition of the long legacy of abolitionist resistance and struggle for liberation undertaken by Black women.

The Combahee River Collective was comprised of activists and political theorists influenced by the Civil Rights Movement, the Black Power movement, the feminist movement, and the lesbian politics of the 1960s and 1970s. Founding members include Barbara Smith, Demita Frazier, Cheryl Clarke, Akasha Hull, Margo Okazawa-Rey, Chirlane McCray, and Audre Lorde.

Through consciousness-raising sessions, shared study, and ongoing emotional support, the Collective's sustained engagement generated a political economy of *simultaneity* – "the idea that their lived experiences and everyday realities as well as their challenges to oppression were all guided by the combined influences of class, race, gender, and sexuality" (Clark, Matthew, and Burns, 2017, p. 12).

During the second wave of the US feminist movement in the late 1960s, Black women confronted racism and Western elitism – i.e., the view that the societies of the US and Western Europe are superior to all others. Black feminists offered their solidarity with women of the "Third World" – what Western development economics call the lower-income countries of Asia, Africa, and Latin America – recognizing that gendered and sexual oppression is racialized. Within the movements for Black liberation of the 1960s and 1970s (i.e., those of Civil Rights, Black Nationalism, and the Black Panthers), they confronted sexism and heteronormativity. In this very spirit, members of the Combahee River Collective contended with alienation in the movements of the 1970s. As socialists, they confronted the uncritical view of capitalism espoused by the "bourgeois feminist[s]" of the National Black Feminist Organization (NBFO). At the same time, as racialized women, members of the Collective also rejected the uncritical view of socialism promoted by the National Socialist Feminist Conference of 1975.[1]

Ultimately, the Combahee River Collective realized they needed to develop their own lived understandings of their economic situation in pursuit of their own kind of complex economic analysis: "We realize that the liberation of all oppressed people necessitates the destruction of the political-economic systems of capitalism and imperialism as well as patriarchy ... we are not convinced, however, that a socialist revolution that is not also a feminist and anti-racist revolution will guarantee our liberation." As part of this project, the Collective published a statement that set forth their analysis. In it, they reflect on the establishment of their union – "the overwhelming feeling that we had is that after years and years we had finally found each other." During the four years of the Combahee River Collective's existence, hundreds of women had been active members – predominantly Black women who, in recognition of the little value ascribed to their lives across "four centuries of bondage in the Western Hemisphere," realized they were the only ones who would work consistently for their liberation. They understood that this would be a lifelong struggle against a whole range of interlocking oppressions.

Now regarded as a seminal text in the history of Black feminist thought, the "Combahee River Collective Statement" connects modern Black feminist thought to "generations of personal sacrifice, militancy, and work" undertaken by Black women activists.[2] Some of the women in this lineage are known to us – such as Harriet Tubman, Sojourner Truth, Frances E.W. Harper, Ida B. Wells, and Mary Church Terrell – while countless others remain unknown. The 1977 statement recognizes that Black women have always embodied "an adversary stance to white male rule." Today, the impact of the Combahee River Collective's statement continues to reverberate through political life in the United States, providing the inspiration and foundational elements for intersectionality theory (Tracey, 2022).

Written by Daniella Medina

4.2. How Does Intersectionality Advance Stratification Economics?

In this section, we outline the three critical functions that intersectionality theory performs in our analysis of how racism creates a stratified economic system in the US. We illustrate each function with specific examples from the US political economy.

4.2.1. Getting the Quantities Right

We start with the most straightforward way in which an intersectional analysis improves our understanding of the US' stratified economy: an intersectional analysis requires that we disaggregate data sufficiently to observe socio-economic measures – such as income, wealth, wages, etc. – for social groups with *overlapping* marginalized identities. According to economist Rhonda Sharpe, failing to do so will likely lead to misunderstanding the dimensions of a social problem or mismeasuring a policy remedy's success.[3]

4.2.1.1. Wage Inequality

Take, for example, the 2016 study by economists Valerie Wilson and William Rodgers on wage inequality by race and gender. In their study, they examine how wages differ, on average, between four social groups. More specifically, they estimate the wage disadvantage associated with being a member of each of the following groups, from 1979 to 2015, relative to White men: Black men, White women, and Black women. We have reproduced a figure from their study in figure 4.1, which shows the percent wage disadvantage for each group, relative to White men. For example, over this time period, Black men have been losing ground: their wage disadvantage relative to White men who are comparable – along the dimensions of full-time status, education, potential work experience,[4] region and metropolitan residence – has risen from 16.9% in 1979 to 22.0% in 2015.

What is immediately apparent in this figure is that the relative wage trend for each social group is distinctive. In contrast to the situation among Black men, women – both Black and White – have experienced a dramatic decline in their wage disadvantage relative to White men through the early 1990s. The wage disadvantage for White women, however, started lower than among Black women (37.8% vs. 42.3%) in 1979, and fell by a larger amount by 1993 (−14.7 percentage points to 23.1% vs. −11.4 percentage points to 30.9%). After 1993, the wage

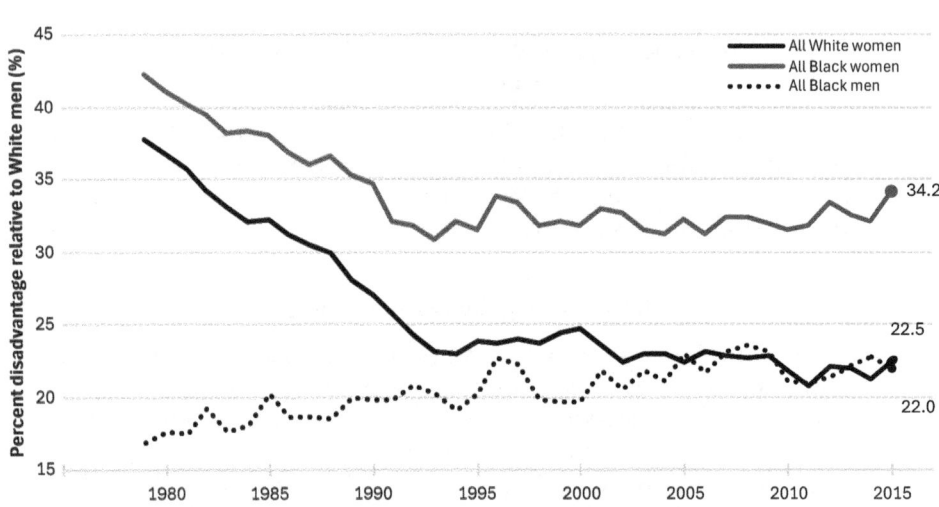

Note: The adjusted wage gaps are for full-time workers and control for racial differences in education, potential experience, region of residence, and metro status.

Figure 4.1 Adjusted average hourly wage gaps relative to White men by race and gender, 1979–2015.
Source: Wilson and Rodgers (2016), p. 14, figure C. *Data source*: EPI analysis of Current Population Survey (CPS) Outgoing Rotation Group microdata.

disadvantage for White women workers declined slightly. Black women workers, on the other hand, experienced an increase to 34.2% in their wage disadvantage between 1993 and 2015.

Meaningful differences between Black and White women's, and Black men's, wage trends are lost when analyses are done only by gender or only by race. An analysis of wage differences by gender largely reflects the experiences of White women relative to White men, as White women and White men make up the large majority of workers in each gender group (90% and 85%, respectively). That is, the trend in wage differences by gender would be approximated by the wage disadvantage as experienced by White women relative to White men – the solid black line in figure 4.1.

Consider further the following dimensions of inequality that we learn by examining wage trends by race *and* gender. First, the wage disadvantage among Black women is worse than for White women in each and every year for the full 35 years. Second, Black women are falling behind White women, in terms of their access to equal pay: the gap between the wage disadvantage among Black and White women is widening over time – a gap of about 5 percentage points in 1979 doubled to roughly 10 percentage points by 2015. Third, the wage disadvantage for Black women relative to White men in 2015 is approximately what the wage disadvantage was for White women (relative to White men) in the early 1980s. In other words, the wage disadvantage among Black women relative to White men in 2015 is similar in magnitude to what White women were experiencing over three decades prior.

Without an intersectional analysis, the persistently greater degree of wage disadvantage experienced by Black women, relative to White women and Black men, would be hidden from view. In particular, a gender-only analysis would overstate the degree of progress toward pay equity between men and women by obscuring the limited progress experienced by Black women. We discuss these dimensions of wage inequality in greater depth in chapters 6 and 7, including discussions of the factors driving these racial and gender disparities.

4.2.1.2. Disparities in Unemployment

As another example of how an intersectional analysis generates a more meaningful understanding of the extent of economic inequality – i.e., in getting the quantities right – we can look at the unemployment rate. The unemployment rate is a bellwether measure of how a country's economy is performing for the vast majority of its residents, one reason why we use it multiple times throughout our book to discuss racial economic inequality. Let's start by looking at trends in unemployment. Figure 4.2 panel A shows the overall unemployment rate for workers by gender (men and women, separately). What this picture shows us is that men and women's unemployment rates tend to move together – both spike during recessions and drop during expansions. Over the past half-century, these rates have remained roughly within the range of between 4% and 10%.

With two exceptions, the unemployment rates for men and women by and large coincide:

(1) A gender gap in unemployment rates exists during the 1970s and 1980s – with higher rates for women. This pattern reflects how at the start of the 1970s, women had less access to jobs and, correspondingly, less labor force experience, relative to men. In 1970, the majority – 57% – of women were not active in the labor force, while 43% were labor force participants. Women's labor force participation rose dramatically during the 1970s and 1980s so that, by 1988, these shares flipped: 57% of women had landed

A. All Women & All Men

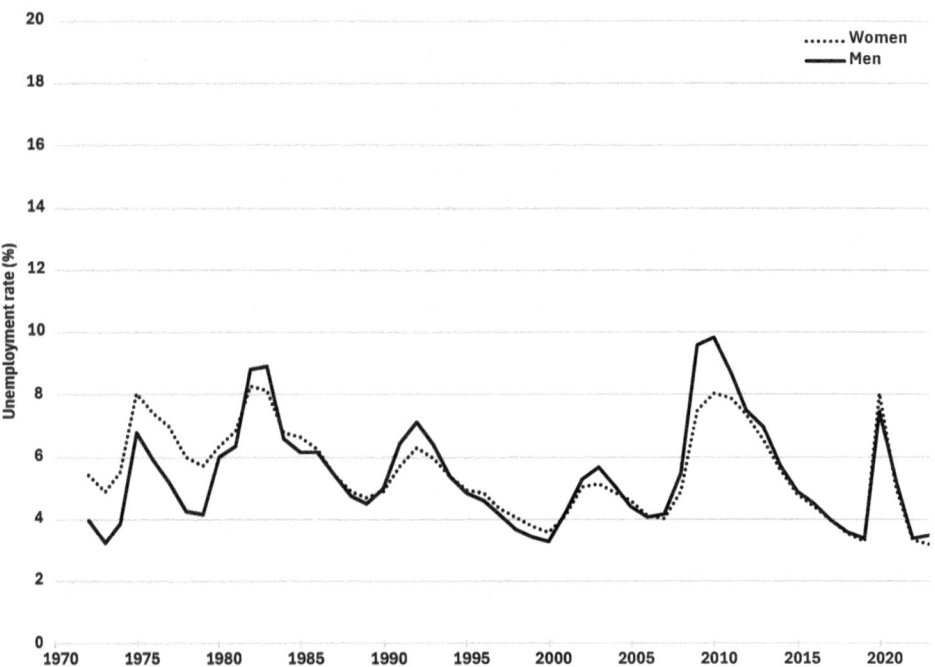

Figure 4.2 Trends in unemployment rate by gender among workers age 20 years and older, 1972–2023.

Data source: Seasonally adjusted unemployment rate, BLS – Current Population Survey, 1972–2023.

jobs or were actively seeking them, and 43% remained out of the labor force.

(2) During recessionary periods, men's rate of unemployment tends to surpass the rate among women. This reflects how men tend to be employed in businesses more vulnerable to economic slowdowns, including jobs in goods-producing sectors such as manufacturing and construction. Women tend to have higher rates of employment in sectors that are relatively "recession-proof," such as jobs in services including government, health, and education. These are services that people are likely to continue to use, or use even more of, during economic downturns. These sectors include

B. White Women & White Men

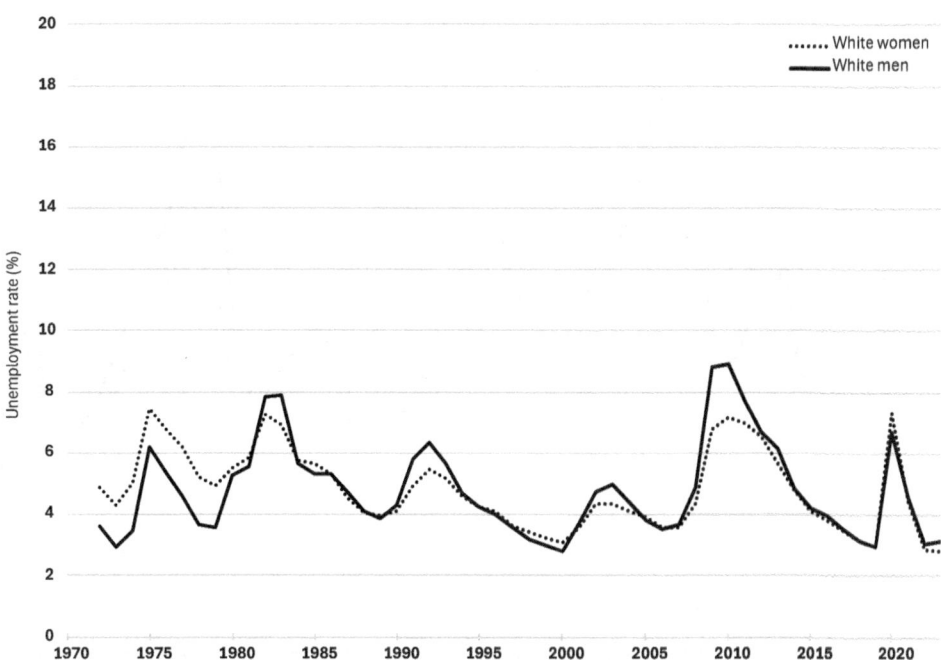

Figure 4.2 (*continued*) Trends in unemployment rate by gender among workers age 20 years and older, 1972–2023.
Data source: Seasonally adjusted unemployment rate, BLS – Current Population Survey, 1972–2023.

occupational categories with high concentrations of women such as nurses, teachers, and social service workers.[5]

Panel B of figure 4.2 presents unemployment trends now for White men and White women only, and panel C of figure 4.2 presents unemployment trends for Black men and Black women only. The same gendered patterns appear in both panels B and C. That is, while the trend lines of men and women generally track each other, men, relative to women, have greater unemployment rates when the economy is contracting. What is striking about these unemployment trends, now shown by race, is how the trends in panel A largely reflect

Figure 4.2 (*continued*) Trends in unemployment rate by gender among workers age 20 years and older, 1972–2023.

Data source: Seasonally adjusted unemployment rate, BLS – Current Population Survey, 1972–2023.

the experiences of White men and women shown in panel B. On the one hand, this is not surprising, since White men and White women comprise the majority of the working-age population. On the other hand, the dramatically higher unemployment rates shown in panel C among Black men and women compared to their White counterparts illustrates how poorly panel A captures the labor market experience of Black workers. For example, the worst unemployment rates experienced by White women – i.e., during economic recessions – average 6.3%. Compare this to the best unemployment rates experienced by Black women – i.e. during economic expansions – which averages at 7.9%. The best labor market conditions (i.e., lowest jobless rates) for Black women are typically *worse* than the most difficult labor market conditions (i.e., highest jobless rates) for White women. Additionally, the cyclically driven *volatility* in the unemployment rate among Black women is much greater – i.e., in terms of the up-and-down percentage-point fluctuations in the rate – than among White men.

A similar pattern emerges when we compare the unemployment rates between Black and White men: Black men's unemployment rates are markedly higher than those among White men, as is the volatility of the rate. What becomes clear from this picture is that Black men experience both greater levels and volatility in unemployment than any of the other groups of workers: White men, White women, or Black women. Consequently, Black men experience the most severe levels of unemployment.

To sum up, a gender analysis of unemployment rates will capture how men – Black or White – tend to have higher unemployment rates during economic downturns due to occupational segregation by gender. However, without an intersectional analysis, we miss the fact that Black women not only experience dramatically higher levels of unemployment relative to White women, but also more volatility than that experienced by White men. Moreover, Black men consistently experience greater volatility and magnitudes of unemployment relative to all the other three groups of workers.[6]

4.2.2. Getting the Qualities Right

An intersectional approach helps to reveal forms of oppression unique in *quality* to social groups at the intersection of marginalized identities. "Getting the qualities right" is about identifying how overlapping marginalized identities may experience different *types* of oppression, as opposed to different magnitudes of the *same type* of oppression (e.g., insufficient employment). In other words, the oppressive conditions experienced by a social group at the intersection of marginalized identities can differ in quality – not just quantity – from the oppressions experienced by each separate identity.

4.2.2.1. Occupational Segregation

Occupational segregation – by gender, by race, by both – is a well-documented form of social stratification (Alonso-Villar and del Río, 2017; Beller, 1982; Branch, 2011; Darity Jr. and Mason, 1998; Hamilton and Darity Jr., 2012; Holder, Jones, and Masterson, 2021; Reskin, 1999; Spriggs and Williams, 1996). Occupational segregation is the over- or under-representation of a social group within an occupation, relative to that group's share of the workforce. In the US, occupational segregation remains a significant method by which economic resources – such as favorable compensation, schedule stability, adequate employment, safe and/or fulfilling working conditions – can be reserved for dominant social groups and withheld from marginalized social groups. In this section, we provide illustrations of the phenomenon. Later in the book, in chapter 6, we review the body of existing research on the patterns and causes of occupational segregation.

A gender-only analysis of occupational segregation will overlook the different qualities of oppression experienced by Black and White women. An intersectional analysis, in contrast, reveals how Black women have historically, and presently, not only been *more* segregated into a limited set of occupations relative to White women, but also segregated into occupations of worse *quality* – particularly in terms of how an occupation serves to assign a person's relative position in the social hierarchy.

Let's start with a picture of occupational segregation as of 1940. Data from the US Census indicate that a high level of gender segregation in employment existed by occupation. Over 70% of working men held jobs in one of the following four occupational groupings: (1) business owners or managers (24%); (2) operatives and related workers (19%); (3) craftsmen, foremen, and related workers (17%); and (4) non-farm laborers (11%). Likewise, over 70% of working women were concentrated in four occupational groupings. All but one of the top four occupational groupings among women differed from those among men; they include: (1) clerical and related workers (22%); (2) operatives and related workers (21%); (3) private household service workers (17%); and (4) nurses, librarians, and teachers (12%). This occupational segregation provided men with an upper hand in earnings: men dominated the occupational groupings with the highest average pay – protective service occupations (99% men; 1% women) and professionals and scientists (84% men and 16% women). At the same time, men also earned higher pay within each occupational grouping.

Table 4.1 also shows how women had access, in 1940, to three occupational groupings that offered above-average earnings: (1) nurses, librarians, and teachers; (2) clerical and related occupations; and (3) operatives and related workers.

Table 4.2 presents the occupational distribution of women by race. This intersectional analysis – by gender and race – show how among the occupations available to women, the better-paying positions were

Table 4.1 Occupational distribution by gender and average annual earnings in 1940

Occupational group	% of men	% of women	Average earnings (1940$)
Professionals and scientists	5.3	3.4	1,476
Nurses, librarians, teachers	1.0	11.8	1,241
Business owners and managers	23.9	6.1	597
Clerical and kindred workers	7.0	22.3	1,314
Sales workers	6.2	7.3	1,267
Craftsmen, foremen, and kindred workers	17.1	1.6	1,244
Operatives and kindred workers	18.8	20.5	944
Private household service	0.4	16.5	311
Service, except private household	2.4	7.0	647
Protective service	1.4	0.1	1,583
Farm labor	4.8	2.5	287
Non-farm labor	11.6	1.0	677
All occupations	100.0	100.0	930

Source: Authors' analysis of 1940 US Census data; data are from Ruggles et al. (2024), IPUMS USA: Version 15.0 [data set], Minneapolis: University of Minnesota.

Table 4.2 Occupational distribution of women by race, 1940

Occupational group	% of White women	% of Black women
Professionals and scientists	3.9	0.6
Nurses, librarians, teachers	13.1	4.6
Business owners and managers	6.4	4.2
Clerical and kindred workers	26.1	1.1
Sales workers	8.5	0.8
Craftsmen, foremen, and kindred workers	1.8	0.5
Operatives and kindred workers	22.6	8.6
Private household service	8.6	61.1
Service not private household	7.0	6.6
Protective service	0.1	0.0
Farm labor	1.0	10.8
Labor, not farm	0.9	1.1
All occupations	100.0	100.0

Source: Authors' analysis of 1940 US Census data; data are from Ruggles et al. (2024), IPUMS USA: Version 15.0 [data set], Minneapolis: University of Minnesota.

effectively only open to White women. Take for example, clerical and related workers. Fully 26% of employed White women occupied such positions. Only 1% of employed Black women held such jobs. Similarly, 13% of White working women were nurses, librarians, and teachers, compared to 5% of their Black counterparts. Finally, 23% of White women workers held operative positions, compared to only 9% of Black women workers.

Table 4.2 also shows how Black women were hyper-segregated into the worst positions available to women: fully 61% of Black women held jobs in private household service. The next highest fraction of Black women workers found employment in farming (11%) – again, dramatically higher than the 1% of White women workers. This distinct pattern of occupational segregation in private household services and farming mirrored the dominant types of labor that the US's slave economy compelled Black women to provide prior to 1865. Historian Jacqueline Jones (1985) remarks that, "Despite the significant shift in white working women's options, the paid labor of black women exhibited striking continuity across space – urban areas in the North and South – and time – from the nineteenth century to the early twentieth century" (p. 161).[7]

Another insidious dimension of these racist employment practices that continued to limit Black women to private household work is how such practices subjected them to sexual harassment, sexual assault, and other types of violence. As noted above, US law, in the main, did not criminalize the sexual assault or rape of enslaved women. The racial segregation of Black women into private household service work continued their high exposure to sexual violence. The pervasiveness of this abuse is indicated by the organized political actions taken against it, as by the National Association of Colored Women (NACW). In 1919, the NACW made a formal statement objecting to the working conditions of domestic service, specifically calling for protection against sexual violence with a euphemistic phrase: "protection in white homes against exposure to moral temptations."[8] In fact, Angela Davis (1983) wrote in the early 1980s that "From Reconstruction to the present, Black women household workers have considered sexual abuse perpetrated by the 'man of the house' as one of their major occupational hazards. Time after time they have been victims of extortion on the job, compelled to choose between sexual submission and absolute poverty for themselves and their families" (p. 91).

Racist social and employment policies have maintained a degraded status for these jobs. Take, for example, the Fair Labor Standards Act

(FLSA) of 1938, a major component of President Franklin Delano Roosevelt's New Deal agenda. The FLSA is arguably one of the most significant labor policies in modern US history – best known for its establishment of the federal minimum wage, as well as the right to premium pay for overtime hours. The FLSA excised domestic servants and farm laborers from protection. As legal scholar Juan F. Perea explains: "During the New Deal Era, the statutory exclusion of agricultural and domestic employees was well-understood as a race-neutral proxy for excluding blacks from statutory benefits and protections made available to most whites. Remarkably, despite these racist origins, an agricultural and domestic worker exclusion remains on the books today, entirely unaltered after seventy-five years" (2011, p. 96).

The occupational segregation of Black women to lower-status, lower-quality occupations has, over time, become less severe, but persists to the present day. Economists Alonso-Villar and del Río (2017) document a sharp decline in occupational segregation for Black women after 1940, in part due to the civil rights organizing of that era. In particular, they measure how much "the employment distribution of African American women across occupations departs from the occupational structure of the economy." According to one of their broadest measures, they find that in 1940, 69% of African American women would have had to change occupations to achieve zero segregation. By 1980, this percentage fell to 38%. In the decades that followed, progress slowed and then stalled, falling only to 32% during 2008–10. In other words, close to one-third of Black women would need to change occupations in order for their occupational distribution to match the occupational structure of the economy.

More recent labor market data show how the persistence in occupational segregation experienced by Black women continues to shape the qualitative differences in employment opportunities between Black and White women. Take the occupational distribution of Black and White women presented in table 4.3. Table 4.3 presents data originally published by Holder, Jones, and Masterton (2020) to show how both White and Black women are concentrated in certain occupations. They do this by using a metric called "the concentration ratio," a measure typically used to gauge the degree to which an industry's market is concentrated to a limited number of firms. For example, the five-firm concentration ratio (CR5) is a measure of how much of an industry's output is concentrated in the top five firms of that industry. Holder et al. (2020) estimate the CR5 in terms of occupational concentration – i.e., the concentration ratio of the five

Table 4.3 Occupational employment shares and wages among Black and White women, 2020

Occupational group	Average hourly wage (2020$)	of total workforce	of Black women	of White women	Difference (of White women – of Black women)
Management	60.81	11.9	7.8	11.0	3.2
Legal	54.00	1.2	1.1	1.4	0.3
Computer and mathematical	46.53	3.6	1.6	1.6	0.0
Architecture and engineering	43.41	2.1	0.5	0.5	0.0
Healthcare practitioners and technical	41.30	6.2	9.2	9.8	0.6
Business and financial operations	38.79	5.8	6.8	6.5	–0.3
Life, physical, and social science	38.15	1	0.4	1.1	0.7
Arts, design, entertainment, sports, and media	30.96	2.1	1.1	2.2	1.1
Educational instruction and library	28.75	6.2	6.9	10.3	3.4
Construction and extraction	25.93	5.1	0.3	0.5	0.2
Installation, maintenance, and repair	25.17	3.1	0.4	0.3	–0.1
Protective service	25.11	2	2	0.9	–1.1
Community and social service	25.09	1.8	3.3	2.4	–0.9
Sales and related	22.00	9.5	9.8	10.1	0.3
Office and administrative support	20.38	10.4	16.3	16.7	0.4
Production	20.08	5.3	3.4	3.1	–0.3
Transportation and material moving	19.08	7.4	4.6	3.0	–1.6
Farming, fishing, and forestry	16.02	0.7	0.2	0.5	0.3
Building and grounds cleaning and maintenance	15.75	3.3	3.6	3.1	–0.5
Personal care and service	15.68	3.3	4.1	4.1	0.0
Healthcare support	15.50	3.2	10.4	5.0	–5.4
Food preparation and serving related	13.30	5.4	6.1	6.2	0.1

Source: Wage data are from the US Labor Department's May 2020 Occupational Employment and Wage Statistics; data in columns 3–5 are reproduced from Holder et al. (2020).

occupations with the highest shares of employment among White (or Black) women.

In February 2020, the top five occupations that White women are concentrated in (the five occupations that make up the CR5) include: (1) management, (2) healthcare practitioners and technical, (3) educational instruction and, (4) sales and related, and (5) office and administrative support. The CR5 for White women is 57.9%, as 57.9% of White women held jobs in these five occupations. The fact that this 57.9% figure is much higher than the share of *total* employment that these five occupations represent – 44.2% – indicates that White women are over-represented in these occupations.[9] Similarly, the occupations that make up the CR5 for Black women include four of these five occupations: (1) management, (2) healthcare practitioners and technical, (3) sales and related, and (4) office and administrative support. In place of educational instruction and library occupations, the fifth occupation in the CR5 for Black women is healthcare support occupations.[10] The CR5 for Black women is 53.5% – i.e., 53.5% of Black women held jobs in these five occupations. This is, again, higher than the share of total employment that these occupations represent, or 41.2%. Ranking the occupational groups from highest to lowest pay in table 4.3, we can see how Black women tend to be concentrated in lower-paying occupations. As standout examples, 10.3% of White women held educational instruction and library occupation jobs, with above-average pay ($28.75 vs. the average pay across all occupations of $27.07), and 10.4% of Black women held healthcare support occupation jobs, with below-average hourly pay ($15.50).

4.2.2.2. Racism and Labor Force Participation

Another dimension of working life that sets Black and White women's experiences apart qualitatively is rooted in their decision around *whether or not* to enter the labor market. As we discuss in greater depth in chapter 6, anti-Black racism has created the double standard that Black women should seek paid work and White women should not.[11] These patterns show up in the economic data through the "labor force participation rate" (LFPR) – the share of the population participating actively in the labor market by seeking work or holding a job. Black women's LFPR has exceeded, substantially, the LFPR of White women from at least since 1940 when the US Census Bureau adopted the current definition of labor force participation (see figure 6.4).

This social expectation to enter the paid workforce also has had the consequence of limiting the ability of Black women to provide their households with essential unpaid work. This unpaid work, traditionally expected of women generally within patriarchal systems, includes maintaining their homes and looking after their children. Put another way, the White-dominant society puts greater value on Black women's labor outside their homes, and less value on Black women's labor inside their homes. Economist Nina Banks (2019) explains, "Since the era of slavery, the dominant view of black women has been that they should be workers, a view that contributed to their devaluation as mothers with caregiving needs at home."[12]

One of the largest means-tested welfare programs in US history – the Aid to Families with Dependent Children (AFDC) – provides a caustic illustration of this racist gender norm. Blank and Blum (1997) explain how the AFDC (preceded by Aid to Dependent Children, or ADC) operated on the premise that White single mothers should not work and should stay at home to raise their children. The program did not provide the same benefit to Black single mothers. States largely denied Black single mothers these welfare benefits by deeming them "undesirable" or their homes "unsuitable." As a result, the ADC/AFDC nearly explicitly provided financial support for White single mothers to stay home and raise their children and not for Black single mothers. Civil rights advocates forced states to end these racist policies during the 1960s.[13]

The contrasting racialized labor market positions among Black and White women, however, has been changing over time. The civil rights and feminist movements that reduced gender and racial discrimination in the labor market for women generally have also promoted a new social norm of fuller employment for White women, particularly White married mothers (Beller, 1982; Darity Jr. and Mason, 1998; Goldin, 1988, 2006; Pepin and Cotter, 2018). As a result of these changing social conventions, the choice of staying outside the labor force for White women has become decoupled from their racial and economic privilege (Wicks-Lim, 2025). Goldin (1977) describes this transformation: "The revolutionary increase in the participation of women in the labor force mainly involved whites. Black women have been abundantly represented in the labor market as slaves and had remained so as freed persons" (p. 87).

These qualitative differences in how sexism operates to shape the economic opportunities for Black women and White women would remain out of view without an intersectional analysis. And again, as we saw above, failure to examine the distinctiveness of social oppression at the intersection of race and gender inevitably prioritizes the experience of White women since White women make up the large majority of women in the US. Put another way, any analysis that examines inequality by gender only will effectively see the features of inequality as experienced by White women, and the experience White women have relative to White men.

4.2.3. Getting the Coalitions Right

The third major advantage of an intersectional approach is in revealing the incentives for creating, maintaining, or breaking political coalitions between social groups. That is, an intersectional approach puts a spotlight on the *social intersections between social groups* that may facilitate political alignment and solidarity – points of political leverage to achieve liberation. An intersectional approach also focuses our awareness of the potential for simultaneous *social divisions within social groups* based on other aspects of social group members' identities – identities that can occupy unequal positions in the social hierarchy.

For example, social groups at the intersection of marginalized and dominant social groups – such as White women or Black men – have a strong incentive to ally closely with the dominant group as a means to leverage the power associated with that group. In this scenario, White women have a strong incentive to ally with White men. Black men likewise may have a strong incentive to ally with White men.

Conversely, these same groups – White women and Black men – have a strong incentive to break alliances with the marginalized group that each intersects with to insulate themselves from the oppression experienced by the marginalized group. This feature can weaken alliances between White and Black women, and Black men and Black women. Those in social groups at the intersection of two marginalized groups – such as Black women – face precarious and limited opportunities to access power through coalitions because their own political power is precarious and limited. Gender-only and race-only analyses fail to study the full range of dynamics and coalitions that enable social groups to gain – or block – access to desirable economic and social resources. Understanding the incentives and disincentives for political coalitions is central to understanding the political economy of any society. This is because such alliances between social groups can enlarge the political power of each group, improving their ability to access economic and social resources.

4.2.3.1. The Woman Suffrage Movement[14]

The evolution of the woman's suffrage movement – the movement to grant women the right to vote – in the US vividly illustrates these dynamics. In particular, the history of the transformation of the universal suffrage movement to a narrower woman suffrage movement exemplifies the instability of the political alliances between White women and Black women, and how the political alliances between White men and White women can weaken or supplant such interracial alliances. Moreover, the history of the suffrage movement plainly demonstrates how closely the political rights of a social group track with the group's access to economic resources. It does so by illustrating how a social group's access to suffrage advances the group's representation in the political institutions that, in turn, arbitrate access to economic resources through policies.

The clear correspondence between gains and losses in voting, political, and economic rights during this period arises from the suffrage movement's overlap with one of the most turbulent phases of race relations in American history. The suffrage movement began roughly around the time of the Civil War – the military war that culminated in the end to legal slavery. The passage of the 19th Constitutional amendment establishing women's right to vote concluded the suffrage movement during the Nadir – the historical low point for civil rights resulting from White supremacists' terror campaign to claw back the economic and political gains of Black Americans. In other words, radical changes to the rules that governed the social hierarchy, in terms of race, coincide with the start and end of the woman suffrage movement. The incendiary and revolutionary nature of these times must clearly be in view to understand the evolution of strategies advanced by Black and White women, each social group pursuing their collective self-interest – at times competing against, and at other times allying with, each other.

The Rise and Fall of the Universal Suffrage Movement, 1848–1877
Many historians mark the start of the US women's suffrage movement with the women's rights convention held at Seneca Falls, New York, in 1848.[15] At the time, White males – "male citizens" – had a basic monopoly on voting rights across the country.[16] Multiple social groups – White women, non-White women, and non-White men – had a stake in expanding access to this privilege.

Social reformers active in the abolitionist movement – an interracial coalition including White and Black Radical Republicans, free Black people, and enslaved Black people – launched the suffrage movement.[17] Abolitionists' political work and the onset of the Civil War would eventually produce one of US history's most profound shifts in economic and political rights: the abolition of slavery. These efforts to fundamentally restructure the social hierarchy cross-pollinated with feminist efforts to empower women within their homes, communities, and government.[18]

Action by the federal government eliminated legal slavery in fits and starts, producing seismic convulsions in the social hierarchy. These quakes created both openings and obstacles to radically redistributing political power, social status, and economic resources. These events provide extreme examples of the consequential nature of voting rights and political representation in government.

Consider, for example, the profoundly life-changing potential for Black families offered by Union Army General Sherman's Special Field Order 15 issued under the Lincoln administration on January 16, 1865, a few months before the end of the Civil War. After consulting with local Black Southern community leaders about the needs of freed people, General Sherman's order called for the redistribution of land confiscated by the Union Army from slaveowners: 40-acre parcels for formerly enslaved families would be allocated from land running along the coast of South Carolina, Georgia, and into northern Florida – a total of about 5.3 million acres. The order's potential was never realized: after Lincoln's assassination, Vice-President-turned-President Andrew Johnson, a Democrat, took an accommodative stance toward the former Confederacy and enacted policies that effectively annulled Special Field Order 15. Only about 40,000 families had the chance to resettle on 400,000 acres of land, for less than a year.[19]

The Black Codes that began in 1865, after the end of the Civil War, serve as another example of the high stakes attendant to voting rights and political representation. President Andrew Johnson permitted former Confederate leaders to take control of the newly formed Southern state governments.[20] These leaders put in place a new legal rubric – the Black Codes – in order to approximate a slave-like status for Black residents.[21] Republican abolitionists, with a majority in the US Congress, revolted against the Johnson administration,[22] and took control of the post-Civil War transition. On March 2, 1867, Congress passed the Reconstruction Act of 1867 and imposed martial law in the Southern states. Civilian rule would not resume until these states met the following demands: (1) adopt a state constitution voted in by a majority that included Black voters; (2) ratify the 13th amendment, which abolished slavery, except as a criminal punishment; and (3) ratify the 14th amendment which effectively granted all free Black people citizenship, and stipulated a punishment for states that blocked male residents from voting.[23] By 1868, the Black Codes had largely been removed. Within less than a decade, the nation witnessed a group of people transition from being enslaved to freed, freed to re-enslaved, and then freed again.

The Civil War's racial reckoning weakened the interracial alliances that the suffrage movement inherited from the abolition movement. White and Black women had different stakes in how the social hierarchy would be reordered after the war. On the one hand, both groups of women had a common interest in reforming patriarchal norms, and social and economic policies that limited their political rights and lowered their position in the social hierarchy. On the other hand, White women exercised economic and political power as members of the White community – power that was successfully being contested during this same period. For White women, woman suffrage held the potential to both promote their position relative to men within the White community as well as strengthen the White community's ability to maintain their dominant position relative to the Black community. Black women's position in the social hierarchy was similarly tied to their racial group membership, in addition to their gender. However, for Black women, suffrage for themselves *or* Black men represented a major political advance for the Black community since neither group had the franchise.[24] Suffrage for any part of the Black community would increase the entire Black community's ability to combat racism.

The interracial universal suffrage movement eventually fractured into two factions. One faction focused on "woman-suffrage-first," prioritizing achieving suffrage for women before extending the franchise to Black men. The other faction prioritized "Negro suffrage" – voting rights for Black men. The ratification process of the 14th amendment that took place between 1866 and 1868, and the controversial 1867 Kansas election (see below for further discussion), catalyzed this fracture.[25] As noted above, the 14th amendment explicitly tied voting rights to men, allowing for the enfranchisement of all men – including Black men. Political support for the 14th amendment came from three different groups of abolitionists: (1) abolitionists who opposed suffrage for women on the grounds of political expediency, viewing woman suffrage as less politically viable than Black voting rights; (2) abolitionists who opposed suffrage for women on principle;[26] and (3) abolitionists who viewed the franchise for Black men as meeting a more urgent need: the need to protect the Black community. Prominent suffragists such as Elizabeth Stanton and Susan B. Anthony (both White women) attempted, but failed, to have the word "male" stricken from the 14th amendment so that it would expand suffrage universally, enfranchising women as well as Black men. The Republican leaders' refusal to change the amendment weakened the alliance of these White women and their colleagues within the party that championed the civil rights of Black Americans.

The Kansas election weakened these alliances further. In 1867, Kansas voters faced two state referenda that had the effect of pitting supporters of woman suffrage against supporters of "Negro suffrage."[27] One referendum would grant suffrage to Black men by striking the word "white" from Kansas' constitution and expand the male electorate to include White and Black men. The other referendum would extend the franchise to White women by striking the word "male" from its constitution, expanding the White electorate to include White men and White women. The passage of both state referenda would achieve universal suffrage. However, the increasingly polarized political environment split suffragists on strategy, many choosing one referendum over the other, observably operationalizing their political priorities.

Anthony and Stanton spearheaded a woman-suffrage-first campaign independent of the Republican Party. This new strategy relied, in part, on an alliance with Democratic Party supporter and Whites-only voting proponent George Francis Train. As a result, the woman-suffrage-first faction effectively narrowed their focus to achieving gender equality between White men and White women, and actively opposed Black men receiving the vote.[28] A mutual interest in maintaining a dominant racial position served to strengthen this intra-racial, inter-gender coalition. Stanton, in a letter to the *Anti-Slavery Standard*, articulates her fundamental predisposition for this intra-racial alliance saying, "In fact, it is better to be the slave of an educated white man, than of a degraded ignorant Black one."[29] Ultimately, this strategy failed in overcoming the opposition to woman suffrage, even White woman suffrage, among the White-men-only Kansas electorate.

"Negro suffrage" supporters, on the other hand, prioritized extending the franchise to Black men over suffrage for women. The limited historical documentation of Black women's voices suggests that at least some prominent Black women suffragists took up the Negro suffrage position as part of their Black Nationalist feminist agenda.[30] Take for example, Frances Harper, who viewed advocating the voting rights of Black men as a means to politically empowering the whole Black community – a community existing in an extraordinarily precarious position. At the 1869 convention of the major national suffrage rights organization American Equal Rights Association (AERA), Harper is quoted as saying, "If the nation could only handle one question, [I] would not have Black women put a single straw in the way, if only the men of the race could obtain what they wanted."[31] Despite Congress' approval of the 14th amendment in 1866 and Kansas' legislature's early ratification of the amendment in January 1867, the White-men-only Kansas electorate voted down the Negro suffrage state referendum.

Under the weight of this conflict, in 1869, AERA folded and two new groups replaced it: the "women-suffrage-first" faction split off to create the National Woman Suffrage Association (NWSA), and the "Negro suffrage" faction, i.e., the faction of suffragists that actively supported Black voting rights, created the American Woman Suffrage Association (AWSA).

From the "Mystic Years" to the Nadir and the Ascent of White Woman Suffrage, 1870 to 1920

The years 1867 to 1873, described by Du Bois as "seven mystic years," overlap with the split in the suffrage movement. These years had a magical quality, according to Du Bois, because Black Americans achieved key political rights that meaningfully, if temporarily, reshaped the racial hierarchy.[32] The 15th amendment, passed by Congress in 1869 and ratified in 1870, reinforced Black men's franchise rights by precluding race as a voting criterion. By this time, Republicans came to control most Southern state legislatures.[33]

White supremacists reacted brutally to the changing political climate, engaging in terrorist acts organized by the Ku Klux Klan (KKK), Red Shirts, and the Knights of the White Camelia, among others. In an effort to protect Black Americans' newly established civil rights, Congress passed three Enforcement Acts between 1870 and 1871, and authorized federal troops to curb the rising White supremacist violence.[34]

During the early 1870s, however, under President Ulysses Grant's leadership, the federal government's commitment to protecting the civil rights of Black citizens in the South weakened. His position reflected the greater focus of many Northerners on their own economic situation, destabilized by the financial crisis dubbed the "Panic of 1873" and the economic depression that followed. Insufficient federal protection of Southern Black and White Republican voters enabled Democratic supporters to violently wrench control of state governments in the South from the Republican Party. By 1874, Democrats had taken control of state governments in Virginia, Tennessee, North Carolina, Georgia, Texas, Alabama, and Arkansas.[35] Congress passed its last major civil rights legislation for nearly 90 years, the Civil Rights Act of 1875, which guaranteed equal treatment in places of public transportation, public accommodations, and jury service. The Supreme Court ruled the Act unconstitutional in 1883.[36]

The resurgence of the Democratic Party, including retaking of the US House, culminated in the Hayes Act of 1877 – a compromise made between the Democrats and Republicans to resolve a contested presidential election. The Democratic Party agreed to accept Republican Rutherford B. Hayes as the president-elect in exchange for greater control over the South, including the withdrawal of federal troops from the only Southern states under Republican control: Florida, Louisiana, and South Carolina.[37] This withdrawal of federal protection marks the end of Reconstruction and the start of the Nadir – the period roughly between 1870 and 1930 – characterized by reversals of core political gains that had been achieved by Black Americans during Reconstruction, and a rising campaign of violence by White supremacist organizations. During this low point in US race relations, White supremacist campaigns of racial massacres, lynching, theft, and land-taking peaked.[38] Jim Crow laws became widespread as a legally codified system of racial segregation operating to socially elevate White people and degrade Black people, as well as to hoard political and economic resources for the White community – e.g., public transportation, schools, and hotels. This period also witnessed the near-complete disenfranchisement of Black men in the South by the early 1890s. Black women, who newly gained the right to vote in 1920, lost the ability to functionally exercise this right by the end of the decade.[39]

Prior to 1877, 16 Black men achieved national offices in Congress, including 2 senators. Additionally, Black men held more than 600 state offices and even more local positions.[40] By 1901, this progress had vanished: Black men held no seats in the US Congress and would not again until 1929. According to Du Bois (1935a), by the early 1900s, "In the former slave states, from Virginia to Texas, excepting Missouri, there are no Negro state officials ... and very seldom even a policeman" (p. 694). As in the preceding decades, restructuring the racial hierarchy progressed in fits and starts, and demonstrated again the extreme consequences of gaining and losing the franchise, as well as gaining and losing representation in government.

The dynamics of the suffrage movement combined with, reflected, and shaped the dynamics of the post-Reconstruction civil rights movement. Leaders of NWSA continued their narrow focus on achieving woman suffrage after the 14th amendment's passage, including arguing against the 15th amendment on the grounds of political expediency – i.e., that it distracted from enfranchising women – and on principle that White women should have the right to vote before Black men.[41] In contrast, the Republican Party's agenda strongly influenced that of AWSA, including in its push *for* the 15th amendment. After securing the amendment's passage, AWSA then also shifted its focus to woman suffrage. The rival suffrage organizations eventually reunited in 1890, forming NAWSA, to achieve greater political leverage with a united front.

NAWSA's national strategy invested more strongly in intra-racial alliances between White Northerners and Southerners, and further weakened interracial coalitions between Black and White suffragists. To attract White Southern women to the organization, NAWSA leadership defended woman suffrage as a means to strengthen White dominance in the South. Leading suffragist Stanton advocated for "educated suffrage," a position supported by NAWSA through a 1903 resolution stating that literate, White, native-born women outnumbered literate Black and foreign-born women combined, so that "the enfranchisement of such women would settle the vexed question of rule by literacy, whether of home grown or foreign born production." In other words, "educated suffrage" would mostly enable White women to vote, thereby adding to a White voting bloc capable of maintaining the social practices and institutions of White supremacy. As another example, in 1903, at the (Whites-only) New Orleans NAWSA convention, the executive board publicly endorsed a strong states' rights position on the question of whether or not woman suffrage would be extended to Black women. Historian Rosalyn Terborg-Penn describes these developments thus: "the feminists' fight for the most part was for white women to be included in the rights and privileges of a racist society."[42]

Black suffragists responded in a range of ways to the increasing enthusiasm of major feminist organizations – e.g., NAWSA and the National Women's Party – for "White woman suffrage" rather than universal suffrage. These responses include both building up intra-racial coalitions within the Black community, as well as attempting to shape the agenda of the wider suffrage movement through interracial coalitions, especially to curb its White supremacist tendencies.

A feminist, nationalist agenda framed the political goals of many of the Black women suffragists – i.e., suffrage rights were seen as vital to promoting civil rights legislation and public policies to secure the welfare of the Black community, a community increasingly menaced during the Nadir. Women's clubs – networks of women-led organizations advocating for social reforms and providing community service – comprised an important part of this organizing work. Black women developed their clubs separate from White women, in part reflecting the nationwide spread of Jim Crow, and actively pursued a political agenda that included Black civil rights.⁴³ Take the statement of Margaret Murray Washington, vice-president of the National Association of Colored Women (NACW), who reported the organization's goals for the fourth volume of *The History of Woman Suffrage*: "The Convict Lease System, 'Jim Crow' Car Laws, Lynching and other barbarities are thoroughly discussed, in the hope that some remedy for these evils may be discovered" (quoted in Terborg-Penn, 1998, p. 89).

These organizing activities significantly relied on inter-gender, intra-racial alliances between Black men and women to promote the cause, including the use of the Black press, Black universities and colleges, and the Black church, controlled primarily by Black men at that time.⁴⁴ The threat of White supremacy to the Black community as a whole strengthened this inter-gender coalition, with both prominent Black men and women advocating for woman suffrage – woman suffrage, that is, that included Black women.⁴⁵

Black suffragists also continued to cultivate alliances with White suffragists, challenging anti-Black proposals within NAWSA. Evidence of this appears in the sometimes contradictory positions taken up by NAWSA leadership on the question of universal suffrage. While the NAWSA leadership clearly indicated support for White-woman-suffrage, NAWSA leaders such as Carrie Catt, NAWSA president between 1916 and 1920, also sought to ally with the politically powerful Black suffragists in the North. Catt would express support for universal suffrage when speaking to Black audiences, including readers of the *Crisis*.⁴⁶ Black men were still enfranchised in the North, and in some states, such as New York and Illinois, state-level woman suffrage rights enabled Black women to vote in significant numbers. Black suffragists also argued for the necessity of building an intra-gender alliance to effectively combat sexism. Take the 1916 statement from the National Baptist Woman's Convention, which included these words: "The longer and farther apart the women of the races remain, the greater will be the encroachment by White men" (Terborg-Penn, 1998, p. 126).

The 19th amendment extended the franchise to all women in 1920 at a time when no members of Congress were Black. This racial exclusion reflects the success of Southern Whites in blocking Black men's votes – the South being the region of the country where potential Black voters were most numerous. Note that, in 1875, eight Black US congressmen were seated – the highest number until 1969 – and all eight men were from states of the former Confederacy. The disenfranchisement process repeated with Black women in the South – but at a faster pace. Black Southern women fought to protect their franchise, including filing legal suits against malfeasant states and making appeals to Congress for bills to protect their vote. Despite this, White Southerners succeeded in disenfranchising Black Southern women regionwide by the end of the decade. The major women's suffrage organizations – NAWSA (renamed League of Women Voters in 1921) and the National Women's Party (NWP) – did not respond to the appeals of Black women for their assistance.[47]

The ratification process of the 19th amendment overlaps with the "Red Summer" – the period between April and November 1919 during which a multitude of White riots took place across 25 major cities.[48] Among them, in Chicago, a riot erupted on July 27 after a White mob stoned to death a Black teenager accused of crossing a "color line" in a Lake Michigan swimming area. As a result of the violence, "25 blacks and 13 whites were killed, 537 people injured – some of them severely – and over 1,000 black families lost their homes after they were torched by rioters" (Darity Jr. and Mullen, 2020, p. 13). In 1920, the year that the 19th amendment was certified, an armed White mob attacked Black residents of Ocoee, Florida, because some had attempted to exercise their right to vote in the 1920 presidential election. After several days of violence, these White assailants murdered or chased out an estimated 500 Black residents. After the massacre, the town remained all-White for a half-century.[49] In other words, the woman's suffrage movement ascended to its peak achievement while Black civil rights suffered profound setbacks.[50]

Examining the intersectional character of the various social groups propelling the suffrage movement helps explain the rationale behind the coalitions that emerged, as well as how competition for economic and political resources operated to undermine or undergird these coalitions. In the absence of an intersectional approach, the following important elements of the suffrage movement may be missed:

(1) Many Black men and Black women were active proponents of the suffrage movement, and had as a primary goal universal suffrage that would support a broader civil rights movement; and
(2) The preponderance of White suffragists actively supported White women's suffrage but not universal suffrage, and for those in the South, in particular, extending suffrage to White women would serve as a means to maintain White supremacy.

It would take nearly a half-century more of political activity to produce the Voting Rights Act of 1965 which finally ended the widespread Black disfranchisement in the South.

4.2.3.2. A Legacy of Intra-Racial, Inter-Gender Alliances

The voting patterns of the 2016 presidential election echo the strong intra-racial alliances – between White men and White women, as well as between Black men and Black women – evident during the woman's suffrage movement. Correspondingly, interracial disunity among Black and White women appears to persist. To see this, consider the two major contenders for the presidential office. The 2016 Republican candidate Donald Trump was widely viewed as racist – more so than any other major presidential candidate in recent history – as well as misogynist.[51] Democratic candidate Hillary Clinton, on the other hand, became the first female presidential nominee for a major political party, and as such represented a major achievement for women.

According to a study of voters by the Pew Research Center, men voted in greater numbers for Trump (52% of men voted for Trump, and 41% for Clinton) and more women for Clinton (54% of women voted for Clinton vs. 39% for Trump). At this level of analysis, the voter's gender appears correlated, though somewhat weakly, with the gender of the candidate (Pew Research Center, 2018).

Examining voting patterns by gender and race – in particular, among White women and Black men – provides insight on whether the alignment of interests by race dominate interests by gender, or vice versa. As guideposts, we can use White men and Black women who, as a crude first cut, can be expected to support in greater numbers Trump and Clinton, respectively. White men could be expected to support Trump in greater numbers on the basis of Trump's pro-White and pro-male orientation (e.g., White men made up 73% of Trump's initial cabinet choices, as compared to 32% of President Obama's; Black judges made up 4% of Trump's federal judge appointments, compared to 18% of President Obama's).[52] And, in fact, 62% of White men supported Trump, as compared to 32% supporting Clinton. Black women, on the other hand, nearly unanimously voted for Clinton (98% of Black women voted for Clinton), the candidate with a political agenda that was pro-female, and a critic of Trump's pro-White views (Pew Research Center, 2018). What about White women and Black men? Did their gendered interests dominate their racial interests? Or vice versa? White women appear conflicted: similar shares voted for Trump and Clinton, with their support for Trump edging out their support for Clinton (47% vs. 45%). For Black men, race dominates: an overwhelmingly larger share of Black men voted for Clinton, compared to Trump (81% vs. 14%). Racial alliances appear to trump – or greatly strain – gender alliances: White men and women together formed a sufficient, if weak, coalition to back Trump that offset the near-unanimous support that Black men and women formed to back Clinton.

The 2020 presidential election that followed put then-incumbent President Trump against former Vice President Joseph Biden. In this presidential race, voters had before them two White male candidates. At the same time, as a historic first, Senator Kamala Harris ran as Biden's running mate – the first time a Black and Asian woman appeared on a major party ticket for the vice presidency. Moreover, Biden's decades-long career as Pennsylvania's senator and then vice-presidency to President Barack Obama placed Biden's political agenda in close alignment with that of Hillary Clinton. In 2020, Trump again received the majority of White men's vote: 57% vs. 40% for Biden. Biden received the near-unanimous support of Black women: 95% vs. 5% for Trump. Looking now at White women and Black men, we see that, again, racial alliances appear to prevail over gender alliances. The majority of White women (53%) voted for Trump, while Biden received overwhelming support from Black men (87%).

4.3. Conclusion

The goal of this chapter has been to explain how an intersectional approach to stratification economics produces a higher quality of analysis of the dimensions of a stratified economy, as well as a higher quality of analysis of the rationale and processes that produce a stratified economy.

To review, intersectionality theorizes that forms of discrimination and marginalization differ depending on race, class, ethnicity, gender, sexual orientation, ancestry, and so on. In addition, the overlapping of various forms of exclusion and bias create distinctive and new forms of oppression and marginalization. A disjointed analysis, in contrast, tends to restrict its focus to the experience of oppression faced by a social group that is otherwise privileged: racism, for example, as experienced by Black men; sexism, as another example, as experienced by White women. We use an intersectional approach within the stratification economics framework to understand how racism operates in the US.

We then used empirical and historical examples to demonstrate the application of an intersectional approach to stratification economics. Within the stratification economic framework, an intersectional approach makes it easier to:

(1) *Get the quantities right.* Ignoring the intersection of marginalized identities can lead to underestimating a problem's severity,

such as wage inequality and disparate unemployment rates, and, consequently, overestimating the country's progress toward racial equality.
(2) *Get the qualities right.* Social groups at the intersection of marginalized identities can experience forms of oppression unique to them, differing in quality – not just quantity – from the oppressions experienced by each separate identity. These qualitative differences can be seen in which jobs Black women have greatest access to, as well as how their choices around labor force participation have differed historically from those of White women.
(3) *Get the coalitions right.* An intersectional approach helps explain incentives for creating, maintaining, or breaking coalitions between social groups. These coalition dynamics are dramatically illustrated by the overlap of the first phase of the Black Civil Rights Movement and the women's suffrage movement.

PART II

DEMONSTRATING HOW ANTI-BLACKNESS STRATIFIES THE US ECONOMY

Primer to Part II

P1. Introduction

In chapters 1–4, we presented the main components of our analytical approach to studying racism and how it operates in the US political economy. Specifically, we use a stratification economics approach – which is built on the principle that race is socially constructed – combined with intersectionality theory.

In our introductory chapter, we laid out the basic tenets of stratification economics. Most critically, we laid out how stratification economics' core organizing theory is that group inequality is the result of how social groups rationally pursue their collective self-interest. That is, in the pursuit of their collective self-interest, social groups compete and/or collaborate with other social groups to attain and maintain their relative position in a social hierarchy. An important corollary of this tenet is that, just as collective action creates group inequalities, such as racial inequality, collective action through politics and policies is required to eliminate group inequalities. In the remaining chapters of Part I, we set out the historical record that explains how, in the United States, social groups developed around the social construct of race and formed the basis for anti-Black racism.

In contrast, neoclassical economics focuses primarily on self-interested individuals as the primary economic agent. This means that individuals pursue *individual* – as opposed to *collective* – goals. The first major neoclassical theory of discrimination – *Becker's taste for discrimination theory* – has as its basic assumption that individuals' personal tastes or preferences motivate racist behavior. In this framework, individuals make choices according to what brings them greater happiness – or, in economics jargon, greater "utility." For example, employers who use racist hiring practices do so because of their own personal preferences to interact (or not interact) with workers from a specific racial group. In the case of neoclassical economics, as we will discuss further below, the competitive forces of markets that reward individuals based on their individual attributes are all that is needed to eliminate racial inequalities.

The purpose of this primer is to provide the reader with a more detailed explanation of how the neoclassical and stratification economics approaches to racism differ in the areas of education, the labor market, wealth, and the criminal legal system. We will then follow this primer with our application of the stratification economics approach to each of these areas.

P2. Education

We begin with common ground between the stratification and neoclassical economics approaches. Both approaches hold that education is a means for skill acquisition which, in turn, better positions an individual to earn income in the labor market, and, in the longer run, to accumulate wealth.[1] On a larger scale, raising the overall education level of a nation can lead to greater macroeconomic growth through improved public health and technological advancements, increasing a nation's income. In sum, both conventional economics and stratification economics assign significant economic value to education.

The two economic approaches, however, examine the role of education in the political economy with sharply different analytical lenses. Conventional economics typically takes a narrow view of education's role in the US economy, focusing solely on educational institutions as the main channels through which individuals obtain the skills they need to contribute to the production of economic value (e.g., goods and services). This, in turn, enables individuals to earn economic rewards (i.e., income).

In neoclassical economics, individuals choose to acquire education based on their individual preferences. The process of skill acquisition itself is seen as a relatively individualistic activity, with the individual's capacity to learn dependent mainly on the individual's innate abilities (developed by one's family). In this view, the social context – for instance, how teachers view or treat their students or the social dynamics within a classroom – is not a major focus.[2]

In addition, neoclassical economics assumes that the competitiveness of the labor market requires that employers reward a worker's education and skill level based only on their productivity within the firm. As a result, determining the rewards from education (i.e., wages or salary) is largely a technical matter – i.e., the reward depends on how a firm (employer) organizes the production of its output or service (more on this below).

Prominent research questions within this framework focus on which measures accurately distinguish between different levels of educational attainment and what skills new technologies require (or make obsolete). In other words, this research is primarily concerned with understanding which skills enhance a worker's productivity in the existing or emerging economy. The objective of this research is to understand the market factors that affect how educational attainment determines an individual's earnings, level of employment, and/or labor force activity.

Conventional economics' conception of education supports the popular belief that education is "the great equalizer."[3] In this view, it is assumed that competitive markets enable individuals – regardless of background – to earn economic rewards commensurate with their abilities, abilities that can be increased by education. Therefore, anyone with the determination and discipline to acquire the educational credentials that employers – or, more generally, markets – desire will receive a corresponding set of economic rewards. Conversely, differences in economic success between individuals can largely be explained by differences between the individuals' skills and education – what economists call an individual's *human capital*. This is the basic logic of human capital theory. The popular assumption here is that these skills and educational achievements depend on an individual's talent or intelligence – qualities one is "naturally" endowed with at birth, nurtured by one's family upbringing, and/or developed with hard work.

Neoclassical economics research in education tends to gloss over the question of whether individuals have equal *access* to education. In chapter 5, we document how US history is riddled with racist laws, policies, and practices that have created unequal educational opportunities for Black and White Americans. Racial inequality in accessing education, in other words, is easily traceable to racism. Such racism, however, is viewed by conventional economics as primarily occurring outside competitive markets – in so-called "pre-market" processes.[4] This is because the provision of education in the US is dominated by public and non-profit institutions that operate largely outside market competition. Neoclassical economics generally cedes the research area of how education is obtained to the other social sciences.

Economists Dania Francis, Bradley Hardy, and Damon Jones (2022) explain how the "Economics of education, as a field of study, emerged from the human capital debates of the 1960s and 1970s, as economists pondered the economic value of schooling, on-the-job training, and other skills and traits that could impact worker productivity" (p. 460). That is, conventional economics is more concerned with assessing the economic returns to obtained educational credentials, as opposed to the process of obtaining credentials (see also Teixeira, 2000). Further, these neoclassical models assume that competitive market forces squeeze out of the labor market any influences on wages unrelated to productivity. Therefore, the task at hand is identifying education's relationship to the productivity-related factors that determine wages.

The racial identity of workers, however, persists as an important explanatory variable of wages. This is true even while controlling for various measures of education, intelligence, and training.[5] Unwilling to permit persistent racial discrimination as an explanation for the significance of racial identity in wage determination, and constrained by social norms from explicitly racist assertions about intellectual capacity, human capital theorists point to *unobservable* productivity-related skills, such as "soft-skills" or "cultural values," as underlying the explanatory power of racial identity. But as Steinberg and Darity Jr. (1985) have argued, such invocations are tautological: neoclassical economists assert that competition in the labor market only allows for productivity-related factors to influence the determination of wages, and, therefore, conclude that any factors that play a role in determining wages are purely productivity-related.

In addition to this logical weakness, human capital theory implies a set of implausible social machinations to discount the potential role of racism and racial discrimination in the labor market. Spriggs (2020) refers to these social machinations as the "Two-bus theory." In particular, Spriggs points out that these theorists deny racism in the labor market and only narrowly allow that "'the deficiency' in African Americans is caused by systemic policies that disadvantage Black people's *participation in the economy as equals*" [emphasis added]. He goes on to explain that:

> [The human capital theorist] proclaims that there is a set of actors who have devised rules to prevent African Americans from adequate schooling (this is the primary claim), mostly through housing segregation and, depending on the economist, some learned or absorbed frustration on the part of African Americans that compounds their disadvantage. That is a difficult model to accept, because it means these actors who act with animus direct all their efforts at human capital accumulation but then act objectively in all of their other interactions with African

Americans. I call this the two-bus theory because it requires busing out those negative actors and busing in new actors to make all other economic decisions on jobs and, in total contortion, home mortgage and home purchase decisions (since animus is accepted in creating residential segregation). Far too often, these same economists reject the modern social science theory of race as a social construct, designed to achieve and maximize outcomes for the benefit of those who created the racial definition, because those economists "fail to see where the agency is" for this. The inconsistency, of course, is that this contorted view accepts clear agency for the actions to segregate housing and create poor schooling.

Historian Jeanne Theoharis puts an even finer point on the irony of how conventional economists disassociate inequalities in educational attainment from inequalities in labor market outcomes: "Schooling seems to be the area where inequality is foundationally built and also where inequality is most resolutely and historically supported ... And yet educational inequality is the bedrock of how differential [labor market] outcomes are justified and maintained."[6]

Stratification economics, in contrast, provides a logically coherent analytical framework consistent with the persistently important role of race in both educational attainment as well as wage determination. Stratification economics posits that racial identities define social groups that compete over access to, and control of, educational resources to provide in-group members with greater political power, agency, and self-actualization, and access to better economic rewards in the labor market.

Stratification economics approaches the topic of education and its relationship to economic rewards by focusing on the questions of *who has access to the resources* needed to acquire skills and *who has access to the rewards* associated with the acquired skills. This is consistent with stratification economics' core understanding of how the US economy works: as a social arena within which social groups compete over resources.

Stratification economics also differs from conventional economics in how it views education and skill acquisition as an inherently social activity. That is, stratification economics advances the view that education and skill acquisition depend crucially on how teachers and students and peers interact, not narrowly on an individual's upbringing or intellectual capacity to learn. These social interactions within the classroom – between social groups, as well as within social groups – can serve as either conduits or obstacles to skill acquisition. In other words, the process of obtaining an education is embedded in a political process. As a result, a student's ability to obtain an education depends, in part, on the political power the student has relative to the teacher and their classmates.[7]

Finally, stratification economics holds that a critical feature of education is its role in supporting one's political agency, civic engagement, and efficacy, all of which contribute to the collective power of the social group in which one has membership. In the educational setting, teachers, students, and their peers impart judgments of worth and capability between each other, alongside oratory and writing skills, methods of persuasion and leadership, ethics, and philosophies of governance and social justice. All of these are related to the skills needed to operate as effective agents in the political arena. Civil rights activist and writer James Baldwin (1963) eloquently explains the critical role of education in generating one's political agency:

> The purpose of education, finally, is to create in a person the ability to look at the world for himself, to make his own decisions, to say to himself this is black or this is white, to decide for himself whether there is a God in heaven or not. To ask questions of the universe, and then learn to live with those questions, is the way he achieves his own identity. But no society is really anxious to have that kind of person around. What societies really, ideally, want is a citizenry which will simply obey the rules of society. If a society succeeds in this, that society is about to perish. The obligation of anyone who thinks of himself as responsible is to examine society and try to change it and to fight it – at no matter what risk. This is the only hope society has. This is the only way societies change.[8]

Two research questions hold center stage in the stratification economics of education: (1) How do social groups hoard valuable school resources – including not only the physical school structures, materials, and equipment, but also teaching quality, methods, and content – for in-group members, and withhold such resources from out-group members? (2) How do dominant social groups organize the distribution of economic rewards linked to skills?

In sum, stratification economics' orientation toward education emphasizes how educational attainment can operate as a great *differentiator*. Social group membership influences access to quality education, as well as the opportunities to convert any educational attainment into economic rewards. That is, individuals from different backgrounds have varying levels of access to skill acquisition and educational credentials, even whilst their intellectual capacities are the same. Moreover, differences in the individual's social group membership and their group's position in the social hierarchy contribute to, in part, individual differences in economic success even whilst their skills and educational attainment are the same.

In chapter 5, we use the stratification economics framework to explore how racism and collective racial identities are used to control, or gain access to, education and its rewards. We do this by surveying, in particular, the history of political activity and public policies that have shaped how education is provided within the US.

P3. Labor

In this section, we provide a basic comparison of how neoclassical and stratification economic theories approach racial inequality in the labor market.

We start with the taste for discrimination theory, mentioned at the start of the Primer. This is the neoclassical economic theory proposed by Gary Becker (1971) to explain how racial discrimination would operate within the US economy. In this model, Becker theorizes that racial wage disparities between equally productive Black and White workers are the result of employer preferences about what types of workers they wish to interact with or employ. In Becker's model, employers with a taste for discrimination who pay Black and White workers differently for doing the same work gain some type of utility or satisfaction from doing so.

A major theoretical challenge for this theory is that, under the conditions of robust market competition in the labor market, employers who hold such preferences get competed out. Imagine an extreme case of an employer with a "preference" for White workers who, therefore, hired only White workers. This employer would be at a competitive disadvantage relative to an employer with no such preference. This is because the employer without a taste for discrimination would have a larger supply of workers to hire from (Black *and* White workers) and as such would have more workers competing for their jobs. According to the basic economic laws of supply and demand, all else being equal, the larger labor supply enables the employer to hire workers at a lower wage than the employer with a more limited, Whites-only labor supply. In a competitive market, the discriminating employer would be pushed out as that employer's labor costs would be higher than the non-discriminating employer's, resulting in profits insufficient to remain in the market. Thus, according to the conventional economics approach, this type of discrimination should not persist in the long run; market competition should eliminate wage gaps resulting from discriminatory preferences (Darity Jr., 1989).

Another major economic theory that neoclassical economics offers to explain racial differences in economic outcomes is human capital theory. Recall from the preceding section that human capital theory proposes that labor market outcomes are primarily the result of differences in human capital endowments, where "human capital" refers to such measurable attributes as educational attainment, work experience, and training. Given this, human capital theory, therefore, explains group differences in labor market outcomes as primarily the result of differences in average human capital endowments. The major challenge to this theory, which we discuss in detail in chapter 6, is the large body of empirical evidence that shows that racial wage differences exist between workers with the same human capital.

Neoclassical economists have reformulated the human capital theory to try to reconcile its logic with the persistence of racial inequality evident in the empirical data. In chapter 6, we will delve deeper into the details of these updated theories (for example, the Labor Quality theory), as well as take a look at the contemporary evidence of racial inequality in the US labor market.

Alternatively, stratification economics focuses on how privileged social groups have a material interest in sustaining discrimination in the labor market because of the benefits that it accrues to the group as a whole. Here we quote at length from Wilson and Darity Jr.'s explainer on stratification economics:

> [discrimination] serves the functional role of preserving hierarchy. Therefore, persistent racial inequality arises when a dominant group seeks to maintain the hierarchy that affords it some degree of social or economic privilege. Under this framework, identity can be structured so that investing in, or associating with, a group identity can lead to economic returns and benefits. This treatment of identity as endogenous represents a major departure from more conventional economic models but is consistent with a set of alternative theories for explaining stubborn racial gaps in economic outcomes, and these theories help to operationalize stratification economics.
>
> [These theories] ... present models of a hierarchical wage or occupational structure and the existence of white worker "coalitions" that allow those who share this group identity to maintain a higher position in that hierarchy by limiting other (i.e., black)

workers' access to higher-status and higher-paying occupations and funneling them into lower-status and lower-wage jobs. The coalitions' ability to exercise such an influence is based on their position as the majority group, which is a numerical and historical advantage. (2022, pp. 23–4)

In sum, stratification economics focuses on how privileged social groups operate within the labor market to achieve and preserve their preferred position in the social hierarchy.

The stratification economics approach provides rich insights into how racial groups can maintain cohesion even when other, intersecting social identities, such as economic class, have the potential to weaken intra-racial alliances. Take, for example, the situation of White and Black workers. A strong interracial alliance between Black and White workers has the potential to benefit workers of *both* social groups. This is because an interracial worker coalition, such as that formed through an interracial labor union, increases the collective power of Black and White workers to bargain for higher wages – again, a benefit to *both* White and Black workers. However, if racism enables White workers to benefit from racial discrimination in other arenas, such as access to education or political power or in relative terms within the labor market (i.e., higher wages than Black workers), then White workers may be willing to accept lower overall wages. In other words, the benefits of an *intra-racial* alliance between White workers and White employers may trump the benefits of an *interracial* alliance between White and Black workers. This may occur even while White employers benefit from both the greater profits they can earn by paying all workers less, as well as their racial advantage in access to education or political power. This is an example of the stratification economics basic tenet that, while all individuals of the privileged group – in this case, White Americans – have a material interest in maintaining racism, the benefits from racism to White Americans are not always distributed evenly across all in-group members.

In chapter 6, we will present empirical data and discuss theories consistent with the stratification economics approach, such as occupational crowding. We also discuss various contemporary public policies to reduce labor market inequalities.

P4. Wealth

Neoclassical economics conceives of wealth primarily as the outcome of how individuals accumulate savings out of income, especially labor income.⁹ As a result, the preceding discussion of neoclassical approaches to understanding racial inequality in labor outcomes generalizes to the racial disparities in wealth. Put another way, the neoclassical explanations of racial wealth inequality are simply extensions of theories of racial inequality in the labor market. That is, neoclassical economics explain racial wealth inequality as the accumulated effect of racial inequality in income, within one's lifetime and across generations.

Stratification economics, on the other hand, examines the specific ways in which wealth operates to preserve the existing social hierarchy. The focus of this approach is on centuries of policies and practices that have enabled the transfer of wealth among White American families, from one generation to the next, while simultaneously limiting the ability of Black American families to do the same. These policies and practices include, among others, slavery, Black Codes, land theft and domestic terrorism by White supremacists, Jim Crow laws, racist housing policies such as redlining, and mass incarceration.

Recall the bathtub analogy that we introduced in chapter 2 to distinguish wealth from income. Neoclassical economics focuses on the individual choices and behaviors that affect the flow of income that accumulates into wealth, and the flow of consumption that drains wealth. In the study of racial wealth inequality, stratification economics differs from neoclassical economics in two main ways. First, stratification economics examines the full range of inputs to racial wealth inequality – not just the flow of income and patterns of consumption, but also the consequences for wealth accumulation from theft, race-based terrorism, and racist policies that amount to removing stocks of wealth from Black households and/or dumping stocks of wealth into White households. And, because wealth begets wealth, racial wealth inequality tends to persist. Thus, stratification economics conceives of present-day wealth inequalities as the cumulative sedimentation of historical racial inequalities (Mason, 2023; Shapiro, 2006). Second, stratification economics examines how the choices and behavior of *social* groups, rather than individuals, participate in shaping this full range of inputs into wealth.¹⁰

We illustrate a stratification economics approach to analyzing racial wealth inequality in chapter 7. Specifically, we present empirical data and analysis on the full range of inputs into wealth among Black women. We also discuss barriers that inhibit Black women from accumulating wealth relative to other social groups, such as White men, and policies that could be adopted to break these barriers down, such as reparations.

P5. The Criminal Legal System

The criminal justice system is, according to one textbook, "the system of law enforcement that is directly involved in apprehending, prosecuting, defending, sentencing, and punishing those who are suspected or convicted of criminal offences."[11] The criminal justice system is, in other words, the conglomeration of people and institutions – police, prisons, jails, juvenile detention facilities, criminal laws, criminal attorneys, and so forth – involved in managing people engaged in behavior officially prohibited by society. Economists Patrick Mason, Samuel Myers Jr., and Margaret Simms (2022) refer to this system as the "criminal legal system," preferring to anchor the label more accurately to its grounding in laws, rather than justice, since justice is an ethical dimension that may or may not characterize the system's operations or goals.[12] We follow their practice in our book.

As with the other areas we have discussed above, the main theoretical problem of neoclassical economics is to explain the individual's decision-making process, i.e., to construct an accurate individual-level rational choice model. In the context of the criminal legal system, neoclassical economics has focused on the decision-making process that guides individuals' participation in criminalized behavior. Put another way, individuals' behavioral choices serve as the primary driver of criminal behavior, and the analytical objective is to understand the conditions under which an individual is likely to choose criminal behavior rather than being deterred from such behavior, or alternatively, identify the qualities of an individual who is likely to choose, rather than refrain from, criminal behavior. This neoclassical economics approach builds from the assumption that the locus of control over whether one becomes ensnared in the criminal legal system lies with the individual.

In the early years of neoclassical economics – during the late nineteenth century – the founding members of the American Economic Association (AEA), such as Frances Amasa Walker, Richard Ely, and Walter Willcox, expressed explicitly racist views in their research. In particular, they held the view that members of the Black race were immoral, shiftless, and generally inferior to members of the White race (see textboxes on pp. 124 and 129). Within this analytical framework, such explicitly racist theories explained the hyper-racialization of the carceral system: an individual's race determined whether an individual would engage in criminal behavior and, therefore, whether an individual would become ensnared by the criminal legal system.

Who Founded the American Economic Association?

The AEA was formed in 1885 under the leadership of Francis Amasa Walker, Richard Ely, and Walter Willcox, among other influential members.[13] These principal co-founders planned to construct the AEA on the foundation of the progressivist German Historical School – an intellectual tradition which, in contrast to American *laissez faire* economics, recommends *more* government intervention to reform and correct the capitalist system. Social scientists of the American Progressive era (1896–1917) also fell within the *Social Darwinist* tradition, characterized by the belief that people of certain races and ethnicities are better fit for survival.[14] Eugenic and racist approaches to social and economic reform were not only popular and widespread in the budding American Progressive Era, but the scientific community respected and valued such approaches (Leonard, 2005, p. 208).[15] As such, the "progressive reformers" who developed the AEA contributed to the construction and scientific legitimization of racial theories. In what follows, we describe some of the theories promoted by leading members of the AEA.

Francis Amasa Walker (1840–97) was perhaps the most respected American economist of the early Progressive Era and became the first president of the AEA in 1886. Walker was also president of MIT (1881–97), director of the census (1870–80), vice president of the National Academy of Sciences, and chief of the US Bureau of Statistics (Leonard, 2005, pp. 210–11; Myers, 2023). His account of *race suicide* theory (see more on this below) argued that the natural fertility of superior "native" Anglo-Saxon Europeans would be limited by the immigration of inferior "foreign born" populations. Walker thought southern Italian, Russian, Hungarian, and Austrian immigrants were "beaten men from beaten races; representing the worst failures in the struggle for existence" (1899, p. 447). He endorsed eugenic policies, believing poverty and "pauperism" could be eliminated from social life by "strain[ing] ... the taint inherited from a bad and vicious past" out of "the blood of the race" (1899, p. 469).

Richard Ely (1854–1943) was an American economist and professor of political economy. As leader of the German Progressive movement, Ely left Johns Hopkins University with a cohort of other professors, including John R. Commons. A principal co-founder of the AEA, he served as the organization's first secretary in 1885 and remained a senior statesman until his death. Ely wrote *Outlines for Economics* (1893) – one of the first mass-produced institutional works in the field and a remarkably popular textbook in American colleges. From the 1890s to the 1930s, generations of college students learned economics from the text; in it, students encountered race suicide theory, first termed by Ely's student, Edward A. Ross. Ely argued, "the race is dying at the top, the ablest and most successful people have the smallest families ... the problem lies in the apparent failures of the most efficient individuals [white Northern Europeans] ... to multiply as rapidly as certain classes of the less efficient" (1898, p. 60). For Ely, the Negro race were "for the most part grown up children" and, in general, he believed that "there are certain human beings who are absolutely unfit, and should be prevented from a continuation of their kind" (1898, p. 781; 1918, pp. 144–5).[16]

Walter Willcox (1861–1964) was a professor of economics at Cornell University and statistician at the US Census Bureau (1899–1931) who was among the leading figures in the formative years of the AEA, serving as president in 1915. A former president of the American Statistical Association (ASA) (1912) and a prominent economic demographer and statistician of his time, Willcox believed "objective statistical facts" would reveal the truth of all social problems, including the American "race" problem (Darity Jr., 1994, p. 47). He believed "negroes" had made no progress since emancipation, attributed Black criminality to dysfunctional family structure, and denied that racial segregation and discrimination produce labor market disparities (Myers, 2023; Willcox, 1899). Willcox was principally involved in the development of American social science with respect to the nature of race and racial difference; in 1900, Willcox handpicked members for an AEA committee to "Investigate the Conditions of the Negro." This committee formed the Willcox School, which advanced the *Black disappearance hypothesis* and facilitated the publication of such racist and eugenicist works as Frederick Hoffman's *Race Traits and Tendencies of the American Negro* (1896) and Joseph Tillinghast's "The Negro in Africa and America" (1902).

> The Black disappearance hypothesis is the idea that the Negro race in America would deteriorate to the point of extinction – due not to "the conditions of life" faced by African Americans, but to "race traits and tendencies" of moral, physical, and intellectual inferiority in relation to Whites (Hoffman, 1896, pp. 52, 95). For more on the Willcox School, see the textbox "The Willcox School at the American Economic Association" on page 129.
>
> *Written by Daniella Medina*

The neoclassical economics approach has evolved over time, moving away from explicitly racist assumptions about Black individuals' moral capacity to include environmental factors – such as an examination of how an individual's social conditions may change their individual calculus around the costs and benefits of engaging in criminal behavior. Within this framework, the primary locus of control remains with the individual: the individual chooses to engage in criminal behavior based on rational calculations within the context of their environment, and the criminogenic features of "being Black" derive from the environment rather than having an innate, biological, source. Neoclassical economics assumes that the individual-based, rational choice model remains central, and individuals operating with similar structural disadvantages will, on average, experience similar criminal legal system outcomes. The racist assumption that being Black is an innately criminogenic attribute no longer serves as the basis for explaining racial disparities in the criminal legal system. Instead, in more contemporary neoclassical economics models of criminal behavior, being Black serves as a proxy for criminogenic factors that correlate with being Black, such as, for example, higher rates of poverty.[17] The extent to which being impoverished may be related to engaging in criminal behavior, in other words, may confound the relationship between being Black and criminal behavior because of the higher rate of poverty among Black Americans. In sum, at the center of neoclassical economics is the basic question: Why do some individuals choose to behave criminally?

Also, as in the case of labor markets, this rational choice model allows for individuals to have Becker-style tastes for discrimination, at least in the short run. This is what economics professor Harold Winter refers to as a *prejudicial discrimination*.[18] The fact that discrimination occurs in the criminal legal system is a less controversial conclusion at this point in the development of economic theory and research.[19] At the same time, neoclassical economics' theoretical implication that racial discrimination can only exist in the short run applies to the criminal legal system as well if it is required to run efficiently. That is, in the long run, discriminatory behavior should not persist in any system where efficiency dominates as the organizing force in how the system operates – such as in competitive markets. As a result, the neoclassical framework attributes observations of discrimination to either market failures: insufficient competition to root out inefficient prejudicial behavior; political failures: inability to adopt effective policies; or a failure in analysis: the omission of factors correlated with race and unrelated to prejudicial beliefs.

As a consequence, neoclassical economists who accept that racial – as well as other forms of – bias exists in the criminal legal system maintain the following basic features in their approach to analyzing the criminal legal system. Criminal legal systems can and do operate with racial bias. These systems will not persist in doing so in the long term if the demands for efficiency are strong. And finally, the existence of confounding factors can cause an efficient criminal legal system to produce disparate outcomes by racial group that are not the result of "prejudicial discrimination." Operating within this framework, neoclassical economists such as Harold Winter (2019) adopt the following default position in their approach when analyzing a situation for the presence of bias: an assumption of no racial bias. Winter advises that economists should conclude that bias exists only after all confounding factors can be ruled out:

> In all, there is almost universal acceptance that racial discrimination exists in the criminal justice system. Among the numerous studies discussed … there is evidence that such bias may be found at all levels of the system … However, and importantly, the fact that different racial and ethnic groups, as well as different genders, are treated differently by the criminal justice system is not proof that bias based on animosity alone is present … [I]f defendants are truly different based on a number of confounding factors related to criminal behavior and criminal history, an efficient system should be expected to treat defendants differently …
>
> The main contribution of economic analysis in this case is to explicitly recognize that a demonstration of racial discrimination requires a careful consideration of the many other factors that can lead to how suspects, defendants, prisoners, death row inmates and so on, are treated. (2019, p. 83)

Stratification economics takes a distinctly different approach to analyzing the role of racial discrimination and racism in the US criminal legal system. Two central features of stratification economics include: (1) all individuals operate as a member of a racial social group, including within the criminal legal system; (2) individuals operate as a member of a racial social group because these groupings serve a rational purpose: to protect or improve one's position – one's group's position – in the existing racial hierarchy which organizes access to political, economic, and social resources within a society. We discuss each in turn.

First, stratification economics assumes that all individuals engaging with criminal legal institutions and processes do so as members of a social group, and therefore, their social group membership colors all such interactions.[20] As we have discussed in the previous chapters, race-based social group identities are among the most profound in US society.

More specifically, stratification economics starts with the assumption that, in the US, we can expect that racial identity, and discriminatory behavior that enforces the hierarchy of such identity, to operate across all social arenas unless major interventions to prohibit such behavior have taken place. These arenas include the criminal legal system, as well as the educational system, the labor market, healthcare, government, and so on. Mason, Myers, and Simms explain:

> Economic historians and analysts of the legacy of racial separation and subordination in American life recognize that this underlying assumption of no racism or no historical underpinning for systemic inequality based on race is inaccurate. Instead, the standing assumption ought to be that there is a race effect until or unless countervailing influences – such as corrective or remedial efforts designed to reduce racial disparities – are accounted for. (2022, p. 496)

These scholars illustrate this with the important example of how racial identities operate in knowledge creation *about* the criminal legal system:

> For many Black researchers, race is a statistically significant, substantively large, and causally significant variable *because* of racial differences in treatment by police, prosecutors, courts, probation officers, and parole officers, according to this view. This is so not just because of conjecture or speculation. Rather this is

because of lived experiences and intergenerational transfers of knowledge that in many ways has been sequestered because of the marginalization of this scholarly knowledge and insights within the dominant paradigms of economics. (2022, p. 496)

Evidence of this point are the results of Mason, Myers, and Simms' meta-analysis – an analysis of the empirical research results produced across many studies – examining the relationship between the racial identity of a scholar and whether the scholar's research concludes with a "finding of discrimination." After examining more than 600 economic studies published between 1973 and 2020 that examine race or racism and the criminal legal system, they find that, "the odds of finding discrimination are 2.9–4 times higher for Black authors than for non-Black authors."

The Willcox School at the American Economic Association

The so-called Willcox School on the American race question consisted of AEA members selected by Walter Willcox to "investigate the condition of the American Negro." The committee applied the empiricism of the German Historical School to American economics, believing statistics to be capable of revealing the truth of all social problems, including the "American race problem." Proponents of the Willcox School's alarmist race suicide theory advanced the Black disappearance hypothesis, responding to the popular fear among Whites that "degenerate" African Americans would drive the White population out of existence. What was overwhelmingly common among the progressivist social scientists of the Willcox School was their embrace of the notion of the "constitutional inferiority" of African Americans (Darity Jr., 1994, p. 48).[21]

Frederick Hoffman (1865–1946) was an American actuary and statistician for Prudential Life Insurance Company and president of the ASA in 1911. In 1896, the AEA devoted three full issues to the publication of Hoffman's *Race Traits and Tendencies of the American Negro*. In it, Hoffman responded to the fear-stoking race suicide theory with a comprehensive statement of the Black disappearance hypothesis. In a paper on Black longevity and disease patterns, Hoffman concludes that "the colored race" possesses a "race proclivity to disease and death"

(1892, p. 585).[22] He argued that the "gross immorality, early and excessive intercourse of the sexes, premature maternity, and general intemperance in eating and drinking" cause "the colored people" to be susceptible to venereal disease (1892, p. 534). He concludes: "the colored race is showing every sign of an undermined constitution, a diseased manhood and womanhood; in short, all the indications of a race on the road to extinction" (1892, p. 537).

Alfred Holt Stone (1870–1955) was a non-academic member of the AEA. The Mississippi planter and aristocrat was a long-time friend of Willcox, with whom he co-authored and published a collection of his own works in an AEA volume called *Studies in the American Race Problem* (1906).[23] Stone conducted an "experiment with negro labor" on his own Mississippi plantation comparing Black farmers who rented land to those who sharecropped. He concluded that "the motives of self-interest do not operate with the negro" as they are "controlled far more by their fancies" and lack the "calculating powers and stick-to-it-ness of homo economicus" (Darity Jr., 1994, p. 56). Like Hoffman, Stone believed that competition between Black and White Americans would lead to the extinction of Black Americans. He attributed all gains of the race to infusion with White blood, using W. E. B. Du Bois and Booker T. Washington as examples (Aldrich, 1979, p. 9).

John R. Commons (1862–1945) was an American institutionalist economist who served as AEA president in 1917. His book *Races and Immigrants in America* (1907), which opens with an outright dismissal of Jefferson's famous declaration that all men are created equal, offers a eugenic rationalization of American slavery (Dimand, 2005, p. 842). For Commons, African Americans were "indolent and fickle," which justified and necessitated slavery – "The negro could not possibly have found a place in American industry had he come as a free man" (1907, p. 136; Myers, 2023). He believed that Black inferiority could only be alleviated by interbreeding with superior races (Leonard, 2003, p. 689). He echoed race suicide theorists, arguing that "the race with the lowest necessities" – for Commons, Jews and African Americans – "displace others" (1907, p. 151). He remains an honored figure of the AEA in the twenty-first century.

William Z. Ripley (1867–1941) was an American economist and "race anthropologist" who served terms as vice president and president of the AEA.[24] Ripley used cartography to represent and legitimize racial categories, constructing biological, intellectual, and moral geographies related to racial distributions in both the US and Europe (Winlow, 2006, p. 119). In 1899, he produced "the most influential racial taxonomy of the progressive era," *The Races of Europe*, which argued that race is the central engine to understanding history (Leonard, 2003, p. 690; Myers, 2023). Ripley used the cranial index (ratio of skull width to length), height, eye color, and hair color to classify Europeans into three distinct races (Ripley, 1899, p. 272). In a later article publicized by the *New York Times* (1908), Ripley argues that "abnormal intermixture" may revert civilization to a "primitive type of European" he supposed existed in "a time before the separation of European varieties of men began." This primitive type, according to Ripley (1908), was "brunette with black eyes and hair and a swarthy skin."

Edward A. Ross (1866–1951) was an American sociologist, economist, eugenicist, and founding member of the AEA. A leading public intellectual of his time, Ross coined the concept of race suicide, featured in Ely's popular economics textbook and often cited by Theodore Roosevelt. He believed that under industrial capitalism, "native" Anglo-Saxons were well suited to rural life, whereas the inferior immigrant races – "Latins, Slavs, Asiatics, and Hebrews" – were better adapted to urban life (Ross, 1901). Ross was fired from Stanford University in 1900 after a racist speech in which he proclaimed, "California, this latest and loveliest seat of the Aryan race, shall not become, if we can help it, the theater of such stern wolfish struggle for existence as prevails throughout the Orient." In response, the AEA appointed a committee to inquire into his firing and to condemn the violation of his academic freedom (Magness, 2020).[25] In the twenty-first century, he is remembered as a "martyr to academic freedom" and is still a celebrated founder of the AAUP and the American Sociological Association (Leonard, 2005, pp. 208–10).

Written by Daniella Medina

The second fundamental feature of stratification economics is that it assigns a rational basis for these racial identities in the criminal legal system and elsewhere, i.e., that these racial identities function to support or improve an individual's position in a social hierarchy. Stratification economics' main analytical goal is to understand the criminal legal system's functional role in maintaining the racial hierarchy, and how the members of dominant social groups use the criminal legal system to resist changes to the existing social hierarchy. Likewise, members of subaltern social groups, rationally, seek ways to reform or radically change the criminal legal system to improve their position in the social hierarchy.

In chapter 8, we trace the stratifying function of the criminal legal system from its colonial-era roots to its contemporary form of mass incarceration.

In this primer, we have presented what we view as the major differences in approach between neoclassical and stratification economics to the topics of education, labor, wealth, and the criminal legal system. In the next four chapters, we will dive deeper into each of these topics, applying the stratification economics approach.

5

Education: Unequal Access, Unequal Outcomes

5.1. Introduction

In the "Primer to Part II" we discussed fundamental differences between how neoclassical and stratification economics approach analyzing racial inequality in education. To recap, neoclassical economics conceives of education as *the great equalizer*. That is, conventional economics assumes that competitive markets enable individuals – regardless of background – to earn economic rewards commensurate with their abilities, abilities that can be increased by education. Anyone with the determination and discipline to acquire the educational credentials that employers – or more generally, markets – desire will receive a commensurate corresponding set of economic rewards. In contrast, the stratification economics' orientation toward education emphasizes how educational attainment can operate as a *great differentiator*. Social group membership influences access to quality education, as well as the opportunities to convert any educational attainment into economic rewards. That is, individuals from different backgrounds have varying levels of access to skill acquisition and educational credentials, even whilst their intellectual capacities are the same. Moreover, differences in individuals' social group membership and their group's position in the social hierarchy contribute to differences in economic success even whilst their skills and educational attainment are the same.

In this chapter, we examine how education operates to racially stratify economic outcomes in the United States. That is, the goal of this chapter is to use the stratification economics framework to explore how racism and collective racial identities are used to control, or gain access to, education and rewards therefrom.

5.2. Looking at the Numbers

Before diving into what a stratification economics approach – as opposed to a conventional, neoclassical approach – reveals about education's role in the US economy, we first preview some empirical data. These data describe basic patterns in educational attainment, the rewards associated with educational credentials, and the racial dimension of these numbers.

In figure 5.1, we show the historical trends in educational attainment for Black and White Americans from 1940 to 2020.[1] The first panel shows the share of the American population 25 years and older that have obtained at least a high school degree. The second panel shows the share that has obtained at least a 4-year college degree.

We can see from figure 5.1 that achieving a high school diploma transformed from a relatively notable accomplishment of about 1 in

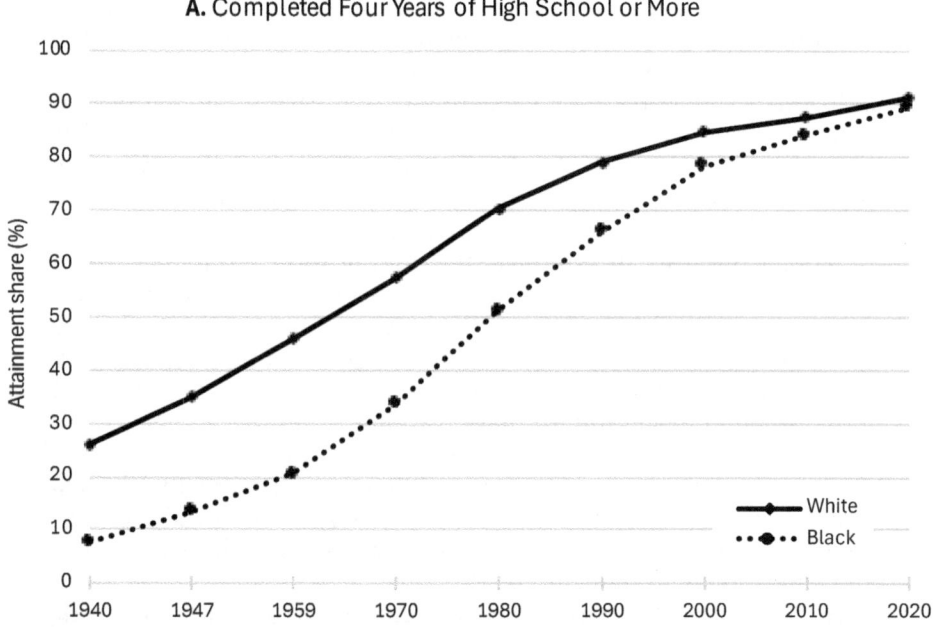

Figure 5.1 Trends in the share of US adult education attainment by race, 1940–2020.
Data source: US Census Bureau, 1947, and 1952 to 2002 March Current Population Survey, 2003 to 2021 Annual Social and Economic Supplement to the Current Population Survey (noninstitutionalized population, excluding members of the Armed Forces living in barracks); 1950 Census of Population and 1940 Census of Population (resident population).

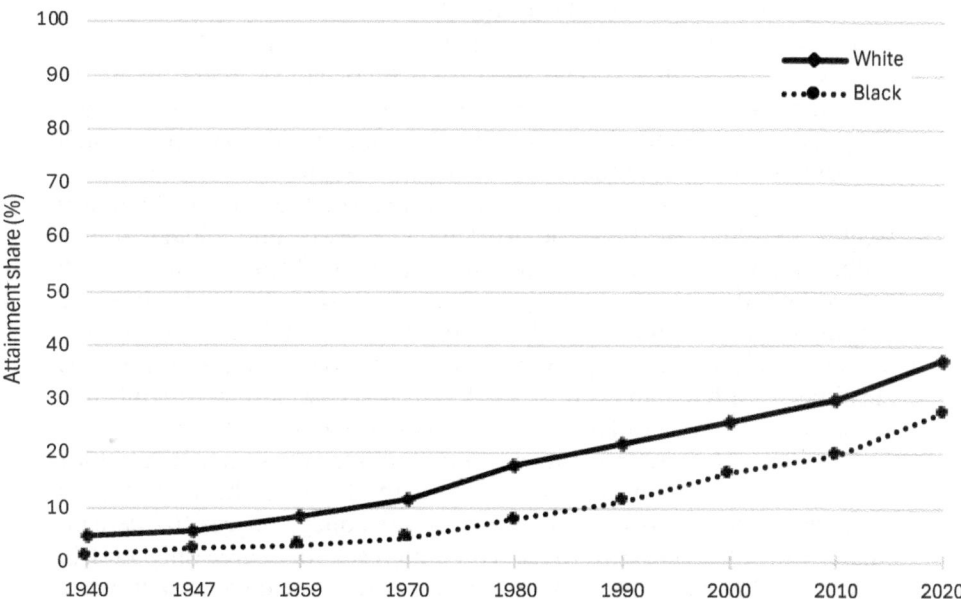

Figure 5.1 (*continued*) Trends in the share of US adult education attainment by race, 1940–2020.
Data source: US Census Bureau, 1947, and 1952 to 2002 March Current Population Survey, 2003 to 2021 Annual Social and Economic Supplement to the Current Population Survey (noninstitutionalized population, excluding members of the Armed Forces living in barracks); 1950 Census of Population and 1940 Census of Population (resident population).

4 White Americans and 1 in 10 Black Americans in 1940 to a near universal achievement for both groups by 2020 (about 90 percent). Over the same period, the share of adults obtaining a 4-year college degree or more also increased, but at a slower pace. In 1940, few achieved such levels of education, Black or White. About 40 years later, in 1980, securing a 4-year college degree or more remained a privilege and the racial gap in educational attainment widened to 10 percentage points. By 2020, the same 10 percentage point racial gap remains, with 38 percent of White Americans completing four years of college compared to 28 percent of Black Americans.

Whether this convergence in educational achievement – at least in the rate of high school graduation – narrows the racial gaps in economic outcomes depends crucially on whether racial groups obtain similar *rewards* for their educational achievements. As we will show in the next set of tables, the economic rewards to educational attainment are clear, and clearly racially stratified.

We start with three basic measures of economic well-being: (1) weekly earnings of full-time workers, which gauges one's access to earnings when fully employed; (2) the unemployment rate, which gauges one's access to any work-related earnings; and (3) wealth, which accounts for the accumulation of economic resources over time.

In the first column of table 5.1, we present the average (median) weekly earnings of full-time workers (25 years and older) at five different levels of educational attainment for 2019.[2] That is, each row shows the weekly earnings for workers with the same level of employment (full-time), by the amount of education workers have achieved. These figures provide a view of how earnings *rates* (i.e., earnings for a fixed amount of work – in this case, a week of full-time work) are related to different levels of educational attainment.

We see right away that the earnings rate improves considerably for workers as they gain educational credentials, with the largest gain occurring when a worker achieves a 4-year college degree (67 percent higher earnings relative to those with a high school degree only, and 46 percent higher earnings relative to those with some college experience but no 4-year degree).

Column 2 provides analogous figures related to unemployment rates by educational attainment level.[3] Here again, we see that economic outcomes improve as educational attainment levels increase. Those

Table 5.1 Economic outcomes in 2019 by educational attainment level

Educational attainment levels	Median weekly earnings (full-time workers only) (2019$)	% unemployment rate	Wealth (net worth) (2019$)
High school drop-out	592	5.4	18,000
High school graduate, no college experience	746	3.7	79,000
Some college experience, no degree, or Associate's degree	856	3.0	102,000
4-year college degree	1,248	2.2	243,000
Some post-college experience	1,567	1.9	484,000

Source: US Department of Labor; Federal Reserve Bank of St. Louis (www.stlouisfed.org/open-vault/2020/december/has-wealth-inequality-changed-over-time-key-statistics).

Education: Unequal Access, Unequal Outcomes 137

with a high school degree only have an unemployment rate that is two-thirds again that of those with a 4-year college degree.

As a final measure, we look at differences in net worth in column 3.[4] This measure serves as the most comprehensive measure for differences in economic opportunities because it captures differences in contemporaneous earnings rates and employment access as well as the cumulative effects of economic opportunity gaps over time, including for prior generations.[5] The largest jump in wealth between educational attainment levels occurs between high school drop-out and high school graduate where the net worth of high school graduates is more than quadruple that of high school drop-outs. The net worth of 4-year college degree holders comes in next at nearly 2.5 times the net worth of those with only some college experience.

What these figures illustrate is the clear and dramatic relationship between economic rewards and educational attainment levels. What these figures cannot tell us is the direction of causation: does one's educational attainment level lead to access to greater economic resources, or does one's access to greater economic resources lead to higher levels of educational attainment? Conventional, neoclassical economics primarily focuses on investigating the former relationship while stratification economics primarily examines the latter. That is, stratification economics focuses on the question: How much does one's educational attainment reflect one's access to economic resources, access that is facilitated by one's social group membership?[6]

Table 5.2 presents the three economic outcome measures we have been discussing – weekly earnings rate of full-time workers, unemployment rate, and net worth – by educational attainment *and race*.

In Panel A, we can see right away that for both Black and White workers, weekly earnings rates rise with each additional educational credential. It is also true that at each educational credential level, full-time White workers earn more than their Black counterparts. In fact, Black workers with at least some college experience typically earn less than not only their White counterparts with some college experience, but also White workers with a high school degree and no college experience. Similarly, Black workers with graduate coursework or an advanced degree, i.e., education beyond a 4-year college degree, typically earn less than their White counterparts. Instead, these highly educated Black workers earn nearly the equivalent of White workers with only a 4-year degree.

In Panel B, we see the same racialized pattern in unemployment rates. For both racial groups, the unemployment rate falls with each advance in educational credentials. It is also clear that among those

Table 5.2 Economic outcomes in 2019 by educational attainment level and race

Educational attainment levels	Black (2019$)	White	% racial gap (White/Black ratio)
A. Median weekly earnings of full-time workers			
High school drop-out	536	604	113
High school graduate, no college experience	635	778	123
Some college experience, no degree, or Associate's degree	720	894	124
4-year college degree	1,007	1,270	126
Some post-college experience	1,284	1,568	122
B. Unemployment rate			
High school drop-out	9.9	4.9	49
High school graduate, no college experience	6.2	3.2	52
Some college experience, no degree or Associates	4.4	2.7	61
4-year college degree	3.1	2.1	68
Some post-college experience	2.3	1.7	74
C. Wealth (net worth)			
High school drop-out	8,000	47,000	588
High school graduate, no college experience	14,000	115,000	821
Some college experience, no degree or Associates	43,000	132,000	307
4-year college degree	51,000	298,000	584
Some post-college experience	115,000	597,000	519

Source: US Department of Labor; Federal Reserve of St. Louis (www.stlouisfed.org/on-the-economy/2021/january/wealth-gaps-white-black-hispanic-families-2019).

with up to a 4-year degree, Black workers are roughly 1.5 to 2 times more likely to be unemployed than their White counterparts. In fact, access to employment for Black workers with some college is not much better than among White high school *drop-outs*. Black workers with a 4-year degree fare about the same in the labor market as White workers with only a high school degree.

Panel C shows how the racial gaps in net worth by educational credential are an order of magnitude larger – on a different scale from earnings or employment rates. The gaps within and across educational levels are larger than any of the gaps we have encountered thus far. Within each educational credential level, White households have between 3 and 8 times the wealth of their Black counterparts. Moreover, the wealth of the typical Black college graduate ($51,000) is similar to that of the typical White high school drop-out ($47,000). The net worth of the typical Black household headed by a person with more than a 4-year college degree is comparable to that of a White household headed by a person with only a high school diploma.

In table 5.3, we show the pattern of median earnings and unemployment by race and gender.[7] Here we see a similar pattern to that in table 5.2: as educational credentials increase, earnings rise and unemployment rates fall. Two other patterns with regard to earnings, however, emerge: a male earnings premium among both White and Black workers alongside a White earnings premium, among both male and female workers. Combining these observations, we see that, for every level of educational credential, Black women are situated at the bottom of the earnings hierarchy and White men are at the top. The largest gaps between social groups occur between White men and Black women with at least a high school degree.

The patterns in unemployment rates differ. The main differences in unemployment rates are along race, rather than gender, echoing the figures we presented in chapter 4. That is, Black men and Black women similarly have higher unemployment rates than both White men and White women. And while Black men have the highest unemployment rates, for at least some educational levels, Black men and Black women fare similarly. Finally, while White men have the lowest unemployment rates, White men and White women fare similarly. In sum, White men and White women appear to have greater access to employment relative to Black men and Black women, while White men have the greatest access to earnings when employed.

Three major features emerge from this brief data sketch of the economic returns to education credentials. First, greater education is linked to greater access to economic resources. In other words, those with access to greater levels of education also have greater economic advantages. Second, White racial group membership confers greater *access* to education as well as greater economic *returns* to education. That is, each increase in education for White Americans is linked to a greater rise in economic resources. Third, White men, in particular, experience the greatest increase in economic returns to education in terms of the opportunity to work as well as what they earn when employed. These features have the effect of sustaining economic inequality between racial groups, even as racial group members converge in their educational attainment levels and especially since

Table 5.3 Economic outcomes in 2019 by educational attainment level, race, and gender

Educational attainment levels	Black (2019$)		White		% gender gap by race (men/women ratio)		% racial gap by gender (White/Black ratio)	
	Men	Women	Men	Women	Black	White	Men	Women
A. Median weekly earnings of full-time workers								
High school drop-out	575	478	658	497	120	132	114	104
High school graduate, no college experience	696	586	888	653	119	136	128	111
Some college experience, no degree, or Associate's degree	791	662	1,030	755	119	136	130	114
4-year college degree	1,056	970	1,489	1,107	109	135	141	114
Some post-college experience	1,434	1,231	1,880	1,359	116	138	131	110
B. Unemployment rate								
High school drop-out	9.3	10.6	4.4	5.8	88	76	47	55
High school graduate, no college experience	6.6	5.6	3.1	3.3	118	94	47	59
Some college experience, no degree, or Associate's degree	8.5	8.6	4.9	5.9	99	83	58	69
4-year college degree	3.2	3.0	2.1	2.1	107	100	66	70
Some post-college experience	2.1	2.4	1.8	1.7	88	106	86	71

Source: US Department of Labor.

men and women of each race tend to combine into households. These data suggest that even as increasing levels of educational attainment improve economic outcomes, increasing levels of *racial equity in educational attainment* is unlikely to result in *racial economic equality*.

5.3. Knowledge Is Power: Governing Access to the Value of Education

We turn next to the main objective of this chapter: to investigate the link between access to educational resources and access to political and economic resources. We do this over the next four sections.

Sections 5.3.1 and 5.3.2 provide a brief historical survey – first of the South and then the North – to describe how the dominant racial group in the US, White Americans, explicitly built a racial monopoly on educational resources to protect their claim on political and economic resources. Conversely, and simultaneously, Black Americans resisted domination by breaking this monopoly, creating new access points to formal education. Sections 5.3.3 and 5.3.4 link this historical foundation of racialized access to education to the contemporary education system in the US. In particular, section 5.3.3 examines the extent to which access to educational resources remains racialized, and section 5.3.4 explores the limits to racial integration in providing racial equity in education.

5.3.1. The Political Economy of Education, Illustrations from the South

The profound shifts in the educational landscape that occurred in the South around the time of the Civil War lay bare education's role as a conduit to political, economic, and social power. During Reconstruction, formerly enslaved people immediately set to revolutionizing access to formal education, articulating a view that education was a means to the power they needed to improve their position in the social hierarchy.[8] White Americans, conversely, provide clear articulations of their social group's opposing interest in making education inaccessible to the formerly enslaved in order to protect White Americans' dominant position in the social hierarchy.

5.3.1.1. Education as a Source of Political Power

Prior to the Civil War, laws in Southern states prohibited the education of enslaved persons.[9] Enslaved persons who defied these laws risked severe consequences – including gruesome acts of physical mutilation as well as considerable financial fines.[10] Slaveholders, and others invested in the operation of the slave system, controlled access to knowledge as one element of political control. Withholding literacy from enslaved persons made political knowledge harder to access and spread – such as through books and periodicals, restricting the channels through which they could organize.

Take, for example, the 1829 anti-slavery political treatise *Appeal to the Coloured Citizens of the World*. David Walker, a free Black man who migrated from North Carolina to Boston, Massachusetts, wrote this series of essays, and published them in a political pamphlet, to inspire enslaved people to revolt. The *Appeal* spread to Georgia within weeks of its publication and then, within months, across the states of Virginia and Louisiana. This occurred even while individuals found in possession of the publication in those states were charged with inciting insurrection. According to historian Clement Eaton, it was in response to the clandestine circulation of the *Appeal* that these states passed laws against the distribution of seditious literature and against teaching enslaved persons to read and write.[11]

Scholars William Darity Jr. and A. Kirsten Mullen speculate that Walker's treatise may have inspired the Nat Turner rebellion, an uprising emblematic of "the worst fears of slaveholders about the consequences of enslaved blacks acquiring literacy" (2020, p. 88). What is known about Nat Turner, an enslaved man, is that his reading and writing abilities assisted him in using the Bible to inspire an armed rebellion, in 1831, against slavery in Southampton, Virginia. The uprising, involving at least 40 allies, resulted in the death of 55 Whites. Du Bois observes that "after the Nat Turner insurrection in Virginia, these laws [prohibiting the education of enslaved people] were strengthened and more carefully enforced" (1935a, p. 638). Research by historian Carter J. Woodson distinguishes the period from 1800 to the mid-1830s as a repressive one for the education of Black people in the US as White Americans attempted to derail Black individuals' access to literacy, education, and, thus, political power (Evans, 2007, p. 25).

After the Civil War, acquiring education supported the Black community's efforts to realize the economic independence and political freedom that their new status made possible. In the short term, literacy improved Black people's bargaining power in any manner of negotiation with White people – political, economic, or social. Historian James Anderson explains how, for example, "The uses and abuses of written labor contracts made it worthwhile to be able to read, write, and cipher. Frequently, planters designed labor contracts in ways that would confuse and entrap the ex-slaves" (1988, p. 18).

Looking over a longer time-horizon, Anderson also describes the widely held view among freedpeople that education played an essential role in cultivating the political leadership necessary to secure their freedom long into the future:

> any significant reorganization of the southern political economy was indissolubly linked to their education in the principles, dues, and obligations appropriate to a democratic social order. Ex-slave communities pursued their educational objectives by developing various strata, but the one they stressed the most was leadership training. They believed that the masses could not achieve political and economic independence or self-determination without first becoming organized, and organization was impossible without well-trained intellectuals – teachers, ministers, politicians, managers, administrators, and businessmen. (1988, p. 28)

5.3.1.2. Education as a Source of Economic Power

Limiting the education of the Black community helped to insure that planters had access to the labor supply they desired: an abundant supply of workers with weak bargaining power. Preventing freedpeople from accessing formal education limited the range of skills they could acquire, and thus the range of income-generating activities freedpeople could access. Du Bois' scholarship documents how Southern property owners "believed that laborers did not need education; that it made their exploitation more difficult; and that if any of them were really worth educating, they would somehow escape their condition by their own efforts" (1935a, p. 641). In other words, the desire for education on the part of freedpeople – and fear on the part of White Southerners – derives from education's potential to enable economic gains, including economic self-sufficiency within the Black community. Blocking freedpeople's access to formal education also benefited White employers another way: doing so removed the time demands of educational activities – among adults and children – thereby increasing the available supply of labor.[12]

In these ways, the prohibition of enslaved persons – and then freedpeople – from obtaining an education served as an important support for the intensely repressive labor system of the Southern White supremacist political economy. Indeed, Anderson, drawing on the historical research of Jonathan Wiener, describes how, "Faced with the possibilities of moving toward a northern-style system of free labor and mass literacy or remaining with their coercive mode of labor allocation and control, the planters chose the labor-repressive system, which rested at least partially on the absence of formal schooling among agricultural and domestic laborers" (1988, p. 21).[13]

5.3.1.3. Education as a Source of Social Power

Du Bois also points to the significance of how the absence of education, for the enslaved, and then freedpeople, served as a hallmark of their subordination. According to Du Bois, "The very feeling of inferiority which slavery forced upon them [Black Americans] fathered an intense desire to rise out of their condition by means of education" (1935a, p. 638). Education's role as a symbol of intellect likewise energized the White community's efforts to block freedpeople's access to it. Anderson describes the educational impulse among freedpeople as a "frontal assault on the racist myth of black inferiority, which was critical to the maintenance of the South's racial caste system" (1988, p. 27). Accessing education, in other words, operated to contradict this social status. To maintain their claim to racial superiority, White Southerners reacted violently to the breach to White supremacy represented by freedpeople's attempts to obtain education. Consider this observation by the American Freedmen's Aid Commission – a federal commission formed in 1865 "to promote the education and elevation of the Freedmen, and to cooperate to this end with the Bureau of Refugees, Freedmen, and Abandoned Lands";[14] Du Bois quotes the Commission's assessment that "attempts at education provoked the most intense and bitter hostilities, as evincing a desire to render themselves equal to the whites. Their churches and schoolhouses in many places were destroyed by mobs" (1935a, p. 645).

In sum, the Southern states' use of exclusionary educational policies and the opposing determination of enslaved, and then freed, people to obtain education demonstrate the intense link each social group made between education and power – political, social, and economic power. Anderson documents the contemporaneous recognition of this interdependence among freedpeople, quoting Freedmen Bureau's Superintendent of Schools and Finance John W. Alvord who reported that, "Perhaps the most trying period in the freedmen's full emancipation has not yet come. But we can distinctly see that the incipient education universally diffused as it is, has given these whole four millions an impulse onward never to be lost. They are becoming conscious of what they can do, of what they ultimately can be" (1988, p. 15).

5.3.1.4. A Black Revolution in Southern Education

The Civil War's rupture of the Southern White supremacist political and economic institutions profoundly expanded the opportunities for the Southern Black community to organize internally – as well as in coalition with other communities – an educational system they could access. Even before the war concluded, grassroots efforts to create classes and schools cropped up in places relatively shielded from Confederates, such as at Union army camps or on land abandoned by Southern planters.[15]

After the end of the Civil War in 1865, Alvord observed freedpeople immediately forming schools to realize their newly acquired right to an education. Alvord refers to these schools – fully resourced by members of the Black community – as "native schools," and describes how, "throughout the entire South, an effort is being made by the colored people to educate themselves." According to Alvord's observations, in 1866, there were "at least 500 schools of this description ... already in operation throughout the South" (Alvord quoted in Anderson, 1988, p. 7). Alongside these activities, the Republican-dominated federal government expanded the Freedmen Bureau's powers and funding to develop public schools in the former Confederacy. The Bureau, in coalition with benevolent societies such as missionaries, and freedpeople, established public schools across the South.[16]

Freedpeople further insured their access to education by formalizing their educational demands in legal terms, such as "educational clauses." The "educational clause" was a novel labor contract term that required employers to furnish educational services to their workforce. The South's labor shortage – the result of newly freedpeople quitting the plantations – enabled freedpeople to bargain for these clauses. In 1867, Alvord reports in the *Fourth Semi-Annual Report on Schools for Freedmen*:[17]

> The freedman who works faithfully for his employer can, and does, not only obtain fair wages, but also school privileges for his children. The planter's interest yields to this claim. He obtains a better laborer, with more character and permanent, in the person of the man who makes the education of his family paramount ... and thus schools are everywhere springing up from the soil itself at the demand of those who till it. (p. 83; quoted in Anderson, 1988, p. 21)

Republican allies and freedpeople also worked within the reconstructed state legislatures to insert meaningful commitments to the development of public schools into Southern state constitutions.

Anderson describes how, "By 1870, every southern state had specific provisions in its constitution to assure a public school system financed by a state fund" (1988, p. 19).

Prior to this, no meaningful public school system existed in the South, for Black or White Southerners. This is despite the fact that former Confederate states had language about public schools in either their laws or constitutions. Du Bois' taxonomy of former Confederate states' public school provisions reveals that they inadequately funded their educational goals, mismanaged existing funds, or simply failed to implement any effective plans to provide a public school system.[18] This absence stood in contrast to the North's common school movement that started in the 1830s.

The Southern public schools' failure to develop can be explained, in part, by the alliance between lower-income Whites and property-owning Whites. For both social groups, opposition to Black education was a means to re-establish the antebellum racial hierarchy. White planters' opposition to the education of Blacks, Anderson notes, "sprang from their clear economic and ideological interests in preserving the racially qualified system of coercive agricultural labor" (1988, p. 25). Lower-income Whites, similarly, had the possibility of taking advantage of their racial qualifications to climb up the social hierarchy by becoming property owners themselves. This ambition could be furthered by fortifying the White supremacist institutions on which propertied Whites relied, instead of through acquiring a formal education (Du Bois, 1935a, p. 641). Consequently, propertied White Southerners and Southern Democratic legislators formed a coalition with lower-income White Southerners to block – with violence – freedpeople's access to public schools. The continued presence of federal troops in the South after the Civil War proved crucial in protecting – at least some – public schools serving Black communities.[19]

By the late 1870s, however, the Northern Republicans largely abandoned their alliance with freedpeople and their project of reconstructing the South.[20] Democrats recaptured Southern state governments and pushed back against the universal public education established by freedpeople and their allies. After the 1877 Hayes Compromise, federal troops withdrew from the Southern states. Democrats' opposition to public education, however, failed to reverse all progress. Here we quote Du Bois at length, describing the situation in Alabama during this tumultuous period:

> But the demand for education was now strong, and the effect of the Northern opinion too great, so that the new Constitution

made by Democrats in 1875 kept something of the system, but abolished the Board of Education, and sought, as far as possible, to return to the ante-bellum status. Separate schools for the races were ordered; the administrative expenses were reduced; no money was to be paid to any denominational school or private school. And the constitutional provision of one-fifth of the state revenue for school use was abolished. (1935a, p. 653)

Across the South, more generally, Du Bois observed that:

In the Reconstruction constitutions, state taxation for schools was a new feature, unknown in the previous school laws of Alabama, Florida, Arkansas, Georgia, Mississippi, North Carolina, and South Carolina ... It was perpetuated in all the revisions of these constitutions after 1876, except in Alabama. The victory of home rule in 1876 was followed by a period of hostility or at least indifference to public education. (1935a, p. 664)

Anderson provides the following empirical data that track with Du Bois' observation that while the end of Reconstruction dramatically changed the South's course on public education, it was not a complete U-turn: "Their [Southern Black Americans'] 95 percent illiteracy rate in 1860 had dropped to 70 percent in 1880 and would drop to 30 percent by 1910" (1988, p. 31). Furthermore, Du Bois records the establishment, by 1879, of secondary and postsecondary institutions, educational institutions critical to the development of political leaders within the Black community: 84 normal and high schools, and 16 colleges, with over 12,000 students.

To sum up, the social conflicts and educational experiments in the Southern states, after the Civil War, illustrate explicitly how the dominant social group – White Americans – monopolized educational resources to protect their claim to the economic and political rewards therefrom. Also evident are the freedpeople's efforts to leverage the cataclysmic impact of the Civil War that made radical change in the Southern states possible. Freedpeople, in service of realizing their newly acquired entitlement to economic and political resources, organized to gain access to educational resources. Their efforts produced new educational organizations: an incipient public school system and higher learning institutions accessible to Black students.[21] Still, Anderson takes care to note that, even in the context of these notable achievements, educational opportunities for most southern Black residents remained scarce: "For the majority of black children in the South during most of the period under study (1860–1935), not even public elementary schools were available. High schools were virtually nonexistent, and the general unavailability of secondary education precluded even the opportunity to prepare for college" (1988, p. 285).

5.3.2. The Political Economy of Education, Illustrations from the North[22]

In this section, we describe how Northern White communities stockpiled resources within schools to protect their privileged position in the racialized social hierarchy. Black community members in the North used a range of strategies to gain access to these resources, including fighting *against* segregation to gain access to adequately resourced schools, as well as fighting *for* segregation in order to control their own schools and ensure that Black students received a high-quality education.

5.3.2.1. The Common School Movement in the Antebellum North: 1830–1865

A common school movement surged in the North during the 1830s and aimed to establish a widespread network of publicly funded schools.[23] This movement embraced policies of racial exclusion and racial segregation rather than a universal system of public schools. The schools provided the training grounds for White students, specifically, to develop a unified White Protestant cultural identity, as well as civic skills for their active participation in the country's democratic political institutions. Historian Davison Douglas quotes Ohio Governor Jeremiah Morrow from 1823 on this point: "No sentiment is more generally held to be incontrovertible among enlightened free men than that morality and knowledge are necessary to good government. The necessary dependence which civil liberty and free institutions in government have on the moral qualities and intelligence of the people give importance to the provisions for the encouragement and regulation of common schools" (Douglas, 2005, p. 15).

The common school movement intended to culturally assimilate the large number of White immigrants arriving in the US, inculcating them into a White American citizenry to promote social cohesion and stability. The practice of excluding Black children from, or segregating Black children within, the common school system produced three significant social effects: (1) it hardened the social distinction between racial groups and weakened those between White European nationalities;[24] (2) it expressed the White community's view of Black people as ill equipped, morally and intellectually, to act as full citizens; and, at the same time, (3) it blocked members of the Black community from obtaining the skills to do so.[25]

Documentation of the Northern Black community's fight for educational resources reveals their view that education was critical to empowering Black people to exercise their rights and responsibilities as full citizens. Education would provide the skills necessary to oppose racist policies and practices through litigation and the legislative process, as well as the knowledge needed to create institutions to serve their own communities (e.g., legal services, newspapers, schools, banks, healthcare). As Du Bois put it directly: "In the professions, college men are slowly but surely leavening the Negro church, are healing and preventing the devastations of disease, and beginning to furnish legal protection for the liberty and property of the toiling masses. All this is needful work. Who would do it if Negroes did not?" (1903, p. 103).

Additionally, a well-educated Black community would prove false the White supremacist belief that Black people were intellectually and morally inferior, refuting the ideological justification for slavery. For these reasons, abolitionists embedded educational goals in their political platform. Black abolitionist Alexander Crummel made this connection explicit to abolitionists in London in 1851, "As the *free* coloured population go up in the scale of intelligence, increase in mental capacity, and demonstrate their intellectual power, the whole fabric of slavery proportionably crumbles and totters" (quoted in Douglas, 2005, p. 18).

This antebellum period witnessed a rapid expansion of public school education, but segregation and Black exclusion policies directed most of these educational gains to White children. Douglas describes how, by the Civil War, two-thirds of more than 6.3 million school-age White children in the free states in the North and West attended school, as compared to 35 percent (roughly 30,000) of school-age Black children.[26]

The degree of racial segregation and exclusion varied across the Northern states and corresponded with the levels of White residents' fear of having to compete over jobs and other economic resources. Midwestern states, particularly their Southern regions, experienced a significant influx of Black migrants between the 1820s and 1840s.[27] This movement of Black migrants reflected, in part, the efforts of free Southern Black residents to escape life under the increasingly severe restrictions on their rights imposed by Southern states. Take, for example, the case of Cincinnati, Ohio. Douglas chronicles how the Black population in this area grew from 600 to more than 2,000 during the late 1820s. The area also experienced a surge of German and Irish immigrants.[28] The city's population, overall, grew from 9,642 in 1820 to 24,831 in 1830 to 46,388 in 1840.[29]

White Midwesterners reacted to these changes with mob violence against Black residents and severe anti-Black laws, such as prohibiting the entry of Black migrants (e.g., in Illinois, Indiana, and Iowa; also in the West, in California) and Black Laws that tightly regulated the movement and activity of Black people (e.g., Ohio, Indiana, Illinois, and Michigan).[30] Midwestern states typically excluded Black children altogether from public schools.

The relatively smaller Black population shares in the states farther north and east moderated White communities' anxieties about competing with Black residents for economic resources, and concomitant anti-Black policies and laws. Moreover, a strong presence of abolitionist activists – especially in the New England region – advocated Black children's access to educational resources. Schools in these states more commonly adopted policies of racial segregation rather than Black exclusion. Similarly, upper Midwest and mid-Atlantic states provided some segregated public schools (e.g., New York, Pennsylvania, and New Jersey). In 1865, Massachusetts was alone in abolishing school segregation by statute.

Racial segregation of schools clearly served as a means for White communities to hoard educational resources, even while providing public schooling to Black children. The Blacks-only schools were of worse quality than Whites-only schools along multiple dimensions, including: being housed in dilapidated buildings with ill-equipped, crowded classrooms; providing a deficient educational curriculum; paying teachers poorly; and staffing the schools with poor-quality teachers.[31]

The Northern Black community and their allies – Quakers, White abolitionists and Radical Republicans – used a range of strategies to provide quality education for Black children. These strategies included, among others: creating educational institutions specifically for the Black community (e.g., "African Free Schools," Sunday schools, and Black literary societies); litigating to gain access to Whites-only schools or resources for local Blacks-only schools; lobbying for related legislation; and boycotting poorly resourced Blacks-only schools.[32]

The situation in the mid-1800s in Boston highlights the Black community's multi-pronged approach to political organizing. Some Boston Black families supported segregation so that their children could learn in a supportive and safe environment, as opposed to being subjected to the racial hostility of White teachers and students in an integrated school. Other Boston Black families boycotted the local Black school, Smith School, to protest for integration. And still other Black families turned to litigation: the Roberts family filed suit against the Boston School Committee because it had blocked their daughter from enrolling into several White public schools located closer to their home than Smith School.

In this 1845 case of *Benjamin Roberts v. The Boston School Committee*, the Massachusetts State Supreme Court decided in favor of the School Committee. It argued that the state had the prerogative to segregate students by race.[33] An important feature of this case is that it underscores how New England education administrators *created* segregated schools through explicit racial assignments of students; segregation was not a side effect of residential segregation. That is, school policy drove racial segregation in schools.

5.3.2.2. Postbellum Legislative Reform: 1865–1890

Two countervailing forces shaped how the movement for racial equity in public school education developed during the postbellum period. First, campaigns by Black and White abolitionists to pass anti-segregation laws surged in this period with the support of Republican-dominated state legislatures. The enfranchisement of Black men by the 15th Amendment in 1870 boosted the success of these legislative efforts, as Republican Party legislators had to curry favor with this new and growing voting bloc in close election contests. By 1890, "every northern state, aside from Indiana, that had allowed racial segregation reversed course explicitly or implicitly" (Douglas, 2005, p. 83). Several western states followed suit. These legislative reforms represented meaningful political gains as courts generally did not rule in support of integrating schools, particularly in states without legislative measures calling for integration –the 14th amendment of 1868 that guaranteed equal protection by the law notwithstanding.[34]

Second, the growing population flow of Black Americans north and west, in response to expanding employment opportunities and their newly gained ability to leave the South, accelerated the rise in anti-Black sentiments within receiving White communities. We quote, at length, Douglas' report of these trends:

> During and immediately after the war, approximately 80,000 freed slaves left the South, which further provoked antiblack sentiment. Most of the migrants headed to the Midwest. Since

Missouri and Kentucky, of all the slave states, had the longest contiguous borders with free territory, the most common route was simply to cross the Ohio River into Ohio, Indiana, or Illinois or to move west into Kansas. As a result, the black population in the Midwest more than doubled during the 1860s (and increased twenty-seven-fold in Kansas). Ohio had the biggest increase in black population (more than 26,000), followed by Illinois (more than 21,000), Kansas (more than 16,000), and Indiana (more than 13,000). Blacks still constituted a fraction of the northern population in 1870, comprising no more than 1 percent of the population in the North as a whole, but the population increase of the late 1860s contributed to an upsurge in antiblack feelings in parts of the North, particularly in the lower Midwest. Wanton violence against blacks sharply increased after the Civil War. (2005, p. 64)

This flow of Black migrants surged again, in the 1890s: "Whereas only 88,000 blacks left the South during the 1880s, 185,000 departed during the 1890s, and 194,000 during the first decade of the twentieth century. Between 1890 and 1910, about 2.5 percent of the South's black population moved north" (2005, p. 124).

Recall from the discussion above that this coincides with the start of the Nadir – the period when the Republican Party effectively withdrew from advocating the rights of newly freed people in the South, including withdrawing federal troops that had been critical to enforcing their new civil rights. The increasing number of Black Americans moving into Northern White communities intensified interracial resource competition. White supremacists responded with anti-Black violence and discrimination. In the late nineteenth and early twentieth centuries, the North witnessed a rise in White terrorism, including lynchings, anti-Black discrimination in public accommodations and employment, and racial segregation in housing, particularly in the Midwestern states.[35]

The growing anti-Black sentiments fueled White communities' resistance to the new integration laws, crosscutting the Republican tailwinds that propelled anti-segregation laws to passage. White communities often refused to comply with new laws and judicial rulings requiring integration, their resistance supported by the absence of strong enforcement mechanisms. Echoing the patterns of the antebellum period, the degree of White resistance to integrating schools increased directly with greater Black shares of the local population.[36]

5.3.2.3. Segregation Entrenched: 1890–1940

Black Americans' migration north and west continued through most of the twentieth century. Increasing White terrorism and a dearth of employment caused by a contracting agricultural sector in the South pushed growing numbers of migrants out of the South. At the same time, increasing demands for labor among Northern employers – unmet by the slowing flow of European immigrants – pulled migrants North. The pace of this Black northern migration grew to an order of magnitude larger than what occurred during the postbellum period. Douglas details the dimensions of what historians refer to as the first phase of the "Great Migration" (1910–40):[37]

> Between 1915 and 1920, about 500,000 blacks left the South moving to northern cities. Another 800,000 to 1 million southern blacks migrated north during the 1920s. All told, about 10 percent of blacks living in the South moved to the North between 1915 and 1930. Whereas in 1920, 90 percent of the country's black population lived in the South, those demographics would dramatically shift over the course of the next half century. By 1960, half of the nation's black population lived outside the South.
>
> Those states receiving the largest number of black migrants during WWI were, in descending order, Pennsylvania, Illinois, Ohio, New York and Michigan. (2005, pp. 131–2)

As before, Northern White communities responded to the growing population share of Black Americans with anti-Black animus and violence, including a resurgence in White terrorism organized by the KKK during the 1920s and 1930s.[38] White communities intensified the extent of their economic resource-hoarding, as well as the violence they used to safeguard their economic advantage. Emblematic of these trends is the emergence of severely segregated neighborhoods, as well as Jim Crow practices enforced across social spheres.[39] Douglas notes that racial segregation in schools became more widespread by the late 1930s than at the start of the twentieth century.[40] Local school boards and school administrators used explicitly racial school assignments and racially gerrymandered school districts, if residential segregation did not sufficiently segregate schools, operating in defiance of anti-segregation laws.[41]

Moreover, early in the twentieth century, *integrated* schools commonly turned to the practice of "tracking," or providing a poor-quality curriculum for Black children that prepared them, at best, for low-paying jobs (e.g., cooking, sewing, and manual work) and a higher-quality curriculum for White children that prepared them for more preferred positions (e.g., math, typing, and training for skilled trades). Such curricular differences insured that, once students finished their public education, White workers would join the labor market better prepared than their Black counterparts to compete for high-quality jobs. Stratifying educational programs in this way made racially discriminatory employment practices easier to implement. For many such jobs, for example in the skilled trades, White employers and workers simply blocked Black workers from applying.[42] Some Black families organized against these practices by advocating the supply of sufficient resources to segregated, Blacks-only schools rather than access to integrated schools.[43]

Black girls and women faced additional challenges in gaining access to a rigorous education that met their needs, as compared to their male counterparts. These challenges primarily occurred at the higher educational levels, particularly in postsecondary education. Take, for example, the following figures chronicling firsts in education by historian Stephanie Y. Evans. According to Evans' research, the first Black woman to obtain a Bachelor of Arts degree, in 1865, was "200 years after a white male, 40 years after a black man, and nearly 25 years after 3 white women received a BA from Oberlin in 1841" (2007, p. 25). As another comparison, Evans notes that "Approximately, one hundred African Americans, including only three women, earned a BA before the War's end" (2007, p. 26). These figures provide a rough metric for how Black women had to wait much longer to gain access to the levels of education available to their White and male counterparts.

In sum, the inspiration for a common education – common schools – originated during the mid nineteenth century in the Northern states to equip American children with a shared national identity, the civic skills to support the country's yet-young republican democracy, and the academic skills to become productive members of society. These schools, in other words, served to impart skills that had economic, social, and political value to their students.

The ways in which White communities decided whether, or how, to provide this common school education to Black Americans illustrates explicitly how the dominant social group – Whites – hoarded educational resources to protect their claim to the economic, social, and political rewards therefrom. First, most White Northerners argued against Black Americans' entitlement to a common school education as White Northerners eschewed Black Americans' claim to the American national identity and obstructed their ability to participate in governing. Second, Black Americans' access to the growing network of common schools depended on White Americans' sense of competition with Black Americans for resources, as well as the level of political power Black Americans had harnessed. Black Americans eventually acquired political power through the franchise, and also by creating alliances with White Americans (e.g., Quakers and White abolitionists). In other words, how secure White Americans felt in their ability to maintain their position in the racial hierarchy, and the capacity of Black Americans to change it, influenced the degree to which Black children could access this newly developing resource of public education. The onset of the Great Migration significantly increased the level of negotiation over resources between Black and White Americans. White communities responded by entrenching greater levels of racial segregation across all spheres of life and by giving White children an upper hand in the labor market with the provision of more and better educational resources, disadvantaging Black children with the deprivation of the same.

By the 1940s, the practice of racially segregating schools operated widely – across Northern and Southern states both. The primary difference between the two regions is which public institutions White communities used to implement segregation policies. In the North, schools and local authorities enforced segregation in defiance of the anti-segregation laws passed by state legislatures. In the South, in contrast, state legislatures operated as chief enforcers of school segregation. As of 1954, the 11 former Confederate states had laws that *required* segregation. The 5 so-called border states – Delaware, Kentucky, Maryland, Missouri, and West Virginia – did as well, as did Oklahoma. Several western states – Arizona, Kansas, New Mexico, and Wyoming – provided racial segregation as a legal option.[44] This pattern of state segregation laws corresponds directly with Black communities' power at the ballot box: Black residents in the North had begun to build up meaningful voting blocs through migration whereas Southern states continued to block Black residents from voting.

5.3.3. Racial Segregation into the Twenty-First Century

The efforts of Black Americans to wrest equitable educational resources from White Americans entered a new phase in the 1940s. The nation began to turn away from *de jure* (by law) racial segregation in schools and other public spheres, and to sustain de facto (in practice) segregation through other channels.

The second swell of the Great Migration, from roughly 1940 to 1970, added energy to the countervailing forces of the prior decades – a growing Black voting bloc in the North and increasing White animus against Black migrants. The million-plus African Americans who left the South during this period constituted an internal migration that was an order of magnitude larger than during the turn of the century. Competition intensified in the North between racial groups over resources.[45] This massive relocation also fortified the Black Civil Rights Movement since Black Americans had maintained their suffrage rights in the North, even while segregationist Jim Crow policies breached other civil rights.[46]

This emerging bloc of Black voters meaningfully challenged Jim Crow policies by creating alliances with Democratic and Republican legislators, depending on each party's demonstrated commitment to desegregation.[47] Large protests in Northern urban areas by Black residents further increased the pressure on state governments to adopt anti-segregation and antidiscrimination reforms.[48] Black Americans' contributions to the US military performance in World War II (1939–45) further energized this political activity by amplifying their claims to full citizenship and their grievances against Jim Crow.[49] White public opinion began to turn against explicitly racist Jim Crow policies.[50]

These political winds helped the National Association for the Advancement of Colored People's (NAACP's) legislative strategy gain ground in dismantling *de jure* segregation in the North. By the end of the 1950s, Northern legislatures largely put an end to school segregation policies.[51] The NAACP's litigation strategy similarly met success, culminating in the landmark *Brown v. Board* US Supreme Court ruling in 1954. These Supreme Court rulings reversed the *Plessy v. Ferguson* "separate but equal" doctrine and declared *de jure* racial segregation policies unconstitutional.

White Americans largely resisted this change. In the South, this resistance took the form of ignoring the *Brown v. Board* ruling and using violence to deter Black families from exercising their rights. In the North, where anti-segregation laws had been enacted prior to *Brown v. Board*, White Americans leveraged an array of institutions – both private and public, local, state, and federal – to more severely segregate neighborhoods, ensuring the same for their neighborhood schools. In cases where neighborhood segregation did not achieve sufficient school segregation, school districts continued their use of racial gerrymandering, bussing students, and school transfers.[52]

A review of the institutions – within the private sector as well as at all levels of government – that promoted racially segregated neighborhoods in Northern states is beyond the scope of this chapter.[53] However, we highlight here the federal government's decisive role in promoting racially segregated housing. During the period following World War II, the federal government actively intervened in the housing market to boost the housing supply and to put homeownership within reach of middle-income households. The federal government's sizable intervention in the housing market, including providing mortgage loan guarantees through the Federal Housing Authority (FHA), helped increase the homeownership rate from 44 percent in 1940 to 62 percent by 1960 (Fetter, 2014). The racial priorities of White Americans clearly shaped how these programs operated. Consider that, according to historian Andrew Wiese (2004), "By the late 1950s, only 2 percent of the homes built with FHA support since World War II were occupied by African Americans or other minorities" (p. 109). African Americans and other minorities made up 11 percent of the US population in 1960.[54]

These federal programs, supported by local and private institutions, both promoted homeownership specifically among White Americans and enabled White Americans to encircle their newly acquired wealth within the confines of White neighborhoods. Douglas provides this broad-brush description of the flow of White residents out of urban centers and into suburban neighborhoods, neighborhoods blocked from Black residents by the FHA's racist housing policies:

Between 1940 and 1960, the nation's suburban population increased by more than 30 million, twice the comparable increase in the nation's center city population. This suburban migration would have profound consequences for residential segregation. The overwhelming majority of these suburban migrants were white, leaving major northern cities populated increasingly by racial minorities who continued to migrate from the South. Between 1950 and 1970, the percent of residents in large northern cities who were black more than doubled. (2005, p. 268)

In sum, federal housing policy subsidized the development of new housing through the creation of predominantly White, suburban neighborhoods. And, conversely, these policies restricted the resources available to improve or expand the housing stock of Black neighborhoods, draining value from them as their neighborhoods became overcrowded and their homes dilapidated.

This protracted battle – persisting more than three centuries – between social groups to either gain access to educational resources (the general case for Black Americans) or hoard educational resources (the general case for White Americans) serves as a barometer of its value to each social group. Another measure is the extraordinary level of political force Black Americans had to harness so that federal intervention meaningfully desegregated schools. Massive demonstrations, direct actions, and large-scale boycotts protesting racial segregation and discrimination surged during the 1960s.[55] This phase of the Civil Rights Movement, including the famous 1963 March on Washington for Jobs and Freedom, succeeded in extracting legislation that ended segregationists' evasions of the *Brown* v. *Board* ruling – at least in the South.

During President Lyndon B. Johnson's administration (after the assassination of President John F. Kennedy), three major civil rights acts passed: the Civil Rights Acts (CRA) of 1964, 1965 (a.k.a. the Voting Rights Act), and 1968 (a.k.a. the Fair Housing Act). The 1964 CRA empowered the Department of Health, Education, and Welfare (HEW) to withhold federal funds from school districts that refused to abandon their explicit policies of racial segregation, and the Attorney General to sue violating districts. The passage in 1965 of Title I of the Elementary and Secondary Education Act (ESEA) made the level of federal funds consequential. Federal funding increased five-fold from 1959–60 to 1969–70, representing a rise from 4.4 percent of total public school funding to 8.0 percent.[56] This new enforcement mechanism meaningfully compromised White communities' ability to use school segregation policies to hoard educational resources.

The threat of withholding federal funds or extracting resources through lawsuits from school districts was observably pivotal in desegregating schools in at least three ways.

First, racial segregation in Southern schools dramatically declined immediately after the passage of the 1964 and 1965 CRAs and the 1965 ESEA. In figure 5.2, we present trend data on the percentage of Black students attending majority-White schools from 1954 to 2011 for the 11 former Confederate states, states that to this day enroll the majority of Black students in the country.[57] The trend line in figure 5.2 tracks the resistance among White communities to the *Brown* v. *Board* ruling in 1954: the percent of Black students in majority White schools barely budging from zero in 1954 to 2.3 by 1965. After the passage of the CRAs and the ESEA, we see this percent increase six-fold to 13.9 percent in 1967 and then continue to increase substantially from 1967 to 1970. Progress continued, if slower, until 1988.

Second, Northern states did not progress in desegregating schools, reflecting a carve out in the 1964 CRA crafted by Northern legislators

Education: Unequal Access, Unequal Outcomes 159

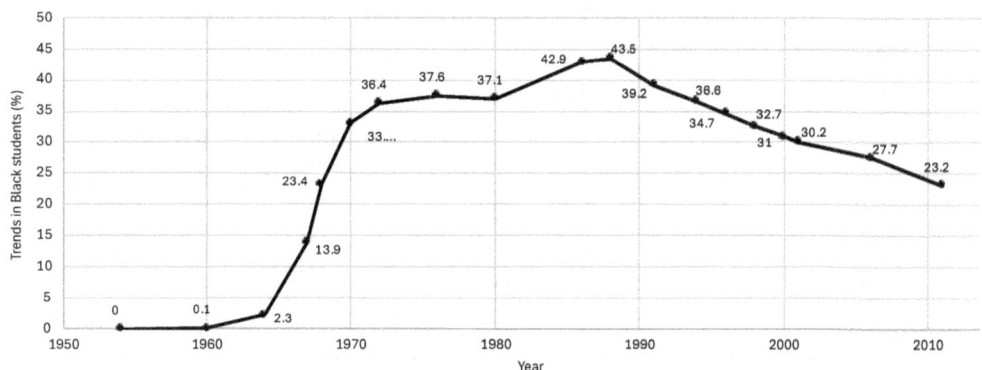

Figure 5.2 Trends in the percentage of Black students at majority-White schools in Southern states, 1954–2011.
Source: Orfield et al. (2014), p. 10, table 3; US Department of Education, National Center for Education Statistics (NCES), Common Core of Data, Public Elementary/Secondary School Universe Survey data, and Office of Civil Rights data.

to effectively exempt de facto segregation, that is, school segregation via residential segregation as opposed to state law or formal school policy. Historians Matthew Delmont and Jeanne Theoharis explain:

> In drafting the 1964 Civil Rights Act ... the bill's northern sponsors drew a sharp distinction between segregation by law in the South and so-called racial imbalance in the North, amending Title IV, section 401b, to read: "Desegregation" means the assignment of students to public schools and within such schools without regard to their race, color, religion, or national origin, but "desegregation" shall not mean the assignment of students to public schools in order to overcome racial imbalance. (2017, p. 24)

In other words, the 1964 CRA permits desegregating schools through the elimination of explicit racial assignments between schools or between classrooms within schools. However, the 1964 CRA *does not* permit schools to racially balance schools that are segregated because of reasons aside from explicitly race-based assignments. Data in table 5.4 show how the amendment de-fanged the 1964 CRA's credible threat of withholding federal funds for much of the Northeast due to the region's reliance on neighborhood segregation to segregate their schools. In the Northeast, the percentage of Black students in

Table 5.4 Percentage of Black students in 90–100% minority schools, select years from 1968 to 2018

Region	1968	1988	2001	2011	2018	% Change from		
						1968 to 1988	1988 to 2018	1968 to 2018
South	77.8	24.0	31.0	34.2	37.0	−53.8	13.0	−40.8
Border states	60.2	34.5	41.6	41.0	42.1	−25.7	7.6	−18.1
Northeast	42.7	48.0	51.2	51.4	51.5	5.3	3.5	8.8
Midwest	58.0	41.8	46.8	43.2	40.7	−16.2	−1.1	−17.3
West	50.8	28.6	30.0	34.4	38.2	−22.2	9.6	−12.6
National	64.3	32.1	37.4	38.8	40.1	−32.2	8.0	−24.2

Note: Border states include Delaware, District of Columbia, Kentucky, Maryland, Missouri, Oklahoma, and West Virginia.
Source: Orfield and Jarvie (2020), table 12 and figure 4, p. 29.

90–100% minority schools actually rose between 1968 and 1988, from 42.7% to 48.0%. This contrasts sharply to the dramatic fall in this same measure between 1968 and 1988 from 77.8% to 24.0% in the South.

Third, after the federal government began to retreat from enforcing the 1964 CRA, beginning with the Nixon administration (1969–74), school integration declined.[58] In addition, a series of court rulings, including three Supreme Court rulings, weakened court oversight of school desegregation plans and progress.[59] The figures in table 5.4 track the reversal (or halt) of progress toward integration in every region after 1988, aside from the Northeast which never gained ground since 1968. As of 2018, 40 percent of Black students are enrolled in highly segregated (90–100% minority) schools.

The material consequences of school segregation also remain evident into the twenty-first century. Neighborhood segregation has proven effective in reserving White Americans' wealth for their racial group by geographically encircling their economic resources, and at the same time, depriving other groups of such resources. As discussed above, the housing policies that supported neighborhood segregation and cultivated wealth in White neighborhoods also withdrew housing value from Black neighborhoods by causing overcrowding and limiting credit available for improvements. Those policies, combined with past and present employment discrimination, and the cumulative nature of racial wealth inequality, has produced high poverty rates in neighborhoods with high shares of non-White residents. Local neighborhoods fund neighborhood schools, therefore resource-strapped neighborhoods have resource-strapped schools. Consequently, neighborhoods with high shares of non-White residents also tend to have high poverty rates and poorly resourced neighborhood schools. Figure 5.3 illustrates the persistence of this pattern that Orfield, Frankenberg, and Kuscera (2014) refer to as "double segregation."

Figure 5.3 shows how few schools (1.7%) with low percentages of Black and Latinx students (0–20% Black or Latinx – white bars) are schools with high shares of impoverished students (91–100% poor). Many more predominantly White schools (11.0%) are schools with low shares of impoverished students (0–10% poor).[60] Conversely, a high percentage (44%) of predominantly Black and Latinx schools (80% to 100% Black or Latinx – black bars) are schools with high shares of impoverished students (91–100% poor). Few schools with high percentages of Black and Latinx students (2.2%) are among schools with low shares of impoverished students (0–10%).

5.3.4. The Limits to Racial Integration in the Twenty-First Century

5.3.4.1. Primary and Secondary Education

History has demonstrated that hoarding of educational resources *within* racially integrated school facilities also occurs (see above). Racialized academic tracking, for example, disproportionately directs school resources to White students and undersupplies them to Black students. Darity Jr. and Jolla (2009) develop this point further by identifying three specific educational benefits that are allocated through academic tracking, especially in the earlier grades. These are: (1) the enrichment effect, "the intellectual gain from exposure to more challenging and interesting content and the development of critical thinking skills"; (2) the anointment effect, "the confidence and validation that students receive by being identified as 'gifted'"; and (3) the cumulative learning effect, "the increased capacity to take harder courses later in schooling as a result of exposure to and mastery of relevant preparatory material in the earlier years of schooling" (p. 108). Through academic tracking, schools can direct these beneficial effects to create, extend, and accentuate differences in existing academic capabilities among students, including differences due to economic and social disadvantages that precede as well as overlap with the educational setting.

The uneven distribution, by race, of these educational benefits is evident in data from the National Center for Education Statistics (NCES). In 2017, 6.6% of primary and secondary public school students enrolled in "Gifted and Talented" programs. If students were

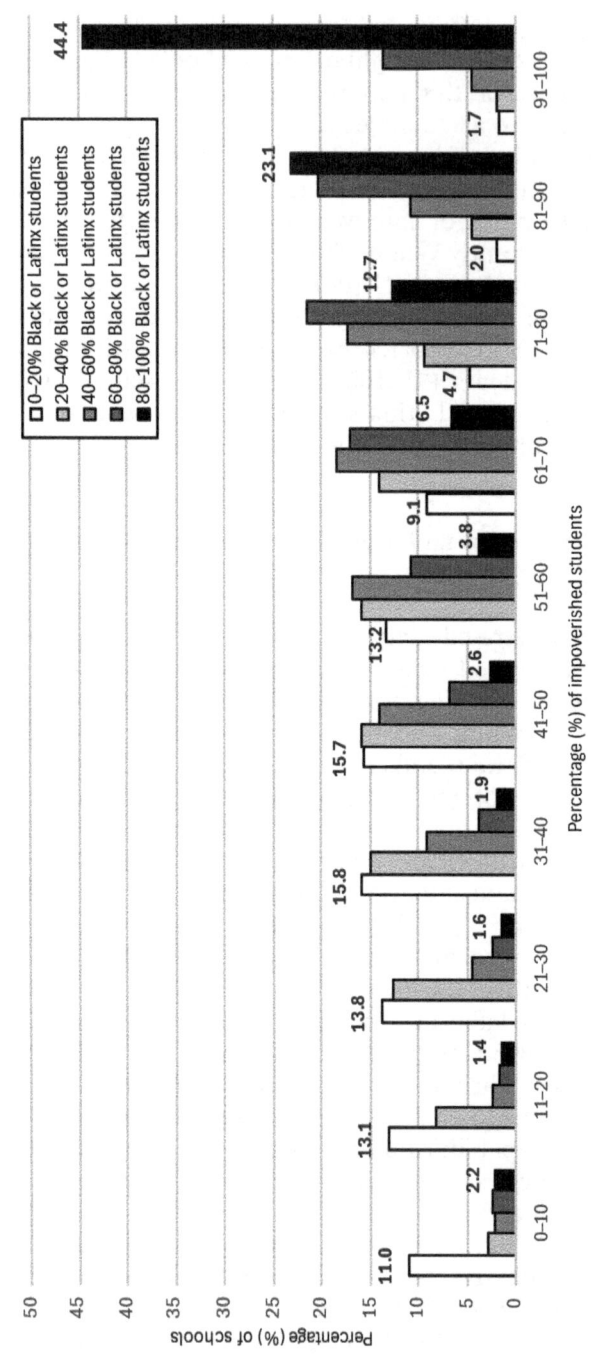

Figure 5.3 Segregation by race and poverty, 2011–2012.

Source: Orfield et al. (2014), p. 16, table 7; US Department of Education, NCES, Common Core of Data.

allocated equal distributions of this educational resource, then the share of each racial group would be roughly equal to 7%. Instead, White students have a close but higher share (8.1%) and Black students have a notably smaller share (3.5%). Asian students, on the other hand, are markedly over-represented in these programs at 12.5%. These figures provide an indicator of how schools are cultivating more knowledge among White and Asian students and less among Black, Latinx, Pacific Islander, and Indigenous students.[61]

In addition to comparable school facilities, equally qualified teachers and high-quality curriculums, equitable access to learning requires supportive social interactions. Due to the social nature of knowledge production, interactions between students and teachers, and between students and their peers, must be equally validating for learning to be cultivated equally across racial groups.

The undersupply of social validation for Black students in many integrated schools during the early twentieth century gave cause to Du Bois' favorable view of segregated schools:

> It is saying in plain English: that a separate Negro school, where children are treated like human beings, trained by teachers of their own race, who know what it means to be black in the year of salvation 1935, is infinitely better than making our boys and girls doormats to be spit and trampled upon and lied to by ignorant social climbers, whose sole claim to superiority is ability to kick "ni__ers" [*authors' modification*] when they are down. I say, too, that certain studies and discipline necessary to Negroes can seldom be found in white schools ... Sympathy, Knowledge, and the Truth, outweigh all that the mixed school can offer. (1935b, p. 335)

Du Bois' concerns expressed nearly 90 years ago remain relevant today: schools administer a disproportionate share of disciplinary actions against Black students relative to students of other races. For example, Morris and Perry's 2016 study of Kentucky public schools found that, "black students are estimated to be 7.57 times as likely to be suspended as white students, and Latinos are over twice as likely as whites" (p. 76). This large difference captures variations between schools, as well as the impact of socio-economic status, gender, special education service needs, and family structure. Even while accounting for the racial variation in these factors – much of which derives from the broader racial social hierarchy that we document throughout this book – Black students are still 2.5 times more likely to be suspended than

White students. Morris and Perry conclude, "the racial achievement gap for black students is reproduced, in part, through disproportionate exposure to exclusionary discipline in public schools" (p. 18).[62] In sum, to the extent that racism colors how teachers, counselors, and administrators evaluate their students or preclude a "sympathetic" touch, the educational system will operate to create racial differences in academic capabilities rather than acting as an equalizing force.

5.3.4.2. Postsecondary Education

Differential access to educational resources at the primary and secondary school levels extends to postsecondary education. We discuss here three major ways in which the systemic racism that operates at the primary and secondary school levels continues into postsecondary schools.

Hoarding of Resources

The mechanisms through which White communities hoard educational resources at the primary and secondary school levels put Black students at a disadvantage relative to White students in accessing postsecondary education. Take, for example, the case of Advanced Placement (AP) courses. These courses provide students early exposure to college-level curriculum. Moreover, AP courses prepare students for AP exams that give them the opportunity to earn college credits in advance of matriculating into a college program. Finally, college admissions officers look favorably on such coursework when making acceptance decisions since, through this coursework, students can demonstrate their ability to master college-level material. The Assistant Secretary for Civil Rights of the US Department of Education Catherine Lhamon wrote in her Letter to Colleagues, dated October 1, 2014, that "almost one in five black high school students attend a high school that does not offer Advanced Placement (AP) courses, a higher proportion than any other racial group" (p. 3). The specific figures for Black, Asian, Latinx, and White students are 19%, 6%, 12% and 14% respectively. In a study of North Carolina students, Francis and Darity Jr. (2021) present estimates that indicate an even greater racial disparity when considering which students take the AP courses offered in their schools. The share of White students who are both eligible for AP Calculus and enrolled in the AP course was 28% compared to 14% among Black students.[63] Consequently, AP coursework operates as a conduit through which racialized academic tracking within primary and secondary schools

Lack of Wealth

Wealth substantially improves a student's ability to access a postsecondary education. In 2020–1, the average annual cost of a 4-year college program, including tuition, fees, and on-campus room and board, was $35,500.[64] Even among the less expensive public universities which enrolled over 70% of students in the fall of 2021, the annual cost exceeds $25,700, equal to more than one-third of the 2021 annual median household income ($71,200). Costs of this magnitude mean that having access to some form of savings – i.e., wealth, not just income – is crucial to achieving a 4-year college degree. We have already discussed in this chapter, and will again in chapter 7, the racist practices, policies, and institutions throughout US history that have created and maintained an acutely unequal distribution of wealth by race in the US. Consequently, racial wealth disparities forecast racial disparities in the ability to pay for postsecondary education. Take Scott-Clayton's (2018) analysis of US Department of Education data which tracks students for up to 12 years after college entry in 2004. That study finds that, among college graduates receiving a BA degree, Black students have the highest borrowing rates, highest loan amounts, and highest default rates relative to other racial groups (see table 5.5). In other words, the ability of White Americans to hoard and maintain wealth has constructed a solid foundation from which they are better

Table 5.5 Debt and default among BA graduates, by race: 12 years after college entry, 2004 entry cohort ($)

	Undergraduate amount borrowed	Total amount borrowed	Total owed	Ever defaulted
White	10,848	26,005	20,770	4
Black or African American	21,149	55,667	64,142	20.6
Hispanic or Latino	10,854	28,599	27,969	8.6
Asian	6,618	30,612	22,234	1.4
Black–White gap (level)	10,301	29,662	43,372	16.6
Black–White ratio	1.9	2.1	3.1	5.2

Source: Reproduced Table 3 from Scott-Clayton (2018). Estimates are produced by Scott-Clayton's calculations using NCES Power Stats with Beginning Postsecondary Student (BPS)-04 data.

able to access postsecondary education than exists among Black Americans.

Racist Admissions Criteria
Selective postsecondary institutions employ gatekeeping mechanisms for their college admissions using demonstrably racist criteria.[65] One example is legacy preferences, a policy that originated around the 1920s at elite private schools to boost the admission chances of children (or grandchildren) of college alumni. This occurred at a time when White, Protestant men dominated college campuses, and therefore provided a distinct advantage for White, Protestant applicants. Measuring the degree to which legacy preferences tip the balance of favor for such students is difficult since relevant data are hard to obtain. However, the racial advantage for White students is clear. Figures from a 2004 study of a prestigious state university, University of Virginia (UVA), are illustrative (Howell and Turner, 2004). Data from 1980 to 2001 show a lopsided distribution of degree recipients: only between 4 and 9 percent of UVA's degree recipients were Black, even while Black residents make up roughly one-fifth of the state's population.[66] This fact is coupled with legacy acceptance rates between about 50 percent and 80 percent higher than among non-legacies.

A 2023 study, *Diversifying Society's Leaders? The Determinants and Causal Effects of Admission to Highly Selective Private Colleges*, by economists Raj Chetty, David J. Deming, and John N. Friedman generalizes this observation about the legacy advantage by examining 1998–2015 data from 12 colleges – so-called Ivy League colleges plus Stanford, Massachusetts Institute of Technology (MIT), Duke, and Chicago. In particular, Chetty et al. find that coming from a high-income family doubles the chances that a student will attend one of these Ivy-Plus schools relative to middle-income students with comparable standardized test scores, and legacy status contributes substantially to this advantage. Chetty et al. summarize their findings saying that:

> Children from families in the top 1% [of the income distribution] are more than twice as likely to attend an Ivy-Plus ... as those from middle-class families with comparable SAT/ACT scores ... The high income admissions advantage at private colleges is driven by three factors: (1) *preferences for children of alumni*, (2) weight placed on non-academic credentials, which tend to be stronger for students applying from private high schools that have affluent student bodies, and (3) recruitment of athletes, who

tend to come from higher-income families. (emphasis added; *Abstract*)

The political, economic, and social value of having access to these educational institutions is remarkable. Chetty et al. note that:

> Leadership positions in the United States are held disproportionately by graduates of a small number of highly selective private colleges. Less than half of one percent of Americans attend Ivy-Plus colleges ... Yet these twelve colleges account for more than 10% of Fortune 500 CEOs, a quarter of US Senators, half of all Rhodes scholars, and three-fourths of Supreme Court justices appointed in the last half-century. (2023, p. 1)

A more recent development in admissions that began in the 1990s is the use of "Early Decisions" (ED). The ED application process enables college applicants to receive an acceptance decision at an earlier date than "regular decision" applications, in exchange for the applicant's binding commitment to enroll in that college if accepted. A critical benefit of applying ED is that, among competitive schools, the acceptance rates among ED applicants is often substantially higher than among regular decision applicants. Fallows (2001) reported that:

> during the 1999–2000 school year, Yale admitted 37% of early applicants but only 16% of regular applicants; Amherst 35% of early applicants and 19% of regular applicants; and the University of Pennsylvania 47% of early applicants and 26% of regular applicants ... among Princeton's 1,825 ED applicants ... 31% were accepted ... among its 11,900 regulars ... 11 percent got in.[67]

A critical disadvantage of applying ED is that applicants are required to commit to enrolling in a school without being able to compare – or negotiate – financial aid packages from multiple schools. ED, in other words, boost the acceptance rates among students with fewer financial constraints, particularly in terms of wealth. This is because, as we note above, postsecondary education represents a major financial expense relative to the average household's income – as opposed to an incremental rise in living costs.[68] In effect, ED policies operate as a gatekeeping mechanism that gives students from families with more wealth – an economic resource with an acutely racist distribution – a leg-up in the application process at competitive schools. ED application rates by race are not widely available. However, the *Journal of Blacks in Higher Education* (1999) conducted its own survey of 12 competitive colleges and universities and found that in 1999 Black students make up an exceedingly small share – 3 percent – of all ED applicants. This compares to Black students' roughly 12 percent share of enrolled college students at the same time.[69]

On the one hand, the racially disparate outcomes of these gatekeeping mechanisms are predictable and easy to link to the economic and educational resource-hoarding practices of White Americans, some explicitly racist. The archetypal example of this type of practice is racial segregation of neighborhoods. On the other hand, White Americans' racially conscious hoarding strategies have rooted racial inequalities sufficiently into the economic landscape for racially disparate educational outcomes to flow therefrom, without relying on *de jure* racial segregation or explicitly racist positions (e.g., claims of biological inferiority of Black people relative to White people). Consequently, an allegiance to explicitly racist beliefs is unnecessary for White Americans to protect their greater access to educational resources. They need only to resist remedies to racially biased practices and policies that provide them with a race-based advantage.

Take, for example, affirmative action policies in college admissions. The language of affirmative action policies – related to racism – first appeared in federal policy when Lyndon B. Johnson was vice president, which he then expanded as president. President Johnson articulated the intent of these affirmative action policies in a 1965 commencement speech at Howard University. In his speech, Johnson equates anti-racist policies with color-conscious ones, that is, policies that work to eliminate existing racial disparities in access to educational resources and that judge policy success based on racial equality in educational outcomes:

> You do not take a person who, for years, has been hobbled by chains and liberate him, bring him up to the starting line of a race and then say, "you are free to compete with all the others," and still justly believe that you have been completely fair. Thus, it is not enough just to open the gates of opportunity. All our citizens must have the ability to walk through those gates. This is the next and the more profound stage of the battle for civil rights. We seek not just freedom but opportunity. We seek not just legal equity but human ability, not just equality as a right and a theory but equality as a fact and equality as a result.[70]

In the context of postsecondary education, one objective of affirmative action policies is to serve as a partial remedy to known, ongoing racial inequality in access to educational resources. This racial disparity limits the supply of Black college applicants who can "walk through the gates" of competitive colleges relative to the supply of White college applicants. Consequently, to meet the goal of "equality as a result" at the stage of college admissions, when confronted with a pipeline of candidates made inadequate because of racist policies and practices in the K-12 grades, requires taking affirmative action – color-conscious action – such as boosting the acceptance rates of qualified Black, Indigenous, and Latinx students. Resistance to such affirmative action – by promoting and advocating for a *color-blind* system – White students protect and extend their K-12 educational advantages through to their postsecondary education.

The Black Studies Movement

It is the opinion of many Black writers, I among them, that the Western aesthetic has run its course ... We advocate a cultural revolution in art and ideas ... In fact, what we need is a whole new system of ideas.

Larry Neal (1968)[71]

After the assassination of Malcolm X in 1965, a cohort of politically motivated artists, dramatists, musicians, and writers – including Maya Angelou, James Baldwin, Nikki Giovanni, Gil Scott-Heron, Sonia Sanchez, Audre Lorde, and June Jordan – emerged within the cultural nationalist camp of the budding Black Power movement. It was in that year that poet Amiri Baraka opened the Black Arts Repertory in Harlem, New York, and the Black Arts and Aesthetics movements began.

The Black Studies movement emerged in tandem with the Black Arts and Aesthetic movements. These movements were politically reinforced by the "separatist Black Power" thrust of the Civil Rights Movement, which sought to awaken Black consciousness and achieve liberation through the establishment of separate Black art, aesthetic, and educational institutions.

Jamaican writer and cultural theorist Sylvia Wynter recovers the history of the existence of "a network of extracurricular institutions" that began to call for the establishment of a Black university, including inter-allied institutions such as the National

Association for African American Research, the Black Academy of Arts and Letters, the Institute for the Black World, the New School of Afro-American Thought, the Institute of Black Studies in Los Angeles, and Forum 66 in Detroit (Wynter, 2006).

Wynter attributes the momentum that would soon grow in the struggle to institute Black Studies programs and departments within mainstream institutions to both: (1) the cultural nationalists of the Black Arts and Aesthetic movements, who produced poetry, novels, visual arts, and theater that reflected pride in Black history and culture and politically affirmed the autonomy of Black artists to create Black art; and (2) the intellectual fervor that led to the integrationist phase of the Civil Rights Movement – led by Dr. Martin Luther King Jr. – in the mid-1950s.

The April 1968 assassination of Dr. King Jr. and the revolts/riots in inner cities that followed activated these movements. These events changed the terrain of struggle for the Black Studies movement. Quite suddenly, mainstream university administrators were willing to yield to Black students' demands for Black Studies programs at universities across the country. Thus, as Wynter notes, the establishment of Black Studies programs and departments was enabled by "trauma that gripped the nation," as protests broke out on college campuses across the United States (Wynter, 2006).

The institutionalization of Black Studies was led by a new and growing cadre of Black student activists at what were until then virtually all-White student- and faculty-populated universities. In May 1968, three events in the political history of Black Studies rapidly unfolded. First, over 90 Black student activists successfully occupied the Bursar's building of Northwestern University for almost 40 hours after weeks of demonstrations and lobbying for extensive changes to university policy to reckon with its institutionalized forms of racism, to which the university was previously unreceptive (Fenderson, Stewart, and Baungarter, 2011). Second, the Black Student Alliance (BSA) and administrators at Yale University held a symposium entitled "Black Studies in the University," where predominantly White university administrators and educational powerbrokers and a few Black activists gathered to deal with "the essential intellectual objection of Black Studies, namely, whether such studies are valid, academically responsible, and intellectually defensible" (Fenderson et al., 2011, p. 3). At the conference, where no mentions of the break-out of protests across the country were made, and large-scale student participation was prohibited, Yale administrators and BSA members voted to approve the first Black Studies program in a dual program model.[72]

Lastly, Black political magazine *Jet* issued a "Special Report on Student Unrest at Black Colleges," which, in contrast to the conventional narrative of the emergence of Black Studies at historically White universities, recovers significant historical precursors. The issue documents heightened political activity and rebellion by Black students at Historically Black Colleges and Universities ("HBCUs," such as Howard University [DC], South Carolina State, Texas Southern State, Cheyney State [PA], Bowie State [MD], Tuskegee [AL], Virginia Union, Kentucky State, and Shaw [NC]) occurring *before* the events of Northwestern and Yale. For instance, at Tuskegee University (AL) Black students called for the untethering of American higher education "from the military industrial complex by calling for an end to compulsory ROTC [Reserve Officers' Training Corps]" (Fenderson et al., 2011, p. 5).[73] This political activity also exemplifies that the demands of the Black Studies movement far exceeded the goal of instituting Black Studies at predominantly White universities. Rather, the Black Studies movement called for the creation of *separate* institutions and spaces of education and critical thinking that did not rely on and perpetuate White supremacist systems of violence and conquest.

While the institutionalization of Black Studies at historically White universities was achieved, the Black Arts and Aesthetic movements, Wynter notes, "disappeared as if they had never been" (2006, p. 109). This disappearance was, in part, due to differing class-based interests within the Black community. The Black middle and socially mobile lower-middle classes prioritized an integrationist goal of establishing Black Studies within primarily White institutions. The development of radical, Black-centered institutions was, in contrast, the priority of members of the Black lower-income and working classes. With the end of the Vietnam War, radical new-Left politics waned as conservative politics swelled in response to the expressions of social unrest of the 1960s (Wynter, 2006).

During this time, the establishment of the new programs and departments of Black Studies – joining the host of other "Ethnic Studies" – drew the work of some of the major figures of the Black

> Arts and Aesthetic movements into the academic mainstream. As a former member of the Black Studies movement, Wynter finds its original transgressive intentions to have been *defused*, and "their energies rechanneled as they came to be defined in new 'multicultural terms' as African American Studies" by their co-optation by and into mainstream academia, whose hierarchy of knowledge the movement arose to contest (2006, p. 109).
>
> *Written by Daniella Medina*

This result is evident from the experience at the University of California and the University of Michigan campuses before and after each state passed legislation that banned the use of race as a factor in college admissions: Proposition 209 in California in 1996 and Proposal 2 in Michigan in 2006. In both cases, the racial profile of voters in support of banning affirmative action policies is consistent with the strategy of White residents voting largely to protect their racial group's greater access to educational resources (i.e., for Prop. 209) and Black and Latinx residents voting to gain greater access (see table 5.6).

In the case of the California university system, two of its highly competitive campuses – University of California, Los Angeles (UCLA) and University of California, Berkeley – experienced dramatic declines in their shares of Black undergraduates. UCLA, for example, saw its Black undergraduate enrollment fall from 5.6% to 3.5% after the ban

Table 5.6 Exit poll results of affirmative action bans in California and Michigan by race (%)

Racial group	Proposition 209: California, 1996		Proposal 2: Michigan, 2006	
	Support	Oppose	Support	Oppose
White	63	37	56	44
Black	26	74	14	86
Latinx	24	76	31	69

Sources: *LA Times*' exit poll on November 5, 1996, available at: https://ballotpedia.org/California_Proposition_209,_Affirmative_Action_Initiative _(1996); *Detroit News* exit poll data reported in Peter Schmidt, "Michigan Overwhelmingly Adopts Ban on Affirmative-Action Preferences," *Chronicle of Higher Education*, November 17, 2006, available at: www.chronicle.com/article/michigan-overwhelmingly-adopts-ban-on-affirmative-action-preferences.

went into effect in 1998. The University of Michigan–Ann Arbor similarly saw Black undergraduate enrollment fall from 7% in 2006 to 4.5% in 2014.[74]

The low shares of Black college students at these competitive schools – both with and without affirmative action policies – also make evident the significant, persistent differences in access to educational resources at the postsecondary education level. According to an analysis of NCES data by the *New York Times*, "After decades of affirmative action black and Hispanic students are more underrepresented at the nation's top colleges and universities than they were 35 years ago ... The share of black freshmen at elite schools [100 schools out of nearly 4,000, including public and private universities and colleges] is virtually unchanged since 1980. Black students are just 6 percent of freshmen but 15 percent of college-age Americans."[75]

On June 29, 2023, the US Supreme Court invalidated affirmative action elements of the admissions programs at Harvard and the University of North Carolina. According to reporting by National Public Radio's Nina Totenberg, the consequence of this decision is that, "It ends the ability of colleges and universities – public and private – to do what most say they still need to do: consider race as one of many factors in deciding which of the qualified applicants is to be admitted." By disallowing race-conscious admissions policies, the ruling against affirmative action policies eliminates one of the few public policies that explicitly operates to remedy current-day racially biased practices and policies. Justice Sonia Sotomayor's dissenting opinion says so much: "The [Supreme] Court subverts the constitutional guarantee of equal protection by further entrenching racial inequality in education, the very foundation of our democratic government and pluralistic society." Justice Ketanji Brown Jackson expresses the same point more bluntly, "With let-them-eat-cake obliviousness, today, the majority pulls the ripcord and announces 'colorblindness for all' by legal fiat. But deeming race irrelevant in law does not make it so in life."[76]

For all of these reasons – anti-Black bias in teaching, advising, tracking and admissions – HBCUs continue to serve as an important access point to postsecondary educational resources for Black students.[77] HBCUs were established prior to the CRA of 1964 when *de jure* racial segregation persisted on a wide scale for the purpose of educating Black students. Of particular importance is the ability of HBCUs to provide Black students with what Du Bois denoted as "Sympathy, Knowledge, and the Truth." Higher-education scholar Marybeth Gasman describes how HBCUs provide their students with "an empowering, family-like environment of small classes, close faculty–student relationships, and life without the daily racial tensions experienced off campus."[78] In 2021, 99 HBCUs were in operation, serving 287,000 students.[79] A 2018 analysis shows how HBCUs enroll a disproportionate share of Black students, enrolling 9% of Black students in 2015 while representing only 3% of bachelor's degree-granting institutions. HBCUs also produce a disproportionate share of graduates with degrees in areas that Black students are significantly underrepresented in, such as math and statistics. In 2015, Black students represented 9.5% of BA degree recipients across all majors, but only 4.4% of math and statistics majors.[80] Nearly one-third – 29% – of these math and statistics majors graduated from an HBCU, even while HBCUs represent, again, only 3% of bachelor's degree-granting institutions. Systematic studies of the specific impact of HBCUs on Black students' economic and social status observe that these postsecondary institutions improve economic mobility (Koch and Swinton, 2023), labor market earnings, and psychological well-being (Price et al., 2011).[81]

5.4. Conclusion

This broad sweep over history to contemporary times of the laws, institutions, policies, and practices governing the provision of education in the US highlights the central role that education has played in fortifying a White-dominated, racially stratified society. Not until roughly the last half-century of the country's four centuries of development did Black Americans achieve significant progress in the integration of schools – the primary means by which this social group could access meaningful levels of educational resources. This progress sparked by the Civil Rights Movement of the 1950s and 1960s took hold, however, for only a couple decades. Since the 1980s, school segregation has again begun to rise.

We highlight these features of the US educational system to make clear how education serves as a means to political power (e.g., meaningful exercise of suffrage rights); social power (e.g., refuting charges of intellectual limits), and economic power (e.g., acquisition of credentials necessary for income-generating activities). As such, White Americans reinforce their advantaged position in the US social hierarchy by capturing disproportionate shares of educational resources: historically, through such actions as legal segregation, and presently through the continuance of residential segregation and neighborhood schools and bans against affirmative action, among

However, as previously noted, economic research regarding racial differentials in labor market outcomes shows that, even after controlling for human capital variables such as educational attainment, as well as other variables which could contribute to wage differentials such as industrial and occupational "crowding" of demographic groups (see explanation of Bergmann, 1971, below), negative and statistically significant coefficients of "dummy variables"[4] for race and/or gender in regression analyses are data evidence of discrimination, with such conclusions largely supported by labor market audit studies.

Mainstream economic theory, however, includes other concepts which, in effect, double down on the productivity argument by suggesting that unexplained residuals in regression analyses of labor market outcomes by race are, in fact, capturing productivity-related characteristics that could not be captured by other variables. The productivity deficiency argument can be illustrated by the Labor Quality theory, which indicates that Black people as a group come to the labor market with inferior abilities due to African American culture, biology (!), or pre-market structural racism (i.e., the impact of structural racism on individuals before they enter the labor market – for example, poorer-quality schools in minority neighborhoods).[5] Labor Quality theorists such as Heckman (1998) and Hernstein and Murray (1994) would argue that there are no unexplained residuals attributable to labor market discrimination in this formulation.

In general, mainstream economic theory, including HCT and the Labor Quality theory, assert that discriminatory behavior on the part of employers cannot be sustained in competitive markets. However, Darity Jr. (2005) has argued that discrimination and competitive markets are not necessarily at odds. According to his construction of the subfield of stratification economics: (1) privileged groups have a material interest in sustaining discrimination because benefits accrue to the privileged group as a whole; and (2) discrimination persists in market-based economies, and only policy intervention can correct that, but such intervention can be difficult to accomplish if the privileged group is overrepresented in, and holds outsized power in, the political system.

In conjunction with stratification economic theory's proposition that discriminatory practices can endure in competitive markets, we return to a major shortcoming of neoclassical economics in explaining persistent labor market differentials between Black and White workers: as pointed out in chapter 1, disparate labor market outcomes based on race are perpetuated not only by employers, but also by institutions designed with anti-Black policies and practices as outlined in critical race theory scholarship. For example, ample literature exists on the racist underpinnings of criminal legal system policies in the US which have led to an overrepresentation of Black and Latinx men among the prison population (see Alexander, 2012; Reiman and Leighton, 2016; Schlosser, 2003; Taibbi, 2014; as well as chapter 8). There's also research which shows a direct link between prior incarceration and lower wages (see Western, 2002; Western, Kling and Weiman, 2001). In the case of Black men with prior felony convictions, research shows that policies and practices within the criminal legal system that result in disparate Black male incarceration rates can *also* be blamed for lower wages among Black male ex-felons, in addition to employer biases. Here is an example of how institutional racism, as practiced by the criminal legal system as well as some employers in the American labor market, contributes to structural racism toward Black male workers as evidenced by lower average wages compared to White males.

6.2.1. The Role of Employers in Anti-Black Practices

Most workers in the US have supervisors who may or may not have also been the persons charged with decision-making in hiring. Whoever is involved in the decision to hire or promote someone, these individuals are presumed to be qualified to make such judgments. Along with possessing qualifications required to make such decisions, these persons have not only the best interests of the organization in mind, but also thoughts and ideas about what characteristics make someone not just a competent employee, but a good "fit" for the company.

We're all, to some degree, subject to preferences regarding whom we'd like to work with. Do they have a sense of humor? Are they easy to get along with? Will they be a team player? Are they too chatty? Are they likely to be hard-working? When individuals are in positions to influence hiring, it can be difficult to put aside personal preferences in order to maintain objectivity as well as elevate the interests of the company above one's own interests or biases. Indeed, in the economist Barbara Bergmann's formulation of the *occupational crowding model* (1971), she suggested that Black workers are "crowded" into low-wage jobs due to employer behavior; the model posits that Black workers are largely funneled into low-wage work by employers due to the latter's desire not to associate with Black people (assuming the employer is non-Black), employers' perception that Black workers aren't as productive as White employees, employers' fear of reprisal from White others. Similarly, Black Americans have sought to alter their position in the social hierarchy by seeking equal access to education either by pushing for the full integration of educational institutions or by seeking resources for segregated institutions under their control.

6

Unemployment, Occupational Crowding, Wage Inequality, and Anti-Blackness in the Labor Market

6.1. Introduction

The experience of the Black community in the US is one defined by historically higher unemployment rates and lower wages than those for the Whites. This seemingly perpetual resignation of Black workers to secondary or tertiary status in the American labor market is perplexing if viewed through the lens of mainstream economic theory; neoclassical economics points to differences in "human capital" endowments – for example, educational attainment, work experience, training, etc. – as the primary reason for differential labor market outcomes based on race. However, economic studies show that, after controlling for factors which could contribute to racial wage differentials, unexplained residuals exist, or variables regarding race show a negative coefficient, in regression analyses. It's been argued that these kinds of findings are data evidence of discrimination (Darity Jr., 1982; Darity Jr. and Mason, 1998; Holder, 2020). In addition, employer surveys and audit studies of the American labor market show discrimination by race is still routinely practiced by employers (Bertrand and Mullainathan, 2004; Kline, Rose, and Walters, 2022; Pager and Western, 2005; Quillian et al., 2017). This chapter uses the framework of stratification economics to explore why the prediction of neoclassical economic theory that discrimination cannot be sustained in markets in a capitalist system has resoundingly failed. It also explores the role of practices on the part of employers that are rooted in anti-Blackness, which result in enduring disparities by race in the American labor market. Note that the "Primer to Part II" of this book outlines for our readers the differences between how mainstream economic theory and stratification economics explain differential outcomes by race in the labor market.

6.2. Economic Theories Explaining Racial Discrimination

The American labor market is, and has been, characterized by well-defined cleavages along racial, ethnic, and gender lines, certainly at least since the postbellum period in the late nineteenth century. Women are overrepresented in the low-wage service sector, as was so clearly revealed during the COVID pandemic (Holder, Jones, and Masterson, 2021), Black workers on average earn less than White workers, and the Latinx community has a higher average unemployment rate than that of Whites. Cleavages along racial lines in the US workforce can be traced to long-standing policies and practices which overtly and covertly excluded – specifically, but not exclusively – Black Americans from full and equal participation. One illustration of the impact of exclusionary hiring practices based on race is the dramatic change in the occupational distribution of Black women after the passage of the 1964 Civil Rights Act in the US, which made employment discrimination based on race and other protected categories illegal.

In the American psyche, the Civil Rights Act of 1964 (CRA) is associated with ending state-sanctioned legal segregation as well as protecting the rights of Black people to vote, given the foci of the Civil Rights Movement at the time. However, during the evolution of the legislation, which initially did focus on segregation and voting, the prohibition of discrimination in employment was added and codified into law through Title VII of the CRA. As we will discuss in chapter 7, Conrad (2005) notes that before 1964 the occupation with the highest share of Black women in the US (38 percent in 1960) was private household service (i.e., domestic servants). White employers were largely uninterested in hiring Black women for positions in which they could hire White men or women, which left private household work as one of the few viable occupational arenas in which Black women could find steady, though low-paying, work in the early to mid twentieth century. Conrad also indicates that by 1980 the occupation with the highest share of Black women had changed from private household to clerical; once employment discrimination based on race and gender in the private sector became illegal, Black women began streaming into low-wage clerical occupations en masse (see Albelda, 1985). Underscoring how pivotal the Act was in changing the trajectory of Black Americans in the workforce, Darity Jr. (2005) noted that the greatest decline in "measured" discrimination against African

Americans occurred during the period 1960–80, after the passage of the CRA – one measure was the Black–White earnings ratio, which rose for over a decade after 1964.[1] Unfortunately, however, there are still contemporary policies and practices, some of which possessing anti-Black underpinnings[2] – such as barring ex-felons from certain occupations – that contribute to present-day disparate outcomes for Black Americans.

While economists have traditionally posed numerous explanations for different intergroup labor market outcomes, two broad categories are especially influential in this vein – namely, human capital theory (HCT) and stratification economics. Though not an exhaustive list, these broad categories nevertheless help to contextualize pivotal research related to disparities in the labor market. On the one hand, HCT proposes that group differences in labor market outcomes are primarily due to differences in average human capital endowments between groups. Human capital refers to quantifiable attributes such as educational attainment levels, work experience, and training. HCT evolved out of economist Gary Becker's model seeking to explain wage disparities based on race in which he posited that differences in wages between equally productive Blacks and Whites performing the same work were due to employers' "taste" or preference for discrimination. In Becker's model, employers who paid Blacks and Whites differently for the same work and productivity levels presumably gained some type of utility or satisfaction from doing so.

On the other hand, other economists (Darity Jr. and Mason, 1998) emphasize the explanatory power of labor market imperfections. Predominantly White unions exercising exclusionary practices, or monopolistic White-owned and White-managed firms, for instance, practicing discrimination in hiring (see related discussion in chapter 4). Nevertheless, Becker's hypothesis on wage discrimination was critiqued by several economists, including Darity Jr. (1982).[3] Darity Jr. explained that even if some employers experience utility or satisfaction from practicing racial discrimination, then employers who do not discriminate could take advantage by luring productive Black workers to their firm with higher wages. This process would continue until Black and White wages were equal. After these critiques, Becker's hypothesis required modification. An updated framework contended that, in fact, Black workers were, as a group, less productive than White workers, and therefore a wage differential would exist between Black and White workers in favor of the latter group. This revised framework did not allow for discrimination in the American labor market as a structural feature.

race theory scholarship. For example, ample literature exists on the racist underpinnings of criminal legal system policies in the US which have led to an overrepresentation of Black and Latinx men among the prison population (see Alexander, 2012; Reiman and Leighton, 2016; Schlosser, 2003; Taibbi, 2014; as well as chapter 8). There's also research which shows a direct link between prior incarceration and lower wages (see Western, 2002; Western, Kling and Weiman, 2001). In the case of Black men with prior felony convictions, research shows that policies and practices within the criminal legal system that result in disparate Black male incarceration rates can *also* be blamed for lower wages among Black male ex-felons, in addition to employer biases. Here is an example of how institutional racism, as practiced by the criminal legal system as well as some employers in the American labor market, contributes to structural racism toward Black male workers as evidenced by lower average wages compared to White males.

6.2.1. The Role of Employers in Anti-Black Practices

Most workers in the US have supervisors who may or may not have also been the persons charged with decision-making in hiring. Whoever is involved in the decision to hire or promote someone, these individuals are presumed to be qualified to make such judgments. Along with possessing qualifications required to make such decisions, these persons have not only the best interests of the organization in mind, but also thoughts and ideas about what characteristics make someone not just a competent employee, but a good "fit" for the company.

We're all, to some degree, subject to preferences regarding whom we'd like to work with. Do they have a sense of humor? Are they easy to get along with? Will they be a team player? Are they too chatty? Are they likely to be hard-working? When individuals are in positions to influence hiring, it can be difficult to put aside personal preferences in order to maintain objectivity as well as elevate the interests of the company above one's own interests or biases. Indeed, in the economist Barbara Bergmann's formulation of the *occupational crowding model* (1971), she suggested that Black workers are "crowded" into low-wage jobs due to employer behavior; the model posits that Black workers are largely funneled into low-wage work by employers due to the latter's desire not to associate with Black people (assuming the employer is non-Black), employers' perception that Black workers aren't as productive as White employees, employers' fear of reprisal from White

However, as previously noted, economic research regarding racial differentials in labor market outcomes shows that, even after controlling for human capital variables such as educational attainment, as well as other variables which could contribute to wage differentials such as industrial and occupational "crowding" of demographic groups (see explanation of Bergmann, 1971, below), negative and statistically significant coefficients of "dummy variables"[4] for race and/or gender in regression analyses are data evidence of discrimination, with such conclusions largely supported by labor market audit studies.

Mainstream economic theory, however, includes other concepts which, in effect, double down on the productivity argument by suggesting that unexplained residuals in regression analyses of labor market outcomes by race are, in fact, capturing productivity-related characteristics that could not be captured by other variables. The productivity deficiency argument can be illustrated by the Labor Quality theory, which indicates that Black people as a group come to the labor market with inferior abilities due to African American culture, biology (!), or pre-market structural racism (i.e., the impact of structural racism on individuals before they enter the labor market – for example, poorer-quality schools in minority neighborhoods).[5] Labor Quality theorists such as Heckman (1998) and Hernstein and Murray (1994) would argue that there are no unexplained residuals attributable to labor market discrimination in this formulation.

In general, mainstream economic theory, including HCT and the Labor Quality theory, assert that discriminatory behavior on the part of employers cannot be sustained in competitive markets. However, Darity Jr. (2005) has argued that discrimination and competitive markets are not necessarily at odds. According to his construction of the subfield of stratification economics: (1) privileged groups have a material interest in sustaining discrimination because benefits accrue to the privileged group as a whole; and (2) discrimination persists in market-based economies, and only policy intervention can correct that, but such intervention can be difficult to accomplish if the privileged group is overrepresented in, and holds outsized power in, the political system.

In conjunction with stratification economic theory's proposition that discriminatory practices can endure in competitive markets, we return to a major shortcoming of neoclassical economics in explaining persistent labor market differentials between Black and White workers: as pointed out in chapter 1, disparate labor market outcomes based on race are perpetuated not only by employers, but also by institutions designed with anti-Black policies and practices as outlined in critical customers or employees, or employers' fears that having Black workers will diminish their company's status among peers.[6] Bergmann's model is currently a half-century old, but its assumptions are still quite relevant if we examine contemporary audit studies and other research which shows that anti-Black hiring preferences on the part of employers still occur with regularity in the American labor market.

Are employers, or, more specifically, the aggregation of those individuals who substantively influence employment decisions in the US, therefore, to blame for all other disparate labor market outcomes based on race aside from occupational crowding, key among these being higher unemployment rates and lower average wages among Black workers? Ironically, mainstream economic theory, it turns out, is helpful in answering at least part of this question.

Certainly, factors other than employer discrimination play a role in the long-standing higher average unemployment rate among Black workers compared to White workers. Chief among these would be differences in human capital acquisition in the form of college completion by race. While the gap in high school completion rates by race has narrowed considerably between Black and White adults over time, there still remains a sizable gap in college completion between these groups; in 2021, 38 percent of White women and men 25 years of age and over possessed a bachelor's degree or higher, compared to 28 percent of Black women and men at least 25 years old – see figure 7.3 in chapter 7. Unemployment rates are strongly inversely correlated with educational attainment in the US – see figure 6.1. Thus, some, but not all, of the gap in unemployment rates between Black and White Americans may be explained by the lower average college completion rate of Black adults compared to White adults.

However, the educational attainment gap at the level of college completion only partially explains differential wage and unemployment rates by race in the US. As previously noted, empirical studies of labor market outcomes by race which control for factors such as educational attainment differences show results which suggest discrimination still occurs. While these studies don't necessarily prove that employers regularly engage in racist and sexist employment practices, what does conclusively prove that biased behavior along racial lines still occurs in the American job market are employer surveys and audit studies. For example, Neckerman and Kirschenman (1991) found that not only did employers in Chicago prefer White candidates to Black candidates, but also these employers preferred immigrant (non-Black) Latinx candidates over Black candidates as well. And a more recent meta-analysis of audit studies by Quillian et al. (2017) examined 24 field studies from

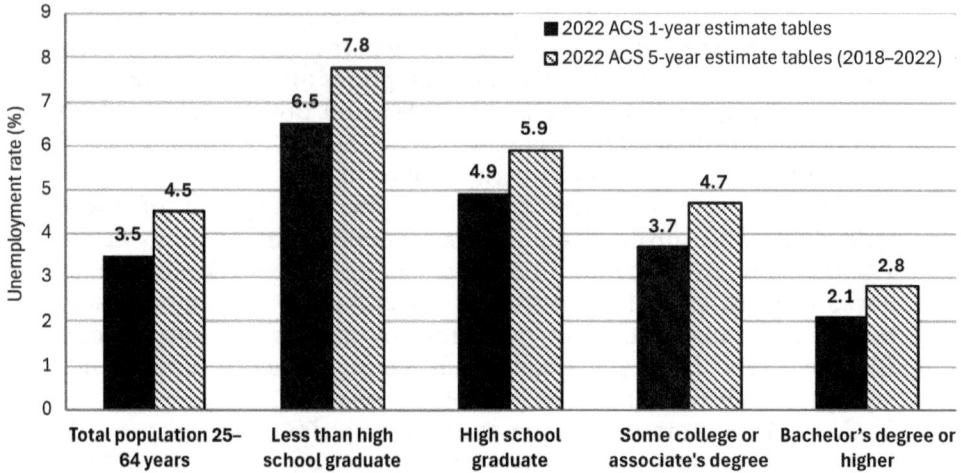

Figure 6.1 Unemployment rates by education level, 2022.
Data source: United States Census Bureau American Community Survey (ACS) Employment Status data, 1- and 5-year estimates, 2022. Table S2301.

1989 to 2015 in the US and concluded that racial and ethnic discrimination are still prevalent in the American labor market.

6.2.1.1. Employers and Statistical Discrimination

The *statistical theory of discrimination* posits that employers use group characteristics in making decisions; from a mainstream economic standpoint, this behavior is explained as *objectively rational*, and not *subjectively discriminatory*, since employers are relying on purportedly widely accepted quantitative information about different demographic groups to inform their decisions, at no cost. This theory may be illustrated by the following equation:[7]

$$y = q + u$$

where y measures productive capability, such as an employment test score, and is directly observable; q measures "true" productive ability, which is unobservable to a potential employer; and u is an error term. While the assumption is that u is normally distributed for Whites and Blacks, q is not assumed to be normally distributed; employers believe the variance of q is larger for Black workers than for White workers, which makes y a less accurate predictor of productive capability for

Blacks compared to Whites. Employers assume that the accuracy of y as a predictor of productivity for Black workers is less than that for White workers because of group characteristic(s) attributable to Blacks which make them less productive, but which cannot be accurately reflected in q. Given this, employers will *also* rely on information about job candidates given average group characteristics possessed by the demographic group(s) to which the job candidate belongs.

There are two key features of the statistical theory of discrimination applicable to anti-Black behavior on the part of employers: (1) employers in the US can, and likely do, make assumptions about the productivity of Black workers based on their race, using as the basis for their assumptions average group characteristics; and (2) by using race as a proxy for productivity, employers push back against the notion that they are engaging in racist behavior by suggesting this is rational behavior – what's wrong, they might argue, with using group characteristics to inform hiring decisions about a job candidate who is a member of a group for whom employers believe they possess accurate information? There are a few problems with this hiring strategy: for starters, average group characteristics for non-White groups in the US are shaped by institutions which historically disenfranchised these groups. Second, how accurate is the information on the group – what is the source? If the sources are "intelligence" test scores, a bevy of academic literature shows the proclivity of tests to be culturally biased (Bazemore-James et al., 2017; Gersh, 1987; Helms, 2008). Moreover, using average characteristics will mean that employers will miss out on hiring above-average candidates. A competitive marketplace should motivate entrepreneurs to develop a more precise and accurate screening tool, and thereby gain a competitive edge against employers who rely on imprecise and/or inaccurate group averages (see Mason, 2000).

6.2.1.2. Do Networks Play a Role in "Anti-Black" Hiring Behavior of Employers?

Granovetter (1995) estimated about half of jobs in the US are filled through social contacts – that is, through informal routes. One potential explanation is that employers can acquire a large pool of candidates at no additional human resource cost. Fernandez, Castilla, and Moore (2000) conceptualized this explanation as the "richer pool" theory, which indicates that by relying on current employees for referrals for open positions employers obtain an increased quantity of quality candidates for openings. Because incumbents are risking their reputation, they will likely refer qualified potential candidates. In addition, incumbents can provide other qualitative information about referred applicants as well as assist the latter in settling into new positions (Elliot, 2001; Fernandez, Castilla, and Moore, 2000; Granovetter, 2005).

Other research, however, indicates that Black Americans tend to rely on formal routes in employment – that is, job ads or recruiting firms (Elliot, 2001; Holzer, 1987). Holzer (1987) noted this is because it is harder for ascriptive characteristics – such as race – to play a role in hiring since personnel offices are typically involved in hiring processes from start to finish. Stainback (2008) pointed out networks can, in fact, maintain segregated labor markets by race and gender since position openings are shared through homogeneous networks from which employers draw job candidates.

When employers choose to fill positions by relying on incumbent referrals, they are choosing to limit their candidate pool to the predominant racial, ethnic, and gender make-up of their current employees. While the richer pool theory suggests that this may be rational behavior on the part of employers charged with acting in the best interests of their organizations, such a practice can lend itself to the reproduction of racially and ethnically homogeneous workforces. As an example, from 2002 to 2006, an estimated 2.3 percent of persons employed in management occupations in the US were Black men (Holder, 2017), even though this group accounts for about 6 percent of the labor force. While human capital differences such as lower college completion rates for Black adults compared to White adults account for some of this disparity, they do not account for all of it. If White workers are overrepresented in management occupations in the US (see Holder, 2017, p. 55, which illustrates that White men are overrepresented in management occupations), then tapping this pool of workers for referrals of candidates for openings in management would likely result in a disproportionate number of those referrals being other White individuals.

6.3. Economic Indicators of Racial Disparities in the Labor Market

6.3.1. Unemployment Rate Differentials

Among economists in the US there has been a long-standing unofficial rule of thumb supported by historical trends: the Black unemployment rate is typically twice that of the White unemployment rate – see figure 6.2, and figure 1.1 from chapter 1.

Indeed, during the current period of a four-decade high in inflation rates in the US, one of the criticisms of the Federal Reserve Board's strategy of raising interest rates to cool down the economy is that the current chair of the Board is willingly ignoring the reality that strategies to increase slack in the American labor market will have a disparate impact on African Americans and Latinxs (see Bernstein and Jones, 2020).

Unemployment rate differentials between Blacks and Whites seem to be an intractable feature of the American labor market. Discrimination by employers could partially explain why the Black unemployment rate is *always* higher than the White unemployment rate: employment audit studies noted in this chapter show persistent employer preferences for White and other non-Black job candidates. But it's difficult to show empirically that employer discrimination alone accounts for the Black–White unemployment rate gap. The roles of institutional and structural factors must be explored.

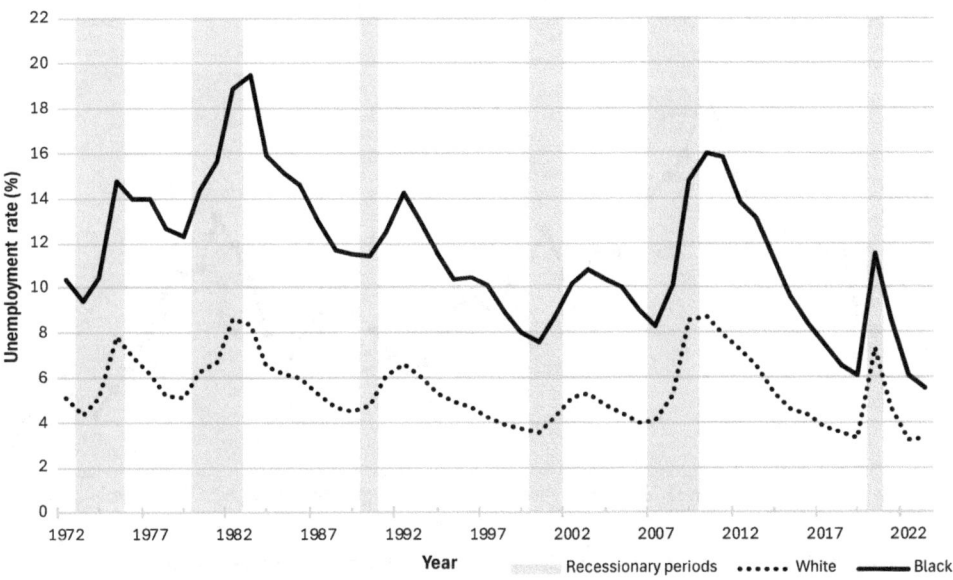

Figure 6.2 Black and White annual unemployment rates, US 1972–2023.
Data source: US Department of Labor, BLS Current Population Survey (CPS), seasonally adjusted employment rates.

As noted in chapter 1, racism can take a few different forms. These forms include: individual/personal and/or group prejudice or bias against another group; laissez-faire racism; institutional racism; and structural racism. In the case of persistent unemployment rate differentials based on race arguably all of the aforementioned forms of racism are contributing factors. While the impact of personal prejudice on employment outcomes can appear obvious, the roles of institutional and structural racism are not as easily perceived. Institutional racism in employment outcomes shows up in the form of organizational policies and practices that disadvantage Black job applicants and/or employees, such as conducting credit checks of job candidates, and requesting prior salary histories from job applicants. The role of structural racism in employment outcomes would include factors – as noted earlier too – such as the college degree attainment gap between Black and White adults, as well as weaker access for Black Americans to informal networks where job information is shared. Notably, however, the unemployment rate gap between Black and White Americans has narrowed – see figure 6.3 – with the Black unemployment rate hitting its lowest level in 50 years in April 2023.[8] While this does not mean personal prejudice, institutional racism, and structural racism no

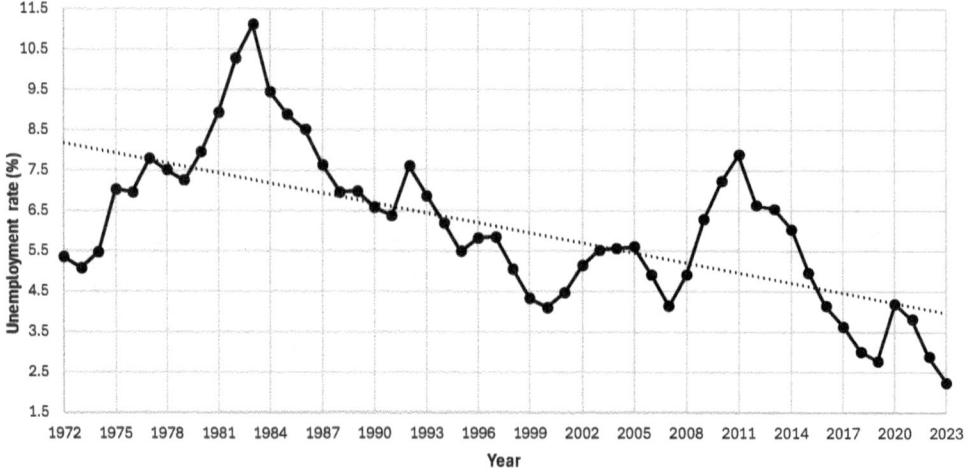

Note: Black-White unemployment rate gap is calculated as the Black unemployment rate minus the white unemployment rate.

Figure 6.3 Black–White unemployment rate gap, US 1972–2023.
Data source: US Department of Labor, BLS CPS.

longer impact Black labor market outcomes, it does underscore that a robust American labor market, which occurred during the post-pandemic recovery in the US, is good for Black employment.

6.3.2. Labor Force Participation Rate Differentials

In this section, we examine the interesting case of racial differentials in labor force participation rates in the US and anti-Black beliefs, using as our starting part the historical difference in labor force participation rates between Black and White women.

The labor force participation rate is, arguably, the second most closely tracked labor force statistic in the US after the unemployment rate. Unlike the unemployment rate, which measures what fraction of the *labor force* is unemployed, this statistic tells us what fraction of the *population* is either working or looking for work. In this sense, it gives an indication of the magnitude of attachment the adult population has to legal work in an area. In a robust economy, high labor force participation rates are desirable, as these are typically associated with higher growth rates in gross domestic product (GDP), and in societies where public assistance is provided to the poor, elderly, and disabled, those who work and pay taxes are contributing to a system where benefits and transfer payments can be provided to those unable to perform wage work. In such societies, when labor force participation rates decline, proportionally fewer adults are contributing to a system in which non-working adults receive pecuniary and other benefits.

Historically, women's labor force participation rates have been consistently lower than those for men, and this is usually ascribed to the assignation of family caregiving responsibilities to primarily women (Amott and Matthaei, 1991; Blau, Ferber, and Winkler, 2014; Hochschild and Machung, 1989). However, when comparing historical differentials in labor force participation rates by gender and race, while Black men's labor force participation rate is routinely lower than that for White men, the reverse is true for Black and White women: Black women currently have – and, with few exceptions, consistently had – higher labor force participation rates than White women (see figure 6.4).

In the case of Black women, it can be argued that anti-Black sentiments played a key role in this demographic's historically higher labor force participation rate in comparison to their White counterparts in at least two distinct ways (see related discussion in chapter 4, "Racism and Labor Force Participation" section). In the first instance,

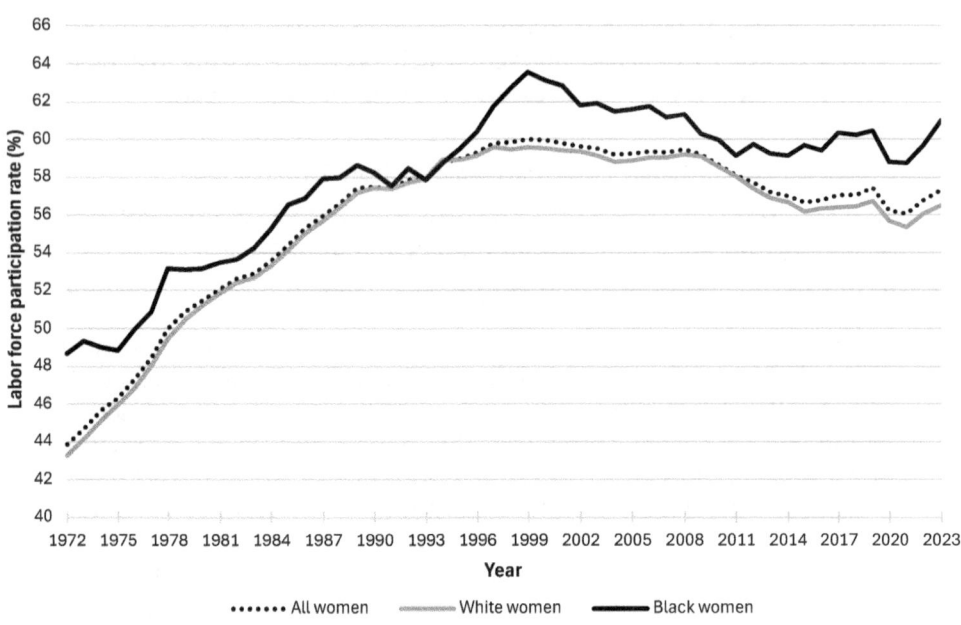

Figure 6.4 Annual labor force participation rates of Black women and White women, 1972–2023.

Data source: US Department of Labor, BLS CPS – seasonally adjusted civilian labor force participation rates age 16 years or older.

after emancipation, there was the belief among Whites that formerly enslaved Black women would continue to labor *outside* the home. There was no "cult of womanhood" or "cult of domesticity" that would be applied to formerly enslaved Black women as was applied to middle-class, married White women. Sojourner Truth alluded to this in her renowned and powerful speech "Ain't I a Woman?" where she pointedly and eloquently noted that while White American society at that time treated White women – especially married, middle-class White women – as delicate and unsuitable for heavy and dangerous work, the same sentiments were not held for formerly enslaved Black women.[9]

After the end of the Civil War, the majority of formerly enslaved Black women worked as agricultural laborers and field hands in a share-cropping system in the rural South. Many of these women were married, but illiterate and poor. Simultaneously, White American society began to enforce a sexual division of labor by recognizing the husband as the head of the house, in contrast to the treatment of Black men and women during slavery. Prior to emancipation, Black men and women were perceived, and treated, similarly with regard to productive capacity, with the critical exception that Black women were also exploited for their reproductive labor – giving birth to children – and often subject to racialized sexual violence by White men (Black men were undoubtedly subject to racialized sexual violence by White men as well). Contrary to what popular American culture has depicted, Black enslaved women worked as hard as Black enslaved men, primarily in agricultural fields. Only an estimated 5 percent of the enslaved worked as domestic servants (Jones, 1985). Cotton production, the most lucrative product of the slave economy, by its very nature required an "all hands on deck" approach. Therefore, enslaved Black women were worked as hard as men, and were subject to the same punishments. This was backbreaking work, sun-up to sun-down, 11–16 hours per day. Pregnant women had to work, and children too, girls as well as boys. Davis (1983) noted that while children were considered "quarter hands," women were considered "full hands," just like men. Thus, within slave households, there was "equality" between enslaved men and women. Nevertheless, enslaved Black women still tried to preserve a somewhat gendered domestic role within their own households as resistance to the slave structure, even as slaveowners had no incentive to enforce a sexual division of labor. Ironically, the sustenance of the cult of domesticity or "cult of womanhood," which wasn't beneficial for White women because it provided a cultural context in which their oppression and subordination could flourish, was precisely enabled in large part because of slave labor, including the slave labor of Black women.

After emancipation, Black women worked in wage and other labor outside the home in greater proportion than White women out of economic necessity – the wages or other forms of compensation accorded to Black male heads of households were so low compared to White men's that the paid labor of Black wives and mothers was overwhelmingly necessary to support Black families.

6.3.3. Occupational Crowding and Wage Differentials

Another long-standing feature of the American labor market is the lower average wage of Black workers compared to White workers. See figure 6.5 for median wages in 2023 by race and gender from the BLS.

Some factors which contribute to wage differentials based on race include differences in median educational attainment levels between groups as well as the industrial and occupational distribution of workers based on race. However, while these factors may account for

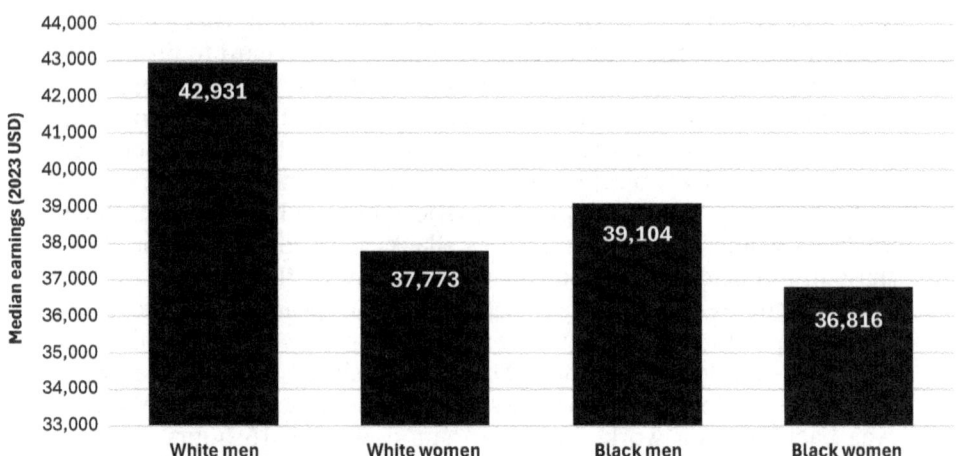

Figure 6.5 Estimated median annual earnings by race and gender, 2023.
Data source: Median annual earnings estimates based on annualized BLS CPS data for median hourly earnings of wages and salary workers paid hourly rates, age 16 years or older, 2023.

most of the difference in median earnings between Black and White workers, they do not account for all of the difference. Nevertheless, a major source of earnings differentials between Black and White workers is occupational segregation.

Metrics of occupational segregation measure the degree of representation of a demographic group in an occupation given that group's *expected* level of representation; the expected representation level is calculated using the share of the group with the level of educational attainment possessed by most workers for the occupation in question (Bergmann, 1971).

What is the explanatory power of the occupational crowding model for the unequal position of Black workers, relative to White workers, in the American labor market? Stratification economics has built on other models to explain persistent labor market disparities. One primary example is the occupational crowding model. As Aigner and Cain (1977, p. 172) noted, labor market discrimination has been traditionally defined as "[different] pay for workers of the same ability." In addition, as Mason (1999) indicated, "[racial] job segregation is one of the mechanisms through which racial wage discrimination is maintained in the presence of competitive labor markets." Occupational crowding research attempts to explain persistent labor market disparities in part by examining how occupational segregation is key to understanding wage differences.

In examining Black men in the American labor market, this demographic group is overrepresented in low-wage occupations and underrepresented in high-wage occupations, even after controlling for education (Bergmann, 1971; Gibson, Darity Jr., and Myers, 1998; Hamilton, Austin, and Darity Jr., 2011). This occupational status of Black men in the US workforce was reaffirmed in original research conducted by one of the co-authors of this book (Holder, 2017). In this research, it was found that Black men were overwhelmingly underrepresented in high-wage occupations both before the Great Recession of 2007–9 and immediately after it. With regard to the concentration of Black men in low-wage occupations, the picture is more complicated given demographic shifts in the American workforce over the last several decades.

The results of quantitative analysis conducted for the years 2010 through 2011 (Holder, 2018) showed a more complex picture than what Bergmann's occupational crowding model once predicted. According to this research, and consistent with Bergmann's model, African American men were underrepresented in high-wage occupations. However, unlike what Bergmann's model predicts, African American men didn't appear to be overrepresented in major low-wage occupational sectors when examined in the aggregate. Holder's approach therefore differs from – but does not contradict – prior research approaches, such as research conducted by Gibson, Darity Jr., and Myers (1998) and Hamilton, Austin and Darity Jr. (2011), insofar as the latter scholar teams examined the distribution of Black men within occupations and across sub-occupations. Both teams of researchers found that Black men were crowded in lower-wage sub-occupations within major occupational sectors, regardless of whether the sector was low-, mid-, or high-wage. Holder's approach differed from, and added value to, this previous research by illustrating that, when all sub-occupations are aggregated and divided into low-, mid-, and high-wage sectors, Black men share representation in low-wage sectors with women and undocumented workers, which they didn't to the same degree when Bergmann developed her model, due to large demographic shifts in labor force composition in the US since the 1970s.

What is the role of anti-Blackness in the occupational crowding of Black workers? Anti-Blackness comes in the form of employer actions that are biased, produces discriminatory outcomes, creates or accommodates an environment where Black workers are mistreated by them or other employees engaging in "opportunity hoarding" (see related discussion in concluding paragraph), or which impacts the occupational sorting of Black workers such that Blacks become crowded in less preferable low-wage occupations. Regarding the latter, Pager and Western (2005) noted in their audit study that it was not uncommon for Black and Latinx male applicants – compared to White male applicants – for sales jobs to be steered or "downward-channeled" into the lower-paying occupation of stock worker.

6.3.3.1. Black Women, Occupational Crowding, and the "Double Gap" in Wages

Research conducted in 2020[10] by one of the co-authors of this book supports the proposition that, while the occupational crowding of Black women into lower-paying jobs partially explains the disparities in wages between this group and non-Latinx White men, it does not explain it all. The wage/earnings gap faced by Black women in the American labor market encompasses both the "gender wage gap" and a "racial wage gap," which Holder has termed the "double gap."[11] The double gap, however, does not simply mean that you either double the gender wage gap, or you double the racial wage gap, and voilà – you have estimated the wage penalty that the average Black female worker encounters in the US labor force. The term "double gap" is simply codifying what the average Black woman in the US labor market faces in terms of the interaction of earnings penalties given her gender and her race.

Data from the US Department of Labor's BLS confirms the existence of both a "gender wage gap" and a "racial wage gap" in the American workforce. The gender wage gap is typically a straightforward comparison of the average or median full-time earnings/wages of all working women to the average or median full-time earnings/wages of all working men. The racial wage gap follows a similar formulation – it consists of a comparison of the average or median full-time earnings/wages of all Black workers to the average or median full-time earnings/wages of all White workers in the US. According to BLS data for 2022, men working full-time earned a median of $1,154 per week (approximately $60,000 annually) and full-time working women earned $958 per week (approximately $49,800 annually);[12] women thus received an estimated 83 cents for every dollar men received. BLS data for 2022 also indicated that Black workers earned a median of $896 weekly working full-time approximately ($46,600 annually) while White workers earned a median of $1,111 weekly working full-time (approximately $57,800 annually),[13] so Black workers were receiving approximately 81 cents for every dollar White workers received. (Note that the estimates above differ from those appearing in figure 6.5 due to annual earnings calculated for the latter being based on a 40-hour-only workweek, with exclusion of overtime pay, commissions, or tips.)

As noted earlier in this section, a variety of factors play a role in gender and racial wage gaps, such as the industrial distribution of workers and median educational attainment differences by group. However, Holder's (2020) research, which compared the earnings of full-time Black female workers directly to those of full-time non-Hispanic White male workers, showed that, even after controlling for factors that would contribute to wage differentials based on race and gender, Black women on average earned approximately $20,000 per year (in 2017 dollars) less than comparably skilled, educated, and experienced non-Hispanic White men. This suggests Black women are systematically underpaid, compared to equally qualified and skilled non-Hispanic White men, by employers, with the only remaining differences between these two groups which could explain this disparity being Black women's race and gender.

6.4. Anti-Black Employment Practices and Policy Solutions

It would seem reasonable to posit, in the context of this book, that in order for any policy to be effective in ameliorating or extinguishing one or more (or all!) of the varied disparate labor market outcomes faced by Black Americans, the role of anti-Blackness embedded in many current employment policies and practices must be acknowledged and addressed. This is not to suggest that *any* employment policy or practice which results in disparate outcomes based on race was designed with the specific intention of disenfranchising Black job applicants and workers. Having noted that, however, any employment policy or practice which has been repeatedly and/or convincingly shown to disaffect Black people, which employers or policymakers refuse or neglect to rectify, is a policy or practice that *has become* anti-Black, regardless of whether its original intent was to be race-neutral.

A historical example of an employment policy at the federal level that was not intended to be race-neutral was the first incarnation of the Social Security Act of 1935. After the decline of the sharecropping system and the subsequent Great Migration of African Americans in the beginning of the twentieth century from the South to the North and Midwest, Black workers continued to labor in large numbers in agricultural or domestic occupations which were excluded (with such exclusion heavily influenced by Southern legislators at the time [Katznelson, 2005]) from President Franklin Delano Roosevelt's New Deal policies establishing Social Security and other important benefits for workers.

Contemporary employment practices which may not have been intended to marginalize Black job applicants, but which nevertheless do, include, but aren't limited to, the following:

(1) Requesting previous salary histories from job applicants and candidates: in the case *Rizo* v. *Yovino*, the Ninth Circuit Court of Appeals found in 2018 the practice of requesting previous salary histories from job applicants had a discriminatory impact on women. This is because of the gender wage gap; if women are, on average, paid less than men, then salary histories of women will show lower wage trajectories compared to men. Because Black workers earn, on average, less than White workers given the racial wage gap, this practice also disadvantages Black job applicants and candidates. Unfortunately, the Ninth Circuit Court of Appeals ruling in *Rizo* v. *Yovina* was vacated, on a technicality, by the US Supreme Court.[14]
(2) Employment credit checks: there are some states that ban the use of credit checks for job applicants, but employers still routinely use this practice. According to the Society for Human Resource Management, employers use this practice to reduce the probability of theft as well as liabilities associated with "negligent hiring."[15] However, the Federal Reserve Board has pointed out the association between racial and ethnic community demographics and the proportion of the community with low credit scores; the higher the share of people of color in a community, the greater the likelihood that community has lower median or average credit scores.[16] Thus, such an employment practice has a discriminatory impact on Black job applicants and workers.
(3) Questions on job applications about previous arrests or convictions: because Black men in the US are overrepresented with respect to criminal legal system involvement, questions on employment applications inquiring about whether an applicant had been convicted of a crime have a disproportionate and deleterious impact on Black male job applicants.

Given the examples above, some policy approaches which would be effective seem clear:

- Enactment of federal legislation banning employers from requesting salary histories from job applicants: recognizing that requesting previous salary histories from job applicants perpetuates pay disparities,[17] as of January 2023 16 states as well as Puerto Rico have enacted statewide bans.[18]

- Enactment of federal legislation banning the use of credit checks for employment: in 2020 the US House of Representatives passed legislation prohibiting the use of credit checks in making employment decisions, but the legislation didn't make it to the Senate,[19] and in 2021 the House once again introduced similar legislation (HR 4144 –Restricting Credit Checks for Employment Decisions Act), when it was sent to committee. As of 2020 11 states have passed laws banning employers from conducting credit checks of job candidates.[20]
- Enactment of federal legislation to "ban the box" – remove questions on job applications about prior arrests or convictions: in Wisconsin, "ban[ning] the box" has been shown to improve employment outcomes for persons who had formerly been imprisoned,[21] and as of 2021 37 states have implemented ban the box laws.[22]

While the aforementioned policies are designed to eliminate racial and other disparities in employment outcomes, much of the current academic and policy literature on eliminating wage/pay gaps tends to focus on the need for more pay transparency (Baker et al., 2023; Kim, 2015; National Women's Law Center, 2020), while some literature discusses the impact of affirmative action on pay equity (Darity Jr., 2013; Holzer and Neumark, 2000; Leonard, 1990; Wicks-Lim, 2013). Currently eight states have enacted salary range transparency laws, requiring employers (with some restrictions) to provide wage or salary ranges for, primarily, job openings.[23] However, movement has stalled on a bill at the federal level which would mandate salary range transparency by employers nationwide – HR 1599, the Salary Transparency Act, was introduced in March 2023 and referred to committee.

6.5. Conclusion

The American labor market is rife with a history of anti-Black policies and practices. Even the labor movement of the early twentieth century, designed to empower workers across a spectrum of race and ethnicity, has a tragic history of exclusion of and violence toward Black American workers (Aronowitz, 1973; Cayton and Mitchell, 1939; Du Bois, 1902; Foner and Lewis, 1983; Hill, 1988). However, consistent with one of the tenets of stratification economics, policy interventions, particularly at the national level, appropriately targeted, can be effective tools to ameliorate and eradicate disparate outcomes based on race; the persistence of disparities based on race underscores the need for such interventions. Further, the current period of a robust labor market also shows that policies and approaches to spur the economy are beneficial for Black workers; one of the so-called "dual mandates" of the Federal Reserve Board, the US central bank, is to use monetary policy "to promote effectively... maximum employment."[24] There exist clear roadmaps for what can be done to eliminate racially disparate outcomes from the American workforce, but the will to act – stymied by the interests of those who want to preserve privileges being enjoyed primarily by White Americans, and/or who believe the US labor market has fair outcomes – must be present and strong among employers, companies, policymakers, legislators, and the American public.

7

Wealth Attainment and Anti-Blackness: The Case of Black Women

A Prefatory Note to Chapter 7

Even as anti-Blackness persists in the US, some economic indicators for Black Americans have improved vis-à-vis those for white Americans: earnings, employment, and educational attainment. However, the gap between Blacks and Whites for one particular economic indicator has remained consistently large since slavery ended in the US – wealth. Wealth is defined as a person, family, or entity's assets minus liabilities, and it is critically important regarding the economic security of individuals and households. Given the constancy of the relative size of the Black–White wealth gap over time, arguably the roles of anti-Black policies and practices in the US have had the most enduring impact on this metric of well-being.

Because income and wealth are correlated, and – as discussed in chapter 6, "Unemployment, Occupational Crowding, Wage Inequality, and Anti-Blackness in the Labor Market" – among Black and White communities in the US, Black women have the lowest median earnings while White men have the highest, co-author of this book Michelle Holder undertook research to examine how the racial and gender wage gaps Black women encounter in the US labor market affect this group's ability to build wealth. The 2023 research and policy brief which resulted from this research, "How Do Wage Gaps Affect Black Women's Wealth Attainment, and Where Do Expenditures Fit In?" – written for the Urban Institute in Washington, DC, with funding from the Goldman Sachs "One Million Black Women: Closing the Wealth Gap" initiative – follows. Also discussed are the role of expenditures Black women disparately face, which constrain wealth-building for them, as well as anti-Black policies and practices involved in wealth stripping and constraining of wealth-building for the Black American community.

This brief is illustrative of how applying an intersectional lens to tenets of stratification economics can help us understand the particular position of Black women in the American economy. While the report does not delineate specific theoretical paradigms, given its original audience were policymakers and advocates, the applicability of the frameworks of stratification economics and intersectional theory in explaining the size, persistence, and gender impacts of the racial wealth gap are present in the following ways: (1) absent effective policy intervention, racial and gender disparities are likely to continue in a competitive, market economy given the benefits that are reaped by White Americans; and (2) intergenerational wealth transfers have played a definitive and crucial role in the size and persistence of the racial wealth gap. In addition, as stratification economics also posits, in order to move the needle in impactful and durable ways, actionable as well as existing policy interventions are outlined at the federal, state, and local levels, including reparations.

HOW DO WAGE GAPS AFFECT BLACK WOMEN'S WEALTH ATTAINMENT, AND WHERE DO EXPENDITURES FIT IN?*

7.1. Introduction

Even as the wage gap between Black and White Americans in the United States has narrowed over the last several decades, the wealth gap between these two groups remains alarmingly wide. Access to wealth, particularly in the form of liquid assets, facilitates income smoothing during periods of joblessness, offers the capital necessary to make large purchases such as homes and cars, and allows individuals and families to invest in educational, business, or other opportunities. Ever since the promise of 40 acres and a mule upon emancipation from slavery went unfulfilled, Black Americans have struggled to build individual and collective wealth. Most expositions on the barriers that have prevented Black wealth accumulation tend

---

* This research and policy brief was written for the Urban Institute by Michelle Holder, and funded by the Goldman Sachs – Urban Institute One Million Black Women Research Partnership. The author would like to thank Tom Masterson for his expert assistance in conducting quantitative analysis for this brief, Joshua Moyse for his research assistance, and Daniella Medina for their research assistance as well as quantitative work. Any changes to the previously published material in the chapter are due to the desire to keep the material consistent with the style of the rest of the book.

to focus on the household. However, research has shown that, when broken down by gender and race, Black women in the US possess the lowest levels of wealth compared with White men, White women, and Black men.

This brief focuses on Black women and wealth in the US. It establishes a framework for examining the Black women's wealth gap from the perspective of earnings gaps as well as expenditure burdens that Black women disproportionately face which can drain income and asset accumulation. The research questions being asked are: *In what ways do racial and gender wage gaps borne by Black women in the American workforce affect their ability to accumulate wealth, and how do expenditures disparately faced by Black women factor into this?*

7.2. Measuring Wealth and Contributors to Wealth Accumulation

An asset is defined in Merriam Webster's dictionary as "the entire property of a person, association, corporation, or estate applicable or subject to the payments of debts."[1] The word asset is often used synonymously with the terms wealth or worth, though it has a more nuanced definition. However, individual or household wealth is typically equal to an individual's or household's net assets, which are assets less any outstanding debts or liabilities.

According to researchers Thomas Shapiro and Jessica Kenty-Drane (2005), wealth accumulation in the US occurs primarily through three pathways: inheritances, earnings, and savings (savings in this context likely meaning whether an individual or household actually saves, since savings are derived from income, including earnings). In addition, these researchers posit that the most important contributor to wealth accumulation is income, but, at the same time, suggest that African Americans cannot necessarily "earn their way out of the racial wealth gap." Shapiro and Kenty-Drane (2005) make an important distinction between "net worth" and "net financial assets" – net worth is everything an individual or household owns of monetary value less any debts owed, while net financial assets are equal to net worth less home equity. This is a critical distinction, given that, according to the US Census Bureau, the biggest contributor to household wealth in the US is home equity, and home equity along with retirement accounts accounted for 65 percent of a household's wealth in the US as of 2019.[2]

Wealth vs. Income

Wealth represents the sedimentation of historical inequalities in the American experience, in a sense the accumulation of advantages and disadvantages for different ... groups. In this way, wealth provides a window to explore how our past influences the realities of today. This is not simply a story about counting money; families think about using wealth first as a private safety net, and second as a vehicle to launch mobility into middle-class status, homeownership, business development, or a more secure retirement.

Thomas Shapiro (2006)

While inequality and poverty measures have historically focused on income, wealth enables a particular understanding of racial stratification in the United States and its persistence. Income is comprised of earnings from labor, or earning substitutes, such as unemployment insurance, social assistance, disability benefits, and pensions. Professor of law and social policy Thomas Shapiro (2006) defines **wealth** as "the total value of a family's financial resources minus all debts." As a special kind of money, wealth accumulation confers resource control and ownership, while income via earnings or payments is used to replace previous earnings consumed. **Income** is a *flow*, used primarily for everyday consumption. **Assets**, on the other hand, are *stocks*, and may be invested or stored as savings. As such, assets can be considered a special form of money – a "surplus resource available for improving life chances, providing further opportunities, securing prestige, passing status along to one's family, and securing economic security for present and future generations" (Oliver and Shapiro, 1995; Shapiro, 2006). Wealth secures livelihood in terms of its ability to finance the development of human capital, facilitate homeownership, allow for greater choice in terms of community location, and promote health and long-term economic security. Wealth is used to facilitate social mobility and increase social status. The accumulation of household wealth has implications for the future of inequality, as intergenerational transfers provide advantages to offspring in their lifetime. A wealth-oriented perspective provides the ability to represent a point-in-time accumulation of past inequality, assess present-day differences in resources, and allow for inferences related to future patterns (Medina, 2017). Thus wealth is a mechanism that allows us to connect our historical memory of racial and gendered inequality to contemporary racial and gendered inequality.

Written by Daniella Medina

7.2.1. Households Versus Individuals

Wealth data are collected at both the household and individual level. However, most analyses of wealth status in the US focus on household, rather than individual, wealth because people tend to spend longer periods experiencing the advantages of wealth (or disadvantages of zero or negative net worth) as part of a household than as a single person. The implication here is that analyses of individual wealth may obscure the impact of the wealth statuses of other household members if an individual is a member of a multiperson household. Nonetheless, to study the issue of Black women's wealth at the individual level is important. As noted by Valentino and Yadon (2023, p. 5), "Using single households is a common approach used by scholars when investigating gender gaps in wealth (e.g., Chang 2010), but it hampers scholars' ability to speak to the full patterns of wealth inequality in the US."

7.2.2. The Racial Wealth Gap

Putting aside the issue of gender, as well as individuals vs. households, for the moment, different approaches have been used to measure the magnitude of the racial wealth gap; in this brief, the racial wealth gap is the average or median difference in net assets between Black and White households. Thus, one frequently employed approach is to compare the median wealth of Black households to the median wealth of White households. A second approach is to compare the percentage of total wealth White Americans in the US hold with the percentage of total wealth Black Americans hold and determine how closely these figures track to each group's respective population size. A third approach is to estimate, in aggregate, the amount of the racial wealth gap.

With the first approach, according to US Census Bureau 2019 data, the median wealth of White, non-Hispanic households was $187,000; for Black households, it was $14,000 (Aliprantis and Carroll, 2019). Thus, White non-Hispanic households in the US have more than 10 times the wealth of Black households. Using the second approach, according to the Federal Reserve Bank of Minneapolis, Whites make up 60 percent of the US population but hold 84 percent of the wealth in the country, while the Black community makes up 13 percent of the population but holds only 4 percent of total wealth.[3] A third novel approach attempted to aggregate the racial wealth gap; according to Vanessa Williamson (2020), senior fellow at the Brookings Institution, "If Black households held a share of the national wealth in proportion to their share of the US population, it would amount to $12.68 trillion in household wealth, rather than the actual sum of $2.54 trillion. The total racial wealth gap, therefore, is $10.14 trillion." However one measures it, the current racial wealth gap in the US is enormous.

7.2.3. Drivers of the Racial Wealth Gap

Research confirms a positive link between income and wealth. According to a Federal Reserve Bank of Cleveland 2019 report, which noted that some research on the racial wealth gap finds it is too large to be explained by income disparities alone, the racial income gap is the biggest driver of the racial wealth gap *over time*, and thus policies designed to close income gaps will also be beneficial for closing wealth gaps (Aliprantis and Carroll, 2019). In the web feature "Nine Charts about Wealth Inequality in America," the Urban Institute also draws a link between rising income inequality and rising wealth inequality in the US.[4]

However, other scholarship posits that another factor is as important, and some may argue more important, than income as a critical driver in the current racial wealth gap. Research published by Derenoncourt and colleagues (2022) indicates that where Black Americans stood after emancipation with regard to wealth – which was effectively zero, as they were, indeed, considered a form of wealth to others before emancipation – is to blame for about half the current racial wealth gap. The researchers point out that in 1870 the racial wealth gap ratio between Whites and Black Americans was 23 to 1, and by 2020 that ratio had narrowed to 6 to 1. Derenoncourt and colleagues (2022) then derive a counterfactual figure: if the wealth of Black and White Americans remained unchanged in 1870, but the rate of wealth accumulation of Black Americans had been equal to that of Whites, then as of 2020 the racial wealth gap ratio should have narrowed to 3 to 1, which suggests that where Black and White Americans stood after the Civil War with respect to wealth mattered a great deal for the contemporary wealth status of the Black community.

Since these researchers estimate the current racial wealth gap ratio is 6 to 1, and according to their methodology about half the current racial wealth gap can be traced to the functionally zero individual wealth of the overwhelming majority of Black American adults after emancipation, the other half of the racial wealth gap requires explication. The researchers attribute that half to racist laws, policies, and practices that constrained wealth accumulation for Black households after emancipation, like Jim Crow laws, redlining, outright theft of land by Whites, inflated mortgage interest rates, workforce discrimination and occupational segregation of Black women and men into lower-paying occupations, and widening overall wealth inequality since 1980 in the US.

7.2.4. Trends in the Racial Wealth Gap

Obtaining current estimates on the size of wealth gaps by race and gender in the US is important, but arguably as important is examining trends in wealth gaps over time to discern whether policy approaches to narrow and close them are working. One study conducted by Valentino and Yadon (2023) used 11 waves of Survey of Consumer Finances data from 1989 to 2019 and found little evidence of convergence of racial and gender wealth gaps; instead, these researchers found consistency across time in wealth gaps between single White men and other single individuals from racial, ethnic, and gender groups, including Black women. Derenoncourt and colleagues (2022) indicate that there were at least two periods in American history since 1860 (excluding the immediate post-emancipation period) when the racial wealth gap shrank: during World War II, when the demand for civilian labor increased; and after the passage of the Civil Rights Act of 1964. But, like Valentino and Yadon, they find convergence in the racial wage gap stalled from 1980 to 2020, which Derenoncourt and colleagues attribute to the trend in growing wealth inequality overall in the US over the past few decades.

7.2.5. The Gender Wealth Gap

Just as the racial wealth gap is a measurement of wealth distribution by race, the gender wealth gap is a measurement of wealth distribution by gender. However, unlike estimates of the racial wealth gap, which have been examined at both the individual and household level, including households with married couples, the gender wealth gap typically examines wealth differentials between individuals, usually single adults, and not households.

Researchers have found intra-racial gender differences in wealth among single individuals are not uniform. The relative difference in wealth between single White men and single White women is smaller than that between single Latinx men and women, which in turn is smaller than that between Black men and women; Valentino and Yadon (2023) found that in 2019 White men had 76 percent more wealth, at the median, than White women, while Latinx men had 117 percent more wealth than Latinas, and Black men had 229 percent more wealth than Black women. While the researchers noted they were unable to explain why relative intra-racial gender differences in wealth were smallest among White Americans but largest among Black Americans, Valentino and Yadon noted that intersectional theory would predict such an outcome given the compounding impacts of both race and gender on economic security.

7.3. Black Women and the Wealth Gap

When examining the wealth gap among Black, Latinx, and White men and women, according to analyses conducted by Valentino and Yadon (2023) using the 2019 Survey of Consumer Finances, Black women in the US have the least wealth (figure 7.1).

7.3.1. Black Women, the Double Gap, and Wealth Accumulation

The relationship between the racial wealth gap and racial and gender wage gaps for Black women in the American workforce seems

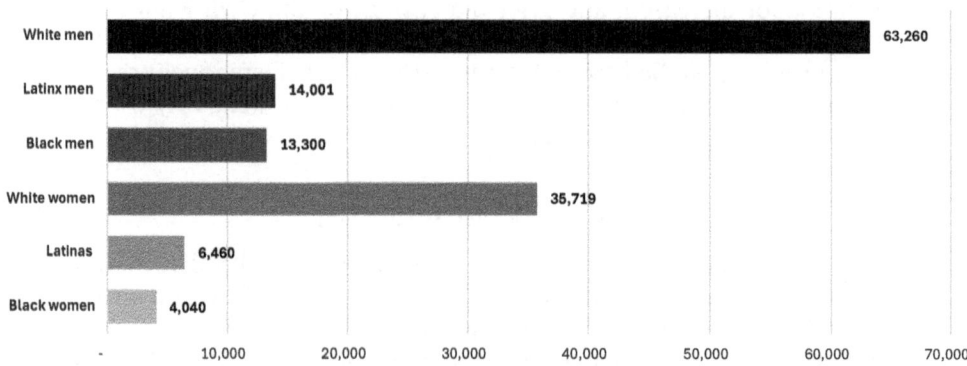

Figure 7.1 Median wealth in the US by race, ethnicity, and gender, 2019.
Source: Valentino and Yadon (2023), p. 8, table 2. Data from the Federal Reserve Board Survey of Consumer Finances (SCF).

straightforward, but the specific ways in which these wage gaps affect wealth attainment are not often explored explicitly. In 2020, this author's research quantified the aggregate earnings loss to Black women attributable to racial and gender wage gaps; approximately $50 billion (in 2017 dollars) in salaries and wages are lost each year from the double gap in wages this group experiences (Holder, 2020). This research indicated that an individual Black woman who works full-time is underpaid, on average, by approximately $20,000 each year. Building on this research, this section explores and highlights the connections between individual gender and racial wage losses that Black women experience and the individual racial wealth gaps their households experience. Part of the goal here is to bring urgency to the undervaluation of Black women's work; it contributes to not only income gaps but wealth gaps between Black and White households. Thus, the case can be more effectively made that policy measures designed to address wage gaps could address wealth inequities too.

The double gap in wages is a result of the intersecting effects of the racial wage gap – Black workers earn on average less than White workers – and the gender wage gap – women on average earn less than men. According to Current Population Survey data for 2022, while women working full-time earned 83 cents for every dollar men working full-time earned, Black women working full-time earned 71 cents for every dollar their White male counterparts earned, resulting in a double gap of 29 percent.[5]

Bureau of Labor Statistics analyses do not account for the complex factors that play a role in wage disparities for women, and women of color in particular. Among these factors are occupational crowding based on sex and race, gender socialization, employer bias, historical exclusionary practices by unions, the "motherhood penalty," and educational attainment gaps, particularly at the level of college completion.

The mechanisms by which Black women's double gap in wages affect wealth attainment include the ability to (1) save and accumulate assets, including buying a home; (2) reduce debt, such as mortgages or credit; and (3) accumulate retirement savings. In addition, expenditures disparately borne by Black women, which can drain income and assets, further constrict Black women's ability to build wealth.

7.3.1.1. Causes of the Double Gap

Occupational Crowding
Current research and data confirm that women are overrepresented in so-called "pink collar" occupations: the three occupations in the

US that employ the largest number of women are administrative assistants/secretaries, teachers, and nurses, and in each of these occupations 80 percent of workers are women.[6] Black women in the US workforce, in line with women generally, are crowded into low-wage occupations, partly because of the kinds of occupations that were open to Black women. This, of course, influences the magnitude of wage gaps Black women face in the workforce. Economist Cecilia Conrad, an editor of *African Americans in the US Economy* (2005), noted that, before the passage of the 1964 Civil Rights Act – particularly Title VII of the Act, which prohibited race- and gender-based discrimination in employment – the occupation with the highest share of Black women in the US (38 percent in 1960) was private household (i.e., domestic servants). Conrad pointed out that by 1980, the occupation with the highest share of Black women had changed from private household to clerical (see economist Randy Albelda's 1985 research for more on this change). Indeed, in 2015, about one in five Black American women worked in office and administrative support occupations, and an additional 17 percent worked in healthcare practitioner and healthcare support occupations (e.g., nurses, nursing assistants, medical records technicians, and home health aides).[7]

Educational Attainment Gap
Earnings and educational attainment are strongly positively correlated in the US: the higher one's educational attainment level, the greater one's earnings are likely to be. Figure 7.2 shows the impact of the gender wage gap: men earn more than women at every level of educational attainment. However, according to Current Population Survey data for 2021,[8] a large educational attainment gap exists between Black and White Americans at the level of college completion: 38 percent of White Americans ages 25 years and older possess a bachelor's degree or higher, compared with 28 percent of Black Americans in the same age group.

By gender, 37 percent of White men ages 25 and older, and 39 percent of White women in the same age group, have a bachelor's degree or higher, compared with 25 percent of Black men and 31 percent of Black women in the same age group (figure 7.3). Without controlling for the educational attainment gap between Black and White workers at the level of college completion or higher, any examination of wage differences between Black women, White men, and White women will, therefore, reflect the impact of higher educational attainment among Whites in the US.

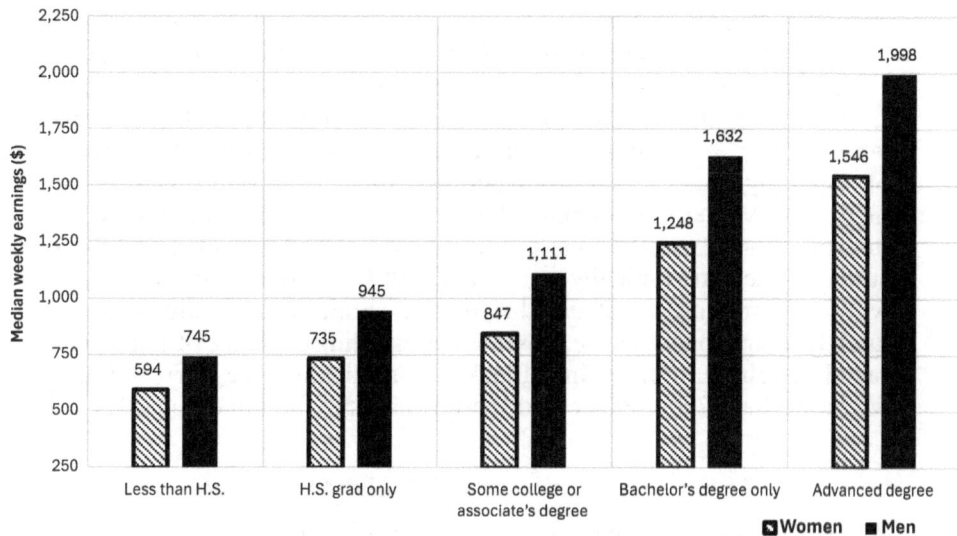

Figure 7.2 Median weekly earnings in the US by gender and educational attainment, 2022.

Data source: Department of Labor Bureau of Labor Statistics CPS, 2022 median weekly earnings of full-time workers age 25 years or older.

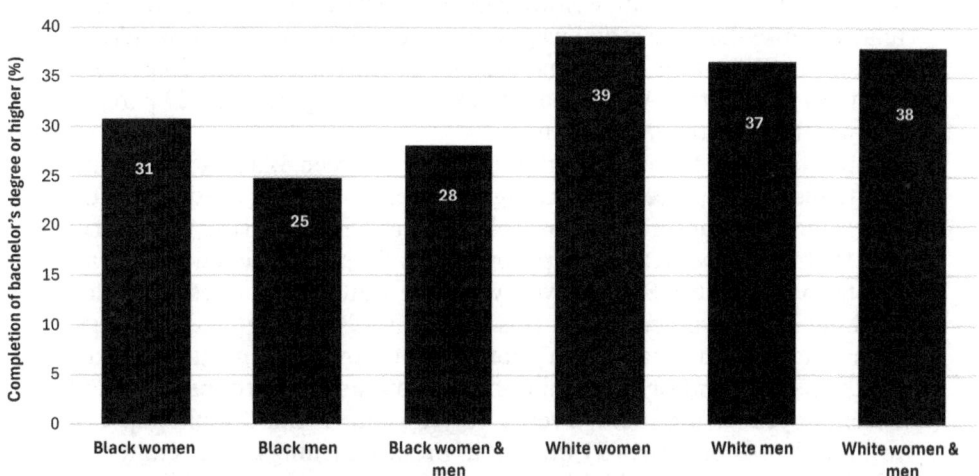

Figure 7.3 Percentage of adults 25+ years of age in the US who have completed a bachelor's degree or higher, 2021.

Data source: US Census Bureau Current Population Survey, 2021 Annual Social and Economic Supplement (CPS ASEC).

Employer Discrimination

Economists and other social scientists use a variety of techniques to either measure or detect racial discrimination in the US labor market. One method uses regression analysis, which controls for various labor market attributes and characteristics to determine the source of, typically, wage differentials between Black and White people (or men and women); unexplained residuals are usually attributed to discrimination. Another method uses field experiments such as "audit studies"; these are typically conducted with Black and White applicants whose résumés are constructed to present similar qualifications. These analytical approaches have presented compelling evidence of persistent racial discrimination against Black job applicants (see Bertrand and Mullainathan, 2004; Pager and Western, 2005; Quillian et al., 2017).

7.3.1.2. The Double Gap and Wealth Accumulation

As noted earlier, income and wealth are positively correlated, and for the majority of adults in the US, income is mostly derived from wages and salaries. Because Black women encounter a double gap in wages/earnings because of both their gender and race, the impact of wage gaps on wealth accumulation for this group is especially deleterious. However, since there isn't a one-to-one relationship between earnings and wealth – the racial wealth gap in America is much larger in a relative sense than the racial wage gap or gender wage gap – it would be an oversimplification to assume because Black women earn 29 percent less than non-Latinx White men, then the former group has 29 percent less wealth than the latter group.

Indeed, while the double gap in wages between Black women and White men is 29 percent according to Bureau of Labor Statistics data, Valentino and Yadon (2023) as well as Bhattacharya, Price, and Perry[9] find that Black women have approximately 90 percent less wealth than White men in the US. However, what the double gap does mean for working Black women is that this group has 29 percent less earnings, on average, to save, pay down debt, allocate toward educational goals for themselves and/or their children, and put aside for retirement than do employed White men. Over a 40-year career, the double gap can result in losses of nearly $1 million in pre-tax earnings, on average, for Black women compared with White men;[10] these dollars could assist in affording childcare costs, shore up retirement savings, allow for large asset purchases such as homes, accommodate the cost of a college education, provide start-up funding for entrepreneurial ventures, or reduce debt burdens.

Black Women and Retirement
One critical way in which the double gap in wages affects Black women's ability to accumulate wealth is in retirement savings. Economist Angelino Viceisza's 2022 brief for the Urban Institute on Black women's readiness for retirement makes a direct connection between the crowding of Black women in low-wage occupations and lower levels of retirement savings. Viceisza indicates that among all major racial, ethnic, and gender groups, Black women have the second-lowest amount available in retirement funds, behind that of Latinas. Importantly, though, he also notes the smaller retirement accounts of Black women can't be attributed to either lower participation rates of these women, compared to other major female demographic groups, in defined benefit pension plans, nor to a financial literacy gap between Black and White women. Notably, after controlling for differences in income, evidence suggests that Black households save at comparable rates to White households (Darity Jr. et al., 2018), so the assumption of a lower propensity to save among Black households also can't be blamed for lower retirement savings among Black women.

7.4. Other Sources of Wealth Accumulation

7.4.1. Black Women and Homeownership

While the homeownership rate among Black women who are heads of their households increased between 1990 and 2019, Black women heads of households have the lowest rate of homeownership compared with White men and women, Latinx men and women, and Black men (figure 7.4). The ability to buy a home typically depends on income, assets, and creditworthiness. Largely because of the double gap in wages, Black women's income is lower than that of White men, White women, and Black men.

While conventional measurements of wealth typically include the value of properties owned (less any outstanding debt on the property), homeownership alone does not guarantee Black women the same access to wealth as it does for other groups, given discriminatory lending practices, lower median home values for Black households than White households, and discrimination in the appraisal value of homes occupied by Black families compared with values assigned to homes occupied by White families.[11]

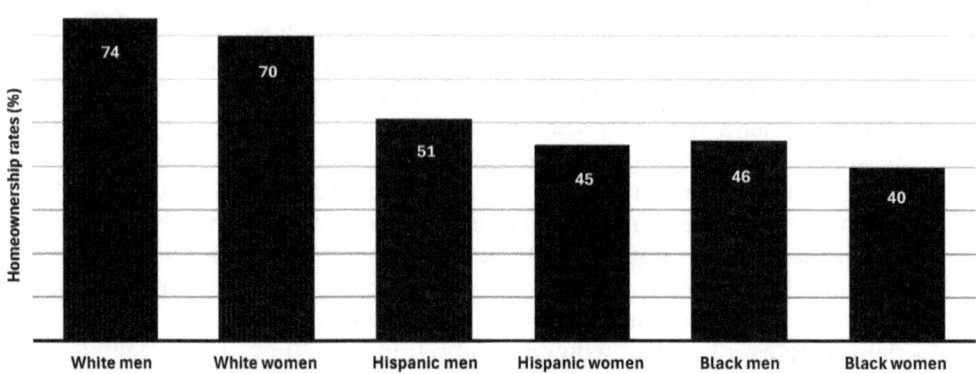

Figure 7.4 Homeownership rates in the US by race, ethnicity, and gender, heads of households, 2019.
Data source: Choi et al. (2021), "A Three Decade Decline in the Gender Homeownership Gap," Urban Institute, Research Report, p. 6 – figure 2; data from the US Census Bureau American Community Survey (ACS).

7.4.2. Intergenerational Wealth Transfers/Inheritance

Research conducted by Paul Menchik and Nancy Ammon Jianakoplos (1997), using data from the Survey of Consumer Finances and the 1976 National Longitudinal Surveys of Mature Men, show the critical role intergenerational wealth transfers play in the racial wealth gap. They found that White households were more than twice as likely to receive an inheritance as Black households; after controlling for other variables, race was significant in determining whether a household received an inheritance and, if so, how large. According to these scholars, racial differences in intergenerational wealth transfers account for 10–20 percent of the racial wealth gap. These findings complement those by Derenoncourt and colleagues (2022) in that the zero wealth status of the overwhelming majority of Black Americans after emancipation, compared with the nonzero wealth status of White Americans during the same period, is likely to blame for about half the wealth gap between Black and White Americans today.

7.5. Black Women and Expenditures

7.5.1. Childcare Costs

In examining the lower wealth levels among Black women, the bulk of empirical analysis typically focuses on drivers of wealth – income, inheritances, and so on. But little is discussed about the costs that Black women may be disparately facing, compared with other racial–ethnic–gender groups, which could play a critical role in constraining their ability to accumulate wealth. One such cost may be for childcare.

According to the Annie E. Casey Foundation, using 2021 data from the American Community Survey, 64 percent of Black children are raised in single-parent homes, compared with 24 percent of White non-Hispanic children.[12] In addition, the Institute for Women's Policy Research noted that the majority of Black mothers were single parents in 2018 (Shaw et al., 2020, p. 3). In single-parent families, a second parent is not available within the home to share childcare responsibilities. While nonresident parents can certainly assist with childcare responsibilities, these tasks often become easier when two parents live in the household. In single-parent families, therefore, childcare duties fall heaviest on the resident parent, who may need to turn to friendship or kin networks as well as childcare providers for assistance.

The majority of Black mothers are also breadwinners for their families. The Institute for Women's Policy Research defines breadwinning mothers as mothers, irrespective of marital status, who contribute a minimum of 40 percent of their income to overall household income (Shaw et al., 2020, p. 3). In popular American culture, a household's primary breadwinner is understood to bring the largest share of income, typically at least 51 percent, of a household. However breadwinning is defined, the data suggest that a higher share of Black mothers are primary breadwinners in their families than White mothers: the Pew Research Center found that in 2011, 40 percent of households with children in the US had a mother who was either the sole or primary breadwinner, with 63 percent of those households headed by a single mother (Wang, Parker, and Taylor, 2013), and the Institute for Women's Policy Research found wide variation of mother-breadwinning by race: in 2018, 79 percent of Black mothers were breadwinners compared with 48 percent of White mothers.

With more than half of Black children growing up in single-parent homes in the US and the majority of single parents in the US being women, it seems likely the cost of childcare is a budgetary item that Black mothers face disparately compared with their White counterparts. Data from the 2019 Survey of Consumer Finances confirm this is the case for single Black mothers. About a third of single Black women are mothers compared with 15 percent of single White women;[13] and, despite the fact that White women working full-time earn more on average than Black women working full-time, single Black mothers face higher average annual childcare costs than single White mothers (Shaw et al., 2020, p. 4) (table 7.1).

7.2. Student Loan Debt

As noted in the educational attainment gap section, 31 percent of Black women ages 25 years and older have a bachelor's degree or higher. However, these achievements are coming at a high cost: Black women have the highest average student debt level of any major racial–ethnic–gender group, which can encumber future earnings and hinder asset accumulation (figure 7.5). Ford and Balu (2023) also point out that Black households are more likely than White households to have both student debt and higher student debt balances.

7.6. Policies, Strategies, and Solutions

7.6.1. The Actors, Federal versus State, and Long-Term versus Short-Term

Narrowing, and eventually closing, the wealth gap that Black women in the US face will require various actors, action on the federal as well as state levels, and both long-term and short-term strategies.

Legislators, employers, advocates, unions, and individuals all have important roles to play; and where long-term policy changes at the national level appear to move excruciatingly slowly, municipal- and state-level changes can help push national discourse and action. Black women can take action individually in addition to strategies they conceive, advocate for, and implement as part of collective work.

Table 7.1 Average annual childcare cost by race for single parents, 2019 ($)

Black women	Black men	White women	White men	Overall
1,131	587	844	576	872

Source: 2019 Consumer Expenditure Survey.

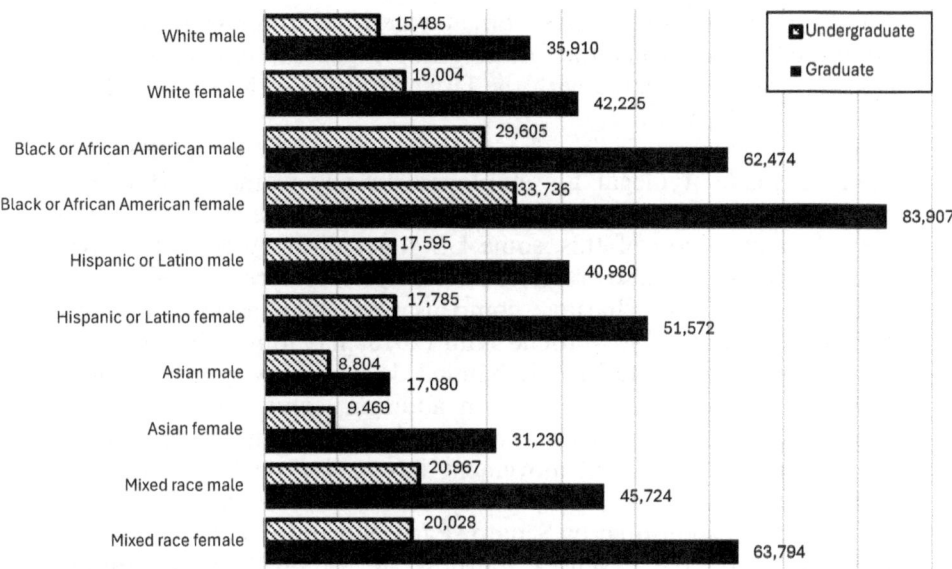

Figure 7.5 Average undergraduate and graduate cumulative federal loan amounts by race and gender, 2016/2017 ($).
Data source: US Department of Education, National Center for Education Statistics, Baccalaureate and Beyond: 2016/2020 (B&B) and National Postsecondary Student Aid Study: 2020 Graduate Students (NPSAS:GR).

7.6.2. Policies, Strategies, and Solutions on the Assets Side

7.6.2.1. Closing the Earnings Gap via Pay Transparency Laws, Policies, and Practices

Closing wage gaps that Black women encounter in the American labor market requires actions that facilitate more pay transparency. Assigning blame to Black women for the double gap in wages they encounter would be incorrect. Research shows that when Black candidates are assertive in salary bargaining, employers may deem them aggressive (Hernandez et al., 2019). Employment or salary offers may then become at risk due to the violation of employers' expectations about how intensely Black candidates should negotiate. In addition, in the 2018 Ninth Circuit Court of Appeals case *Rizo* v. *Yovino* it was found that the often-used employer practice of requesting previous salary histories from job candidates contributed to gender wage gaps.

Finally, other research shows women experience lower salary returns, compared to men, when the former group engages in bargaining strategies typically associated with the latter group (Crothers et al., 2010; Gerhart and Rynes, 1991).

Pay transparency is key for equitable pay. The Equal Pay Act of 1963 made it illegal for employers to pay women and people of color inequitably for the same work being done by Whites and men. In recognition of this, some US states disallow employer "pay secrecy" practices: these practices discourage employees in a company/organization from sharing compensation information amongst themselves. Economist Marlene Kim (2015) has found that in states where pay secrecy practices are banned the gender wage gap is lower among highly educated women. In addition, some states have also passed laws requiring salary ranges to be posted in job announcements.[14] However, federal movement has stalled on legislation that would require more pay transparency from employers: reintroduced in Congress, and sponsored by Senator Patty Murray and Representative Rosa DeLauro, the Paycheck Fairness Act of 2023 would, among other provisions, prevent employers from requesting or using previous salary histories for job applicants and guard against retaliation from employers if employees discuss salaries (National Partnership for Women and Families, 2023). While an earlier version of this bill passed the House of Representatives in 2021, currently there's no movement on the bill in the House, and it remains in committee in the Senate. The private for-profit sector can also take action: one straightforward strategy businesses can pursue to achieve pay parity along gender, racial, and ethnic lines is to voluntarily, and regularly, conduct internal pay parity audits and commit to appropriate course corrections.

7.6.2.2. Better Enforcement of Antidiscrimination Laws

It's important that federal, state, and local government agencies charged with enforcing antidiscrimination in various market activities – including the labor market, housing and mortgage markets, and credit markets – have the resources and staff needed to adequately investigate and enforce antidiscrimination laws. These agencies and institutions may be the last, or the only, option Black women have to seek redress when treated in a discriminatory fashion given their race, gender, or both. As this brief has clearly illustrated, Black women are at the very margins of equitable earnings, homeownership, retirement savings, and wealth, and our economy owes it to this group to provide equal protection under the law when necessary.

7.6.2.3. Baby Bonds

A baby bond is an idea conceived and advanced by economists Darrick Hamilton and William Darity Jr. (2010) to specifically address the US racial wealth gap. Under a baby bond program, a child born in the US would have a publicly seeded and managed trust fund established shortly after birth, with access to it available once the child turns 18 years old, and fund use restricted to only asset-building activities such as paying for college, purchasing a home, starting a business, or investing in retirement accounts (Markoff, 2022).[15] Seed amounts would be determined by the applicable jurisdiction, based on either household assets or income, and contributions would vary inversely with household assets or income – babies from households with lower income or assets could receive higher initial seed amounts, and vice versa. The program could have universal, household income or assets, or other qualifying, eligibility.

Jurisdictions can also decide whether publicly funded contributions would be made after the initial contribution, as well as eligibility for additional contributions, frequency, and amounts. Connecticut is the first US state to implement a baby bond program, with eligibility restricted to babies receiving public health insurance and a seed amount of up to $3,200 for each child.[16] Senator Cory Booker and Representative Ayanna Pressley have proposed legislation at the federal level, the American Opportunity Accounts Act, which has universal eligibility, an initial seed amount of $1,000 for each child, and annual federal contributions with amounts dependent on household income – the lower household income is, the higher the annual contribution.[17]

7.6.2.4. Ask for More

Black women's labor power is largely undercompensated by employers, with tangible implications for income and asset-building in the Black community. Given the double gap in wages, Black women should consider requesting higher compensation – at least 10 percent more – than they assume they will receive or than they are told their labor is worth during salary and promotion negotiations. Clearly it is not up to Black women to fix a system designed to work against them, but by regularly and continually practicing #AskforMore we can take our own singular action to attempt to narrow centuries-old income and wealth deficits. The onus is on policymakers and companies to rectify these inequities that have existed since the end of emancipation (and before) in the US, but Black women can scarcely afford to wait another pay period for true leadership to emerge.

7.6.3. Policies, Strategies, and Solutions on the Expenditures Side

7.6.3.1. Childcare Cost Assistance

For individuals and families in the US with children, the expense of childcare can often be budget-busting. President Biden's Build Back Better framework,[18] which failed to gain the required support from Congress in 2021 for all provisions, included one important provision: individuals and families would pay no more than 7 percent of their income on childcare. For Black women with children, this would be a game-changer. While Congress eventually passed subsequent legislation containing provisions related to other parts of Build Back Better under other Acts, such as the American Rescue Plan Act and the Infrastructure Investment and Jobs Act, both signed into law in 2021, the issue of the burdensome cost of childcare was squarely in the current administration's agenda. If reinvigorated movement can happen on capping childcare costs in the future, this could be beneficial in helping Black women with children achieve more savings, and thus wealth. In 2012 scholars Jessica Gordon Nembhard and Kris Marsh noted the importance of affordable childcare for women of color with regard to wealth-building.

7.6.3.2. Public Colleges and Student Loan Forgiveness

A 4-year college degree is increasingly becoming financially out of reach for families hoping to see their children advance economically as adults. During Senator Bernie Sanders' presidential bid in 2020 a signature proposal of his platform was making public colleges tuition-free. Senator Sanders correctly recognized the important role public colleges play in both increasing economic mobility in the US and offering an affordable option for a college education. Free public colleges are not a new idea in the US; this was the case in the late 1700s and early 1800s, and some states offered tuition-free public college until the 1960s. Free public college, along with student loan forgiveness programs, would be particularly beneficial for Black women with regard to leveling costs for this group, who, as noted earlier, have a higher rate of college completion than Black men but also the highest student loan balances of all racial–ethnic–gender groups.

7.6.4. Reparations

In 1989, Representative John Conyers proposed a bill to establish a commission to study and develop proposals for reparations for Black Americans, and Senator Cory Booker introduced a companion bill in the Senate in 2023. But progress on the passage of HR 40, most recently sponsored by Representative Sheila Jackson Lee, has remained stalled in session after session of Congress for the past three decades.[19] Reparations is not an idea specific to Black Americans in the US context: reparations have been accorded to Japanese Americans, Native Americans, and Alaska Natives in the form of money and land (Darity Jr. and Frank, 2003). As LesLeigh Ford and Rekha Balu noted in a 2023 Urban Institute brief, a reparative program, as delineated by a 2005 United Nations Office of High Commissioner for Human Rights resolution, should have additional components along with restitution to the descendants of African slaves for unpaid labor that was violently coerced from men, women, and children taken from the African continent: "compensation for physical and mental harms" done, "acknowledgement of responsibility," a "formal apology," and "guarantees of non-repetition" (Ford and Balu, 2023).

In analyzing restitution alone, estimates of an appropriate aggregate amount for descendants of enslaved Africans in the US range from $1 trillion to $10 trillion (Darity Jr. and Frank, 2003). Proposals for restitution can take various forms, including not only direct monetary compensation to descendants of enslaved Africans in the US but investments in Black communities. These investments can include education, housing, wealth-building strategies, physical and mental healthcare, and knowledge dissemination throughout the country about all aspects of the institution of slavery, its past and present-day impact on the political and socio-economic status of Black people, and its role in building wealth for America on the backs of enslaved Africans (Ford and Balu, 2023). Black women, constituting more than half the Black population in the US, would have legitimate claims to any reparative efforts the US undertakes. They are uniquely positioned to argue, with respect to restitution, that during American slavery Black women's productive capacities and their *reproductive* capacities were exploited.

7.7. Conclusion

Black women are, and have been for centuries, critical actors in the prosperity of the United States. Yet they have the lowest wealth levels compared with White men, White women, and Black men. Black women should not be left behind with regard to their economic security. This brief outlines why and how the status quo should and can be changed, and it details how lower overall wages for Black women compared with non-Latinx White men and women, and the expenditures – including childcare costs and student loan burdens – Black women disparately face compared with other major demographic groups, can further exacerbate the barriers this group encounters in building wealth in the US. It is incumbent upon us all to delay no further in changing the status quo.

8

The Criminal Legal System: Hardening the Racial Divide

8.1. Introduction

As we noted in the "Primer" above, the criminal legal system is the conglomeration of people and institutions – police, prisons, jails, juvenile detention facilities, criminal laws, criminal attorneys, and so forth – involved in managing people engaged in behavior officially prohibited by society. A cornerstone of this system is the set of socially sanctioned punishments. According to the textbook *Criminal Law*, punishments are generally understood to serve one or more of the following five purposes:

(1) Deterrence – punishment imposes severe costs in order to dissuade an individual from committing a crime;
(2) Retribution – punishment serves as a form of revenge;
(3) Restitution – punishment compensates the victim of the crime;
(4) Incapacitation – punishment eliminates the person's ability to commit a crime, as in incarceration; and
(5) Rehabilitation – punishment changes the criminal's behavior by addressing skills deficits and/or health challenges.[1]

The criminal legal system, however, has demonstrably meted out punishments to serve at least one additional function: to support the existing racial hierarchy in US society. American history is replete with examples of how members of the dominant social group have used the criminal legal system to control the behavior of members of less advantaged, subaltern groups and preserve the social advantages that accrue to the dominant group in the existing social hierarchy. Members of the dominant social group do this by deciding *whose* behavior is criminal, *what types* of behavior are criminal, and even *who can be victims* of crime, and then apply punishments through the criminal legal system to restrict the political, social, and economic resources of members of disadvantaged social groups.

This chapter assesses the stratifying function of the criminal legal system and its role in maintaining the US' persistently anti-Black political economic system. In the next section, we first illustrate the stratifying function of the criminal legal system with examples of how the system contributed to developing the social construct "race" as the United States emerged as a nation. We also present data showing how White Americans have deployed the criminal legal system to resist the major civil rights gains by Black Americans during the postbellum period and Reconstruction, producing a severely racialized pattern of criminal punishment. As we shall show, these patterns persist until the Civil Rights Movement of the 1950s to 1970s. Finally, we apply the analytical framework of stratification economics to make sense of the more contemporary phenomenon of mass incarceration – the paroxysm of punishment of Black Americans by the criminal legal system through the first quarter of the twenty-first century.

8.2. The Stratifying Function of the Criminal Legal System: Constructing Race

Throughout US history, the criminal legal system served as a major institutional tool for reifying the social concept of race. Recall our discussion in chapter 2 that reviewed how, for most of US history – from the colonial period starting in the seventeenth century through the Jim Crow era of the mid twentieth century – the legal system assigned rights to individuals based on their racial group membership. In doing so, the legal system assigned political meaning to each racial category. This process enabled individuals of the privileged racial group – White Americans – to use their racial group membership to benefit themselves and exert power and control over others. One of the most profound expressions of this race-based political power is the legal system operating prior to the Civil War that made members of one racial group – Black – nearly synonymous with slave status.[2] By allocating social protections as well as social controls according to individuals' assigned racial group membership, the legal system added meaning to the social category "race." Economist William Spriggs explains: "in America, race has a specific legal definition to explain exactly which set of people do not have the full protection and exercise of their rights" (2020, p. 3).

For example, during the period when slavery operated widely and legally in the emerging US nation, criminal behavior and the attendant criminal punishment that relied on the deprivation of individuals' rights applied primarily to White individuals. This is because White individuals had the political agency required for the criminal legal system to meaningfully deprive them of privileges as punishment. The political system did not afford enslaved people – most of the Black population at the time – meaningful rights. Activist scholar Angela Davis explains: "Thus, the deprivation of white freedom tended to affirm the whiteness of democratic rights and liberties. As white men acquired the privilege to be punished in ways that acknowledged their equality and the racialized universality of liberty, the punishment of black slaves was corporal, concrete, and particular" (2003, p. 362). In other words, the punishment of enslaved Black individuals – with no meaningful liberties or civil rights – was specific to that social group, and depended on physical harm, including torture.

A feature of the way the legal system served as a means of race-based social control is by defining *crimes and criminal behavior* according to the racial group membership of the perpetrator as compared to their victim. For example, during the colonial period, Virginia Slave Codes defined murder as a felony unless it was committed in the process of disciplining an enslaved Black person.[3] As another example, the colonial criminal legal system broadly deemed the rape of an enslaved woman or girl as generally legal. In contrast, the criminal legal system generally recognized the rape of a White woman as a criminal act (unless the person who raped the woman was her husband).[4] Similarly, in the South, up through the mid nineteenth century, the criminal act of kidnapping – abducting and holding an individual captive – existed nearly exclusively as a potential crime against White individuals. Enslaved individuals' children, for example, could legally be taken from their parents without their consent as long as the abductor had legal ownership of the parents and/or children. In other words, the legality of one's behavior depended, in part, on one's racial identity and the racial identity of one's victim.[5]

The Black Codes that operated primarily in the postbellum period between 1865 and 1867 continued the practice of explicitly defining criminal behavior by race, thus the moniker "Black" Codes. Most well known are vagrancy laws that criminalized poverty and unemployment among newly freed Black people. With the 13th amendment's allowance for enslavement as criminal punishment, the Black Codes enabled White Southerners to re-enslave newly emancipated Black Southerners.[6] The Black Codes operated to criminalize freedpeople with stunning success: prior to emancipation, in 1850, the incarceration rate among Black Southerners was less than half the rate among White Southerners (see figure 8.1). In 1870, the incarceration rate among Black Southerners shot up to nearly three times the rate among White Southerners. In other words, the criminal legal system replaced the equivalence of being Black and slave status (with no civil rights) with being Black and criminal (with their civil rights taken away as punishment). Laws that barred Black Americans from serving as jurors or holding positions in law enforcement reinforced these equivalences. In the North, where slavery had been abolished by the early 1800s (though some individuals remained legally enslaved through the 1850s), the racial content of criminal law – the criminality of being Black – was readily apparent.[7] In 1850, Northern Black Americans' incarceration rate exceeded 10 times the rate of their White counterparts.

During Reconstruction – roughly 1865 to 1877 – the upsurge of political power among Black Southerners and their Northern allies succeeded in eliminating Black Codes. However, as we discuss in chapter 4, White Southerners soon regained political dominance and brought the Reconstruction period to an end. White Southerners did this by using violence, and, crucially, by persuading Northern political

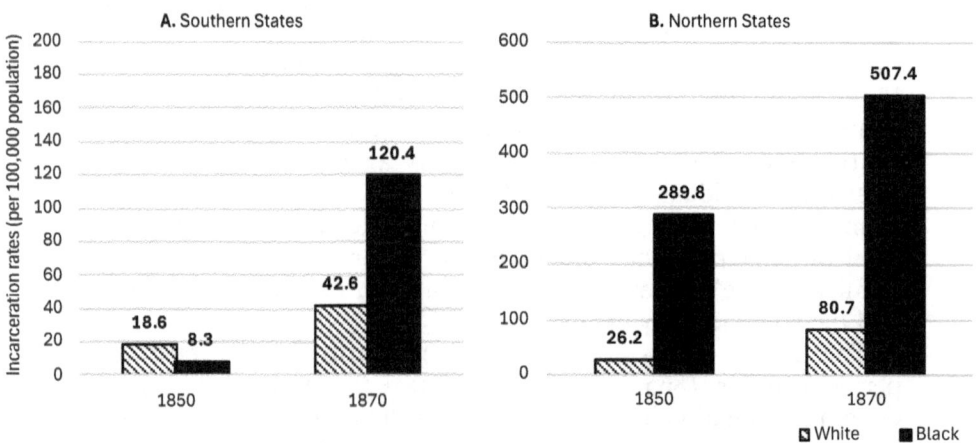

Figure 8.1 Average incarceration rates per 100,000 population by region and race, 1850 and 1870.

Source: Myers and Sabol (1987), table 1: "North–South incarceration rates (average incarceration rates per 100,000)."

leaders to withdraw from the South the federal troops which had been essential in protecting the new legal rights of Black Southerners.

These upheavals in the racial hierarchy provide more examples of how the criminal legal system assigns meaning and political power to racial group membership by what it deems criminal and what it permits. White Americans perpetrated lynchings – the public execution of a person without the due process of law – on Black Americans with increasing frequency during the 1880s.[8] The criminal legal system effectively sanctioned the commission of these murders by White Americans by failing to respond with meaningful legal punishments for the assailants. In 1900, US Representative George H. White, the single Black Congressperson at the time, proposed an anti-lynching bill in response to the failure of local and state public authorities to criminalize acts of terror, murder, and assault by White Americans on Black Americans. The bill, HR 6963, intended to make lynching a federal crime:

> Be it enacted by the Senate and House of Representatives of the United States of America in Congress assembled,
>
> That all persons born or naturalized in the United States, and subject to the jurisdiction thereof, and being citizens of the United States, are entitled to and shall receive protection in their lives from being murdered, tortured, burned to death by any and all organized mobs commonly known as "lynching bees," whether said mob be spontaneously assembled or organized by premeditation for the purpose of taking the life or lives of any citizen or citizens in the United States aforesaid; and that whenever any citizen or citizens of the United States shall be murdered by mob violence in the manner hereinabove described, all parties participating, aiding, and abetting in such murder and lynching shall be guilty of treason against the Government of the United States, and shall be tried for that offense in the United States courts; full power and jurisdiction being given to said United States courts and all its officers to issue process, arrest, try, and in all respects deal with such cases in the same manner now prescribed under existing laws for the trial of felonies in the United States courts.[9]

During the period between World Wars I and II, White vigilantes inflicted an eruption of mob violence on Black communities. Such a conflagration of acts occurred in the summer of 1919 that historians often refer to this period as the "Red Summer." US Representative White's anti-lynching bill languished in the US Congress for more than 100 years. In the spring of 2022, a revised version, HR 55 ("The Emmett Till Antilynching Act"), was signed into law.[10]

In other words, public sanctions through the action or inaction of the criminal legal system operate to define what is, and is not, considered criminal. Over US history, these definitions have caused Americans to think about, and understand, crime and criminal behavior along racial lines. Consider this 2023 exchange between stratification economist Darity Jr. and an attendee to Darity's delivery of the Gamble Lecture, "Does Everyone Lose from Racism?: Insights from Stratification Economics" at the University of Massachusetts Amherst.[11] The attendee asked the question, "Are there any trends within the Black community such as higher crime rates or high illegitimacy rates that could explain their position vis a vis Whites ...?" Darity Jr.'s response illustrates how effectively the US criminal legal system has racialized "crime" and "criminal behavior":

> I guess it depends on what kind of crime you have in mind? If we think about which community in the United States has the highest degree of history of violence that's unquestionably White Americans – unquestionably – I mean, I'm not sure if you're aware of the 100 massacres that were conducted between the end of the Civil War and World War II that were directed against Black communities throughout the United States in which thousands of Blacks were killed and the White terrorists appropriated Black-owned property. So there's no segment of the [US] population that has a greater history of violence than White Americans.

The attendee's question and Darity Jr.'s response demonstrate the criminal legal system's role in defining "crime" and "criminality." By sanctioning massacres (murder and assault) and appropriations (theft and robbery) of Black communities by White Americans, such acts are excepted from the popular notion of crime and criminality.

The criminal legal system also explicitly controlled the behavior of individuals based on their race through Jim Crow laws that began in the North during the mid nineteenth century and spread to the South.[12] These Jim Crow laws used the criminal legal system to clearly define the racial hierarchy and persisted through the mid twentieth century – until the passage of the Civil Rights Act of 1964. These laws dictated individuals' access to physical spaces such as theaters and pools, resources such as schools and hospitals, and intimate matters such as who one could marry. Criminal punishment for infractions by

Black Americans served as a direct means for limiting their political power: through disenfranchisement. Consider the advice provided by a pamphlet published in 1900 titled *What a Colored Man Should Do to Vote: To the Colored Men of Voting Age in the Southern States*. For potential Black voters in 13 Southern states, the pamphlet offers this general rule, "A man convicted of almost any crime may be barred from voting."[13]

We can also observe the stratifying function of the criminal legal system through the racialized pattern in criminal punishment (see figures 8.2 and 8.3). The trend data originally published by Myers and Sabol (1987) show a striking correspondence between the racial profile of who was held by the carceral system and which racial group sat at the bottom of the social hierarchy from the mid nineteenth century to at least 1980. From 1850 to 1980, the incarceration rate of Black Americans was at least 5 times that of White Americans in the North, and usually at least 7 times. In the South, the ratio of the Black to White incarceration rates peaked in 1910, at nearly 6:1, and then hovered between 3:1 and 4:1 through to 1980.

In the next section, we connect the US' contemporary carceral system to this historical context.

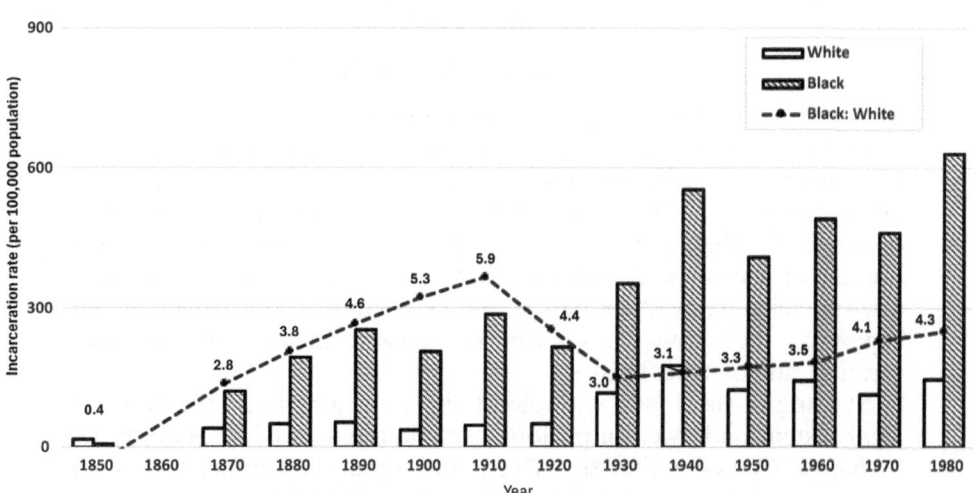

Figure 8.2 Trends in average incarceration rates per 100,000 population in Southern states by race, 1850–1980.

Source: Myers and Sabol (1987), table 1: "North–South incarceration rates (average incarceration rates per 100,000)."

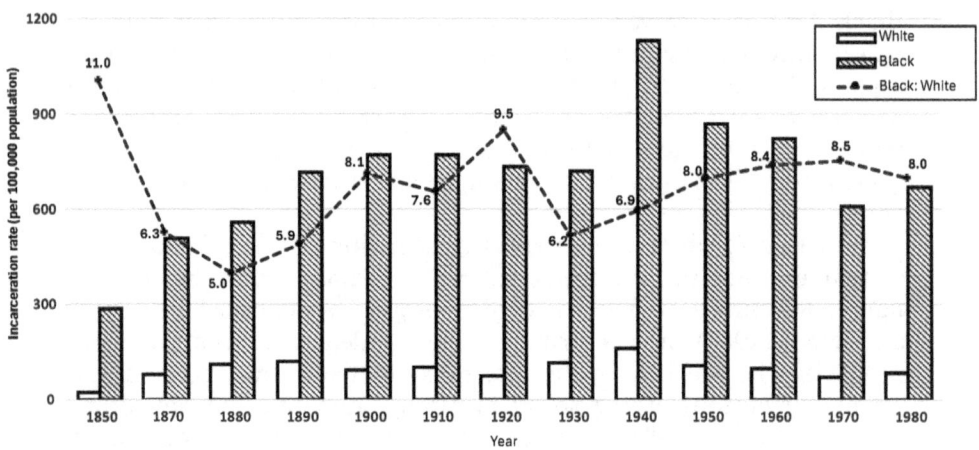

Figure 8.3 Trends in average incarceration rates per 100,000 population in Northern states by race, 1850–1980.
Source: Myers and Sabol (1987), table 1: "North–South incarceration rates (average incarceration rates per 100,000)."

8.3. The Stratifying Function of the Criminal Legal System: Mass Incarceration

8.3.1. Looking at the Numbers

The next set of figures extend Myers and Sabol's data into contemporary times. Specifically, figure 8.4 shows the total incarceration rate (the number of incarcerated per 100,000 members of the working age population) from 1970 to 2022, for prisons (panel A) and for jails (panel B).[14] What is immediately apparent from these figures is that the size of the carceral state relative to the US population underwent a seismic change over this period. Below, we discuss the drivers of this expansion. For now, we describe the massive increase in the incarceration rate of recent years.

Starting in the 1980s, the role of the carceral arm of the criminal legal system underwent a profound qualitative – not just quantitative – change. Consider that the Myers and Sabol data indicate that for the century prior (1880 to 1980), the prison and jail incarceration rate combined hovered between 100 and 300 per 100,000. Then, over the next *quarter*-century, the incarceration rate rose to nearly 1,200 per 100,000 in 2005 – indicating an increase to an order of magnitude higher. In fact, the incarceration rates break away from a pattern of

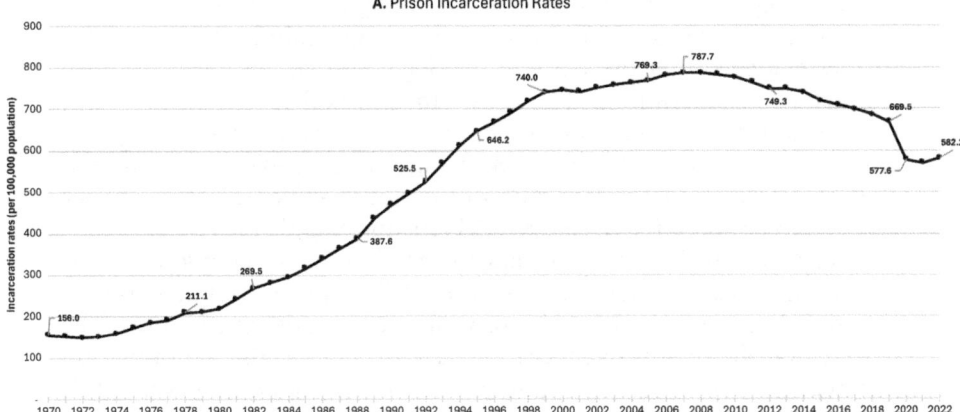

Figure 8.4A Trends in prison incarceration rates, 1970–2022.
Data source: Prison incarceration rates per 100,000 members of the US working age population. Prison population counts estimated using United States Bureau of Justice Statistics, *National Prisoner Statistics*, 1978–2022, distributed by the Inter-university Consortium for Political and Social Research (ICPSR). Prison population counts for years 1970–7 were extracted from US Department of Justice Bureau of Justice Statistics Bulletin *State and Federal Prisoners, 1925–85*, table 1. Population estimates for residents age 15 to 64 produced by the US Census intercensal population estimates.

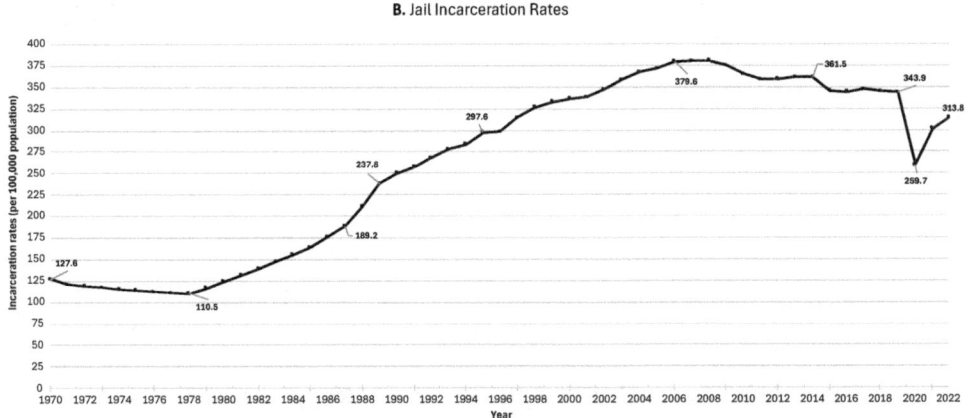

Figure 8.4B Trends in jail incarceration rates, 1970–2022.
Data source: Jail incarceration rates per 100,000 members of the US working age population, 1970–2022. Jail population counts extracted from historical incarceration trends data compiled by the Vera Institute of Criminal Justice Incarceration Trends Project. Population estimates for residents age 15 to 64 produced by the US Census intercensal population estimates.

rising during economic downturns and falling during economic expansions over the 1890–1980 period (Myers and Sabol, 1987, p. 189), further evidence that the US criminal legal system has entered a new chapter in its operations. The only other period in US history that witnessed a similar qualitative change in incarceration is during the country's transition away from enslaving Black people. From 1850 to 1930, the total incarceration rate in the South increased from 15 per 100,000 to about 170 per 100,000 (Myers and Sabol, 1987).

Except for during the slave era in the South, the people confined within the carceral system have been severely disproportionately Black. Figure 8.5 presents data analogous to figure 8.4, this time by race. The closest that the prison incarceration rate among the Black population has been to parity with that among the White population is in 2022,

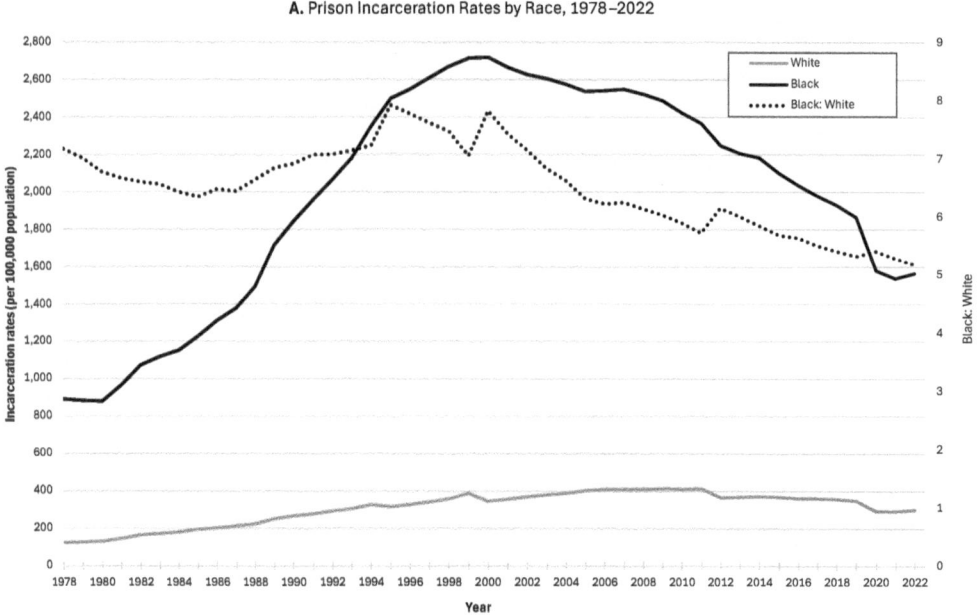

Figure 8.5A Trends in prison incarceration rates by race, 1978–2022.
Data source: Prison incarceration rates per 100,000 members of the US working age population. Prison population counts estimated using United States Bureau of Justice Statistics, *National Prisoner Statistics*, 1978–2022, distributed by the Inter-university Consortium for Political and Social Research (ICPSR). Population estimates for residents age 15 to 64 produced by the US Census intercensal population estimates and Bridged-Race Population Estimates produced by the US Census Bureau in collaboration with the National Center for Health Statistics (NCHS).

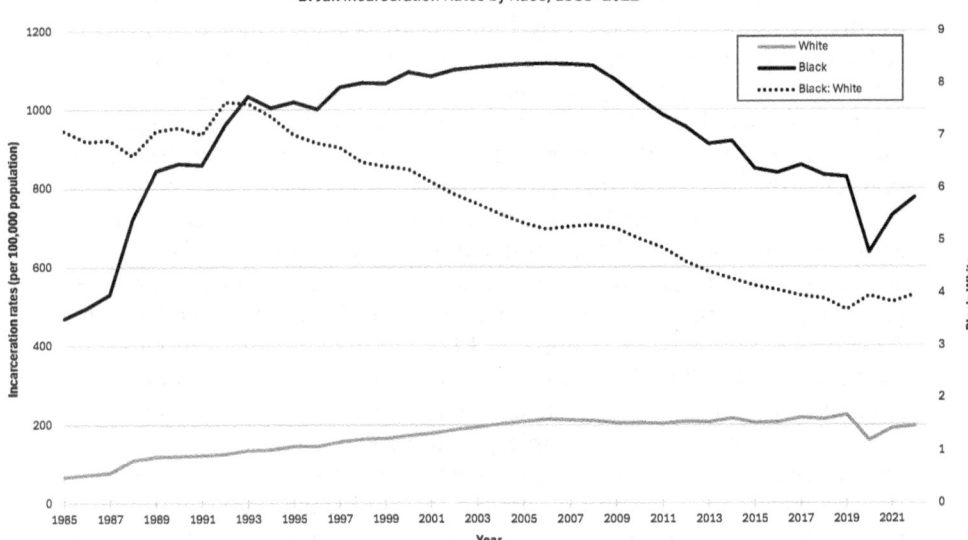

Figure 8.5B Trends in jail incarceration rates by race, 1985–2022.
Data source: Jail incarceration rates per 100,000 members of the US working age population, 1985–2022; historical incarceration trends data compiled by the Vera Institute of Criminal Justice Incarceration Trends Project. Population estimates for residents age 15 to 64 produced by the US Census intercensal population estimates and Bridged-Race Population Estimates produced by the US Census Bureau in collaboration with the National Center for Health Statistics (NCHS).

when the Black incarceration rate stood at five times the White incarceration rate. Among the jailed population, the analogous figure was just under four times in 2019.

These two developments together – the historically unprecedented size of the carceral system combined with its exceptionally disproportionate punishment of Black Americans – has produced an effect on Black communities that is remarkable in scope. For example, according to 2010 US Census data, 1 in 10 Black men between the ages of 20 and 49 resided in an institution. For this age group, the large majority of those living in an institutional setting are incarcerated. The analogous figure for White men is 1 in 50.

In addition to the punishment of confinement, incarceration also subjects inmates in most states to forced labor. As we discussed earlier, the 13th amendment excludes protection for incarcerated people from slavery and involuntary servitude. This carve-out permitted the development of the convict lease systems in the South and contract systems in the North during the late 1800s to the early 1900s. Both systems enabled employers to use convicted people as laborers under slavery-like working conditions. The US labor movement – predominantly made up of White workers at the time – curtailed these systems during the 1890s, and then again in the 1930s, to protect its members from having to compete in the labor market with, effectively, enslaved workers.[15]

Since then, laws regulating prison labor have largely limited it to activities involved in the maintenance of correctional facilities, or activities that produce goods or services for the federal, state, or local governments.[16] According to a 2022 research report produced by the American Civil Liberties Union (ACLU) and the University of Chicago Law School's Global Human Rights Clinic (GHRC), approximately 80 percent of prisoners across state and federal prisons worked to maintain correctional facilities – for example, providing janitorial, kitchen, laundry, and grounds maintenance services.[17] Prison workers are, as a general rule, paid negligible wages, if at all. Among these jobs, the average minimum hourly wage is 13 cents; the average maximum hourly wage is 52 cents.[18] In other words, prisons rely significantly on forced labor for their operation.[19]

Imprisonment is the most visible effect of the criminal legal system. However, felony convictions – whether one is or is not incarcerated – have, on their own, significant social and political effects, curtailing one's civil rights in a range of ways. In most states, ex-felons are barred from certain types of employment, such as occupations that require professional licenses. According to Myers:

> In Texas, for example, convicted felons cannot be employed in work with children (childcare, education), with the elderly (home care) and cannot hold licenses as locksmiths, barbers, electricians or pharmacists. In Minnesota, convicted felons cannot be employed as mortgage originators, insurance agents, nursing or home care assistants, audiologists, physical therapists, dentists or veterinarians. (2017, p. 119)

Ex-felons are also barred access to other critical economic resources, including major social safety-net programs such as federally funded health benefits and educational assistance (Roberts, 2004, p. 1291). We quote legal scholar Michelle Alexander (2012) at length here:

> Once a person is labeled a felon, he or she is ushered into a parallel universe in which discrimination, stigma, and exclusion are perfectly legal, and privileges of citizenship such as voting

and jury service are off-limits. It does not matter whether you have actually spent time in prison; your second-class citizenship begins the moment you are branded a felon. Most people branded felons, in fact, are not sentenced to prison. As of 2008, there were approximately 2.3 million people in prisons and jails, and a staggering 5.1 million people under "community correctional supervision" – i.e., on probation or parole. Merely reducing prison terms does not have a major impact on the majority of people in the system. It is the badge of inferiority – the felony record – that relegates people for their entire lives, to second class status … [F]or drug felons, there is little hope of escape. Barred from public housing by law, discriminated against by private landlords, ineligible for food stamps [i.e., SNAP benefits], forced to "check the box" indicating a felony conviction on employment applications for nearly every job, and denied licenses for a wide range of professions, people whose only crime is drug addiction or possession of a small amount of drugs for recreational use find themselves locked out of the mainstream society and economy – permanently. (p. 94)

A felony conviction, regardless of incarceration status, eliminates an especially important political resource: the franchise. Only 2 states have never curtailed the voting rights of felons (Maine and Vermont). As of December 2023, 23 states deny those who have been convicted of a felony the right to vote while incarcerated. Fourteen other states suspend voting rights of felons until after the completion of their incarceration, parole, and/or probation. The remaining 11 states revoke the right to vote for those convicted of a felony for a period of time after completing their sentence.[20] Some of these 11 states revoke voting rights indefinitely for some crimes, and some require additional action to restore one's voting rights (e.g., a governor's pardon, an approved application for restoration, payment of fines).[21]

Figure 8.6 provides the figures for this proximate population – those ever convicted of a felony, including but not limited to those who are incarcerated. By 2001, the criminal legal system curtailed the civil rights of more than 1 in 3 Black men. The emergence of mass incarceration also distorts political power another way: through *prison gerrymandering* (see textbox "What Is Prison Gerrymandering?" below). Prison gerrymandering exacerbates the imbalance of political power related to the massive, and massively uneven, imposition of felony convictions. Considered in this way, we can see how mass incarceration – and the criminal legal system more generally – has significantly weakened the political power of members of the Black community.

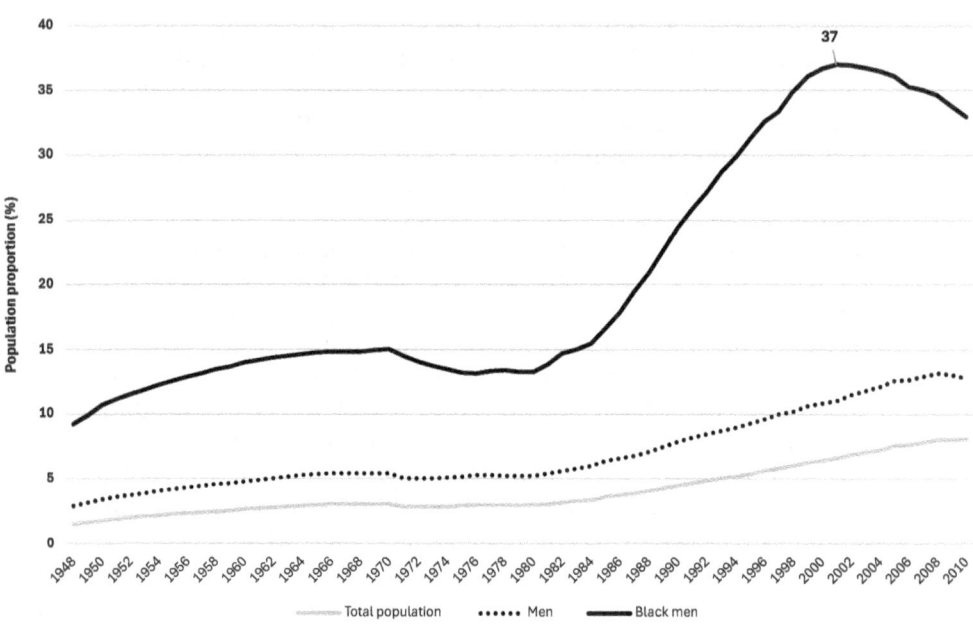

Figure 8.6 Trends in the proportion of voting-age population with a felony conviction, 1948–2010.

Source: Shannon et al. (2017), "The growth, scope and spatial distribution of people with felony records in the United States, 1948–2010," Online Resources 2, Duke University Press.

What Is Prison Gerrymandering?

Prison gerrymandering refers to the practice by which political representation in a state legislative district is distorted by the inclusion of incarcerated people in the region's prisons and jails in census population counts. The practice impacts the drawing of district lines within states while also redirecting power away from urban areas with racially diverse populations and toward rural areas with higher proportions of White residents.

How Voting Districts Are Drawn
Prison gerrymandering is both the result of federal policy and a problem created by the United States Census Bureau's practice of counting incarcerated people "as residents of *prison cells*"

rather than residents of "their *home communities*" (Kajstura, 2023). Every 10 years, state legislators redraw voting districts based on the results of the census. When states use these census counts to draw legislative districts, political representation is distorted; more representation and political voice is unfairly allocated to people who live nearest to prisons at the expense of people living in the communities prisoners call home. And because incarcerated people cannot vote in most states, this practice builds political power on their disenfranchisement and incapacitation.

Impact
The rural House District 8 of eastern Texas, for instance, would not even be considered a political district if it did not include incarcerated persons in its district population count. Given that the majority of inmates in District 8's prisons come from the urban centers of Harris County and Dallas County (home to the cities of Houston and Dallas, respectively), counting incarcerated people at home would allocate an additional House seat to each of these Democrat-leaning districts (Kajstura, 2023).

Prison gerrymandering further distorts political representations by race, compounding the political disenfranchisement racially marginalized communities already experience as a result of partisan gerrymandering (Mansoor and Carlisle, 2021). The underrepresentation of these populations affects whole communities within districts with high rates of incarceration, since it results in a transfer of political power from majority Black and Brown urban communities to predominantly White rural communities (Mansoor and Carlisle, 2021). This overrepresentation in rural communities amasses political power through the disproportionate incarceration of Black and Brown people in US prisons. A study by sociologists at Villanova University estimates that 264,000 people in Pennsylvania – including 100,000 Black residents of Philadelphia – are underrepresented because they live in districts with high incarceration rates, resulting in the overrepresentation of those living in the often rural districts that house state and county prison and jail facilities (Remster and Kramer, 2018).

Current Situation
In the 2010 census, more than 2 million people were counted in the district where they were imprisoned rather than their home

district as a result of the census' default practice. In anticipation for the 2020 redistricting process, advocates worked to urge legislators across the country to change the way they count prisons in the upcoming cycle, as districts drawn on this basis will determine political representation for the next decade (Kajstura, 2023). According to a report from the National Conference of State Legislatures (NCSL), 13 states instituted reallocation policies to adjust census redistricting data after the 2020 census in order to count incarcerated people in their home districts (Williams, 2023).

Proposed Solution
According to prison policy advocates, the most effective and efficient way to address the issue of prison gerrymandering is at the federal level, requiring the US Census Bureau to count an incarcerated person within the district of their last known residence. Another proposed solution is to allow incarcerated people to vote, including in the election of district representatives where they are currently being counted as "ghost constituents," i.e., in the district where they are imprisoned (Wood, 2014).

Written by Daniella Medina

8.3.2. The Gendered Impact of Mass Incarceration

This discussion has so far focused on the Black–White disparities in incarceration. Here we add two dimensions to the discussion: (1) racial disparities in the incarceration rates among women; and (2) racial differences in family- and community-level impacts.

First, we consider the quantitative differences by race and gender of incarceration. Men, by far, encounter the carceral state at higher rates than women, regardless of race (see figure 8.7). Panel A of figure 8.8 shows the incarceration rates among Black, Latinx, and Indigenous men and women from 1990 to 2022.[22] Panel B of figure 8.8 shows the same figures for White and Asian American and Pacific Islander (AAPI) men and women (these two groups in panel B are separated out to make all the trend lines visible). For all five racial groups, the gender division is clear. We can also see from figure 8.8 that the racial differences in incarceration rates we observed

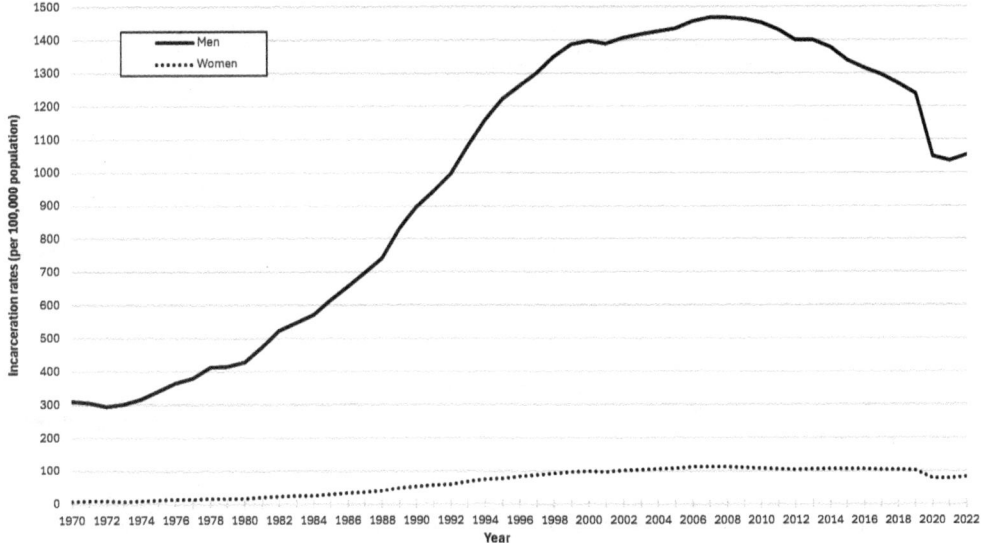

Figure 8.7 Trends in prison incarceration rates by gender, 1970–2022.
Data source: Prison incarceration rates per 100,000 members of the US working age population. Prison population counts estimated using United States Bureau of Justice Statistics, *National Prisoner Statistics*, 1970–2022, distributed by the Inter-university Consortium for Political and Social Research (ICPSR). US working age population counts for residents age 15 to 64 are US Census intercensal population estimates.

between Black and White men are echoed among Black and White women. In 1999, the prison incarceration rate among Black women peaked at 328 per 100,000. This rate is nearly six times the rate among White women (56 per 100,000). These figures demonstrate how one's racial and ethnic group membership is a significant determinant of whether an individual is vulnerable to incarceration for both men and women.

Second, we consider some of the racial differences in the consequences of mass incarceration that result through a different channel: through families, households, and communities. For example, given the gendered role of parenting, the higher incarceration rate of Black women relative to White women means that the effects of incarceration will be experienced by more Black mothers and the children in their custody as compared to White mothers and the children in their custody. Parents can lose their parental rights as a consequence of their incarceration, as well as access to important social safety nets (as

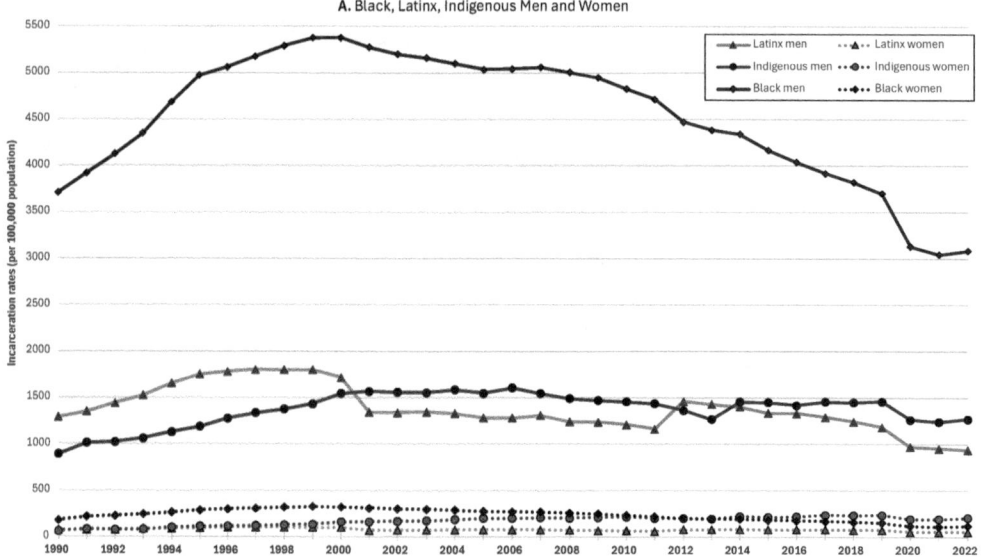

Figure 8.8 Trends in prison incarceration rates by gender and race/ethnicity, 1990–2022.

Data source: Prison incarceration rates per 100,000 members of the US working age population. Prison population counts estimated using United States Bureau of Justice Statistics, *National Prisoner Statistics*, 1990–2022, distributed by the Inter-university Consortium for Political and Social Research (ICPSR). Population estimates for residents age 15 to 64 produced by the US Census intercensal population estimates and Bridged-Race Population Estimates produced by the US Census Bureau in collaboration with the National Center for Health Statistics (NCHS).

noted above) which they may need to support their children (Cox and Wallace, 2016, p. 1064). According to a report by the Bureau of Justice Statistics, in 1999 when mass incarceration was near, but not yet at, its peak, "a majority of state and federal prisoners reported having a child under age eighteen, and almost half lived with their children prior to incarceration." The racial disparity of this impact on children is remarkable: "Seven percent of black children had a parent in prison in 1999, making them nearly 9 times more likely to have an incarcerated parent than white children."[23]

Craigie (2021) examines the impact on the labor market outcomes of women whose *partners* are incarcerated. Across racial groups, these women's weekly earnings are lower than women without incarcerated partners, and their unemployment rates are higher. Craigie provides, as a rough estimate, that having an incarcerated partner reduces a woman's

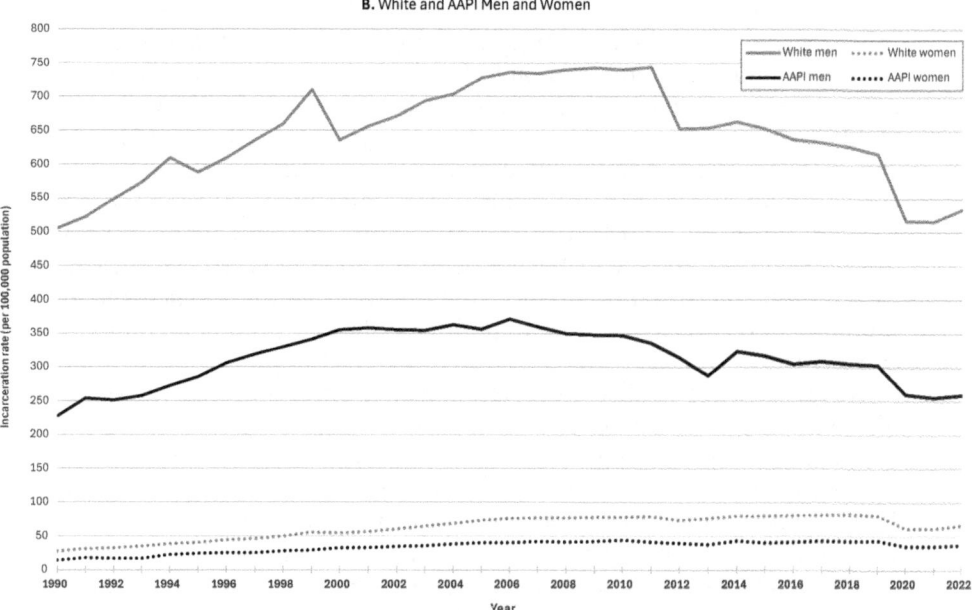

Figure 8.8 (*continued*) Trends in prison incarceration rates by gender and race/ethnicity, 1990–2022.

Data source: Prison incarceration rates per 100,000 members of the US working age population. Prison population counts estimated using United States Bureau of Justice Statistics, *National Prisoner Statistics*, 1990–2022, distributed by the Inter-university Consortium for Political and Social Research (ICPSR). Population estimates for residents age 15 to 64 produced by the US Census intercensal population estimates and Bridged-Race Population Estimates produced by the US Census Bureau in collaboration with the National Center for Health Statistics (NCHS).

annual earnings (in 2010 dollars) by $1,458. Craigie's estimates also indicate a greater negative impact of having an incarcerated partner on earnings for Black women compared to White women. Again, as a rough estimate, this impact is 50 percent greater for Black women – or a loss of $2,187 in annual earnings for Black women.

What underlies this quantitative difference in the impact of incarceration? Qualitative differences between the consequences of mass incarceration for Black and White households and communities can help explain this disparity.

One dimension of the qualitatively different impact of mass incarceration on Black women relative to White women is how the highly racially skewed rates of incarceration among Black men specifically reduce the available number of marriageable Black men (defined as unmarried men in the labor force or in school). Because of the relative infrequency of interracial marriages, particularly among Black women, the lower number of marriageable Black men relative to the number of unmarried Black women reduces heterosexual Black women's ability to form two-parent households (Craigie, Myers Jr., and Darity Jr., 2018; Ruggles, 2022). This pattern has specific consequences for the ability of Black women to form economically secure families. As Craigie, Myers Jr., and Darity Jr. (2018) note, "poverty tends to be a distinctive characteristic of female-headed households" (p. 231). Take, for example, the situation in 2022: the poverty rate for female-headed families (23.0 percent) is more than double the rate among all families (8.8 percent).[24]

Ruggles (2022) confirms this relationship, observing that the more disadvantaged economic circumstances of Black men, relative to White men, including higher incarceration rates, "are sufficiently large to account for most of the disproportionately low marriage rates of Black men in all but the most recent period" (p. 10). He also observes that, due to the falling prevalence of "male breadwinner households" as a modal household across all households, including White ones, the explanatory power of the economic status of Black (or White) men in explaining men's marriageability rates has been diminishing since the turn of the twenty-first century. At the same time, even in the most recent period of 2017–19, the factors associated with economic status (income, occupation, and employment/institutionalization) account for 44 percent of the racial difference in marriage rates (Ruggles, 2022, table 5, p. 20).

Legal scholar Dorothy Roberts (2004) argues for the importance of researching the impact of mass incarceration at the community level because of the phenomenon's scale and geographic concentration. Roberts provides the following metrics from research that demonstrate how "the exit and reentry of inmates is geographically concentrated in the poorest, minority neighborhoods" (p. 1276). This research finds, for example, "As many as 1 in 8 of the adult male residents of these urban areas is sent to prison each year, and 1 in 4 is behind bars on any given day."[25] As another example, Roberts cites the findings of an Urban Institute study (La Vigne et al., 2003) that looks at the situation in Illinois, near the peak of mass incarceration in 2001. This study finds that, "In Illinois, releasees are not only most highly concentrated in Chicago, the largest metropolitan area within the state, but they are even more concentrated within a few communities in the Chicago area. Just 6 of 77 Chicago communities – Austin, Humboldt Park, North Lawndale, Englewood, West Englewood, and East Garfield Park

– account for 34 percent of prisoners returning to Chicago" (Roberts, 2004, p. 1276; La Vigne et al., 2003, p. 51).[26] As another example to make her case, Roberts highlights the research of public health scholar Ernest Drucker:[27]

> How can researchers measure the impact of mass incarceration on these communities? Ernest Drucker approached this problem with a quantitative public health method – "years of life lost" – commonly used to measure the population impact of large-scale adverse events that affect entire populations. He treated person-years of incarceration as years of life "lost" to estimate the magnitude of impact associated with mass imprisonment in New York State during the period from 1973 to 2002. Drucker concluded, "[T]hirty years of forced removal to prison of 150,000 young males from particular communities of New York represents collective losses similar in scale to the losses due to epidemics, wars, and terrorist attacks – with the potential for comparable effects on the survivors and the social structure of their families and communities." (2004, p. 1277)

Sociologist Youngmin Yi (2023) demonstrates that comparisons of incarceration rates by race alone inadequately measure racial disparities in incarceration. Yi does this by pointing to the significant racial differences in the rate of incarcerated household and extended family members. Yi finds that "Black adults in the United States are not only more likely to have experienced family incarceration but are more likely to have had more family members incarcerated ... and to have had family members from more generations ever incarcerated" (p. 1). This reflects how race operates as a central social organizing force across all domains, including in the formation of families. Because most Black men and women and White men and women tend to form intra-racial, heterosexual households, the impact of the higher incarceration rates among Black men and women is concentrated within Black men and Black women's *households*. Moreover, the impact of mass incarceration is concentrated within Black neighborhoods and has been operating over multiple decades. Therefore, the incidence of incarceration is more extensive across Black men and women's family networks. This is particularly consequential for Black households as compared to White households since Black households are more likely to receive and offer support to extended family members.[28] Yi finds, "White respondents report having 0.75 immediate and 1.17 extended family members ever incarcerated, while those numbers are more than twice as high among those who are Black (2.11 immediate, and 3.29 extended family members)" (p. 26).

Mass incarceration can also have a qualitatively different impact on Black women, relative to White women, through another channel: unpaid collective work. Economist Nina Banks (2020) introduced the idea that "community" should be treated as a major site of production in the economy – that is, a social arena in which goods and services that members of a community rely on and benefit from are produced. Economics has typically focused on businesses and government as sites of production, a focus that reflects the dominance of men in the economics discipline.[29] Theories developed within feminist economics – a subfield of economics historically dominated by White women – added the household as a site of production to better reflect the economic concerns and activities of women.[30] These feminist theories, however, tend to omit a significant set of economic matters specific to racialized women, including Black women. Banks explains:

> White women's identity as women ... is generally not shaped by racial injustices and so they have developed feminist theories of women's unpaid work that are more attuned to the lived experiences of White women rather than the unpaid work of racialized women. White women's experiences with gender oppression within their homes have shaped their political consciousness about gender oppression and this has led them to develop theories of women's oppression that emphasize private sphere issues between men and women ... Racialized women's membership in racially oppressed communities, however, both shapes their identities as women and provides them with a sense of shared responsibility to a community that exists beyond the private household sphere. (2020, p. 344)

To address this omission, Banks makes the case for treating the community as an equally important social arena in which economic activities take place. For racialized women, the feminized role of caretaker combines with the specific caretaking needs of the oppressed social group of which they are members: protection against racism and advocacy for racial equality. Banks points to the "nonmarket collective work [of Black women] to improve the welfare of community members and address community needs not met by the public and private sectors" (2020, p. 343) as a primary example of this type of economic activity. As members of a community experiencing exceptional levels of incarceration, Black women experience additional stress through their role as provider of nonmarket collective work, that is, their community-organizing work.

Consider again the statistics we discussed above regarding the high degree of concentration of incarcerated individuals within low-income neighborhoods with high concentrations of Black residents – neighborhoods that can be described as urban ghettos. These include neighborhoods in cities such as New York and Chicago. In such cities, largely Black residents who suffered under ghetto conditions during the 1960s had been able to organize collective actions of political protest. The regime of mass incarceration directly obstructs such political organizing. Roberts (2004) makes this observation: "One of [mass incarceration's] most pernicious features is its destruction of community-based resources for contesting prison policy and other systemic forms of disenfranchisement." Roberts contrasts features of mass imprisonment with one of the social advantages that sociologist Loïc Wacquant attributed to living in a segregated, Black neighborhood: "Unlike the black urban ghetto, 'which enabled African Americans to fully develop their own social and symbolic forms and thereby accumulate the group capacities needed to escalate the fight against continued caste subordination,' prisons break down social networks and norms needed for political solidarity and activism" (2004, p. 1300).[31]

The political interests of Black men and Black women overlap because of these common experiences with mass incarceration – in both quantitative and qualitative terms. This contrasts with the differing experiences with mass incarceration – especially what we have referred to as qualitative differences – between White women and Black women. As is the case with other areas of racial inequality, these differences create overlapping political interests between Black men and Black women, and a strong basis for inter-gender, intra-racial political coalitions, and weaken the potential for interracial, intra-gender political alliances.

Next, we use the stratification economics framework to explain how the US' contemporary carceral system emerged.

8.3.3. Racial Threat Theory

What explains the extensive and intensely anti-Black practices of the contemporary US criminal legal system? The sociological *racial threat* theory provides a framework for a coherent explanation of mass incarceration that is consistent with stratification economics.[32] The racial threat perspective theorizes that a dominant racial group will use the criminal legal system as an instrument for social control over a subaltern group if the dominant racial group perceives a racial threat, that is, a perceived challenge to their advantageous position in the racial hierarchy.

The stratification economics analytical framework similarly links the dominant racial group's use of the criminal legal system to the dominant group's desire to hoard economic, political, and social resources from competing groups. Likewise, subaltern groups work to resist, reform, or abolish channels of social control within the criminal legal system to improve their position in the social hierarchy. Therefore, stratification economics and racial threat theory explain racial discrimination in the criminal legal system to be the product of rational, self-interested behavior that, in turn, helps explain its persistence. That is, racial discrimination in the criminal legal system has an instrumental purpose: it serves as a means for the dominant racial group to socially control a subaltern group and reduce the subaltern group's ability to compete for social, political, and economic resources. As Mason et al. explain:

> The racial threat perspective examines the empirical consequences for criminal justice and policing policies when competing racial groups have unequal political economic power. *A fundamental assumption of this approach is that the racial group with greater political economic power uses that power to exercise social control over subordinate racial groups. Hence, racial discrimination within the racial threat perspective has an instrumental objective – social control – and thereby is not necessarily the result of incorrect or insufficient information (prejudice, statistical discrimination) or irrational negative feelings (bigotry, tastes).* From this perspective, the criminal legal system operates to protect the power and privilege of a political economic elite relative to subordinate groups and a dominant racial elite (Whites) relative to subaltern groups, in particular non-White racial and ethnic minorities. (emphasis added; 2022, p. 507)

Mason et al. (2022) outline three hypotheses of the racial threat perspective that can be tested empirically. The first hypothesis is the "Percent minority effect" which proposes that "An economic or racial elite's average assessment of racial threat increases with the fraction of Non-White racial and ethnic minorities within the relevant geographic area but decreases with the extent of segregation of Non-White racial and ethnic minorities." The second hypothesis is the "Demand for crime control" which says that, as the economic or racial elite's average assessment of racial threat increases, the demand for crime control will increase. The third hypothesis, the "Law enforcement response," posits that as demands for crime control rise by the economic and racial elite, law enforcement activity increases. Mason (2023) links the hypotheses together: "Bringing these three observations together, there is an increase in the size of the police force, greater expenditures on policing activities, and greater arrest and imprisonment of racial and ethnic minorities as the percent of minority increases within a particular location" (p. 314).

To assess the explanatory value of the racial threat perspective, researchers look for empirical evidence of the dominant racial group using the criminal legal system to protect its position in the social hierarchy. Economist Ellora Derenoncourt's 2022 economic study of the long-term effects of the Great Migration – one of the most dramatic geographical shifts in racial composition in US history – provides such empirical evidence. Although Derenoncourt's study does not refer to the racial threat theory, the study's findings draw out crucial links in the empirical data supportive of a racial threat perspective, including evidence of how White Americans used the criminal legal system to fortify their dominance in the existing racial hierarchy.

The Great Migration occurred, broadly speaking, in two waves. From 1910 to 1940, roughly 2 million Southern Black Americans migrated primarily to Northern and Midwestern cities such as Detroit, Chicago, Pittsburgh, and New York. Then from 1940 to 1970, another roughly 4 million Southern Black Americans migrated north and even farther west, including to Oakland, California; Los Angeles; and Portland, Oregon.[33] So massive was this Great Migration that, by 1970, only half of Black Americans lived in the South, compared to 90 percent in 1910.[34]

Derenoncourt's study analyzes how the second wave of the Great Migration impacted the racial climate in the receiving Northern areas, and whether these changing dynamics ultimately impacted the economic success of Black migrant families from 1970 to 2015. Derenoncourt documents a rise in racial hostilities among White residents in the receiving Northern communities toward the entering Black Southern migrants.[35] Compared to areas with relatively small influxes of Black migrants, the areas with relatively large influxes exhibited greater support for racial segregationist presidential candidate George Wallace, experienced race riots of greater intensity in terms of duration and extent of injuries and arrests, and racially segregated their neighborhoods and schools more. In other words, Derenoncourt finds that the increasing share of Black residents in an area can be linked to negative reactions (evidence of racial animus) among the White residents in the areas – evidence of the "Percent minority effect."

The study also finds that the communities with relatively large influxes of Black migrants increased government spending on their police forces more than other communities, rather than other typical government functions, such as schooling, healthcare, sanitation, fire, and recreation (Derenoncourt, 2022, p. 402). In other words, Derenoncourt observes that the Northern communities that experienced the largest changes in racial composition were the same areas that experienced greater levels of racial conflict and greater increases in spending on police. Derenoncourt notes the important contextual feature that "Black residents [in the North] largely lived in cities with all-White governments and interacted with all-White police forces" (2022, p. 401). These responses are consistent with the "Demand for crime control" hypothesis.

These observed increases in police spending result in greater rates of incarceration – in particular, the incarceration of Black men. During the early 1990s, Derenoncourt finds that a substantial influx of Black residents into an area is associated with the incarceration of 300 more Black residents per 100,000 people compared to areas that did not experience a similar demographic shift. This compares to the study's estimate that the increase in incarceration among White residents is one-tenth this level: an increase in incarceration of only 30 more White residents per 100,000.[36] That is, in areas in which White residents perceived a rising racial threat, police spending and incarceration rates rose, the latter especially for Black men. These empirical observations support the racial threat hypothesis "Law enforcement response."

Finally, Derenoncourt draws this conclusion about the study's main thesis: that White communities' responses of racial animus to the arrival of significant numbers of Black Southern migrants obstructed the migrants' economic opportunities by a measurable and meaningful amount. Put another way, the White communities' racial threat response hampered the ability of those in the Black community to compete for economic resources. She observes that in areas with large influxes of Black migrants, the racial gap in income mobility widens by about one-third compared to areas with low influxes of Black migrants.[37] Moreover, Derenoncourt attributes these responses as having a particularly harmful impact on Black men due to the expanded criminal legal system and greater incarceration rate.

Alexander (2012) takes this link between the rising challenges to the racial hierarchy and increasing forms of race-based social control through the criminal legal system a step further to explain mass incarceration. Alexander describes how national political leaders aggressively pursued a policy agenda to expand the criminal legal system over roughly the same period, from 1970 to 2010. This policy agenda aimed to shore up the existing, White-dominated racial hierarchy brought under threat by the historic political gains Black Americans achieved through the Civil Rights Movement. Her qualitative evidence further supports the three racial threat hypotheses. In what follows, we describe her evidence, supplemented with the research of others.[38]

8.3.3.1. Percent Minority Effect

Effective political organizing of the Civil Rights Movement that peaked during the 1950s and 1960s overlapped with, and benefited from, the demographic shifts from the Great Migration.[39] In the early 1960s, Black Americans and their allies organized galvanizing political actions such as with the Freedom Riders.[40] These activists saw to it that the Supreme Court decisions that ruled unconstitutional segregated interstate bus transportation had real-life consequences. The Freedom Riders, including among them the late Congressman John Lewis, rode racially integrated buses into the Deep South, purposefully defying the operating Jim Crow laws. National news coverage of the violent attacks by White Southerners, including by the Ku Klux Klan, on these activists eventually compelled intervention by the federal government. More generally, civil rights activists engaged in numerous acts of civil disobedience, subjecting themselves to tens of thousands of arrests; participated in the massive March on Washington for Jobs and Freedom in 1963; and propelled the consequent passage of the Civil Rights Act of 1964, the Voting Rights Act of 1965, and the Fair Housing Act of 1968, among other accomplishments. This metric illustrates the rise in political power among Black Americans: in 1965, 23 percent of voting-age Black Americans were registered to vote. By 1969, this figure jumped to 69 percent.[41]

This new power at the voting booth showed up in political representation in the governing bodies in Congress. By 1965, six Black men held seats in the US House of Representatives, a number achieved only once before: during Reconstruction.[42] In 1968, Shirley Chisholm became the *first* Black woman to hold a seat in Congress; Chisholm went on to run for president in 1972.[43] Responding to these political changes, Lyndon Johnson's administration pushed forward economic policies to reduce poverty. Calling for a "War on Poverty," the Johnson administration signed into law major social safety-net programs such as Medicare and Medicaid,[44] Food Stamps (now known as the Supplemental Nutrition Assistance Program or SNAP),[45] and the Elementary and Secondary Education Act (ESEA). As we discussed in chapter 5, the ESEA was particularly transformative: it turned the federal government into a major funder of the country's public school system. Johnson's administration also transformed affirmative action, through Executive Order 11246, into a meaningful employment policy to proactively eliminate racial discrimination in 1965.[46] Martin Luther King Jr. and other civil rights organizers began to train their focus on achieving equal economic rights, transforming the Civil Rights Movement into the Poor People's Movement, and pursuing a redistribution of economic resources as well as political and social resources.[47]

In other words, the Civil Rights Movement and the Great Migration dramatically changed the racial composition of the national voting population, as well as the political agenda that lawmakers could (or felt compelled to) pursue. Arguably, the political accomplishments of the mid-twentieth-century Civil Rights Movement are only surpassed by those of the late nineteenth-century civil rights movement that includes Reconstruction, thus earning the more recent Civil Rights Movement the moniker the "Second Reconstruction."[48] With these political gains for Black Americans in particular, Alexander (2012) marks this period as the death of Jim Crow – that is, the dismantlement of the laws and social rules governing the racial hierarchy.

At the same time, the civil rights gains thus far did not alleviate the overcrowding, over-policing, under-employment, poor-quality housing, under-resourced schools and infrastructure of urban centers. These conditions produced organized responses such as through the Adult Community Movement for Equality (ACME), the National Welfare Rights Organization (NWRO), the American Indian Movement (AIM), the Brown Berets, and organizations that advocated for armed self-defense (Black Panther Party for Self-Defense).[49] Political organizing also created interracial alliances through the Rainbow Coalition – a cooperative effort between the Black Panther Party, the Young Lords (a Latinx-centered group), and the Young Patriots (a group for the White working-class), led by Fred Hampton of the Black Panther Party in Chicago.[50] Resistance to these conditions also included disorganized social uprisings that included vandalizing and looting of local businesses, setting fires, and inciting general mayhem.

Between the summer of 1964 and 1965, the killing of a Black child named James Powell by an off-duty White police officer in Harlem,

New York, sparked a series of such uprisings. These protests spread from Harlem to nearby Bedford-Stuyvesant, and then up to Rochester, New York, after another alleged act of police violence. Rebellions also occurred among prison inmates – predominantly Black and male – protesting brutal conditions, among the most well known taking place in 1971 at the Attica Penitentiary in Attica, New York.[51]

In these ways, Black Americans – along with other racial and ethnic minorities – made their way into spaces from which White Americans had previously been able to block them: train cars, restaurants, hotels, pools, theaters, voting booths, schools, elected offices, and more. Where Black Americans and their allies found progress was unacceptably slow, they protested with increasing force and visibility, and increasingly in the North. The impact of the Civil Rights Movement spread across the country and in ways that affected White Americans' everyday lives. The activities of the Civil Rights Movement, in other words, increased White Americans' racial threat assessment – their perception of a growing challenge to their advantageous position in the racial hierarchy.

8.3.3.2. Demand for Crime Control

As challenges to the existing racial hierarchy intensified, national White political leaders reacted by equating both the tactics and the demands of the Civil Rights Movement to crime and the need for crime control. Starting with the 1964 presidential election, the Republican campaign messaging provides some of the clearest examples of this political strategy. The Republican Party candidate Senator Barry Goldwater of Arizona avowed a commitment to increase spending on crime control to tamp down both the organized political actions by the Civil Rights Movement (and other social movements such as the anti-Vietnam war movement), and the social unrest erupting in protest of the slum conditions produced by racism in the North. The Republican Party used this message to start cleaving off White Southern voters that helped the Democratic Party put John F. Kennedy in office in 1960.[52]

Numerous illustrative examples of national leaders equating criminal behavior, political demands, and political protest activity exist in public statements. The Republican Party's message helped build their political alliance with the increasingly disenchanted Southern, White flank of the Democratic Party that staunchly opposed the civil rights agenda of the Northern Democrats. Building on this message, Goldwater's 1964 presidential campaign rhetoric tied demands for economic justice to mob violence: "If it is entirely proper for the government to take away from some to give to others, then won't some be led to believe that they can rightfully take from anyone who has more than they? No wonder law and order has broken down, mob violence has engulfed great American cities, and our wives feel unsafe in the streets."[53]

As another example, the then-former Vice President Richard Nixon[54] condemned the political protests of young people as criminal, especially the protests of urban residents – a widely understood euphemism for Black Americans: "To the professor objecting to de facto segregation, it may be crystal clear where civil disobedience may begin and where it must end. But the boundaries have become fluid to his students. And today they are all but invisible in the urban slums."[55]

Southern segregationist political leaders such as 10-term US Congressman John Bell Williams[56] from Mississippi (later, in 1968, the state's governor) and 1968 Independent Party presidential candidate George Wallace linked the political goal of desegregation with increased criminal behavior and social disorder. Congressman Williams is quoted in the Congressional record (86th Congress, 2nd session) as saying: "This exodus of Negroes from the South, and their influx into the great metropolitan centers of other areas of the Nation, has been accompanied by a wave of crime ... What has civil rights accomplished for these areas? ... Segregation is the only answer as most Americans – not the politicians – have realized for hundreds of years."

Similarly, Wallace said in a 1964 interview with *US News and World Report*, "A racist is one who despises someone because of his color, and an Alabama segregationist is one who conscientiously believes that it is in the best interest of Negro and white to have a separate education and social order."[57] As political scientist Vesla Weaver (2007) observed, "Votes cast in opposition to open housing, busing, the Civil Rights Act, and other measures time and again showed the same divisions as votes for amendments to crime bills ... Members of Congress who voted against civil rights proactively designed crime legislation and actively fought for their proposals" (p. 262).

The voting patterns in the 1964 and 1968 presidential elections indicate that wide swaths of White Americans in the North and the South shared the Republican Party's political message that linked the gains of the Civil Rights Movement with rising crime. In 1964, Senator Goldwater's losing Republican presidential bid earned 39 percent of the popular vote. In 1968, Republican candidate Nixon and American Independent candidate Wallace received a combined 57 percent of the vote, 43 percent and 14 percent, respectively. Around this time, Nixon observed that "I have found a great audience response to this [law and order] theme in all parts of the country, including in areas like New Hampshire where there is virtually no race problem and relatively little crime" (quoted in Parenti, 2000, p. 7). Nixon's comment underscores how the law-and-order rejoinder to the Civil Rights Movement had achieved national scope.

Nixon's racially charged "law and order" (later "tough on crime") presidential campaign themes became hallmarks of the Republican Party.[58] Nixon's campaign used the law-and-order theme to create an alliance with White, particularly Southern, Democratic Party supporters strong enough to break their allegiances to the Democratic Party. Republican political strategist and advisor to President Nixon Kevin Phillips explains:

> From now on, the Republicans are never going to get more than 10 to 20 percent of the Negro vote and they don't need any more than that ... but Republicans would be shortsighted if they weakened enforcement of the Voting Rights Act. The more Negros who register as Democrats in the South, the sooner the Negrophobe whites will quit the Democrats and become Republicans. That's where the votes are. Without that prodding from the blacks, the whites will backslide into their old comfortable arrangement with the local Democrats.[59]

In 1972, Nixon's so-called Southern strategy helped him win the presidential election with the support of an unprecedented one-third of Democrats, along with 95 percent of Republicans. This meant that Nixon's support was also racially lopsided: 68 percent of White voters and only 13 percent of non-Whites voted for Nixon.[60]

For roughly two decades, the Republican Party had a winning message for White Americans: the Republican presidential candidate earned a clear majority of the White vote in each of the presidential elections in 1972, 1980, 1984, and 1988.[61] Scholars have pointed to Reagan's campaign as having expertly crafted thinly veiled anti-Black messages with an anti-crime message.[62] Reagan's "War on Drugs" – especially crack cocaine – anti-crime agenda was emblematic of his talent for crafting such oblique messaging. Crack cocaine is a cheaper form of the same pharmacological substance as powder cocaine. The affordability of crack cocaine made it more prevalent in lower-income neighborhoods with higher proportions of Black residents, as compared to the expensive powder form of cocaine that was more prevalent in high-income neighborhoods with higher proportions of White residents.

In similar fashion, Reagan's Vice-President George H. Bush used in his own 1988 presidential bid the infamous ad featuring a mug shot of Willie Horton – a convicted felon who was also a Black man. As Rutgers University Professor David Greenberg explains, "What crossed the line was not that he was raising the issue of crime itself because crime was a big issue, and that's fair game ... But to use the image of this threatening black man – people call it a dog whistle; it was a pretty clear whistle."[63] Black voters responded, in opposition, even more strongly: more than four-fifths voting for the Democratic candidate in each presidential election since (at least) 1972.

Georgetown University African American history Professor Marcia Chatelain points to a second important political effect of the Willie Horton ad: "it wasn't just about a racist ad that misrepresented the furlough process ... it also taught the Democrats that in order to win elections, they have to mirror some of the racially inflected language of tough on crime."[64] For the 1992 campaign, then Governor Bill Clinton, a Democrat, commandeered the Republican's "tough on crime" stance to bring the support of White Democrats back to the Democratic Party. Clinton was famously quoted as saying "no one can say I'm soft on crime" after interrupting his presidential campaign to witness the execution of Rickey Ray Rector in Arkansas.[65] In 1996, he achieved 44 percent of the White vote – a feat not achieved by a Democrat since Jimmy Carter's election in 1976. In sum, the political reaction to the successes of the Civil Rights Movement – a growing, and significant, threat to the existing racial hierarchy – clearly included a mounting "demand for crime control."

8.3.3.3. Law Enforcement Response

Significant (and significantly White) public support for tough-on-crime campaign messages brought into office political leaders who, as we show below, would sharply increase the funding for, and activity of, law enforcement. An upsurge of funding and staffing of federal, state, and local law enforcement agencies answered the escalating political demands for crime control that began in the 1960s and continued at least through the late 1990s. Four major federal policies serve as signposts along the escalation of law enforcement activity and demands for crime control, three of which came during the Reagan administration.

First is President Reagan's War on Drugs, officially declared in 1982. Reagan's War on Drugs was legislated into action with the Comprehensive Crime Control Act of 1984. The bill singled out fighting drug crime as the main objective for funneling federal resources to state and local law enforcement agencies. The Act also severely increased the punitiveness of the criminal legal system, including reinstating the federal death penalty, pretrial detentions, and new mandatory sentencing. According to Hinton (2016), "As a result of these provisions ... the average prison sentence increased 33 percent, from 46 months in 1980 to 61 months in 1986" (p. 312). To accommodate the enlarging prison population, the 1984 Act also provided for block grants to expand penal institutions.

The second major policy was the Anti-Drug Abuse Act of 1986 which "doubled the already unprecedented level of funding Congress allocated to domestic crime and drug control programs during the president's first term and tripled drug enforcement resources" (Hinton, 2016, p. 317). Included in the 1986 law were more mandatory sentences, including the now infamous racially biased sentencing for crimes involving crack cocaine.[66]

Third, the 1988 Omnibus Anti-Drug Abuse Act increased the punitiveness and scope of anti-drug enforcement: mandatory drug testing for all federal employees and using drug offenses to revoke federally funded assistance such as student financial aid and public housing. Over this period, federal spending on anti-drug activities ballooned. By 1991, according to the Bush administration's Office of the National Drug Control Policy (United States Department of Justice, 1992), "Federal spending on drug control programs has increased more than 750 percent since 1981" (p. 139). Hinton (2016) describes how racial bias in sentencing as well as in law enforcement activities became evident in the racial character of mass incarceration:

> the War on Drugs led to the mass incarceration of black and Latino men, who constituted as much as 90 percent of new inmates for drug offenses in many states. And despite the fact that white citizens account for roughly 70 percent of all monthly drug users and 65 percent of drug abuse arrests, and that white high school seniors reported a significantly higher rate of drug use than their African American counterparts between 1979 and 2000, black citizens remain two-thirds of prisoners serving time for drug possession. (p. 318)

The next and final major crime bill came under the Clinton administration in 1994. Sociologist Katherine Beckett describes the following major features of the bill: "The ... legislation authorized $8.8 billion for hiring more police and $7.9 billion in state prison grants, created dozens of new federal capital crimes, and mandated life sentences for some three-time offenders" (2016, p. 61).

Trends in the expenditure on policing and corrections reflect rising levels of police and carceral activity (see figure 8.9). In inflation-adjusted 2022 dollars, the US spent $35.1 billion on policing which amounted to $170 per person on policing in 1971. This per capita figure increased at an annualized rate of 1.8% until 1985, and then increased to an annual rate of 4.8% between 1985 and 2002. By 2002, the US spent $481 on policing per person, for a total of $138.3 billion. The growth in corrections spending per capita similarly rose at a slower pace from 1971 to 1985 (5.3% per year) compared to 1985 to 2002 (6.3% per year). The overall spending figure rose from $13.0 billion in 1971 to $104.3 billion in 2002, or $63 per capita to $363 per capita. Figure 8.4 above presents the figures on the massive increase of incarcerated individuals that began in the early 1980s and peaked in the early 2000s.

By the early 2000s, criminal punishment – through mass incarceration – transformed into "a major stratifying institution in contemporary America."[67] Political leaders fueled this transformation by exploiting the politically effective strategy of conflating "Blackness" with "criminality," and thereby refortifying the stratifying function of race. The process of this transformation shifted the nation's focus away from the anti-poverty and civil rights agenda that animated the political climate of the 1950s through the 1970s and toward a War on Crime and a political platform concerned with individual – rather than social – responsibility. Consequently, the development of this punitive incarceration regime, the term Mason et al. (2022) use to describe the contemporary criminal legal system, effectively halted progress toward a racially equitable distribution of economic, social, and political resources.

Elsewhere in this book, we have documented persistent or worsening trends in these other areas of racial inequality over this period: in unemployment (see chapters 2 and 6), in wages (see chapters 2 and 6), in school segregation (see chapter 5), in wealth (see chapters 2 and 7), in occupational segregation (see chapters 4 and 6), and in the weakening of affirmative action policies (see chapter 5).[68] In other words, starting roughly in the 1970s, the nation's political priorities switched directions and turned back toward protecting the power and privilege of White Americans relative to Black Americans. This review of historical events based on the scholarship of Derenoncourt, Alexander, and others demonstrates the usefulness of stratification economics and the racial threat hypothesis in explaining the phenomenon of mass incarceration.

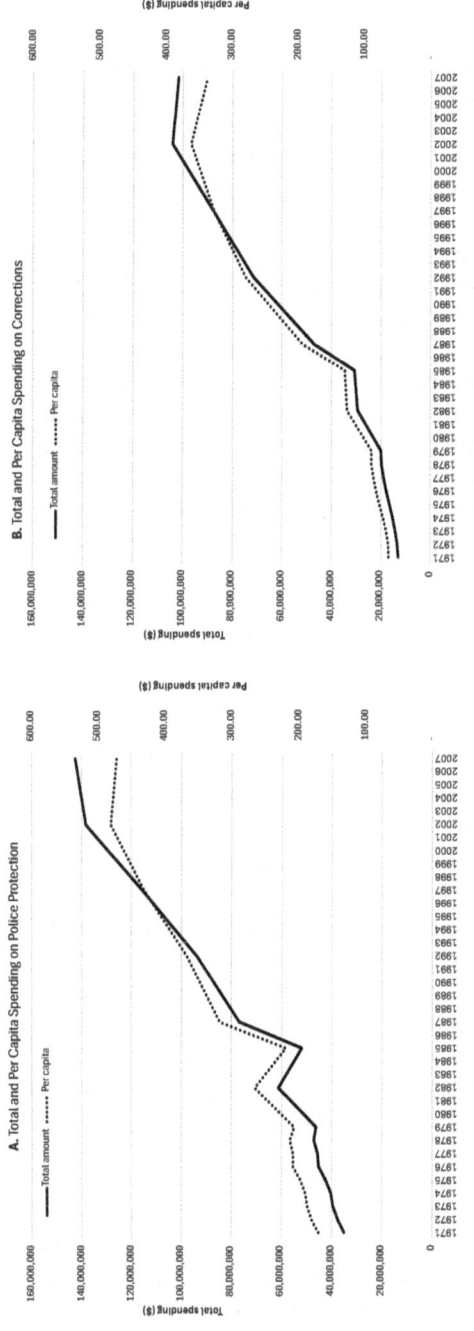

Figure 8.9 Trends in annual government spending on policing and incarceration (2022$), FY 1971–2007.

Sources: 1971–1979 and 1985 expenditure data are from: U.S. Department of Justice, Office of Justice Programs, Bureau of Justice Statistics, *Justice Expenditure and Employment in the U.S., 1985*, "Table F: Total justice expenditure: Total direct and intergovernmental expenditure, by activity and type of government, fiscal years 1971–79 and 1985," July 1989, NCJ-106356, p. xvi. 1982–2007 expenditure data are from: Tracey Kyckelhahn, Ph.D., BJS Statistician, *Justice Expenditures and Employment, FY 1982–2007-Statistical Tables*, "Table 4: Distribution of police protection expenditures, by level of government, FY 1982–2007 (real dollars)," December 2011, NCJ 236218, U.S. Department of Justice, Office of Justice Programs, Bureau of Justice Statistics, p.6.

Dollars are adjusted to 2022 dollars using: (1) "Chain-type price index for the gross domestic product," from: United States President (2001–2009: Bush), *Economic Report of the President: Transmitted to the Congress: Together with the Annual Report of the Council of Economic Advisors*, "Table B-7.—Chain-type price indexes for gross domestic product, 1959–2008," January 2009 (Washington, D.C.: U.S. Govt. Printing Office), p. 292; and (2) United States President (2021–current: Biden), *Economic Report of the President: Transmitted to the Congress: Together with the Annual Report of the Council of Economic Advisors*, "Table B-5. Chain-type price indexes for gross domestic product, 1972–2022," March 2023 (Washington, D.C.: U.S. Govt. Printing Office), p. 442.

Population figures to calculate per capita expenditures are from: (1) U.S. Bureau of the Census, Population Estimates and Population Distribution Branches, "Preliminary Estimates of the Intercensal Population of Counties 1970–1979," April 1982 (https://www2.census.gov/programs-surveys/popest/tables/1900-1980/counties/totals/e7079co.txt); and (2) U.S. Bureau of the Census, "County Intercensal Tables 1980–1990," (https://www.census.gov/data/tables/time-series/demo/popest/1980s-county.html).

8.4. Conclusion

In the "Primer to Part II," we introduced the two basic analytical approaches to studying the US' racialized carceral state in economics: the approach of neoclassical economics – what we refer to as "conventional economics" – and stratification economics. We have distinguished these two approaches by their entry points of analysis: the neoclassical, or conventional, economics framework uses the individual, and stratification economics, in contrast, uses social groups. Economist Samuel Myers Jr. captures the essential differences between these two approaches with two questions. Neoclassical economists focus on why individuals commit crimes, and as a result, the central question that drives their examination of the racial disparities in criminal legal system outcomes, such as incarceration, is: *Why are Blacks so criminal?* In contrast, stratification economists focus on social groups and the operations of the social hierarchy, and organize their research of the criminal legal system's racial disparities around a different question: *Why is the criminal legal system so Black?*[69]

In this chapter, we show how stratification economics provides a useful analytical framework for explaining a major function of the criminal legal system in the United States: to support the existing racial hierarchy in US society. We do this by first providing a survey of US history that is replete with examples of how the dominant racial group, White Americans, has used the criminal legal system to reify the racial hierarchy. We present basic descriptive data on how the criminal legal system has been leveraged primarily against Black American men, but also has disproportionately incarcerated Black women, and has wreaked havoc on the social fabric of Black communities, more generally.

We use the sociological racial threat theory to identify the conditions under which a dominant social group will use the criminal legal system to secure the existing social hierarchy. These conditions include observable indicators that oppressed groups are succeeding in destabilizing the existing social hierarchy. The political reaction of the dominant social group to such conditions is an increased demand for, and then muscular activation of, the criminal legal system and law enforcement.

Consistent with the racial threat perspective, our review of US history shows how the dominant racial group – White Americans – used the criminal legal system as an instrument for social control in response to Black Americans' successes in challenging the existing racial hierarchy through the Civil Rights Movement. The second half of the twentieth century witnessed substantial success in Black Americans' efforts to destabilize the racial hierarchy through the Great Migration and the Civil Rights Movement of the 1950s–1970s. Significant numbers of White Americans reacted to these threats to their privileged position in the racial hierarchy with racial animus, racist resource-hoarding, and support for a massive expansion of the carceral state as a means of social control. In sum, stratification economics theorizes that the criminal legal system serves a functional role in maintaining the racial hierarchy.

9

Conclusion

American-style capitalism has produced a racially stratified society, with racial discrimination operating in a variety of markets and arenas of life. In this volume we've outlined some of the major areas, such as the labor market, the educational system, and the criminal legal system. Moreover, while arguments have been advanced that eliminating racial discrimination would be beneficial for economic growth,[1] US gross domestic product (GDP) has grown, at an annual average rate of 3 percent per year from 1948 through 2024.[2] Economic growth and anti-Black racism, as it seems to have turned out, are not completely at odds. Within this context, the socio-economic status of the White American community has largely improved over the last four centuries in several tangible ways: income, household wealth, and rate of homeownership. On the other hand, the socio-economic status of the Black community has fractionally improved, in comparison to Whites, in some of the same ways, and remained stagnant, or even worsened, in other ways: wealth and the Black incarceration rate. Our goal in writing this book is to provide the reader with a coherent theoretical framework, supported by empirical evidence, that can explain disparate Black outcomes as the result of persistent anti-Black racism in the US economy.

As economists, it's natural for us to turn to economic theory to explain what we observe, but we've found neoclassical economic theory insufficient for interpreting the persistence of anti-Blackness in America. Therefore, we have sought out other economic frameworks with greater potential to help us understand why a phenomenon such as racism, which mainstream economics theorizes should disappear given competition, has remained an enduring and fundamental feature of the American capitalist system for centuries. In our view, a more useful theoretical framework is stratification economics, combined with an intersectional analytical approach.

In our introductory chapter (chapter 1), we describe stratification economics as a theoretical framework that identifies social groups as central agents in creating and maintaining social hierarchies, including especially the economic dimensions of these hierarchies. In chapters 2 and 3, we explain how American society constructed race to serve as a social group identity around which to build its political economy. Anti-Black beliefs, practices, and policies, which have no scientific basis, arose in colonial America as social constructs designed to justify slavery. These beliefs and practices evolved and were sustained to preserve a racial hierarchy in which White Americans would be the prime beneficiaries for centuries to come. In response to the oppressive structure of the racial hierarchy, enslaved Black people and then Black Americans worked collectively to resist domination and develop ways to thrive – by creating, for example, Black schools and churches, Black businesses, towns, and political organizations. In these ways, racial group identities enable individuals to harness the power of a collective that can then be used to resist domination, as in the case of Black Americans, or to dominate, as in the case of White Americans.

Across the other chapters of this book, we provide examples of how racial groups – along with other social identities – developed as individuals organized into factions to take collective action: collective action that would generate political power for in-group members. In economics parlance, we view race as an endogenous variable, not an exogenous one (i.e., a "given" or "natural" category), in explaining economic phenomena.[3] By making clear the political economic function of racial group identities, we hope that our book demystifies the concept of race. This is our first main take-away: *Race is a social construction with a rational basis; race persists as a meaningful social concept because it permits members of a dominant racial group to benefit from an economy defined by racial inequality.*

By understanding the fundamentally political economic basis of the US' race-based social hierarchy, the requirements for eradicating anti-Black racism – in all its forms, but especially the institutional and structural forms that continue to reify race in seemingly race-neutral terms – become clearer. Eradicating racism requires eliminating race as a meaningful determinant of one's life chances, social status, political power, or access to economic resources. In *econometric* terms, this would mean the race variable should ultimately no longer be a significant explanatory variable in our economic models. This requires eliminating racially differentiated relative positions in the social hierarchy. And this requires us to confront a large obstacle to eradicating racism: getting White Americans to accept a lowering of their elevated position in the social hierarchy relative to Black Americans. As Darity Jr. observes, a racially just society "will be hard to attain. It will require intense and sustained struggle – and, finally, a majority of white Americans trade white privilege embodied in exchange for a just society. We cannot produce a racially just society without diminishing the relative position of white Americans; that is virtually tautological."[4]

If our book's historical and contemporary evidence on racial inequality has persuaded the reader – as it has us – that uneven access to political power is a main cause of racial inequality, then our second main take-away is self-evident. Our second main take-away is: *Meaningful progress toward racial equality requires effective political action.* If one accepts that powerful, collective action by White people has supported roughly 350 years of explicitly legal racism, it seems unremarkable that racial inequality has persisted another half-century. Nor does it seem remarkable to deduce from this history that to reverse policies that have disproportionately benefited White Americans requires political action. At the same time, stratification economic theory points out that such policy change can be hard to accomplish, in the case of the US, if White Americans are overrepresented in political leadership, which they are.

Throughout all our chapters, we discuss how such social groups have harnessed political power through social movements – which, in turn generate policy changes – to change or maintain existing social hierarchies. Policies are, after all, the public agreements a society makes about how it will operate. Among the political movements, political actions, and public policies we discuss in this book that aim to *remedy* past and contemporary expressions of racism are: the abolitionist movement (chapter 4), including rebellions among enslaved African people (chapter 5); the organizing of "native" schools and then public schools by communities of newly freedpeople (chapter 5); and the 13th, 14th, and 15th amendments to the Constitution (chapter 4). Other political actions include the en masse migration of Black Americans out of the South that produced one of the US' largest internal migrations: about 6 million Black Americans left the South and relocated to the states north and west from roughly 1910 to 1970 (chapter 8), and the Double V campaign that galvanized the modern Civil Rights Movement of the mid twentieth century (chapter 5). The Civil Rights Movement, in turn, produced major civil rights legislation – the Civil Rights Acts of 1964, 1965, and 1968. These laws – as we observe throughout this entire book – birthed antidiscrimination policies that reached into every dimension of life. In the contemporary context, we discuss public policies such as pay transparency and ban-the-box policies to reduce racial inequality in labor market outcomes (chapter 6), census reforms to reduce prison gerrymandering and increase racial equity in political representation (chapter 8), a federal reparations program to lessen racial wealth inequality (chapter 7), and institutions such as HBCUs in promoting equity in education (chapter 5).

We hope our book has demonstrated that, throughout the history of Black life in the US, Black Americans have been engaged in on-the-ground struggle. From Sojourner Truth to the Underground Railroad to Marcus Garvey's "Back to Africa" movement to the Pullman Porters to the Freedom Riders to Fannie Lou Hamer to Shirley Chisolm's run for US president to the Black Panther Party for Self-Defense to the Rainbow Coalition to Reverend Al Sharpton's National Action Network to the election of President Barack Obama to the Black Lives Matter movement, Black Americans and their allies have continuously agitated for equal opportunity and a better quality of life for the Black community.

These discussions provide evidence that a racial pecking order in which Black Americans are at the bottom doesn't have to remain America's destiny. The liberation of Black Americans from the worst economic outcomes, compared to White Americans, requires political struggle at the individual, collective, local, national, and global levels, even as large-scale social change can be excruciatingly slow. In this volume we've outlined policy approaches across different arenas for which a variety of actors can advocate. We therefore hope, ultimately, that this book inspires our readers to take action in whatever manner they can.

We also specifically highlight the importance of paying attention to *intersections of* social groups (chapter 4). This is because such intersections reveal additional manifestations of oppression, as well as additional means to resist. For example, the intersections may create fault-lines within a social group, weakening that group's political power. We saw this happen within the women's suffrage movement when Black and White women suffragists splintered into two main organizations – the National Woman Suffrage Association (NWSA) and the American Woman Suffrage Association (AWSA) – with the former focusing on voting rights for White women, and the latter focusing on voting rights for Black men and women. Alternatively, intersections can create bridges that support powerful alliances between two social groups. In chapter 3 of the book *Women, Race and Class*, Angela Davis talks about the potential power that a strong coalition between Black and White women would have had, at that time, to move gender equity policies forward. Alas, a rebuilding of this intragender coalition would take another century (from the start of the suffrage movement), with the second wave of the feminist movement.

Importantly, intersectional theory tells us that, where different subaltern groups may experience some forms of discrimination in common – for example Black and White women are vulnerable to gender discrimination – these groups may also *experience the same type of discrimination differently* given the possession, or not, of other identities vulnerable to bias, such as Black women experiencing racism that White women in the US don't. Policy prescriptions, therefore, need input from, and advocacy by, those groups which are disaffected by the absence of such policies.

Finally, if the historical and contemporary evidence that we have presented in our book has persuaded our readers that when racially marginalized communities get access to political power, they have been able to meaningfully reduce racial inequality, then our third main take-away should be unsurprising: when racially marginalized communities lose political power, racial inequality may increase. Put another way, our third main take-away is: *Progress toward racial equity does not move in one direction (it is not "monotonic," as economists would say)*. Depending on each social group's access to political power, society may progress or regress along the various dimensions of racial inequality. The major gains in Black voting rights in the South during Reconstruction that were then lost provide a dramatic example (chapter 4). The toll of mass incarceration, by 1997, compromised the franchise of more than one-third of voting-age Black men (chapter 8). The significant progress in school desegregation produced by tying massive federal government spending on public education to racial integration efforts in 1965 provides another vivid illustration. These major gains in school integration, particularly in the South, slowed with the Reagan administration's pushback against school integration, and then moved in reverse (with the exception of Northeast states that made no school integration gains during this period).

One exception to this general rule may be with respect to racial wealth inequality. Due to the way that the US capitalist economy enables wealth ownership to generate income, wealth inequality has snowballed over time, producing an effectively one-way, path-dependent process. As we discussed in multiple chapters of our book, White Americans achieved their dominance in wealth-holdings with racist violence and policies over most of US history. As a result, recent studies suggest that it could take over two centuries to close the racial wealth gap in the US, and even then the gap could not be closed without significant redistributive policies such as a national reparations program and progressive tax reform.[5] While such projections can be discouraging, they also identify how this will require an exceptional set of policy solutions. This is the challenge – for the Black community, its allies among other groups, and across policy and legislative communities: to think creatively and boldly in their search for policy strategies that will narrow the racial wealth gap, including those discussed in chapter 7.

If we have to choose only one lesson for the reader to take away from reading our book, we hope it is the first take-away: that race is a social construction that evolved out of the political strategies of early American colonists, and then White Americans, to carve out social, political, and economic advantages for their in-group members. Race is not the by-product of Black Americans' moral failings or White Americans' virtue. If this lesson sinks in deeply for our readers – for more Americans, in particular – perhaps the profound injustice of the US racial hierarchy will become impossible to ignore, and this recognition will support us, as a nation, to harness the political power necessary to create a racially just society.

Notes

Acknowledgments

1 C. Savage (2025), "Congress Wrote a Deportation Law to Be Used 'Sparingly.' Trump Has Other Ideas," *New York Times*, April 1, available at: www.nytimes.com/2025/04/01/us/trump-deportations-students-campus-protests.html; M. Matza (2025), "US Judge Scolds Trump Officials for Failing to Return Man Deported in Error," BBC, April 6, available at: www.bbc.com/news/articles/cn4jz3v401yo; T. Bedford (2025), "UMass, Harvard Student Visas Revoked in 'New Stage' of Trump Immigration Crackdown," WGBH, April 7, available at: www.wgbh.org/news/local/2025-04-07/umass-harvard-student-visas-revoked-in-new-stage-of-trump-immigration-crackdown.
2 The White House (2025), "Ending Radical and Wasteful Government DEI Programs and Preferencing" (Press release), Whitehouse.gov, January 20, available at: www.whitehouse.gov/presidential-actions/2025/01/ending-radical-and-wasteful-government-dei-programs-and-preferencing; J. Mark (2025), "Civil Rights Agencies That Once Promoted DEI Now Work to Wipe It Out," *Washington Post*, March 28, available at: www.washingtonpost.com/business/2025/03/28/civil-rights-dei-trump-administration; D. Collins (2025), "NY Public Schools Tell Trump Administration They Won't Comply with DEI Order," *Seattle Times*, April 5, available at: www.seattletimes.com/nation-world/nation/ny-public-schools-tell-trump-administration-they-wont-comply-with-dei-order; J. Offenhartz (2025), "Columbia University Agrees to Policy Changes after Trump Administration Funding Threats," PBS, March 21, available at: www.pbs.org/newshour/education/columbia-university-agrees-to-policy-changes-after-trump-administration-funding-threats.
3 D. T. Tomaskovic-Devey, J. Quesada Velazco, and K. L. Young (2025), "We Analyzed Racial Justice Statements from the 500 Largest US Companies and Found That DEI Officials Really Did Have an Influence," *The Conversation*, March 28, available at: https://theconversation.com/we-analyzed-racial-justice-statements-from-the-500-largest-us-companies-and-found-that-dei-officials-really-did-have-an-influence-249999.
4 E. Singer (2025), "Thousands of U.S. Government Web Pages Have Been Taken Down since Friday," *New York Times*, February 2, available at: www.nytimes.com/2025/02/02/upshot/trump-government-websites-missing-pages

.html; G. Whisnant and A. Stanton (2025), "Trump Says Pausing Government Websites Not 'Bad Idea' Amid Outage Reports," *Newsweek*, January 31, available at: www.newsweek.com/federal-government-websites-going-dark-what-we-know-2024529.

5 Reuters (2025), "Columbia University Caves to Demands to Restore $400m from Trump Administration," *Guardian*, March 21, available at: www.theguardian.com/us-news/2025/mar/21/columbia-university-funding-trump-demands; S. J. Ono, L. K. McCauley, M. S. Runge, and G. S. Chatas (2025), "Evolving Our Approach to DEI and Moving Forward Together" (press release), Office of the President, University of Michigan, March 27, available at: https://president.umich.edu/news-communications/messages-to-the-community/evolving-our-approach-to-dei-and-moving-forward-together; D. Freeman (2025), "3 Ivy League Scholars Plan to Leave US and Teach in Canada amid Trump Administration's Higher Education Battle," CNN US, March 28, available at: www.cnn.com/2025/03/28/us/yale-university-scholars-toronto-trump/index.html.

6 S. Hernandez (2025), "Des Moines Public Schools Ends Some Staff Support Groups after Trump's Anti-DEI Directives," *Des Moines Register*, March 7, available at: www.desmoinesregister.com/story/news/education/2025/03/05/des-moines-public-schools-to-end-support-groups-over-trump-anti-dei-rule-dmps/81164325007; M. Payne (2025), "Iowa House Republicans Pass Bills Barring DEI in Higher Education and across Government," *Des Moines Register*, March 19, available at: www.desmoinesregister.com/story/news/politics/2025/03/19/iowa-legislature-house-republicans-pass-sweeping-restrictions-on-dei-higher-education/82499791007.

7 A. Wong and A. Ma (2025), "Federal Agencies Begin Removing DEI Guidance from Websites in Trump Crackdown," Associated Press, January 24, available at: https://apnews.com/article/trump-dei-education-diversity-equity-inclusion-20cf8a2941f4f35e0b5b0e07c6347ebb; A. Hsu (2025), "Federal Contractors Say They're Stuck Between Nondiscrimination Laws and Anti-DEI Orders," NPR, March 15, available at: www.npr.org/2025/03/15/nx-s1-5325881/federal-contractors-say-theyre-stuck-between-nondiscrimination-laws-and-anti-dei-orders.

8 T. Vanden Brook and C. Mayes-Osterman (2025), "Fort Liberty now Fort Bragg. What's the History behind the Name and Hegseth's Decision?" *USA Today*, February 11, available at: www.usatoday.com/story/news/politics/2025/02/11/hegseth-fort-liberty-bragg-name-change/78408328007; P. Stewart (2025), "Hegseth: 'Diversity Is Our Strength' Dumbest Phrase in Military History," *Arizona Daily Sun*, February 7, available at: https://azdailysun.com/hegseth-diversity-is-our-strength-dumbest-phrase-in-military-history/article_e3f1d58a-d300-5cde-903b-50a9502331e3.html.

9 K. Lazar and L. Kowalcyk (2025), "NIH Abruptly Terminates Millions in Research Grants in Mass. and Around the Country," *Boston Globe*, March 6, available at: www.bostonglobe.com/2025/03/06/metro/trump-kills-science-funding-dei.

10 J. Gelt (2025), "Trump Executive Order Targets the Smithsonian over 'Divisive, Race-Centered Ideology,'" *Los Angeles Times*, March 27, available at: www.latimes.com/entertainment-arts/story/2025-03-27/trump-executive-smithsonian-museums-race-public-monuments; C. Veltman (2025), "Kennedy Center Lays off Social Impact Employees," Houston Public Media, March

26, available at: www.houstonpublicmedia.org/npr/2025/03/26/nx-s1-5340766/kennedy-center-lays-off-social-impact-employees.
11 J. Mcshane (2025), "The NIH Just Officially Killed Diversity Statements in Its Grant Applications," *Mother Jones*, March 25, available at: www.motherjones.com/politics/2025/03/nih-ending-diversity-statements-grant-applications; K. Palmer (2025), "As NIH Pulls Funding, Scientist Worries about 'Frightening Implications,'" *Inside Higher Ed*, March 28, available at: www.insidehighered.com/news/government/science-research-policy/2025/03/28/nih-grant-terminations-have-frightening; C. Y. Johnson, S. Dance, and J. Achenbach (2025), "Here Are the Words Putting Science in the Crosshairs of Trump's Orders," *Washington Post*, February 4, available at: www.washingtonpost.com/science/2025/02/04/national-science-foundation-trump-executive-orders-words.
12 In an email broadly shared among US economists, an administrator at the New York Federal Reserve indicated that, in early 2025, the Federal Reserve System "is working to review the Executive Orders regarding Diversity, Equity, and Inclusion (DEI) programs and the subsequent guidance issued from the Administration. At this time, the [New York Federal Reserve] Research department won't be able to host the CSWEP [Committee on the Status of Women in the Economics Profession of the American Economics Association] reception on February 20 or the CSWEP Summer Economics Fellowship Program."
13 M. Segraves, A. Swalec, and J. Albert (2025), "Removal of DC's Black Lives Matter Plaza Nearly Complete," NBC Washington, April 1, available at: www.nbcwashington.com/news/local/removal-of-dcs-black-lives-matter-plaza-nearly-complete/3880226; L. Sarnoff, M. Crudele, and A. Katersky (2025), "Transgender References Removed from Stonewall National Monument Website," *ABC News*, February 14, available at: https://abcnews.go.com/US/transgender-references-removed-stonewall-national-monument-website/story?id=118804553.
14 W. E. B. Du Bois (1919), "Returning Soldiers," *The Crisis*, 18(1), p. 13, available at: https://dchsny.org/wp-content/uploads/2018/10/Crisis-MAY-1919-Part-1-of-2.pdf.
15 The Williams and Mason quotes are from Banks' speech, "100 Years of African American Economists: Oppositional Knowledge and Scholarly Activism," published in the *Review of Black Political Economy* (2022), 49(1), pp. 9–19.

Introduction

1 Note that when we use the term "Black," unless we specify differently, we are referring to persons of African descent in the United States irrespective of citizenship status.
2 Darity Jr. (2005), p. 145.
3 Wolff and Resnick (2012), p. 14.
4 Claretta Bellamy (2023), "25% of Black Women Say They Were Denied Job Interviews Because of Their Hair, Survey Says," NBC News NBCBLK, March 24, available at: www.nbcnews.com/news/nbcblk/25-black-women-say-denied-job-interviews-hair-survey-says-rcna76006.

Notes to pages 8–19

5 The Crown Coalition (n.d.), "Creating a Respectful and Open World for Natural Hair", available at: www.thecrownact.com/about.
6 Darity Jr. et al. (2018), p. 5.
7 We use the terms "prejudice" and "racism" somewhat interchangeably. Some analysts define racism to be prejudicial views plus the power to oppress the person or people who are the subject of those views. For example, the *Merriam-Webster Dictionary*, as of 2024, defines racism as "the systemic oppression of a racial group to the social, economic, and political advantage of another," and "a political or social system founded on racism and designed to execute its principles" (www.merriam-webster.com/dictionary/racism). In contrast, Merriam-Webster includes no mention of systemic oppression or political power in its definition of prejudice (www.merriam-webster.com/dictionary/prejudice). Because this text is about the political economy of anti-Black views, we primarily use the word "racism," and infrequently use the word "prejudice."
8 US Department of Justice (January 24, 2025), *Laws and Policies*, available at: www.justice.gov/hatecrimes/laws-and-policies.
9 "Laissez faire" is a French term that means "allow to do" and references an economic philosophy that, principally, prioritizes unregulated markets and eschews government economic regulations.
10 Internalized racism is sometimes referred to as internalized racial oppression or internalized White supremacy.
11 Clair and Denis (2015), p. 860.
12 Matthew Bloch, Ford Fessenden, and Janet Roberts (2010), "Stop, Question and Frisk in New York Neighborhoods," *New York Times*, July 11, A16, available at: https://archive.nytimes.com/www.nytimes.com/interactive/2010/07/11/nyregion/20100711-stop-and-frisk.html?searchResultPosition=1.
13 Cambridge Dictionary (n.d.), "Meaning of Structural Racism in English," available at: https://dictionary.cambridge.org/us/dictionary/english/structural-racism.
14 US Census Bureau (2023), "Table A-3: Poverty Status of People by Age, Race, and Hispanic Origin, 1959–2022," available at: www.census.gov/data/tables/2023/demo/income-poverty/p60-280.html.
15 Bottomore (1991), p. 457.
16 Nembhard (2004).
17 Stewart and Coleman (2005), p. 118.
18 Rice (2021), p. 46.
19 Tauheed (2008).
20 Hossein (2019).
21 Y. Ilcheong, F. Farinelli, and R. Landveld (2023), "New Economics for Sustainable Development: Social and Solidarity Economy," United Nations Economist Network, United Nations, p. 7, available at: www.un.org/sites/un2.un.org/files/social_and_solidarity_economy_29_march_2023.pdf.
22 Ray and Gibbons (2021).
23 Carbado et al. (2013).
24 Crenshaw (1991), p. 1243.
25 City of Boston (November 1, 2022), "Black History Boston: Combahee River Collective." Available at: www.boston.gov/news/black-history-boston-combahee-river-collective.
26 Combahee River Collective (1977), "Combahee River Collective Statement,"

available at: https://americanstudies.yale.edu/sites/default/files/files/Keyword%20Coalition_Readings.pdf.
27 Hull, Bell-Scott, and Smith (1982).
28 Rousseau (2013), p. 452.
29 Some Black thinkers, including Glenn Loury and John McWhorter, have offered the criticism that the capitalizing of "black" could inadvertently reinforce essentialism, lead to tokenization, and carry the implication that Black identity is monolithic (Loury and McWhorter, 2022). These perspectives also rightfully name the insufficiency of capitalization for addressing racial inequality – often a performative rather than substantive gesture.
30 Loury and McWhorter (2022).
31 Price (2019).

2 The Construction of Race and the Origins of Racism in the United States

1 See, for example, the treatment of race by the "Libretexts: Social Sciences" website, which includes an excerpt titled "Race as a Social Construct" (https://socialsci.libretexts.org/Courses/Southwestern_College/SWC%3A_SOC_106_Race_and_Ethnicity/Chapter_1%3A_Defining_Race_and_Ethnicity/1.3_Race_as_a_Social_Construct). The Libretexts website is a collaborative project of educators and educational institutions, with major support from the University of California, Davis, to provide learners with open access to educational textbooks and materials.
2 The historical material presented in this section is not original scholarship from this book's authors. Instead, we mine the scholarship provided mainly from two sources. First, the thesis that the construction of the social concept "race" developed out of the economic and political conditions required to operate a slave-based economy is put forward by Eric Williams (2021 [1944]). Williams' thesis, in a nutshell, is that slavery produced anti-Black racism, and that this anti-Black racism acts as a through-line of the Americas' history. Darity Jr. outlines Williams' work on this in the preface of the third edition of *Capitalism and Slavery*:

> In addition to the abolition hypothesis that dominates Williams's dissertation, two additional hypotheses emerge in *Capitalism and Slavery*. One of these appears only briefly in the very first chapter, but the brevity should not diminish its importance. There, Williams argues that slavery produced racism, rather than the reverse. Therefore, for Williams, racism is an ideology that arose to provide a potent rationalization for a wholly immoral but economically lucrative practice.
>
> More recent scholarship, especially the work of the late Cedric Robinson, appears to challenge Williams's position. In his analysis of "racial capitalism," Robinson contends that racism, the practice of designating "the other" as inherently inferior and deserving of subordination, predates the transatlantic slave trade and slavery in the Americas. He points to antecedent racialization of some groups of Europeans by others as part and parcel of intra-European patterns of group-based exploitation and colonialism. But this is beside the point; Williams is directing our attention to the origins of anti-Black racism, not racism writ large. He is

asserting that there was a material foundation for the beginnings of white supremacy.

Second, we rely heavily on the historical material presented by Jacqueline Jones in her 1998 book, *American Work*, particularly chapters 1–4, to add details specific to the slave economies that developed in colonial America. We also use material from Dorothy Roberts' chapter "Race" in *The 1619 Project* (2021), edited by Nikole Hannah-Jones et al., especially pp. 49–54.

3 The Smithsonian National Museum of African American History provides a primer on the historical origins of the terms "race" and "white" on their web page "Historical Foundations of Race," at https://nmaahc.si.edu/learn/talking-about-race/topics/historical-foundations-race.
4 California NewsReel (2003), *Race: The Power of An Illusion, Race Timeline – Go Deeper*, available at: www.pbs.org/race/000_About/002_03_c-godeeper.htm.
5 See discussion above, in section 1.10, "Note on Capitalizing Black and White."
6 Franklin (1961[1751], pp. 225–34) wrote: "Why increase the Sons of Africa, by Planting them in America, where we have so fair an Opportunity, by excluding all Blacks and Tawneys, of increasing the lovely White and Red? But perhaps I am partial to the Complexion of my Country, for such Kind of Partiality is natural to Mankind."
7 In *Black Skin, White Masks* (1967), Frantz Fanon argues that colonialism produced whiteness as a construction in opposition to Blackness, creating psychological associations between whiteness and superiority / proper humanity.
8 As discussed by Kolchin (2009), for anthropologist Edgar T. Thompson, races are created in cultures, not discovered in nature. Kolchin also notes that biologist Stephen Jay Gould critiques the biological determinism (i.e., "the belief that shared behavioral norms ... arise from inherited inborn distinctions") of conceptions of race with which stratification economics is concerned.
9 National Park Service (2022), "A Short History of Jamestown," available at: www.nps.gov/jame/learn/historyculture/a-short-history-of-jamestown.htm.
10 Another historically contingent factor is the active and broad set of trading networks that existed between Europeans and Africans, which involved servants – indentured-type servants, as well as slaves, including chattel slaves. Some historians also attribute kidnapping as a significant source of the people transported from the African continent to the new colonies as slaves (Schwarz, 2022). Whatever the source, the key historical contingency is that colonial settlers sought out, and had access to, a supply of *enslaved* workers to meet their growing demand for a tractable workforce.
11 Boston and Hallam (2004). For brief background material, see "Before There Were 'Red' and 'Blue' States, There Were 'Free' States and 'Slave' States," by J. Gordon Hylton (December 20, 2012), available at: https://law.marquette.edu/facultyblog/2012/12/before-there-were-red-and-blue-states-there-were-free-states-and-slave-states.
12 National Archives, Milestone Documents (2022), "13th Amendment to the US Constitution: Abolition of Slavery (1865)," available at: www.archives.gov/milestone-documents/13th-amendment.
13 Darity Jr. and Mullen (2020). See further discussion of Black Codes in chapters 4 and 8.

14 Darity Jr. and Mullen (2020). See further discussion of the Nadir in chapter 4.
15 For a brief overview of Jim Crow, see *What Was Jim Crow* by Dr. David Pilgrim (2012), Jim Crow Museum, Ferris State University, available at: www.ferris.edu/HTMLS/news/jimcrow/what.htm.
16 National Archives, Milestone Documents (2022), "Civil Rights Act (1964)," available at: www.archives.gov/milestone-documents/civil-rights-act.
17 National Archives, Milestone Documents (2022), "The Voting Rights Act (1965)," available at: www.archives.gov/milestone-documents/voting-rights-act.
18 US Department of Housing and Urban Development History of Fair Housing (n.d.), "History of Fair Housing," available at: www.hud.gov/program_offices/fair_housing_equal_opp/aboutfheo/history.
19 The following is a simple description of capitalism: an economic system based on a relatively small number of individuals (capitalists) who have private ownership of the means of production – e.g., land, factories, equipment and so on. Capitalists hire workers – individuals who have little to no access to capital – to operate the capitalists' means of production to produce goods and services. These goods and services are sold through a market system and generate income for the capitalists (i.e., profit). Workers, of which there are a relatively large number, must compete with other workers to get hired by capitalists to earn a wage income. For further elaboration, see Bowles et al. (2017).
20 Darity Jr. (1989) describes how, from the Marxist viewpoint, competition "gives rise to monopolies … capitalist winners consolidate and concentrate; they can exclude the losers and consolidate their positions for long stretches of time. The 'winners' under Marxist competition can bar, indefinitely, entry of potential rivals. Moreover, the tendency toward centralization and concentration of capital is an immanent law of capitalist development" (p. 357).
21 In 2020, about 67 percent ($7.9 trillion) of the total income reported to the US Internal Revenue Service (IRS) through the IRS Form 1040 consisted of wages and salaries, and 79 percent of tax filers report earning wage income (York and Hartt, 2023).
22 In the 2018 book (first published in 1993), *Persistent Inequalities*, Botwinick develops a Marxist theory of how robust competition produces wage differentials in a capitalist economy, independent of monopolies. Instead, Botwinick theorizes that capitalist competition combines with the existence of a reserve army of labor and uneven worker organization to continually produce wage differentials. This wage hierarchy, in turn, produces the better and worse positions in the labor market over which groups of workers compete.
23 Darity Jr. and Williams (1985), p. 260.
24 Darity Jr. (1983), p. 51.
25 For example, see the scholarship of Alonso-Villar and del Río (2017). They find that "Using well-being measures that allow the assessment of the occupational segregation faced by African American women, this paper has revealed that the strong segregation reduction in the 1960s and 1970s was accompanied by important well-being improvements due to the higher presence of African American women in occupations with (relative) wages higher than those they had in 1940" (p. 219).
26 The immediate impact of the Civil Rights Act of 1964 on school desegregation is documented in *Brown at 60* by Orfield et al. (2014). That study finds that: "Desegregation progress was very substantial for blacks and occurred in the

South from the mid 1960s to the late 1980s. Contrary to many claims, the South has not gone back to the level of segregation before Brown. It has lost all of the additional progress made after 1967 but is still the least segregated region for black students" (p. 2).

27 According to a Congressional report on the 1965 Voting Rights Act (Coleman, 2015), an average of only 12.9 percent of the voting-age Black population across the states of the former confederacy had registered to vote in 1947. By 1966, this figure reached 52.9 percent. In 1969, the number of Black Americans holding US Congressional seats simultaneously (11) exceeded the Reconstruction era's peak figure (6) for the first time. By the 93rd Congress, in 1973, this number rose to 17, including 2 US representatives from Southern states (United States House of Representatives, n.d.a).

28 The actions taken by the AFL–CIO (American Federation of Labor and Congress of Industrial Organizations) during the 1960s provide a particularly illustrative example. The union sought to preserve the privileged position of its White members by establishing seniority policies to determine job classification and promotion procedures. Afro-American studies and Industrial Relations scholar Herbert Hill remarks:

> It must be remembered that the AFL-CIO was willing to support the enactment of Title VII [the employment section of the Civil Rights Act] only if the law insulated established union seniority systems and only if the act would affect future discriminatory practices. The AFL-CIO, as a condition of its support, insisted upon the inclusion of Section 703(H) in Title VII, which they believed would protect the racial status quo of the seniority system for at least a generation. (Hill, 1989, p. 193)

29 Darity Jr., Mason, and Stewart (2006) provide a game-theoretic model to explore how different social conditions support the construction, and persistence, of racial and other group identities.
30 Shulman (1991).
31 For a full discussion of the trends in the racial earnings gap, see chapter 6.
32 Bayer and Charles (2018).
33 For discussion of the trends in labor force participation among women, see chapters 4 and 6.
34 This is the first wave of the Great Migration. For further discussion, see chapter 8.
35 According to the US Labor Department, between 1940 and 1950, the national unemployment rate fell from 14.6 percent in December 1940 to 4.3 percent in December 1950.
36 Other studies similarly find that including nonworkers in an examination of the racial earnings gap diminishes indications of progress toward equity (e.g., Darity Jr. and Myers, 1980; Manduca, 2018; Wicks-Lim, 2023).
37 More formally, wealth is typically measured by a household's net worth or a household's assets minus debt, e.g., the Federal Reserve's Survey of Consumer Finances.
38 See, for example, the CORE-ECON online curriculum's unit on income and wealth, "Unit 9: 9.3 Income and wealth," available at: www.core-econ.org/the-economy/microeconomics/09-lenders-borrowers-02-income-and-wealth.html.
39 Darity Jr. et al. (2018).

40 Shapiro (2006).
41 Jones (1998), pp. 82–3. The economics discipline in the US played a significant role in developing such theories – see our discussion of the American Economic Association founders in the textboxes to our "Primer to Part II" section.
42 NORC is a nonpartisan research organization of the University of Chicago. The survey asked: "Do you think Negroes should have as good a chance as white people to get any kind of job, or do you think white people should have the first chance at any kind of job?" Possible responses were: (1) As good a chance; or (2) White people first. NORC combined its surveys into the General Social Survey (GSS) in 1972, a nationally representative survey of US adults which collects "data on contemporary American society in order to monitor and explain trends in opinions, attitudes and behaviors" (National Opinion Research Center, 2021).
43 Bobo et al. (1997) use sociologist Herbert Blumer's (1958) theorization of racial prejudice. In particular, they adopt Blumer's theorization of racial prejudice as a set of views and beliefs that govern how social groups relate to each other, as opposed to a set of preferences or tastes held by individuals outside their group identity. Blumer's group position theory consists of the following crucial factors: (1) "a sense among members of the dominant racial group of proprietary claim or entitlement to greater resources and status"; and (2) a "perception of threat [resentment] posed by subordinate racial group members to those entitlements" (p. 22). Bobo et al. (1997) argue that such racial prejudice propels "the dominant racial group to strive to maintain a privileged status relative to members of the subordinate group" (p. 22).
44 In terms of the taxonomy of racism we presented in chapter 1, laissez-faire racism is a type of internalized racial bias that is expressed through interpersonal, institutional, and structural racism.
45 For a survey of such studies, see Bertrand and Duflo (2016).
46 The Gallup Poll Social Series has surveys of US adults starting in the 1930s. Survey data are weighted to be nationally representative (Gallup, 2025). For survey figures on equal employment opportunity, see Saad (2019).
47 As these figures indicate, significant shares of White and Black Americans hold views that are in opposition: about 60% of Black Americans disagree with about 60% of White Americans on whether discrimination is a primary cause of racial inequality. At the same time, that still leaves about 40% of Black Americans who agree with about 60% of White Americans that discrimination is not mainly to blame for racial inequality. Among the most prominent Black American voices that hold this view is renowned Brown University's economics professor Glenn Loury. Loury views the "development narrative" to be a more important explanation of racial inequality than the racial discrimination, or the "bias" narrative. The development narrative "puts in center place the incomplete project of empowering African Americans who have been adversely impacted by history to acquire those capacities of functioning and performance that can allow for effective competition on what is basically a level playing field" (Loury, 2021, p. xxi). Other Black intellectuals who point to dysfunction within the Black community as the primary obstacle to reducing racial disparities include Thomas Sowell (see, for example, his 2005 book *Black Rednecks, White Liberals*) and Walter Williams (see, for example, his 2011 book *Race and Economics: How Much Can Be Blamed on Discrimination?*).

48 As evidence of this, the *NBC News* public opinion survey frames its questions about affirmative action policies using phrases such as "rigid quotas" and "unfairly discriminate against whites and Asian Americans" (Hart Research Associates, 2023). In fact, affirmative action policies can only legally adopt numerical quotas as part of a court order that results from a finding that an establishment has engaged in discriminatory behavior – i.e., such quotas serve as an element of a remedy to the court finding of discrimination (Badgett and Lim, 2001).

49 For an overview of the origins of the Black Lives Matter movement, see Howard University School of Law's "A Brief History of Civil Rights in the United States: The Black Lives Matter Movement" at https://library.law.howard.edu/civilrightshistory/BLM. For a discussion on recent changes in racial attitudes, see The Associated Press and NORC (2019). For survey data on racial attitudes by race, see Krysan and Moberg (2021). For evidence of Trump's racist views, we can look to his own words. Take, for example, Donald Trump's 2015 presidential announcement speech in which he denigrated Mexicans – nearly wholesale – saying, "When Mexico sends its people, they're not sending their best.... They're sending people that have lots of problems, and they're bringing those problems with us. They're bringing drugs. They're bringing crime. They're rapists. And some, I assume, are good people" ("Here's Donald Trump's Presidential Announcement Speech," *Time Magazine*, June 16, 2015, available at: https://time.com/3923128/donald-trump-announcement-speech). Later, in 2023, Trump revealed his racist views to be even more extreme, saying at a campaign rally that immigrants in the United States illegally are "Poisoning the blood of our country" (Nathan Lane, "Trump Repeats 'Poisoning the Blood' Anti-Immigrant Remark," Reuters, December 16, 2023, available at: www.reuters.com/world/us/trump-repeats-poisoning-blood-anti-immigrant-remark-2023-12-16).

50 These questions paraphrase some of Darity Jr.'s critique of Chiswick's scholarship on discrimination faced by Asian Americans (Darity Jr., 1989, p. 343).

51 For this section, we plumb the scholarship of Darity Jr. (1989) and Kim (1999, 2018) to sketch some illustrative answers to the above three questions as they apply to Asians.

52 The US Census began collecting data on Asian residents in 1860, but only on Chinese residents in California. In 1870, the census began to collect this data outside California as well. Similarly, the US Census began to collect data on residents with Japanese ancestry in 1870, but only in California. By 1890, the census expanded its collection of data on Japanese ancestry outside California (Humes and Hogan, 2009).

53 See Takaki (1998).

54 In 1882, US Congress passed the Chinese Exclusion Act and President Chester A. Arthur signed it into law. This initial 10-year ban on Chinese workers immigrating to the United States had the effect of reducing the level of competition that White Americans workers would face on the West Coast where many Chinese immigrants had initially located in the wake of the Gold Rush. See Takaki (1998). See also discussion in Gibson and Jung (2002).

55 Immigration History (n.d.), "Chinese Exclusion Act AKA 'An Act to Execute Certain Treaty Stipulations Relating to Chinese.'" Available at: https://immigrationhistory.org/item/an-act-to-execute-certain-treaty-stipulations-relating-to-chinese-aka-the-chinese-exclusion-law. Also, see Humes and Hogan (2009).

56 "Coolie" developed into an anti-Asian slur during this period, casting Asians as willing to work for low wages and poor working conditions. For some history about the term "Coolie," see Lakshmi Gandhi, "A History of Indentured Labor Gives 'Coolie' Its Sting," Code Switch, National Public Radio, November 25, 2013, available at: www.npr.org/sections/codeswitch/2013/11/25/247166284/a-history-of-indentured-labor-gives-coolie-its-sting.
57 United States House of Representatives (n.d.b); Changelab (n.d.).
58 The 1790 Nationality Act established that only free, White men could be US citizens. This status expanded over time and included Asians only after the passage of the Immigration and Nationality Act of 1952, aka the McCarran–Walter Law (Takaki, 1998).
59 See Kim (1999), p. 114, for illustrative examples of legal arguments, made on behalf of Asian immigrants, that Asians were "White" – or at least "not Black" – at the end of the nineteenth and early in the twentieth century.
60 For a timeline of immigration, by region and decade, to the United States from 1821 to 2000, see Johnstown Area Heritage Association, "US Immigration by Region and Decade: 1821–2000," n.d., available at: www.jaha.org/wpcontent/uploads/sites/2/2023/01/immigration_timeline.pdf. Also see Asia Society, "Asian Americans Then and Now: Linking Past to Present," Education Today, n.d., available at: https://asiasociety.org/education/asian-americans-then-and-now.
61 This change to the US immigration policy is the means through which the parents of Jeannette Wicks-Lim (co-author of this book) emigrated from South Korea to the United States.
62 Liu (1992), p. 680.
63 Jessica Semega et al., *Income and Poverty in the United States: 2019*, September 15, 2020, available at: www.census.gov/library/publications/2020/demo/p60-270.html. See "Table A-1. Income summary measures by selected characteristics: 2018 and 2019."
64 Woodrum, Rhodes, and Feagin (1980).
65 Most recently, consider the June 2023 Supreme Court ruling against affirmative action policies in higher education admissions policies. This involved the suit by the Students for Fair Admissions against Harvard University and the University of North Carolina. SFFA's suit alleged that the schools' admissions policies had the effect of discriminating against Asian American students. For an overview, see Nina Totenberg (2023), "Supreme Court guts affirmative action, effectively ending race-conscious admissions," National Public Radio, June 29, available at: www.npr.org/2023/06/29/1181138066/affirmative-action-supreme-court-decision.
66 Quoted in Kim (1999), p. 124, available at: www.washingtonpost.com/archive/opinions/1989/04/16/prejudice-against-excellence/6c2922c3-a858-4594-a7ff-7234fa71c5bf. See also Kim (2018) for discussion of this and other affirmative action cases.

3 Afro-Latinxs and Anti-Blackness

1 See Gonzalez-Barrera (2019) and Davila, Mora, and Stockly (2011).
2 Holder and Aja (2021), pp. 52–74.
3 Holder and Aja (2021), pp. 43–59.

Notes to pages 66–70   273

4 See Darity Jr. et al. (2018); Darrick Hamilton, "The Federal Job Guarantee: A Step Toward Racial Justice," *Dissent Magazine*, November 9, 2015, available at: www.dissentmagazine.org/online_articles/federal-job-guarantee-racial-justicedarrick-hamilton; Janelle Jones and John Schmitt, "A College Degree Is No Guarantee," Center for Economic and Policy Research, Washington, DC, May 2014, available at http://cepr.net/documents/black-coll-grads-2014-05.pdf; Yunju Nam et al., "Bootstraps Are for Black Kids: Race, Wealth, and the Impact of Intergenerational Transfers on Adult Outcomes," Insight Center for Community Economic Development, September 2015, available at https://sanford.duke.edu/articles/bootstraps-are-black-kids.

5 See Alan A. Aja et al. (2019), "The Color of Wealth in Miami," a joint publication of the Kirwan Center on the Study of Race and Ethnicity at Ohio State University, Samuel DuBois Cook Center on Social Equity at Duke University, and Insight Center for Community Economic Development, Oakland, California, available at http://kirwaninstitute.osu.edu/wp-content/uploads/2019/02/The-Color-of-Wealth-in-Miami-Metro.pdf; Darity Jr. et al. (2018); Jones and Schmitt, "A College Degree Is No Guarantee"; Darity Jr., Dietrich, and Hamilton (2010); Darrick Hamilton et al., "Umbrellas Don't Make It Rain: Why Studying and Working Hard Isn't Enough for Black Americans," Samuel DuBois Cook Center on Social Equity at Duke University, the New School, and Insight Center for Community Economic Development, 2015, available at www.insightcced.org/uploads/CRWG/Umbrellas-Dont-Make-It-Rain8.pdf.

6 Darity Jr., Dietrich, and Hamilton (2010), pp. 488–9.

7 Petersen and Omori (2018).

8 See Marc Mauer and Ryan S. King (2007), "A 25-Year Quagmire: The War on Drugs and Its Impact on American Society," The Sentencing Project, Washington DC, available at www.prisonpolicy.org/scans/sp/A-25-Year-Quagmire-The-War-On-Drugs-and-Its-Impact-on-American-Society.pdf; Bruce Western, Becky Petit, and Josh Guetzkow (2002), "Black Economic Progress in the Era of Mass Imprisonment," in *Invisible Punishment: The Collateral Consequences of Mass Imprisonment*, ed. Marc Mauer and Meda Chesney-Lind (New York: The New Press): 165–80; Holder (2017), pp. 14–18.

9 Holder and Aja (2021), p. 2.

10 Holder and Aja (2021), p. 2.

11 López and Gonzalez-Barrera (2016).

12 Qian, Lichter, and Tumin (2018).

13 Qian, Lichter, and Tumin (2018).

14 Sharon M. Lee and Sonya M. Tafoya (2006), "Rethinking US Census Racial and Ethnic Categories for the 21st Century," *Journal of Economic and Social Measurement*, 31(3–4) (January 1), pp. 233–52; Sonya M. Tafoya (2004), "Shades of Belonging: Latinos and Racial Identity," Pew Research Center, Washington, DC, available at: www.pewresearch.org/hispanic/2004/12/06/shades-of-belonging.

15 Holder and Aja (2021), p. 3.

16 See Mary C. Waters, Philip Kasinitz, and Asad L. Asad (2014), "Immigrants and African Americans," *Annual Review of Sociology*, 40(1): 369–90; also see Philip Kasinitz (1992), *Caribbean New York: Black Immigrants and the Politics of Race* (Ithaca, NY: Cornell University Press); for rebuttal on the role of culture and labor market skills, see William Darity Jr. (2011), "Revisiting the Debate on Race and Culture: The New (Incorrect) Harvard/Washington

Consensus," *Du Bois Review: Social Science Research on Race*, 8(2): 467–76; Mason (1997).
17 See Michelle A. Hay (2009), *"I've Been Black in Two Countries": Black Cuban Views on Race in the US*, New Americans (El Paso: LFB Scholarly Pub), and Alan A. Aja (2016), *Miami's Forgotten Cubans: Race, Racialization and the Local Afro-Cuban Experience* (London: Palgrave-Macmillan).
18 Galdámez et al. (2023).
19 Freire et al. (2018). In addition, López and Gonzalez-Barrera (2016) note that Princeton University's "Project on Race and Ethnicity" (PERLA) also estimated that one quarter of the Latin American population is of African descent.
20 Rodriguez (2020).
21 Román (2010).
22 US Census Bureau (2024), "FAQs about the History of Demographic Surveys," available at: www.census.gov/about/history/historical-censuses-and-surveys/census-programs-surveys/demographic/faq.html.
23 Public Broadcasting Service (2003a).
24 Public Broadcasting Service (2003b).
25 B. M. Pratt and L. Hixson (2015), "Infographic: Measuring Race and Ethnicity across the Decades, 1790–2010," Race. United States Census Bureau, available at: www.census.gov/data-tools/demo/race/MREAD_1790_2010.html.
26 Holder and Aja (2021), p. 14.
27 US Census Bureau (2015), "The Hispanic Population in the United States – 2015," Table 2: "Population By Sex, Age, and Hispanic Origin Type: 2015." Data from the Current Population Survey Annual Social and Economic Supplement, available at: www.census.gov/data/tables/2015/demo/hispanic-origin/2015-cps.html.
28 See Hank Baker (2024), "La diáspora," *Sun Magazine*, January, available at www.thesunmagazine.org/issues/577/la-diaspora; and López and Gonzalez-Barrera (2016).
29 López and Gonzalez-Barrera (2016).
30 López and Gonzalez-Barrera (2016).
31 Darity Jr., Dietrich, and Hamilton (2010), p. 490.
32 Darity Jr., Dietrich, and Hamilton (2010), p. 488.
33 Cruz-Jansen (2010), p. 282.
34 Cunningham (2006).
35 Jorge (2010), p. 269.
36 Holder and Aja (2021), p. 9.

4 An Intersectional Approach to Stratification Economics

1 The Collective even rejected the stance of lesbian separatism on the grounds that, as Black women, they find any kind of biological determinism to be a "dangerous and reactionary basis upon which to build a politic" (1977).
2 The statement's articulation of interlocking systems of oppression formed the basis of Kimberlé Crenshaw's concept of intersectionality; see Crenshaw (1989).
3 For further discussion on the need to disaggregate data by gender and race and ethnicity to inform policy, see Sharpe (2019).

4 The term "potential work experience" refers to a measure that economists typically use to approximate a person's *actual* work experience when, as is often the case, they do not have data on individuals' actual work experiences (Mincer, 1974). Potential work experience is defined as a person's age minus the number of years spent in school minus 5 (since most children in the US enroll in school at age 5).
5 Hilary Hoynes, Douglas L. Miller, and Jessamyn Schaller (2012), "Who Suffers During Recessions?" *Journal of Economic Perspectives*, 26(3), pp. 27–48.
6 For a close examination of these trends, see Wilson and Jones (2018).
7 Similarly, racism in the labor market hyper-segregated Black men into among the lowest-paying occupations – farm labor and non-farm labor: 41.4% of Black employed men worked as laborers compared to 14.0% of White men.
8 G. Lerner (1973), *Black Women in White America: A Documentary History* (New York: Vintage Books), p. 462.
9 If White women were distributed evenly across occupations, then the CR5 for White women would be 44.2%.
10 Healthcare support occupations include such jobs as personal care aides, homecare aides, nursing assistants, and orderlies.
11 Figure 6.4 shows these patterns in the economic data on the labor force participation rate (LFPR). Black women's LFPR has exceeded, substantially, the LFPR of White women at least since 1940 when the US Census Bureau adopted the current definition of labor force participation.
12 Banks (2020) extends her analysis of how economics devalues Black women's unpaid labor to include the unpaid communal care to which Black women contribute significant amounts of time and energy. This unpaid communal care includes goods and services that the Black community needs but faces obstacles in obtaining due to the community's marginalized status, including especially community organizing around civil rights. We discuss Banks' work further in chapter 8.
13 The US social welfare system provides a clear example of how economic policy reflects and supports social conventions and, therefore, how social conventions drive the distribution of economic resources.
14 As the citations that follow indicate, this section draws heavily from the scholarship presented in Terborg-Penn (1998) and Darity Jr. and Mullen (2020). Also note that the voting rights for women are variously termed "woman suffrage," "woman's suffrage," and "women's suffrage." We alternate between the terms and treat them as synonymous.
15 Terborg-Penn (1998), p. 7; United States National Archives and Records Administration (2021).
16 The Constitution left the regulation of voting rights to state legislatures. Most states limited the franchise to property-owning citizens, which implied White men only. The language in Section 2 of the 14th amendment made the exclusion of women from voting more explicit by tying sanctions to states that inhibited "male" citizens from voting (National Constitution Center, n.d.).
17 For today's readers, identifying the Republican Party as the major political party pursuing civil rights may feel unfamiliar since the Kennedy and Johnson administrations – both Democrats – held the White House during the passage of the major civil rights laws of the 1960s. The Republican Party, however, was the "party of Lincoln" and the political home of abolitionists before the

Civil War, and the proponents of Reconstruction-era policies. The strong support of Black Americans for the Democratic Party, and the general alignment of the Democratic Party's political platform with the Civil Rights Movement is a relatively new phenomenon. This political alignment grew out of a coalition-building strategy of the Democratic Party across marginalized groups – including the working class and Black Americans, specifically – in the wake of the Great Depression (Kirby, 1980).

18 Terborg-Penn (1998, p. 22) describes how the historians Carter Woodson and Bettina Aptheker both point to the way abolitionists' social change activities inspired a radical view on women's rights.
19 Darity Jr. and Mullen (2020), pp. 157–8, 176.
20 Darity Jr. and Mullen (2020), p. 178.
21 For example, the Black Codes took advantage of the exception in the 13th amendment that allowed slavery to be used as criminal punishment. The Black Codes allowed local law enforcement to arrest and imprison Black people for being poor or unemployed, and then law enforcement could hire out prisoners to White employers in exchange for the White employers paying the prisoners' fines. As another example, the Black Codes effectively legalized the enslaving of Black children by White adults: an accusation of poor parenting against Black parents gave White adults legal authority to abduct Black children and put them to work, under an "apprenticeship" (Darity Jr. and Mullen, 2020, p. 187). Samuel Sloan, a Freedmen's Bureau's agent stationed in Texas, said of the Black Codes that they "enslave the rising generation" of freedmen in "worse conditions" of bondage "than they have ever been" (1866, cited in Darity Jr. and Mullen, 2020, p. 184).
22 The US Congress eventually impeached President Andrew Johnson.
23 US Congress passed the 14th amendment in June 1866, and the amendment then went to the states for ratification (United States National Archives and Records Administration, 2024).
24 Prior to 1920, the vast majority – roughly 90 percent – of Black people lived in the Southern states where they did not have voting rights (Wilkerson, 2016).
25 Terborg-Penn (1998), pp. 27–33.
26 This position, reflects, in part, the long-standing misogyny within both the abolition movement and the Republican Party (Terborg-Penn, 1998).
27 Though Kansas was an early ratifier of the 14th amendment (January, 1867), the amendment did not pass until 1868. See United States National Archives (July 25, 2019), The Center for Legislative Archives, Universal Suffrage, available at: www.archives.gov/legislative/features/suffrage.
28 See, for example, Darity Jr. and Mullen (2020), p. 87; and Terborg-Penn (1998), pp. 21, 28–30.
29 Terborg-Penn (1998), p. 28.
30 Note that Terborg-Penn's book is a deliberate effort to document the voices of Black woman suffragists frequently overlooked by the White woman suffragists, such as in the six-volume tome *The History of Woman Suffrage* (edited by Stanton, Anthony, and Gage, 1881).
31 Terborg-Penn (1998), p. 34.
32 Du Bois (1935a) described these years as a period when "the majority of thinking Americans of the North believed in the equal manhood of the Negroes" (pp. 319–20).
33 Darity Jr. and Mullen (2020), p. 196.

34 Darity Jr. and Mullen (2020), pp. 198–202.
35 Darity Jr. and Mullen (2020), p. 204.
36 US Senate Historical Office (n.d.), *Landmark Legislation: Civil Rights Act of 1875*, available at: www.senate.gov/artandhistory/history/common/generic/CivilRightsAct1875.htm.
37 Darity Jr. and Mullen (2020), p. 166.
38 Darity Jr. and Mullen (2020) report that: "In 1895, former US Representative Robert Smalls reported 53,000 blacks had been killed by white terrorists since the end of the Civil War" (p. 166). Also see Darity Jr. and Mullen (2020), pp. 214–18; Terborg-Penn (1998), p. 79; Michael O'Malley, Spring 1999, "A Blood Red Record: The 1890s and American Apartheid, Part III: Lynching," Jim Crow Museum, Ferris State University, available at: www.ferris.edu/HTMLS/news/jimcrow/links/misclink/1980s.htm; Equal Justice Initiative (2015), "Lynching in America," available at: https://time.com/wp-content/uploads/2015/02/eji_lynching_in_america_summary.pdf; Douglas O. Linder (n.d.), "Famous Trials: Lynchings by Year and Race," available at: https://famous-trials.com/sheriffshipp/1084-lynchingsyear.
39 Du Bois (1935a), pp. 693–5.
40 Hannah-Jones (2021a), p. 16.
41 Recall that the 14th amendment discouraged, but did not disallow, the exclusion of Black men from voting. States that did not provide Black men the franchise lost representation in the US Congress proportional to the extent of the disfranchisement: US Senate Historical Office (n.d.), *Landmark Legislation: The 14th Amendment*, available at: www.senate.gov/about/origins-foundations/senate-and-constitution/14th-amendment.htm.
42 Terborg-Penn (1998), p. 110.
43 For example, Terborg-Penn discusses how in the 1890s, some Black women's clubs voluntarily segregated themselves from White women's clubs. According to Black journalist, civil rights leader, and suffragist Josephine St. Pierre Ruffin, Black women chose to join Black women's clubs in order to tend to "the large field of work open to them there" (Ruffin quoted in Terborg-Penn, 1998, p. 118). See also Lofgren and Davis (2023).
44 Terborg-Penn (1998), p. 61.
45 Terborg-Penn (1998) explains: "African American women's organizations developed to push for the enfranchisement of all Black women as a means to protect Black communities, and for the re-enfranchisement of Black men whose votes had been stolen from them" (p. 82).
46 The *Crisis* is the official magazine of the National Association for the Advancement of Colored People (NAACP). It was founded in 1910 by W. E. B. Du Bois (editor), Oswald Garrison Villard, J. Max Barber, Charles Edward Russell, Kelly Miller, William Stanley Braithwaite, and Mary Dunlop Maclean (Terborg-Penn, 1998, p. 126).
47 Terborg-Penn (1998), p. 155.
48 Anderson (2021), p. 262.
49 Anderson (2021), p. 263.
50 The most documented anti-Black pogrom of this era may be the Tulsa Oklahoma massacre of 1921, in which a mob of more than 2,000 White men set ablaze more than 35 blocks of the thriving Greenwood District, also known as Black Wall Street, displacing in the range of 10,000 Black people (Alexander and Alexander, 2021, p. 115).

51 For evidence of Trump's racist views, see note 49 of chapter 2. Trump has been equally explicit when denigrating women. During his 2016 presidential bid, a video was leaked of Trump bragging about using his celebrity status to kiss and grope women without their consent, saying "grab 'em by the p****. You can do anything" (Mark Makela [2016], "Transcript: Donald Trump's Taped Comments about Women," *New York Times*, October 8, available at: www.nytimes.com/2016/10/08/us/donald-trump-tape-transcript.html).

52 See John Gramlich (2021), "How Trump Compares with Other Recent Presidents in Appointing Federal Judges," Pew Research Center, January 13 (www.pewresearch.org/short-reads/2021/01/13/how-trump-compares-with-other-recent-presidents-in-appointing-federal-judges); Alana Wise (2021), "Biden Pledged Historic Cabinet Diversity: Here's How His Nominees Stack Up," National Public Radio, February 5 (www.npr.org/sections/president-biden-takes-office/2021/02/05/963837953/biden-pledged-historic-cabinet-diversity-heres-how-his-nominees-stack-up).

Primer to Part II

1 See, for example, stratification economist Patrick Mason's discussion of the relationship between education, income, and wealth assumed by both individualist economics (what we are referring to as conventional economics) and stratification economics. He distinguishes the two approaches on the basis of how each explains the differences in education and economic outcomes (2023, pp. 113–18).

2 Examples of neoclassical economists who take such an approach – using *human capital theory* – are Becker (1994) and Mincer (1970).

3 This view is most closely associated with Horace Mann, the nineteenth-century proponent of public education who is quoted as declaring that education is "a great equalizer of the conditions of men" (see Arne Duncan [2023], "Education: The 'Great Equalizer,'" published in *Encyclopedia Britannica*, December 29, available at: www.britannica.com/topic/Education-The-Great-Equalizer-2119678). This general view has been expressed by a range of political leaders, as well as celebrities. For example, the former UN Secretary-General Kofi Annan said in a March 2010 speech, "education is the great equalizer of our time. It gives hope to the hopeless and creates chances for those without" (Annan's speech transcript is available at: "Bartels@100: A Life Dedicated to Education," www.kofiannanfoundation.org/speeches/bartels100-a-life-dedicated-to-education). Talk-show host, actress, and author Oprah Winfrey said in a September 2010 press release by her network (OWN), "I value nothing more in the world than education ... It is an open door to freedom" (Winfrey quoted on the OWN website, "Oprah's Angel Network Grants $6 Million to US Charter School Programs," available at: www.oprah.com/pressroom/oprahs-angel-network-grants-6-million-to-us-charter-school). On the CalKids program website – a program created in 2022 – California Governor Gavin Newsom is quoted as saying, "Education is the gateway to opportunity for all California kids" (see Mary Stringini [2022], "CalKIDS: How to Access the Free Cash California Is Giving Out for Kids to Go to College," Fox 11 Los Angeles, August 11, available at: www.foxla.com/news/calkids-california-college-savings-account).

4 See Albelda, Drago, and Shulman (2001), pp. 108–9.
5 As a recent example, see Wilson and Rodgers (2016). Rodgers and Spriggs (1996) refute past research findings that differences in AFQT scores – a variable meant to measure intelligence – explain racial differences in wages. Wilson and Darity Jr. (2022) provide an overview of the empirical evidence that challenges the ability of AFQT scores to explain racial wage differences. See also Mason (1997), who identifies characteristics, such as effort, that are positively correlated with higher educational attainment and Black identity. Mason argues that this positive relationship between effort and racial identity suggests that any estimated negative effect of a "Black" control variable in an earnings equation is likely related to racism.
6 Quote taken from written material that Theoharis provided for a December 7, 2015 Roosevelt Institute meeting to discuss racism in the operations of the US economy.
7 See section 5.6, "Identity Effects on the Quantity and Quality of Instruction Time," in Mason (2023, pp. 138–9). Also, note that the impact of differential power and racial identities can extend to the principal–teacher relationship, as the principal is the manager of the teachers in their school.
8 Excerpt from James Baldwin's speech to educators, delivered on October 16, 1963, as "The Negro Child – His Self-Image"; published in the *Saturday Review*, December 21, 1963, reprinted in *The Price of the Ticket: Collected Non-Fiction 1948–1985* (New York: St. Martin's Press, 1985).
9 See, for example, the popular economics textbook by Case, Fair, and Oster (2012), *Principles of Economics*, 10th edition (Prentice Hall). Although the textbook discusses wealth as the result of savings from income *and* inheritance, inheritance is characterized as savings from "past income": "Wealth is the amount that households have accumulated out of past income through saving or inheritance" (p. 41). Moreover, in their discussion of how wealth transfers tend to produce wealth inequality because wealth accumulates across generations, they discuss such accumulation as resulting from events like "small businesses become successful large businesses" (p. 376) – i.e., from past increases in income.
10 See a fuller discussion of these social group mechanisms in Mason (2023, pp. 39–42), as well as of how the advantages and disadvantages of racial wealth inequality intersect with racial discrimination in the labor market (see, especially, p. 59).
11 Kassandra Weinberg MSW (2017), "Social Work in Criminal Justice Settings," in *An Introduction to Social Work at Ferris State University*, ed. Gladden et al. Montreal: Pressbooks, available at: https://pressbooks.pub/ferrisintroductiontosocialwork.
12 Mason, Myers, and Simms (2022), p. 494, footnote 1.
13 Other influential members include Frank Taussig and Edwin R. A. Seligman.
14 The economic philosophy of laissez faire (French: "allow to do," i.e., "let it happen") came from the physiocrats, eighteenth-century French economists who believed in the natural efficiency of economic forces, but was further developed by classical economists such as Adam Smith. Laissez faire economics promotes the idea that the government and the law should not interfere with the capitalist economy, since the competitive, self-interested behavior of free individuals – i.e., the free forces of supply and demand – should produce a naturally harmonious and self-regulating system (Hunt,

2011, p. 57). Recall that earlier in chapter 2, we discuss *laissez faire racism*, a term sociologist Lawrence Bobo and his co-authors (1997) introduced to characterize the economic policy environment that followed the Jim Crow era. Laissez faire racism, says Bobo, "involves persistent negative stereotyping of African Americans, a tendency to blame blacks themselves for the black–white gap in socioeconomic standing, and resistance to meaningful policy efforts to ameliorate America's racist social conditions and institutions" (1997, p. 16).

15 Economist John Maynard Keynes considered eugenics "the most important significant, and I would add, genuine branch of sociology which exists," and served as the director of the British Eugenics Society from 1937 to 1944 (Keynes, 1946, p. 40).

16 Although it has since been renamed in recognition of Ely's offensive views, the AEA held an annual distinguished lecture series in his honor from 1962 to 2020 (American Economic Association, 2020).

17 Mason et al. (2022), p. 497. The question of whether the structural disadvantages are specifically, or predominantly, experienced by Black Americans is treated as a separate matter. Whether such proxy measures are themselves indicators of racism is not usually investigated.

18 Winter (2019), p. 70.

19 Winter (2019) notes, "there is almost universal acceptance that racial discrimination exists in the criminal justice system" (p. 83).

20 Assuming otherwise requires, again, the belief in Spriggs' tongue-in-cheek two-bus theory that we discuss above (Spriggs, 2020). That is, Spriggs argues that one must deploy the two-bus theory to explain how obvious acts of racism can take place in one social arena (e.g., housing) and be absent from another (e.g., the criminal legal system). The two-bus theory posits that the racist individuals who produce segregated neighborhoods are bussed out, and non-racist individuals are bussed in to operate the criminal legal system. The two-bus theory points out that it is unlikely that one's social group identity can exist within one social arena such as housing and be absent in another, such as the criminal legal system or the labor market.

21 Additional members beyond the scope of this discussion include the nation's first female statistics professor, Katherine Coman, who deemed abolitionist arguments "unscientific" on the grounds that they "make the mistake of thinking the negro a fully developed man"; and Matthew Brown Hammond, who claimed the inherent inferiority of Black agricultural workers, stressing "the general rule of negro idleness and shiftlessness" (cited in Darity Jr., 1994, p. 56).

22 The paper, "Vital Statistics of the Negro" (1892), was solicited by Prudential to garner "evidence" by which to justify the company's refusal to sell life insurance policies to Black Americans.

23 In the Forward to *Studies in the American Race Problem* (1906), Willcox claimed to have "learned more from Stone than anyone else" on the subject of Black inferiority.

24 Ripley taught at Columbia University, MIT, and Harvard University and spent much of his career studying railroad economics.

25 This committee would later co-found the American Association of University Professors (AAUP) along with Ross, effectively establishing the notion of "academic freedom" (De Witte, 2023).

5 Education: Unequal Access, Unequal Outcomes

1. Ethnicity is not available for earlier years of the US Census. As a result, these racial categories are inclusive of Latinx individuals. See: US Census Bureau (n.d.), "Why We Ask Questions about ... Hispanic or Latino Origin," available at: www.census.gov/acs/www/about/why-we-ask-each-question/ethnicity.
2. Note that these data are similar to what we present in figure 7.2. The main difference is the time period that the data represent and the demographic break-out here is by race instead of gender. We present 2019 data here – as opposed to 2022 data in the later chapter – to make the data consistent with the most recent publication of nationally representative data on wealth by race and educational attainment.
3. The unemployment rate is defined as the share of individuals who are active in the labor force (i.e., either looking for work or employed) and do not have work. Those individuals who are not looking for work because they are unable to work, discouraged from looking for work, or have unpaid responsibilities such as eldercare or childcare, or are enrolled in school are *not* included in the labor force figures (US Labor Department [2015], "Labor Force Statistics from the Current Population Survey: How the Government Measures Unemployment," April 8, available at: www.bls.gov/cps/cps_htgm.htm#unemployed).
4. More formally, wealth is typically measured by a household's net worth or a household's assets minus debt, e.g., the Federal Reserve's Survey of Consumer Finances.
5. See chapter 2 for a definition of wealth, and also chapter 7 for an in-depth discussion of wealth, including wealth disparities by race and gender.
6. See, for example, Hamilton and Darity Jr. (2017).
7. We do not include net worth in this table because individuals usually combine their wealth as members of a household. Therefore, analyzing wealth at the individual level requires more nuance. We provide an example of this type of in-depth examination of wealth by gender and race in chapter 7.
8. This section draws heavily from the scholarship of two historians: Anderson (1988) and Du Bois (1935a), especially ch. 15.
9. Evans (2007) writes that: "In 1740, South Carolina became the first colony to draft a law against teaching black people to read or write, and most southern states quickly followed" (p. 33).
10. Darity Jr. and Mullen note how South Carolina (in 1740) made teaching an enslaved person to write punishable by £100, "an extraordinary sum at the time" (2020, p. 88). Anderson quotes former slave William Henry Heard describing brutal punishments, "it was against the law for any person to teach any slave to read; and any slave caught writing suffered the penalty of having his forefinger cut from his right hand" (1988, p. 16).
11. C. Eaton (1936), "A Dangerous Pamphlet in the Old South," *Journal of Southern History*, 23 (August), pp. 323–34.
12. Anderson notes that the "planters' heavy use of child labor contributed significantly to their opposition to black education" (1988, p. 23).
13. J. M. Wiener (1978), "Planter Persistence and Social Change: Alabama, 1850–1870," *Journal of Interdisciplinary History*, 7(2), pp. 235–60, cited on p. 21 of Anderson (1988).
14. The American Freedmen's Aid Commission (1865), *American Freedmen's Aid Commission, and African American Pamphlet Collection*. New York:

The American Freedmen's Aid Commission, available at: www.loc.gov/item/12003486.
15 Du Bois (1935a), pp. 642–5.
16 Du Bois (1935a, p. 648) reports that between 1868 and 1870 the Bureau appropriated $3,521,934 to support these schools; churches and societies contributed $1,572,287; and between 1866 and 1870, $785,700 in cash came from freedpeople.
17 United States Bureau of Refugees, Freedmen, and Abandoned Lands (1867), *Semi-Annual Report on Schools for Freedmen*. Washington, DC: Government Printing Office, available at: https://archive.org/details/371.974_U58_JUL_1_1867.
18 Du Bois (1935a), pp. 638–44.
19 Du Bois describes the importance of the federal military in protecting public schools from attacks by White Americans in Virginia, Texas, Alabama, Mississippi, Louisiana, Kentucky, Tennessee, and Maryland. In his description, Du Bois references observations documented in Freedman's Bureau reports (1935a, pp. 646–7).
20 For a more detailed description of these political shifts, see chapter 4.
21 These include institutions such as Howard University, Atlanta University, Fisk University, and Talledega College – postsecondary educational institutions now known as Historically Black Colleges and Universities (HBCUs).
22 This section draws heavily from the research of Davison M. Douglas, presented in his 2005 book, *Jim Crow Moves North: The Battle over Northern School Segregation, 1865–1954*.
23 Douglas describes how the number of children in public schools rose during the 1830s and 1840s (2005, p. 14). He provides these specific growth figures for the 1840s: in New York, this figure rose from 27,000 to 675,000; from 52,000 to 484,000 in Ohio; and from 74,000 to 414,000 in Pennsylvania. Also see Purnell and Theoharis (2019).
24 To illustrate, consider a *New York Herald* editorial that articulates how the impending integration of schools in Massachusetts (after the passage of its 1855 anti-segregation law) would soften the social distinction between, specifically, racial groups: "Now the n****** are really just as good as white folks. The North is to be Africanized. Amalgamation has commenced" (quoted in Douglas, 2005, p. 59). Frederick Douglass also argues – though in a different spirit – that integrating schools would soften the racial divide, "The evils of separate colored schools are obvious to the common sense of all. Their very tendency is to produce feelings of superiority in the minds of white children, and a sense of inferiority in those of colored children; thus producing pride on the one hand, and servility on the other, and making those who would be the best of friends the worst of enemies. As we have frequently urged on the platform and elsewhere, prejudice is not the creature of birth, *but of education*" (emphasis added; quoted in Douglas, 2005, p. 47).
25 Consider here the articulated purpose of the Noyes Academy in New Hampshire, a racially integrated school that opened in March 1835: to "afford colored youth a fair opportunity to *show* that they are capable, equally with the whites, of improving themselves in every scientific attainment, every social virtue, and every Christian ornament" (Douglas, 2005, p. 43). Douglas describes how White members of the local community decided to abolish the school five months later, in August 1835, and "literally dragged the school

off its foundation, and into a nearby swamp" (2005, p. 44). Another strategy employed by White Americans to hamper the education of Black students was through disparate treatment within integrated schools. For example, Douglas describes how, "Even in communities like Boston, with a relatively liberal attitude toward free blacks, few black children took advantages of opportunities during the late 18th and early 19th centuries to attend white schools, and in fact, black parents petitioned local school authorities for a racially separate school because of the ridicule and mistreatment their children received from the white classmates and teachers" (2005, p. 48).

26 Douglas (2005), pp. 31 and 60.
27 Douglas (2005), p. 26.
28 Douglas (2005), p. 24.
29 C. Gibson (1998), *Population of the 100 Largest Cities and Other Urban Places in the United States: 1790 to 1990* (Working Paper POP-WP027), June, available at: www.census.gov/library/working-papers/1998/demo/POP-twps0027.html.
30 Note that Black Laws differ from the Black Codes passed in the Southern states immediately after the Civil War. See this description of the Black Laws passed in Cleveland, Ohio, in the early 1800s provided by the *Encyclopedia of Cleveland History* at: https://case.edu/ech/articles/b/black-laws. See also Douglas' (2005) discussion on pp. 20–6.
31 Douglas quotes statements made at a Black national convention that the education for Black children "had been shamefully limited" (2005, p. 45). As another example, the New Haven school board "conceded in 1860 that few black children graduated with sufficient knowledge of arithmetic to permit them to be clerks or conduct independent businesses" (Douglas, 2005, p. 45).
32 Douglas (2005), p. 54.
33 Decades later, the US Supreme Court used the precedence of the *Roberts* case to argue for the constitutionality of school segregation in *Plessy* v. *Ferguson* (see web page "1848 SARAH C. ROBERTS VS. THE CITY OF BOSTON," published as part of the "Long Road to Justice: The African American Experience in the Massachusetts Courts" exhibit created by Primary Source, in partnership with the Massachusetts Historical Society, available at: www.longroadtojustice.org/topics/education/sarah-roberts.php).
34 Basically, through to 1900, the courts for the most part did not see education as protected as part of the privileges and immunities of citizenship (Douglas, 2005, pp. 74 and 82).
35 Douglas (2005), pp. 127–31.
36 Douglas (2005), pp. 97–8 and 104–5.
37 For a brief description of the two phases of the Great Migration, see "African American Heritage: The Great Migration (1910–1970)," published by the National Archives (June 28, 2021), at www.archives.gov/research/african-americans/migrations/great-migration.
38 Douglas (2005), p. 158; see also discussion of the Nadir period in chapters 2 and 4.
39 Du Bois (1935a), for example, describes how "not a single hotel in Boston dared to refuse colored guests" during the earlier part of the century. However, after the start of the Great Migration, there were "few Boston hotels where colored people are received" (p. 134). Douglas reports on how the rising level of racial discrimination in the form of realtor policies, anti-Black covenants, and mortgage policies led to the following developments: "In 1910, only 30

percent of Chicago's African Americans lived in predominantly black neighborhoods. By 1920, a majority did so. In Cleveland, the number of census tracts with no black residents more than doubled between 1910 and 1920, from 17 to 38. Racially restrictive covenants in San Francisco caused one black newspaper in that city to announce in 1927, 'Residential Segregation Is as Real in California as in Mississippi'" (2005, p. 137).

40 Douglas (2005), p. 217. Also, Douglas describes the findings of a 1932 study of New Jersey schools which observed that when the Black population in a given area reaches 10 percent, calls for racial segregation notably increase (pp. 153–4).

41 Douglas (2005), pp. 136–9, and p. 141.

42 Douglas (2005), pp. 164–6.

43 Take, for example, the case of Cincinnati where "700 blacks signed a petition in 1897 complaining of the mistreatment of their children in the city's racially mixed schools. The mistreatment was so severe that by 1901, after most of Cincinnati's separate black schools had been closed, only about half of the city's school-age black children still attended the public schools" (Douglas, 2005, p. 108).

44 J. V. Delinder (2004), "Brown v. Board of Education of Topeka: A Landmark Case Unresolved Fifty Years Later," *Prologue Magazine*, 36(1), available at: www.archives.gov/publications/prologue/2004/spring/brown-v-board-1.html.

45 Black migrants primarily settled in the northern states of New York, Illinois, Pennsylvania, Ohio, Michigan, New Jersey, and one western state, California (Douglas, 2005, p. 227).

46 We refer to states outside the former Confederacy as the North, following the practice of Douglas (2005).

47 For example, between 1932 and 1940, the number of Black registered voters in Philadelphia rose from about 69,000 (46 percent of eligible Black voters) to nearly 135,000 (82 percent of eligible Black voters). At this time, the New Deal Democratic policies put forth by Franklin Delano Roosevelt attracted many of these Black voters, pulling their traditional support away from the Republican Party (Douglas, 2005, pp. 228–31).

48 There were 242 major incidents of racially motivated violence within a ten-month period – from March to December of 1943 (Douglas, 2005, p. 236).

49 The National Association for the Advancement of Colored People's (NAACP's) membership grew tenfold from 1940 to 1946, starting at 50,556 to more than 500,000 (Douglas, 2005, p. 225). Black activists appropriated the political rhetoric used by the US government to inspire national support for its war effort – rhetoric centered on a message of promoting freedom and democracy abroad. This "Double V" (V for victory) campaign underscored how the Civil Rights Movement had duplicate goals on the domestic front, highlighting the hypocrisy of America's lack of civil rights for Black Americans. See F. Hughes (2020), "Jim Crow Museum: Double V Campaign," available at: https://jimcrowmuseum.ferris.edu/question/2020/june.htm#.

50 See description of Herbert Hyman and colleagues' analysis of National Opinion Research Centers data from the 1940s and 1950s in Bobo et al. (2012).

51 Douglas (2005), pp. 237–65. *De jure* segregation persisted in some areas despite these legislative gains. The Boston school district, for example, continued its *de jure* segregationist policies into the 1970s (Delmont and Theoharis, 2017).

52 Douglas (2005), pp. 265–73.

53 For an overview, see, for example, Tatum (2017). For more in-depth analysis, see Rothstein (2017) and Oliver and Shapiro (1995).
54 US Census (September 7, 1961), *1960 Census of the Population: Supplementary Reports: Race of the Population of the United States, by States: 1960*, Report Number PC(S1)-10, available at: www.census.gov/library/publications/1961/dec/pc-s1-10.html.
55 Opposition to the Civil Rights Movement spurred major acts of violence, including in a single year the assassination of civil rights leader Medgar Evers and President John F. Kennedy, and the 16th St. Baptist Church bombing that killed four girls, among other violent incidents. See J. M. Hayter, "To End Divisions: Reflections on the Civil Rights Act of 1964," *Richmond Journal of Law and the Public Interest*, 18(4), pp. 499–514.
56 National Center for Education Statistics (n.d.), "Table 235.10. Revenues for public elementary and secondary schools, by source of funds: Selected years, 1919–20 through 2011–12," available at: https://nces.ed.gov/programs/digest/d14/tables/dt14_235.10.asp?current=yes.
57 These data were originally published by Orfield et al. (2014); National Center for Education Statistics (n.d.), "Table 203.50. Enrollment and percentage distribution of enrollment in public elementary and secondary schools, by race/ethnicity and region: Selected years, fall 1995 through fall 2030," available at: https://nces.ed.gov/programs/digest/d21/tables/dt21_203.50.asp.
58 For example, the Nixon administration favored voluntary, as opposed to mandated, desegregation plans, and longer timeframes to achieve plan goals (Frankenberg and Taylor, 2015). As another example, at its start in 1981, the Reagan administration cut funding from the Emergency School Aid Act, the program created to compel greater desegregation efforts among lagging school districts, incentivized with federal funds (Devins and Stedman, 1984). See also Frankenberg, Hawley, and Orfield (2017).
59 These three cases established: (1) Desegregation plans as temporary and preferably controlled by local authorities. In particular, a school district sufficiently integrated to be deemed unitary (i.e., integrated) did not have to put in place any plans for dealing with any remaining segregation or any segregation that may develop in the future (*Board of Education* v. *Dowell*, 1991). (2) Incremental progress as sufficient. The Supreme Court ruled that school districts could satisfy court orders to desegregate in stages rather than quickly and comprehensively (*Freeman* v. *Pitts*, 1992). (3) School districts only need to correct the outcomes of past discriminatory policies, a limited requirement that could continue to result in segregated schools (*Missouri* v. *Jenkins*, 1995). See discussion of these cases in Orfield et al. (2014, p. 27) and Reardon et al. (2012, p. 877). Reardon et al.'s (2012) statistical analysis of racial integration trends among school districts by court supervision status observes measurable declines in school district integration levels within 10 years of release from court supervision. The authors note that this pattern is consistent with adopting neighborhood assignments.
60 For the purposes of this figure, poverty is indicated by enrollment in free or reduced-cost school lunches. Orfield et al. (2014) stopped using this measure because, as they explain: "While there have always been concerns about the representativeness of using free/reduced lunch eligibility as a measure of student poverty, recent legislation to provide meals to all students in

high-poverty schools may further obscure efforts to use this to measure student poverty." See www.schooldiversity.org/pdf/CEP_Letter_for_ED_3-13-14.pdf for further information (footnote 7, p. 15).

61 As another example, Francis et al. (2019) observed high school counselors recommending significantly fewer well-qualified Black female students for advanced math courses (Calculus Advanced Placement or AP courses) than their male or White counterparts.

62 See also Wallace and Goodkind (2008).

63 These figures are for students who were in high school between 2004 and 2010. See Francis and Darity Jr. (2021), figure 1, p. 193.

64 This figure is in current dollars from National Center for Education Statistics (n.d.), "Table 330.40. Average total cost of attendance for first-time, full-time undergraduate students in degree-granting postsecondary institutions, by control and level of institution, living arrangement, and component of student costs: selected years, 2010–11 through 2020–21," available at: https://nces.ed.gov/programs/digest/d21/tables/dt21_330.40.asp.

65 Across the roughly 4,000 degree-granting colleges and universities in the US, about 2,600 grant 4-year college degrees (National Center for Education Statistics Fast Facts [n.d.], "Educational Institutions – Question: How Many Postsecondary Educational Institutions Exist in the United States?" available at: https://nces.ed.gov/fastfacts/display.asp?id=1122. Of those 2,600, approximately 200 are selective – inviting one-third of their applicant pool to enroll (Drew Desilver [2019], "A Majority of US Colleges Admit Most Students Who Apply," Pew Research Center Short Reads, April 9, available at: www.pewresearch.org/short-reads/2019/04/09/a-majority-of-u-s-colleges-admit-most-students-who-apply).

66 USAFacts (July 2022), "Our Changing Population: Virginia," available at: https://usafacts.org/data/topics/people-society/population-and-demographics/our-changing-population/state/virginia?endDate=2021-01-01&startDate=1980-01-01.

67 J. Fallows (2001), "The Early-Decision Racket," *The Atlantic*, 288(2), pp. 37–52.

68 J. J. Park and M. K. Eagan (2011), "Who Goes Early? A Multi-Level Analysis of Enrolling via Early Action and Early Decision Admissions," *Teachers College Record*, 113(11), pp. 2345–73, available at: https://doi.org/10.1177/016146811111301108; also M. Kim (2010), "Early Decision and Financial Aid Competition among Need-Blind Colleges and Universities," *Journal of Public Economics*, 94(5), pp. 410–20. Avery, Fairbanks, and Zeckhauser (2001) find that the higher ED acceptance rates cannot be fully explained by the quality of ED applications and estimates that applying ED is equivalent to scoring 100 points higher on the SAT exam.

69 National Center for Education Statistics (n.d.), "Table 306.10. Total fall enrollment in degree-granting postsecondary institutions, by level of enrollment, sex, attendance status, and race/ethnicity or nonresident status of student: selected years, 1976 through 2022," available at: https://nces.ed.gov/programs/digest/d23/tables/dt23_306.10.asp.

70 A transcript of President Johnson's 1965 commencement address to Howard University is available at The American Presidency Project, available at: www.presidency.ucsb.edu/documents/commencement-address-howard-university-fulfill-these-rights.

71 Here, "aesthetics" refers to a weave of artistic and stylistic sensibilities, ethics, ideas, and representations of normative experiences of the world. For writer and critical thinker of the Black Arts and Aesthetic movements Larry Neal, the "Western aesthetic" is situated within a White European philosophical tradition that is seen as common sense: "what the Western man calls 'aesthetic' is fundamentally an assembly of dead ideas based on dead people; a people whose ideas have been found meaningless in light of contemporary history. We need new values, new ways of living" (Neal, 2024). Black Aesthetics, in contrast, are fundamentally anti-Eurocentric and intimately connected to Black lived experiences of the world.
72 According to the dual program model, students must supplement their studies of African American experience with that of a traditional discipline.
73 At Columbia University, Black students called for an end to university dealings with American intelligence agencies, including the CIA. Across the HBCUs, Black students insisted on changes to restrictions on student life, inequitable state funding practices, lack of representation on policymaking boards, and many other changes.
74 Tatum (2017), pp. 38–9. Such outcomes had been predicted by simulations conducted by the Office of the President of the UC system as well as at the Admissions Office of UC, San Diego. The simulation models replaced race with socio-economic criteria such as income as a plus-factor and projected a decline in under-represented minorities, such as Black, Latinx, and Indigenous students (Conrad and Sharpe, 1996, pp. 27–9).
75 J. Ashkenas, H. Park, and P. Adam (2017), "Even with Affirmative Action, Blacks and Hispanics Are More Underrepresented at Top Colleges Than 35 Years Ago," *New York Times*, August 24, available at: https://nyti.ms/3s2hFxC.
76 Nina Totenberg (2023), "Supreme Court Guts Affirmative Action, Effectively Ending Race-Conscious Admissions," National Public Radio: Law, June 29, 7:52 p.m. ET, available at: www.npr.org/2023/06/29/1181138066/affirmative-action-supreme-court-decision.
77 Other institutions, such as tribal colleges and universities (TCUs), serve a similar role for Indigenous Americans, and Hispanic-Serving Institutions (HSIs) for Latinx students.
78 M. Gasman (2009), "Historically Black Colleges and Universities in a Time of Economic Crisis: How have HBCUs responded to the current crisis?" *Academe*, 95(6): 26–8.
79 National Center for Education Statistics Fast Facts (n.d.), "Historically Black Colleges and Universities – Question: What Data Do You Have on Historically Black Colleges and Universities in the United States?" available at: https://nces.ed.gov/fastfacts/display.asp?id=667.
80 National Center for Science and Engineering Statistics (NCSES) of the National Science Foundation (2021), "Women, Minorities, and Persons with Disabilities in Science and Engineering," Report NSF 21-321, April 29, available at: https://ncses.nsf.gov/pubs/nsf21321/report/field-of-degree-minorities#blacks-or-african-americans.
81 Price and Viceisza (2023) provide an overview of the extant research evidence on the impact of HBCUs on Black students' outcomes.

6 Unemployment, Occupational Crowding, Wage Inequality, and Anti-Blackness in the Labor Market

1 Darity Jr. (2005), p. 145.
2 Federal Reserve Board Report to the Congress on Credit Scoring and Its Effects on the Affordability and Availability of Credit – Executive Summary, August 2007, available at: www.federalreserve.gov/boarddocs/rptcongress/creditscore/creditscore.pdf.
3 Darity Jr. (1982), p. 73.
4 "Dummy variables" represent different racial groups (Black, Latinx, Asian Americans, for instance) with one group (say, White Americans) serving as a reference group in regression equations. When these dummy variables are negative and statistically significant, it suggests that individuals from those racial groups earn lower wages compared to the reference category (which can be interpreted as a wage penalty associated with their race in relation to White Americans if they are the reference group), even after controlling for factors such as education and occupation. The negative coefficient indicates a decrease in wages/earnings relative to the reference group, and statistical significance implies this observed difference in wages between a group and the reference group is not random, but is instead statistically meaningful, thus indicating the presence of discrimination in the labor market.
5 Mason (2000), p. 321.
6 Bergmann (1971), p. 294.
7 Aigner and Cain (1977), p. 176.
8 US Department of Labor, BLS (2025), "The Employment Situation – July 2023, Table A-2. Employment status of the civilian population by race, sex, and age," available at: www.bls.gov/bls/news-release/empsit.htm#2023.
9 National Park Service (n.d.), "Sojourner Truth: Ain't I a Woman?" available at: www.nps.gov/articles/sojourner-truth.htm.
10 Holder (2020).
11 Holder (2020), p. 4.
12 Retrieved data from the Current Population Survey for men and women, in 2022 current dollars, from the US Department of Labor, Bureau of Labor Statistics series (n.d.) "(Unadjusted) Median Usual Weekly Earnings, Employed Full-time, Wage and Salary Workers," available at: www.bls.gov/cps/data.htm.
13 Retrieved data from the Current Population Survey for Black or African American and White workers in 2022 current dollars from the BLS series (n.d.) "(Unadjusted) Median Usual Weekly Earnings, Employed Full-time, Wage and Salary Workers," available at: www.bls.gov/cps/data.htm
14 Judge Christen, Morgan B. (2020), *Rizo* v. *Yovino*, 950 F.3d. In 16-15372, edited by United States Court of Appeals for the Ninth Circuit.
15 Society for Human Resource Management presentation (August 2010), "Background Checking: The Implications of Credit Background Checks on Hiring Decision," available at: www.shrm.org/Research/SurveyFindings/Articles/Pages/2010SurveyFindings.aspx.
16 Federal Reserve Board Report to the Congress on Credit Scoring and Its Effects on the Affordability and Availability of Credit – Executive Summary, August 2007.
17 See "Asking for Salary History Perpetuates Pay Discrimination from Job to

Job," National Women's Law Center, March 2022 Fact Sheet, Washington, DC, available at: https://nwlc.org/wp-content/uploads/2020/12/Asking-for-Salary-History-2022.pdf.
18 A. Dalrymple (March 2023), "Equal Pay in the United States: Salary History Bans," US Department of Labor Women's Bureau Issue Brief, Washington, DC, available at: www.dol.gov/sites/dolgov/files/WB/equalpay/WB_Brief_Equal_Pay_Salary_History_Bans_03072023.pdf.
19 R. Maurer (2020), "House Approves Ban on Most Employment Credit Checks," Society for Human Resource Professionals, January 30, available at: www.shrm.org/topics-tools/news/talent-acquisition/house-approves-ban-employment-credit-checks.
20 N. Gunzenhauser Popper and A. M. Gomez (n.d.), "House Passes Bill Restricting Employment Credit Checks," *National Law Review*, available at www.natlawreview.com/article/house-passes-bill-restricting-employer-credit-checks.
21 D. Pager (2021), "The Mark of a Criminal Record," *American Journal of Sociology* 108(5), pp. 937–75.
22 B. Avery and H. Lu (2021), *Ban the Box: US Cities, Counties, and States Adopt Fair-Chance Policies to Advance Employment Opportunities for People with Past Convictions*. Fair Chance Employment. New York: National Employment Law Project (NELP).
23 B. Damante, L. Hoffman, and R. Khattar (2023), "Quick Facts about State Salary Range Transparency Laws," Center for American Progress, March 9, Washington, DC, available at: www.americanprogress.org/article/quick-facts-about-state-salary-range-transparency-laws.
24 Federal Reserve Board (July 29, 2021), "Monetary Policy: What Are Its Goals? How Does It Work?" available at: www.federalreserve.gov/monetarypolicy/monetary-policy-what-are-its-goals-how-does-it-work.htm.

7 Wealth Attainment and Anti-Blackness: The Case of Black Women

1 "Asset," *Merriam-Webster.com Dictionary*, Merriam-Webster, available at: www.merriam-webster.com/dictionary/asset.
2 Neil Bennett, Donald Hays, and Briana Sullivan (2022), "2019 Data Show Baby Boomers Nearly 9 Times Wealthier than Millennials," US Census Bureau, August 1, available at: www.census.gov/library/stories/2022/08/wealth-inequality-by-household-type.html.
3 Lisa Camner McKay (2022), "How the Racial Wealth Gap Has Evolved – and Why It Persists: New Dataset Identifies the Causes of Today's Wealth Gap," Federal Reserve Bank of Minneapolis, October 3, available at: www.minneapolisfed.org/article/2022/how-the-racial-wealth-gap-has-evolved-and-why-it-persists.
4 Signe-Mary McKernan et al. (2017), "Nine Charts about Wealth Inequality," Urban Institute, last updated October 5, available at: https://apps.urban.org/features/wealth-inequality-charts.
5 US Department of Labor, Bureau of Labor Statistics (2015), "Table 3: Median usual weekly earnings of full-time wage and salary workers by age, race, Hispanic or Latino ethnicity, and sex, not seasonally adjusted," last modified September 16, available at: www.bls.gov/webapps/legacy/cpswktab3.htm.

6 Hegewisch and Tesfaselassie (2019), p. 3; also see US Department of Labor, Bureau of Labor Statistics, "Table 39: Median weekly earnings of full-time wage and salary workers by detailed occupation and sex, 2018," available at: www.bls.gov/cps/cpsaat39.htm.
7 Author's analysis of American Community Survey data for 2017 from Steven Ruggles, Sarah Flood, Ronald Goekin, Josiah Glover, Erin Meyer, Jose Pacas, and Matthew Sobek. IPUMS USA: Version 9.0 (data set). Minneapolis, MN: IPUMS, 2019, available at: https://doi.org/10.18128/D010.V9.0.
8 US Census Bureau, "Educational Attainment of the Population 18 Year and Over, by Age, Sex, Race, and Hispanic Origin: 2021" for "White Alone" and "Black Alone," available at: www.census.gov/data/tables/2021/demo/educational-attainment/cps-detailed-tables.html.
9 Jhumpa Bhattacharya, Anne Price, and Andre M. Perry (2022), "Why Homeownership Fails to Build Wealth for Black Women," Locked Out: Black Women, Wealth and Homeownership series, *Nonprofit Quarterly,* November 9, available at: https://nonprofitquarterly.org/series/locked-out-black-women-wealth-and-homeownership.
10 Danielle Dickens and Mica Whitfield (2022), "Closing the Pay Gap Facing Black Women in the US," infographic, Urban Institute, available at: www.urban.org/research/publication/closing-pay-gap-facing-black-women-us.
11 Bhattacharya, Price, and Perry, "Why Homeownership Fails to Build Wealth for Black Women."
12 The Annie E. Casey Foundation, "Children in Single-Parent Families by Race and Ethnicity in the United States, 2011–21," available at: https://datacenter.aecf.org/data/tables/107-children-in-single-parent-families-by-race-and-ethnicity#detailed/1/any/false/1729,37,871,870,573,869,36,868,867,133/10,11,9,12,1,185,13/432,431.
13 Analysis of 2019 and 2021 data from the US Department of Labor Bureau of Labor Statistics' Consumer Expenditure Survey.
14 Becca Damante, Lauren Hoffman and Rose Khattar, "Quick Facts about State Salary Range Transparency Laws," Center for American Progress, March 9, Washington, DC, available at: www.americanprogress.org/article/quick-facts-about-state-salary-range-transparency-laws.
15 S. Markoff (2022), "Frequently Asked Questions about Baby Bonds," available at: https://prosperitynow.org/resources/baby-bonds-frequently-asked-questions.
16 Office of Treasurer Erick Russell, "CT Baby Bonds," available at: https://portal.ct.gov/OTT/Debt-Management/CT-Baby-Bonds.
17 Office of Senator Cory Booker (2023), "Booker, Pressley Reintroduce Bicameral 'Baby Bonds' Legislation to Tackle Wealth Inequality," news release, February 15, available at: www.booker.senate.gov/news/press/booker-pressley-reintroduce-bicameral-baby-bonds-legislation-to-tackle-wealth-inequality.
18 The White House, "The Build Back Better Framework: President Biden's Plan to Rebuild the Middle Class," available at: www.whitehouse.gov/build-back-better.
19 Juana Summers (2021), "A Bill to Study Reparations for Slavery Had Momentum, but Still No Vote," *All Things Considered,* NPR, November 12, available at: www.npr.org/2021/11/12/1054889820/a-bill-to-study-reparations-for-slavery-had-momentum-in-congress-but-still-no-vo.

8 The Criminal Legal System: Hardening the Racial Divide

1. See chapter 1 in *Introduction to Criminal Law* by L. M. Storm, Esq. in *Criminal Law, v.1.0* (2012; online: Saylor Academy), available at: https://saylordotorg.github.io/text_criminal-law.
2. For example, the 1860 US Census divides inhabitants of the US states and territories into White, free colored, or slaves (see also our discussion in chapter 3 of eighteenth-century classifications for Black Americans). There is no documentation of any White inhabitants with the status of slave, vs. 89 percent of inhabitants identified as "black" or "mulatto." According to the 1860 Census, 4.4 million Black individuals resided in the US and its territories. Of these, 4.0 million of these individuals (or 89 percent) were enslaved, and 488,000 (or 11 percent) were free (see p. ix of US Census [n.d.], "Population of the United States in 1860: Introduction," available at: www2.census.gov/library/publications/decennial/1860/population/1860a-02.pdf.
3. Roberts (2021), p. 51.
4. Roberts (2021), p. 52.
5. Roberts (2021), pp. 49–54; Darity Jr. and Mullen (2020), pp. 184–94. The legal system also allowed for the children of Indigenous families to be legally abducted. From 1819 to 1969, these abductions were part of a nationwide effort by White communities to eradicate Indigenous culture. See the May 2022 report by Bryan Newland, Assistant Secretary – Indian Affairs, titled "Federal Indian Boarding School Initiative Investigative Report," available at: www.bia.gov/sites/default/files/dup/inline-files/bsi_investigative_report_may_2022_508.pdf.
6. See further discussion in chapter 4.
7. Boston and Hallam (2004).
8. For a historical overview of lynching in the US, see the 2017 report "Lynching in America," 3rd edition, by the Equal Justice Initiative, available at: https://lynchinginamerica.eji.org/report.
9. "Rise Once Again, George Henry White, American Phoenix" (Sept. 17, 2016, updated Dec. 7, 2020), GHW Info: George Henry White and the Anti-Lynching Bill of 1900, available at: www.georgehenrywhite.com/single-post/2016/09/17/george-henry-white-and-the-anti-lynching-bill-of-1900.
10. HR 55 of the 117th Congress, 2nd Session, "Emmett Till Antilynching Act" (see www.congress.gov/117/bills/hr55/BILLS-117hr55eh.xml).
11. A video recording of Darity Jr.'s 2023 Gamble Lecture at the University of Massachusetts Amherst is available here: www.youtube.com/watch?v=PytHIKzs044.
12. The North racially segregated its public (common) schools during the antebellum period, as documented by Douglas (2005), and discussed at length in chapter 5.
13. African American Pamphlet Collection (1900), *What a Colored Man Should Do to Vote: To the Colored Men of Voting Age in the Southern States* (Philadelphia: Press of E. A. Wright), available at: www.loc.gov/item/92838850.
14. Prisons typically house those who have been convicted of a crime and are serving more than a year; jails typically house those who have been charged, but not convicted, of a crime and are awaiting trial, as well as those convicted of a crime but serving less than a year. Note that the trendlines in figure 8.4 measure a slightly different trend from what Myers and Sabol capture. Figure

8.4 rates are for the working age population (15 to 64 years old), rather than the entire population – the base that Myers and Sabol use. As a result, the rates in figure 8.4 (as well as the rates in figures 8.5, 8.7, and 8.8) are higher – but not dramatically so – than those in Myers and Sabol's data due to the rates' different bases. For detailed discussions of the Vera Institute's estimating methodology, see Hinds et al. (2017) and Kang-Brown et al. (2018, 2020).

15 See pp. 333–7 of G. LeBaron (2012), "Rethinking Prison Labor: Social Discipline and the State in Historical Perspective," *WorkingUSA*, 15(3), pp. 327–51. Also see American Civil Liberties Union and the University of Chicago Law School's Global Human Rights Clinic (ACLU–GHRC) (2022), pp. 25–7.

16 Some states have amended their state constitutions to eliminate slavery in all cases, such as Alabama, Colorado, Nebraska, Nevada, Oregon, Rhode Island, Tennessee, Utah, and Vermont. However, it is unclear whether these legal changes have actually eliminated forced labor given the coercive conditions under which people in prison live. With the exception of Rhode Island which eliminated the 13th amendment's exception for forced labor in 1842, these nine states only recently changed their laws – between 2018 and 2022. See S. Spencer (June 17, 2022; updated October 18, 2022), "Emancipation on the Ballot: Why Slavery Is Still Legal in America – and How Voters Can Take Action," Legal Defense Fund, available at: www.naacpldf.org/13th-amendment-emancipation.

17 This figure is based on the ACLU and GHRC's analysis of survey data collected by the Department of Justice in 2016 (ACLU–GHRC, 2022, see p. 28). The ACLU–GHRC report also documents that, according to the 2019 Bureau of Justice Statistics Census of State and Federal Adult Correctional Facilities, 90 percent of private prisons and 95 percent of public prisons had work programs for facilities maintenance and support services (2022, p. 29).

18 ACLU–GHRC (2022), p. 58.

19 Governments also use a limited amount of prison labor to improve their fiscal situation more generally. The 2022 ACLU–GHRC report documents a notable share of prisoners –7 percent –are employed in public works programs such as road work, cleaning up parks, natural disaster preparation, and response work such as fighting wildfires and filling sandbags. Also, 7 percent of prisoners are employed in the "production of goods and services in state-owned prison industries or 'correctional industries' for sale to other state agencies" (p. 27). These "industry jobs" have an average minimum hourly wage of 30 cents; the average maximum hourly wage is $1.30 (p. 58). These correctional industries also sell their goods and services to a wide-ranging variety of private-sector companies, including, among others, the 3M Company, Apple Inc., FedEx, Lowe's, KFC, Pepsi Co., Proctor and Gamble, and Verizon. Therefore, private firms also use forced labor to boost their profits.

20 As of 2020, the District of Columbia also does not restrict the voting rights of those convicted of a felony.

21 The 23 states that withhold voting rights among felons during incarceration include (states followed by a year in parentheses adopted this reform since 2019): Hawaii, Connecticut (2021), California (2020), Washington (2021), Oregon, Nevada (2019), Utah, Montana, Colorado (2019), New Mexico (2023), North Dakota, Minnesota (2023), Michigan, Illinois, Indiana, Ohio, Pennsylvania, Maryland, New Jersey, New York (2021), Massachusetts, New

Hampshire, and Rhode Island. The 14 states that automatically restore voting rights to felons after the completion of the sentence (prison, parole, probation) include: Alaska, Arkansas, Idaho, Kansas, South Dakota, Oklahoma, Texas, Missouri, Wisconsin, West Virginia, North Carolina, South Carolina, Georgia, Louisiana (as of 2019, with the additional condition of not being incarcerated within 5 years). The 11 states that do not automatically restore voting rights after sentence completion, and require some other action, include: Florida, Iowa, Virginia, Wyoming, Arizona, Kentucky (as of 2019, non-violent offenders' voting rights are automatically restored after completing their sentences), Delaware, Tennessee, Alabama, Mississippi, Nebraska (American Civil Liberties Union, 2023, Felony Disenfranchisement Laws [MAP], available at: www.aclu.org/issues/voting-rights/felony-disenfranchisement-laws-map; National Conference of State Legislatures (October 18, 2024), Felon Voting Rights, available at: www.ncsl.org/elections-and-campaigns/felon-voting-rights.
22 Note that the US Census did not begin releasing estimates of Latinx, Native, and Asian American and Pacific Islander populations until 1990.
23 Cited in Roberts (2004), p. 1283.
24 See US Census Bureau (September 12, 2023), "Historical Poverty Tables: People and Families – 1959 to 2022," Table 4: Poverty status of families by type of family, presence of related children, race, and Hispanic origin: 1959 to 2022, available at: www.census.gov/data/tables/time-series/demo/income-poverty/historical-poverty-people.html.
25 Roberts is referring to this research: T. R. Clear, "The Problem with 'Addition by Subtraction': The Prison–Crime Relationship in Low Income Communities," in *Invisible Punishment: The Collateral Consequences of Mass Imprisonment*, ed. Mauer and Chesney-Lind, pp. 181–94.
26 N. G. La Vigne, C. A. Mamalian, J. Travis, and C. Visher (2003), "A Portrait of Prisoner Reentry in Illinois," Urban Institute Research Report, April, available at: www.urban.org/sites/default/files/publication/42776/410662-A-Portrait-of-Prisoner-Reentry-in-Illinois.PDF.
27 E. Drucker (2002), "Population Impact of Mass Incarceration under New York's Rockefeller Drug Laws: An Analysis of Years of Life Lost," *Journal of Urban Health*, 79(3), pp. 434–5.
28 Yi (2023), p. 18.
29 For a critique of mainstream economics' male-centric focus, see P. England (1993), "The Separative Self: Androcentric Bias in Neoclassical Assumptions," in *Beyond Economic Man: Feminist Theory and Economics*, ed. M. A. Ferber and J. A. Nelson (University of Chicago Press), pp. 37–53. Also see N. Folbre (2001), *The Invisible Heart: Economics and Family Values* (New York: The New Press). For a similar critique of Marxist economics, see the 2017 volume edited by T. Bhattacharya titled *Social Reproduction Theory: Remapping Class, Recentering Oppression* (London: Pluto Press).
30 For a discussion of how the perspective of White women tends to dominate feminist economics, see Banks (2021).
31 This Loïc Wacquant quote is from "Deadly Symbiosis: When Ghetto and Prison Meet and Mesh," in *Mass Imprisonment: Social Causes and Consequences*, ed. D. Garland (London and Thousand Oaks, CA: Sage, 2001). Note, too, that in such neighborhoods, women who may need law enforcement protection from domestic violence, a gender-based form of oppression, have less access

to public safety resources. This is because Black women living in communities with high incarceration rates may be especially concerned with protecting their own household members or neighbors from contact with agents of the criminal legal system (Roberts, 2004, pp. 1287–8).

32 Mason et al. (2022) discuss the usefulness of "racial threat theory" for analyzing mass incarceration on pp. 507–9.

33 For a brief description of the two phases of the Great Migration, see *African American Heritage: The Great Migration (1910–1970)* published by the National Archives (June 28, 2021), available at www.archives.gov/research/african-americans/migrations/great-migration.

34 Derenoncourt (2022), p. 373.

35 See Chapter 5, sections 5.3.3, "Racial Segregation into the Twenty-First Century" and 5.3.4, "The Limits to Racial Integration in the Twenty-First Century," for our detailed description of the anti-Black racial hostilities arising during the Great Migration.

36 For a discussion of these estimates, see the accompanying "On-Line Appendix" by Derenoncourt (2022), available at: https://assets.aeaweb.org/asset-server/files/16001.pdf. See, in particular, appendix F, p. 154.

37 See Derenoncourt (2022), table 7, p. 397. Note that Derenoncourt reports the percent *reduction* in the racial gap in upward mobility in table 7. We convert these figures to the equivalent percent *increase* in the racial gap in upward mobility.

38 The material in this section draws heavily on Alexander (2012).

39 See Alexander (2012), pp. 127–8.

40 For a brief description of the Freedom Rides, see The Martin Luther King, Jr. Research and Education Institute at Stanford University (n.d.), "The Freedom Rides," available at: https://kinginstitute.stanford.edu/freedom-rides.

41 Library of Congress (n.d.), "African American Voting Rights," available at: www.loc.gov/classroom-materials/elections/right-to-vote/voting-rights-for-african-americans.

42 By 1967, Senator Edward William Brooke became the first Black senator since Senator Blanche K. Bruce whose term ended in 1881, more than 80 years earlier. Senator Bruce was also the lone Black senator during his term (United States House of Representatives, n.d.a).

43 For a brief biography of Shirley Chisholm, see D. Michals (2015), "Shirley Chisholm, 1924–2005," The National Women's History Museum, available at: www.womenshistory.org/education-resources/biographies/shirley-chisholm.

44 See National Archives, Milestone Documents (February 8, 2022), "Medicare and Medicaid Act (1965)," available at: www.archives.gov/milestone-documents/medicare-and-medicaid-act.

45 J. Shahin (2014), "Commemorating the History of SNAP: Looking Back at the Food Stamp Act of 1964," USDA (United States Department of Agriculture), Oct. 15, available at: www.usda.gov/media/blog/2014/10/15/commemorating-history-snap-looking-back-food-stamp-act-1964.

46 Office of Federal Contract Compliance Programs (n.d.), "History of Executive Order 11246," available at: www.dol.gov/agencies/ofccp/about/executive-order-11246-history.

47 Alexander (2012), p. 39.

48 See, for example, K. K. Gaines (2018), "The End of the Second Reconstruction," *Modern American History*, 1, pp. 113–19, available at: https://doi.org/10.1017/mah.2017.16.

49 For brief background on these organizations see: (1) the on-line resources compiled by Matthew Lassiter and the Policing and Social Justice HistoryLab at the University of Michigan, "Detroit under Fire: Police Violence, Crime Politics, and the Struggle for Racial Justice in the Civil Rights Era," in particular, the web page "Adult Community Movement for Equality" (n.d.), available at: https://policing.umhistorylabs.lsa.umich.edu/s/detroitunderfire/page/adult-community-movement-for-equality, and the web page "Black Panther Party" (n.d.), available at: https://policing.umhistorylabs.lsa.umich.edu/s/detroitunderfire/page/black-panther-party; (2) for the NWRO, see J. Tillmon (1972), "Welfare Is a Women's Issue," *Ms. Magazine*, Spring, available at: https://msmagazine.com/2021/03/25/welfare-is-a-womens-issue-ms-magazine-spring-1972; (3) for AIM, see L. Waterman Wittstock and E. J. Salinas (n.d.), "A Brief History of the American Indian Movement," available at: www.aimovement.org/ggc/history.html; and (4) for the Brown Berets, see J. Estrada (n.d.), "Brown Beret Chapters: 1969–1972," available at: https://depts.washington.edu/moves/brown_beret_map.shtml, and A. Cruz (October 15, 2018), "The Brown Berets, as Explained by Founding Member Dr. David Sanchez," available at: www.teenvogue.com/story/brown-berets-as-explained-by-founding-member-dr-david-sanchez.

50 Readers may be more familiar with the term "Rainbow Coalition" from Jesse Jackson's use of it in his 1984 presidential campaign which echoed the original Rainbow Coalition's idea of forming interracial alliances.

51 Civil Rights Digital Library (n.d.), "New York Race Riots," available at: https://crdl.usg.edu/events/ny_race_riots; H. Thompson (2016), *Blood in the Water: The Attica Prison Uprising of 1971 and Its Legacy* (New York: Vintage Books).

52 Alexander (2012), pp. 101–66; Hinton (2016), pp. 1–26.

53 K. Beckett and T. Sasson (2004), *The Politics of Injustice: Crime and Punishment in America*, 2nd edition (Thousand Oaks, CA: Sage Publications), p. 51.

54 Nixon served as vice president to President Dwight Eisenhower from 1954 to 1961 and then served as president from 1969 to 1974.

55 Richard Nixon (1967), "What Has Happened to America?" *Reader's Digest*, October, pp. 49–54.

56 D. Sansing (2004), "John Bell Williams: Fifty-Fifth Governor of Mississippi: 1968–1972," Mississippi History Now, January, available at: www.mshistorynow.mdah.ms.gov/issue/john-bell-williams-fifty-fifth-governor-of-mississippi-1968-1972.

57 *US News and World Report*, Volume 56.

58 Alexander (2012), pp. 143–4.

59 Quoted in Hoffman (2015), p. 15.

60 "Poll Says Nixon Won Labor Vote," *New York Times*, December 14, 1972, p. L27, available at: https://timesmachine.nytimes.com/timesmachine/1972/12/14/93424437.html?pageNumber=27 or www.nytimes.com/1972/12/14/archives/poll-says-nixon-won-labor-vote-it-finds-that-54-of-union-families.html.

61 The one exception was President Jimmy Carter's election in 1976 following the end of the near criminally charged President Nixon and his administration. Even then the Republican candidate, Gerald Ford, won 52 percent of the White vote, and Carter only won 48 percent (Roper Center [n.d.], "How Groups Voted in 1976," available at: https://ropercenter.cornell.edu/how-groups-voted-1976).

62 Alexander (2012), pp. 151–2.
63 P. Baker (2018), "Bush Made Willie Horton an Issue in 1988, and the Racial Scars Are Still Fresh," *New York Times*, Dec. 3.
64 P. Baker (2018), "Bush Made Willie Horton an Issue in 1988, and the Racial Scars Are Still Fresh," *New York Times*, Dec. 3.
65 M. Kramer (1994), "The Political Interest: Frying Them Isn't the Answer," *Time Magazine*, March 14.
66 Hinton (2016) notes that "Congress included mandatory minimum sentences for 'offenses involving one hundred grams of heroin, five hundred grams of cocaine or five grams of cocaine freebase known as crack cocaine,' among twenty-nine other mandatory minimum sentences stipulated by the Anti–Drug Abuse Act of 1986. As drug-related arrests surged, the disproportionate number of black Americans who abused crack rather than powdered cocaine rendered the law virtual 'apartheid sentencing'" (p. 317).
67 M. S. Phelps and D. Pager (2016), "Inequality and Punishment: A Turning Point for Mass Incarceration." *Annals of the American Academy of Political and Social Science*, 663, pp. 185–203.
68 Chapter 3 of Alexander (2012, pp. 228–98), "The Color of Justice," documents the major setbacks in the legal tools available to identify racial bias in the operations of the criminal legal system.
69 Myers (2021).

9 Conclusion

1 See, for example, Buckman et al.'s (2021) Brookings article "The Economic Gains from Equity" or Zandi et al.'s (2021) Moody Analytics piece "The Macroeconomic Benefits of Racial Integration."
2 We annualized data for 2024. US Department of Commerce, Bureau of Economic Analysis data on United States annual GDP growth rate accessed from Trading Economics (n.d.), *United States GDP Annual Growth Rate*, available at: https://tradingeconomics.com/united-states/gdp-growth-annual.
3 For an in-depth exploration of the endogeneity of race, see Darity Jr. et al. (2006).
4 W. A. Darity Jr. (2024), "Review of Heather McGhee *The Sum of Us: What Racism Costs Everyone and How We Can Prosper Together*, New York: One World 2021 415 pp," *Journal of Economics, Race, and Policy*, May 6, online, available at: https://doi.org/10.1007/s41996-024-00140-8.
5 See, for example, the Prosperity Now / Institute for Policy Studies 2016 report by Asante-Muhammad et al., "The Ever Growing Gap," available at: https://prosperitynow.org/sites/default/files/resources/The_Ever_Growing_Gap-CFED_IPS-Final.pdf; D. Irving (2023), "What Would It Take to Close America's Black–White Wealth Gap?" RAND Corporation 2023 Research and Policy Blog, available at www.rand.org/pubs/articles/2023/what-would-it-take-to-close-americas-black-white-wealth-gap.html; Brookings Institution December 2020 report by Williamson, "Closing the Racial Wealth Gap Requires Heavy, Progressive Taxation of Wealth," available at: www.brookings.edu/articles/closing-the-racial-wealth-gap-requires-heavy-progressive-taxation-of-wealth.

References

Aigner, D. J. and Cain, G. G. (1977) "Statistical Theories of Discrimination in Labor Markets," *Industrial and Labor Relations Review*, 30(2), pp. 175–87.

Albelda, R. (1985) "'Nice Work If You Can Get It': Segmentation of White and Black Women Workers in the Post-War Period," *Review of Racial Political Economics*, 17(3), pp. 72–85.

Albelda, R., Drago, R. W., and Schulman, S. (2001) *Unlevel Playing Fields: Understanding Wage Inequality and Discrimination*. Cambridge, MA: Economic Affairs Bureau, Inc.

Aldrich, M. (1979) "Progressive Economists and Scientific Racism: Walter Willcox and Black Americans, 1895–1910," *Phylon (1960–)*, 40(1), pp. 1–14.

Alexander, L., and Alexander, M. (2021) "Fear," in N. Hannah-Jones, I. Silverman, and J. Silverstein (eds.), *The 1619 Project*. New York: One World, pp. 97–124.

Alexander, M. (2012) *The New Jim Crow: Mass Incarceration in the Age of Colorblindness*. Revised Edition. New York: The New Press.

Aliprantis, D. and Carroll, D. R. (2019) *What Is Behind the Persistence of the Racial Wealth Gap?* Economic Commentary. Federal Reserve Bank of Cleveland, available at: https://doi.org/10.26509/frbc-ec-201903.

Allen, T. (1997) *The Invention of the White Race*. London: Verso Books.

Alonso-Villar, O., and del Río, C. (2017) "The Occupational Segregation of African American Women: Its Evolution from 1940 to 2010," *Feminist Economics*, 23(1), pp. 108–34.

American Civil Liberties Union and the University of Chicago Law School's Global Human Rights Clinic (ACLU–GHRC) (2022) "Captive Labor: Exploitation of Incarcerated Workers," available at: www.aclu.org/wp-content/uploads/publications/2022-06-15-captivelaborresearchreport.pdf.

American Economic Association (2020) "Committee Recommendation regarding Renaming the Ely Lecture Series" (Press release). April 24, 2020.

Amott, T. L. and Matthaei, J. A. (1991) *Race, Gender, and Work: A Multicultural Economic History of Women in the United States*. Boston, MA: South End Press.

Anderson, C. (2021) "Self-Defense," in N. Hannah-Jones, I. Silverman, and J. Silverstein (eds.), *The 1619 Project*. New York: One World, pp. 249–68.

Anderson, J. (1988) *The Education of Blacks in the South, 1860–1935*. Chapel Hill: University of North Carolina Press.

Appiah, K. A. (2020) "The Case for Capitalizing the B in Black," The Atlantic, Ideas, available at: www.theatlantic.com/ideas/archive/2020/06/time-to-capitalize-blackand-white/613159.

Aronowitz, S. (1973) *False Promises*. New York: McGraw Hill.

Associated Press and National Opinion Reseaerch Center at the University of Chicago (2019) "Changing Attitudes about Racial Inequality." The Associated Press – NORC Center for Public Affairs Research, available at: https://apnorc.org/wp-content/uploads/2020/02/APNORC_GSS_race_relations_report_2019-1.pdf.

Avery, C., Fairbanks, A., and Zeckhauser, R. (2001) *What Worms for the Early Bird: Early Admissions at Elite College* (Faculty Research Working Paper RWP01-049). Cambridge, MA: John F. Kennedy School of Government Harvard University.

Badgett, L., and Lim, J. (2001) "Promoting Women's Economic Progress through Affirmative Action," in M. C. King (ed.), *Squaring Up: Policy Strategies to Raise Women's Incomes in the United States*. Ann Arbor: The University of Michigan Press, pp. 179–99.

Baker, M., Halberstam, Y., Kroft, K., Mas, A., and Messacar, D. (2023) "Pay Transparency and the Gender Gap," *American Economic Journal: Applied Economics*, 15(2), pp. 157–83.

Baldwin, J. (1963) "The Negro child – his self-image," *Saturday Review*, December 21, 1963.

Banks, N. (2019) "Black Women's Labor Market History Reveals Deep-Seated Race and Gender Discrimination." Working Economics Blog. Washington, DC: Economic Policy Institute, available at: www.epi.org/blog/Black-womens-labor-market-history-revealsdeep-seated-race-and-gender-discrimination.

Banks, N. (2020) "Black Women in the United States and Unpaid Collective Work: Theorizing the Community as a Site of Production," *Review of Black Political Economy*, 47(4), pp. 343–62.

Banks, N. (2021) "Intersectional Identities and Analysis," in G. Berik and E. Kongar (eds.), *The Routledge Handbook of Feminist Economics. Core Concepts and Frameworks*. New York: Routledge, pp. 118–26.

Bayer, P. and Charles, K. K. (2018) "Divergent Paths: A New Perspective on Earnings Differences Between Black and White Men Since 1940," *Quarterly Journal of Economics*, 133(3), pp. 1459–1501.

Bazemore-James, C., Shinaprayoon, T., and Martin, J. (2017) *Supporting Students Who Experience Cultural Bias in Standardized Tests*. Trends and Issues in Academic Support: 2016–2017. Washington, DC: Commission for Academic Support in Higher Education.

Becker, G. (1971) *The Economics of Discrimination*. 2nd edition. University of Chicago Press.

Becker, G. S. (1994) "Human capital revisited," in *Human Capital: A Theoretical and Empirical Analysis with Special Reference to Education*. 3rd edition. University of Chicago Press, pp. 15–28.

Beckett, K. (2016) *Making Crime Pay: Law and Order in Contemporary American Politics*. London and New York: Oxford University Press.

Beller, A. (1982) "Occupational Segregation by Sex: Determinants and Changes," *Journal of Human Resources*, 17(3), pp. 371–92.

Bergmann, B. (1971) "The Effect on White Incomes of Discrimination in Employment," *Journal of Political Economy*, 79(2), pp. 294–313.

Bernstein, J. and Jones, J. (2020) *The Impact of the COVID19 Recession on the Jobs and Incomes of People of Color*. Washington, DC: Center on Budget and Policy Priorities, available at: www.cbpp.org/research/full-employment/the-impact-of-the-covid19-recession-on-the-jobs-and-incomes-of-persons-of.

Bertrand, M. and Duflo, E. 2016. *Field Experiments on Discrimination* (NBER Working Paper 22014), available at: www.nber.org/papers/w22014.

Bertrand, M. and Mullainathan, S. (2004) "Are Emily and Greg More Employable than Lakisha and Jamal? A Field Experiment on Labor Market Discrimination," *American Economic Review*, 94(4), pp. 991–1013.

Bhattacharya, J., Price, A., and Perry, A. M. (2022) "Why Homeownership Fails to Build Wealth for Black Women," Locked Out: Black Women, Wealth and Homeownership series, *Nonprofit Quarterly*, November 9, 2022, available at: https://nonprofitquarterly.org/series/locked-out-black-women-wealth-and-homeownership.

Blank, S. and Blum, B. B. (1997) "A Brief History of Work Expectations for Welfare Mothers," *The Future of Children*, 7(1), pp. 28–38.

Blau, F., Ferber, M., and Winkler, A. (2014) *The Economics of Women, Men, and Work*. Boston, MA: Pearson.

Blumer, H. (1958) "Race Prejudice as a Sense of Group Position," *Pacific Sociological Review*, 1(1), pp. 3–7.

Bobo, L., Kluegel, J. R., and Smith, R. A. (1997) "Laissez-Faire Racism: The Crystallization of a 'Kindler, Genter' Anti-black Ideology," in S. A. Tuch and J. K. Martin (eds.), *Racial Attitudes in the 1990s: Continuity and Change*. Westport, CT: Praeger, pp. 15–42.

Bobo, L. D., Charles, C. Z., Krysan, M., and Simmons, A. D. (2012) "The Real Record on Racial Attitudes," in P. V. Marsden (ed.), *Social Trends in American Life: Findings from the General Social Survey since 1972*. Princeton University Press, pp. 38–83.

Boston, N. and Hallam, J. (2004) "The Slave Experience: Freedom and Emancipation, Historical Overview." Slavery and the Making of America, *available at*: www.thirteen.org/wnet/slavery/experience/freedom/history.html.

Bottomore, T. (1991) *A Dictionary of Marxist Thought*. Malden, MA: Blackwell Publishing, p. 457.

Botwinick, H. (2018 [1993]) *Persistent Inequalities: Wage Disparity under Capitalist Competition*. Berlin: Brill.

Bowles, S., Roosevelt, Edwards, R., and Larudee, M. (2017) *Understanding*

Capitalism: Competition, Command, and Change, 4th edition. Oxford University Press, 2017.

Branch, E. H. (2011) *Opportunity Denied: Limiting Black Women to Devalued Work*. New Brunswick, NJ: Rutgers University Press.

Buckman, S. R., Choi, L. Y., Daly, M. C., and Seitelman, L. M. (2021) "The economic gains from equity," *Fall 2021 Brookings Papers on Economic Activity (BPEA)*, available at: www.brookings.edu/articles/the-economic-gains-from-equity.

Carbado, D. W., Crenshaw, K. W., Mays, V. M., and Tomlinson, B. (2013) "INTERSECTIONALITY: Mapping the Movements of a Theory," *Du Bois Review: Social Science Research on Race*, 10(2), p. 303, available at: https://doi.org/10.1017/S1742058X13000349.

Cayton, H. R. and Mitchell, G. S. (1939) *Black Workers and the New Unions*. Chapel Hill: University of North Carolina Press.

Chang, M. (2010) *Lifting as We Climb: Women of Color, Wealth, and America's Future*. Oakland, CA: Insight Center for Community Economic Development, available at: https://static1.squarespace.com/static/5c50b84131d4df5265e7392d/t/5c5c7801ec212d4fd499ba39/1549563907681/Lifting_As_We_Climb_InsightCCED_2010.pdf.

Changelab (n.d.) "A Different Asian American Timeline." Available at: https://aatimeline.com/1939-1980.

Chetty, R., Deming, D. J., and Friedman, J. N. (2023) *Diversifying Society's Leaders? The Determinants and Causal Effects of Admission to Highly Selective Private Colleges* (Working Paper 31492). Cambridge, MA: National Bureau of Economic Research (NBER).

Clair, M. and Denis, J. S. (2015) "Sociology of Racism," in J. D. Wright (ed.), *The International Encyclopedia of the Social and Behavioral Sciences*. 2nd edition. Cambridge, MA: Elsevier, pp. 857–63.

Clark, C., Matthew, D., and Burns, V. (2017) "Power, Privilege, and Justice: Intersectionality as Human Rights?" *International Journal of Human Rights*, 22(1), pp. 108–26.

Coleman, K. J. (2015) "The Voting Rights Act of 1965: Background and Overview." Congressional Research Service (online), available at: https://crsreports.congress.gov/product/pdf/R/R43626/15.

Collins, P. Hill (1990) "Black Feminist Thought in the Matrix of Domination," in *Black Feminist Thought: Knowledge, Consciousness, and the Politics of Empowerment*. Boston: Unwyn Hyman, pp. 221–38.

Combahee River Collective (1983[1977]) "The Combahee River Collective Statement," in B. Smith (ed.), *Home Girls: A Black Feminist Anthology*. New York: Kitchen Table: Women of Color Press, Inc.

Commons, J. R. (1907) *Races and Immigrants in America*. New York: The Macmillan Company.

Conrad, C. (2005) "Changes in the labor market status of Black women, 1960–2000," in C. Conrad, J. Whitehead, J. B. Stewart, and P. L. Mason (eds.), *African Americans in the US Economy*. Lanham, MD: Rowman and Littlefield Publishers, 2005, pp. 200–16.

Conrad, C. A., and Sharpe, R. V. (1996) "The Impact of the California Civil Rights Initiative (CCRI) on University and Professional School Admissions and the Implications for the California Economy," *Review of Black Political Economy*, 25, pp. 13–59.

Cox, R., and Wallace, S. (2016) "Identifying the Link Between Food Security and Incarceration," *Southern Economic Journal*, 82(4), pp. 1062–77.

Craigie, T. (2021) "Men's Incarceration and Women's Labor Market Outcomes," *Feminist Economics*, 27(4), pp. 1–28.

Craigie, T., Myers, S. L., Jr., and Darity, W. A., Jr. (2018). "Racial Differences in the Effect of Marriageable Males on Female Family Headship," *Journal of Demographic Economics*, 84, pp. 231–56.

Crenshaw, K. (1989) "Demarginalizing the Intersection of Race and Sex: A Black Feminist Critique of Antidiscrimination Doctrine, Feminist Theory, and Antiracist Politics," *University of Chicago Legal Forum*, 14, pp. 54139–67.

Crenshaw, K. (1991) "Mapping the Margins: Intersectionality, Identity Politics, and Violence against Women of Color," *Stanford Law Review*, 43(6), pp. 1241–99.

Crothers, L. M., Hughes, T. L., Schmitt, A. J., et al. (2010) "Has Equity Been Achieved? Salary and Promotion Negotiation Practices of a National Sample of School Psychology University Faculty," *Psychologist-Manager Journal*, 13(1), pp. 40–59.

Cruz-Janzen, M. I. (2010) "Latinegras: Desirable Women – Undesirable Mothers, Daughters, Sisters, and Wives," in M. J. Román and J. Flores (eds.), *The Afro-Latin@ Reader: History and Culture in the United States*. Durham, NC: Duke University Press, pp. 282–95.

Cunningham, J. (2006) "Center of Attention: Afro Latino Institution Celebrates 30 Years in the Big Apple," *New York Post*, March 22, 2006, available at: https://nypost.com/2006/03/22/center-of-attention-afro-latino-institution-celebrates-30-years-in-the-big-apple.

Cuyahoga Arts and Culture (2019) "Four Levels of Racism." Cuyahoga Arts and Culture, available at: www.cacgrants.org/assets/ce/Documents/2019/FourLevelsOfRacism.pdf.

Darity, W. A., Jr. (1982) "The Human Capital Approach to Black–White Earnings Inequality: Some Unsettled Questions," *Journal of Human Resources*, 17, pp. 72–93.

Darity, W. A., Jr. (1983) "The Goal of Racial Economic Equality: A Critique," *Journal of Ethnic Studies*, 10(4), pp. 51–7.

Darity, W. A., Jr. (1989) "What's Left of the Economic Theory of Discrimination," in S. Shulman and W. Darity Jr. (eds.), *The Question of Discrimination*. Middletown, CT: Wesleyan University Press, pp. 335–76.

Darity, W. A., Jr. (1994) "Many Roads to Extinction: Early AEA Economists and the Black Disappearance Hypothesis," *History of Economics Review*, 21(1), pp. 47–64.

Darity, W. A., Jr. (2005) "Stratification Economics: The Role of Intergroup Inequality," *Journal of Economics and Finance*, 29(2), pp. 144–53.

Darity, W. A., Jr. (2013), "Confronting Those Affirmative Action Grumbles," in J. Wicks-Lim and R. Pollin (eds.), *Capitalism on Trial: Explorations in the Tradition of Thomas E. Weisskopf*. Cheltenham, UK, and Northampton, MA: Edward Elgar, pp. 215–23.

Darity, W. A., Jr., Dietrich, J., and Hamilton, D. (2010) "Bleach in the Rainbow: Latino Ethnicity and Preference for Whiteness," in M. J. Román and J. Flores (eds.), *The Afro-Latin@ Reader: History and Culture in the United States*. Durham, NC: Duke University Press, pp. 485–98.

Darity, W. A., Jr. and Frank, D. (2003) "The Economics of Reparations," *American Economic Review*, 93(2), pp. 326–9.

Darity, W. A., Jr., Hamilton, D., Paul, M., et al. (2018) "What We Get Wrong about Closing the Racial Wealth Gap." Samuel DuBois Cook Center on Social Equality and the Insight Center for Community Economic Development, available at: https://socialequity.duke.edu/wp-content/uploads/2019/10/what-we-get-wrong.pdf.

Darity, W. A., Jr., Hamilton, D., and Stewart, J. B. (2015). "A Tour de Force in Understanding Intergroup Inequality: An Introduction to Stratification Economics," *Review of Black Political Economy*, 42(1–2), pp. 1–6.

Darity, W. A., Jr. and Jolla, A. (2009) "Desegregated schools with segregated education," in C. Hartman and G. D. Squires (eds.), *The Integration Debate: Competing Futures for American Cities*. New York: Routledge, pp. 99–117, available at: https://doi.org/10.4324/9780203890462.

Darity, W. A., Jr. and Mason, P. L. (1998) "Evidence on Discrimination in Employment: Codes of Color, Codes of Gender," *Journal of Economic Perspectives*, 12(2), pp. 63–90.

Darity, W. A., Jr., Mason, P. L., and Stewart, J. B. (2006) "The Economics of Identity: The Origin and Persistence of Racial Norms," *Journal of Economic Behavior and Organization*, 60(3), pp. 283–305.

Darity, W. A., Jr. and Mullen, K. (2020) *From Here to Equality*. Chapel Hill: University of North Carolina Press.

Darity, W. A., Jr. and Myers, S. L., Jr. (1980) "Changes in Black–White Income Inequality, 1968–78: A Decade of Progress?" *Review of Black Political Economy*, 10(4), pp. 354–379.

Darity, W. A., Jr. and Williams, R. M. (1985) "Peddlers Forever? Culture, Competition, and Discrimination," *American Economic Review*, 75(2), pp. 256–61.

Davila, A., Mora, M. T., and Stockly, S. K. (2011) "Does Mestizaje Matter in the US? Economic Stratification of Mexican Immigrants," *American Economic Review 96*, 101(3), pp. 593–7.

Davis, A. Y. (1983) *Women, Race and Class*. First Vintage books edition. New York: Vintage Books.

Davis, A. Y. (2003) "Racialized Punishment and Prison Abolition," in T. L. Lott and J. P. Pittman (eds.), *A Companion to African-American Philosophy*. Oxford: Blackwell Publishing, pp. 360–8.

Davis, K. (2008) "Intersectionality as Buzzword: A Sociology of Science Perspective on What Makes a Feminist Theory," *Feminist Theory*, 9(1), pp. 67–85.

Delmont, M. and Theoharis, J. (2017) "Introduction: Rethinking the Boston 'Busing Crisis,'" *Journal of Urban History*, 43(2), pp. 191–203.

Derenoncourt, E. (2022) "Can You Move to Opportunity? Evidence from the Great Migration," *American Economic Review*, 112(2), pp. 369–408.

Derenoncourt, E., Kim, C. H., Kuhn, M., and Schularick, M. (2022) *Wealth of Two Nations: The US Racial Wealth Gap 1860–2020* (Working Paper 30101). Cambridge, MA: National Bureau of Economic Research (NBER).

Desmond, M. and Emirbayer, M. (2009) "What is Racial Domination?" *Du Bois Review*, 6(2), pp. 335–55, available at: https://scholar.harvard.edu/files/mdesmond/files/what_is_racial_domination.pdf.

Devins, N. and Stedman, J. B. (1984) "New Federalism in Education: The Meaning of the Chicago School Desegregation," *Notre Dame Law Review*, Faculty Publications (387), available at: https://scholarship.law.wm.edu/facpubs/387.

De Witte, M. (2023) "Academic freedom's origin story," Stanford Report, available at: https://news.stanford.edu/stories/2023/05/origin-story-academic-freedom.

DiAngelo, R. (2018) *White Fragility: Why It's So Hard to Talk about Racism*. Boston: Beacon Press.

Dimand, R. (2005) "Economists and the Shadow of 'The Other' Before 1914," *American Journal of Economics and Sociology*, 64(3), pp. 827–50.

Douglas, D. M. (2005) *Jim Crow Moves North: The Battle over Northern School Segregation, 1865–1954*. New York: Cambridge University Press.

Du Bois, W. E. B. (1902) *The Negro Artisan*. Atlanta University Publications.

Du Bois, W. E. B. (1903) *The Souls of Black Folk*. Chicago: A. C. McClurg and Co.

Du Bois, W. E. B. (1935a) *Black Reconstruction in America: An Essay Toward a History of the Part Which Black Folk Played in the Attempt to Reconstruct Democracy in America, 1860–1880*. New York: Harcourt, Brace and Company.

Du Bois, W. E. B. (1935b) "Does the Negro Need Separate Schools?" *Journal of Negro Education*, 4(3 [July]), pp. 328–35.

Du Bois, W. E. B. (1973) *The Education of Black People: Ten Critiques, 1906–1960*, ed. H. Aptheker. New York: Monthly Review Press.

Dukes, K. N. and Kahn, K. B. (2017) "What Social Science Research Says about Police Violence against Racial and Ethnic Minorities: Understanding the Antecedents and Consequences – An Introduction," *Journal of Social Issues*, 73(4), pp. 690–700.

Dyer, R. (1997) *White: Essays on Race and Culture*. London and New York: Routledge.

Elliot, J. R. (2001) "Referral Hiring and Ethnically Homogeneous Jobs: How Prevalent Is the Connection and For Whom?," *Social Science Research*, 30(3), pp. 401–25.

Ely, R. T. (1893) *Outlines for Economics*. New York: Flood and Vincent.

Ely, R. T. (1898) "Fraternalism vs. Paternalism in Government," *Century*, 55(5), pp. 780–4.

Ely, R. T. (1918) *The World War and Leadership in a Democracy*. New York: Macmillan.

Evans, S. Y. (2007) *Black Women in the Ivory Tower, 1850–1954: An Intellectual History*. Gainsville: University of Florida.

Fanon, F. (1967) *Black Skin, White Masks*. New York: Grove.

Fenderson, J., Stewart, J. B., and Baungarter, K. (2011) "Expanding the History of the Black Studies Movement: Some Prefatory Notes," *Springer Journal of African American Studies*, 16(1), pp. 1–20.

Fernandez, R., Castilla, E., and Moore, P. (2000) "Social Capital at Work: Networks and Employment at a Phone Center," *American Journal of Sociology*, 105(5), pp. 1288–1356.

Ferreira da Silva, D. (2007) *Toward a Global Idea of Race*. Minneapolis: University of Minnesota Press.

Fetter, D. K. (2014) "The Twentieth-Century Increase in US Home Ownership: Facts and Hypotheses," in E. N. White, K. Snowden, and P. Fishback (eds.), *Housing and Mortgage Markets in Historical Perspective*. University of Chicago Press, pp. 329–50, available at: www.nber.org/chapters/c12801.

Foner, P. and Lewis, R. (1983) *The Black Worker, Volume 7: The Black Worker from the Founding of the CIO to the AFL–CIO Merger, 1936–1955*. Philadelphia: Temple University Press, available at: https://doi.org/10.2307/j.ctvn1tch8.

Ford, L. and Balu, R. (2023) *How Social Science Research Can Inform a National Reparations Agenda*. Washington, DC: Urban Institute, available at: www.urban.org/research/publication/how-social-science-research-can-inform-national-reparations-research-agenda.

Francis, D., Hardy, B. L., and Jones, D. (2022) "Black Economists on Race and Policy: Contributions to Education, Poverty and Mobility, and Public Finance," *Journal of Economic Literature*, 60(2), pp. 454–93.

Francis, D. V. and Darity, W. A., Jr. (2021) "Separate and Unequal under One Roof: How the Legacy of Racialized Tracking Perpetuates Within-School Segregation," *RSF: The Russell Sage Foundation Journal of the Social Sciences*, 7(1), pp. 187–202.

Francis, D. V., de Oliveira, A. C. M., and Dimmitt, C. (2019) "Do school counselors exhibit bias in recommending students for advanced coursework?" *B. E. Journal of Economic Analysis and Policy*, 19(4), available at: https://doi.org/10.1515/bejeap-2018-0189.

Frankenberg, E., Hawley, G. S., Ee, J., and Orfield, G. (2017) *Southern Schools – More than a Half-Century after the Civil Rights Revolution*. The Civil Rights Project and The Center for Education and Civil Rights, available at: www.civilrightsproject.ucla.edu/research/k-12-education/integration-and-diversity/southern-schools-brown-83-report/Brown63_South_052317-RELEASE-VERSION.pdf.

Frankenberg, E. and Taylor, K. (2015) "ESEA and the Civil Rights Act: An Interbranch Approach to Furthering Desegregation," *RSF: The Russell Sage Foundation Journal of the Social Sciences*, 1(3), pp. 32–49.

Franklin, B. (1961[1751]) "Observations Concerning the Increase of Mankind, 1751," in L. W. Labaree (ed.), *The Papers of Benjamin Franklin*, vol. IV: *July 1, 1750 through June 30, 1753*. New Haven: Yale University, pp. 225–34.

Freire, G., Diaz-Bonilla, C., Orellana, S. S., Lopez, J. S., and Carbonari, F. (2018) *Afro-descendants in Latin America: Toward a Framework of Inclusion*. Washington, DC: World Bank, available at: www.worldbank.org/en/region/lac/publication/afrodescendants-in-LAC.

Gaddis, S. M. (2019) "Understanding the 'How' and 'Why' Aspects of Racial–Ethnic Discrimination: A Multimethod Approach to Audit Studies," *Sociology of Race and Ethnicity*, 5(4), pp. 443–55.

Galdámez, M., Gómez, M., Pérez, R., et al. (2023) *Centering Black Latinidad: A Profile of the US Afro-Latinx Population and Complex Inequalities*. UCLA Latino Policy and Politics Institute, available at: https://latino.ucla.edu/research/centering-black-latinidad.

Gallup (2025) "How Does the Gallup Poll Social Series Work? Methodology." Available at: www.gallup.com/175307/gallup-poll-social-series-methodology.aspx.

Gerhart, B. and Rynes, S. (1991) "Determinants and Consequences of Salary Negotiations by Male and Female MBA Graduates," *Journal of Applied Psychology*, 76(2), pp. 256–62.

Gersh, D. (1987) "The corporate elite and the introduction of IQ testing in American public schools," in M. Schwartz (ed.), *The Structure of Power in America: The Corporate Elite as a Ruling Class*. New York: Holmes and Meier, pp. 163–84.

Gibson, C. and Jung, K. (2002) "Historical Census Statistics on Population Totals by Race, 1790 to 1990, and by Hispanic Origin, 1970 to 1990, for the United States, Regions, Divisions, and States." Washington, DC: US Census Bureau (online), available at: www.census.gov/content/dam/Census/library/working-papers/2002/demo/POP-twps0056.pdf.

Gibson, K., Darity, W. A., Jr., and Myers, S. L., Jr. (1998) "Revisiting Occupational Crowding in the United States: A Preliminary Study," *Feminist Economics*, 4(3), pp. 73–95.

Goldin, C. (1977) "Female Labor Force Participation: The Origin of Black and White Differences, 1870 and 1880," *Journal of Economic History*, 37(1), pp. 87–108.

Goldin, C. (1988) *Marriage Bars: Discrimination Against Married Women Workers, 1920s to 1950* (NBER Working Paper 2747). Cambridge, MA: National Bureau of Economic Research (NBER).

Goldin, C. (2006) "Richard T. Ely Lecture: The Quiet Revolution that Transformed Women's Employment, Education, and Family," *American Economic Review*, 96(2), pp. 1–21.

Gordon Nembhard, J. (2004) "Cooperative ownership in the struggle for African American economic empowerment," *Humanity and Society*, 28(3), pp. 298–321.

Gordon Nembhard, J. and Marsh, K. (2012) "Wealth Affirming Policies for Women of Color," *Review of Black Political Economy*, 39, pp. 353–60.

Gonzalez-Barrera, A. (2019) *Hispanics with darker skin are more likely to experience discrimination than those with lighter skin*. Washington, DC: Pew Research Center, available at: www.pewresearch.org/fact-tank/2019/07/02/hispanics-with-darker-skin-are-more-likely-to-experience-discrimination-than-those-with-lighter-skin.

Granovetter, M. (1995) *Getting a Job: A Study of Contract and Careers*. University of Chicago Press.
Granovetter, M. (2005) "The Impact of Social Structure on Economic Outcomes," *Journal of Economic Perspectives*, 19(1), pp. 33–50.
Grant, M. (1916) *The Passing of the Great Race; or The Racial Basis of European History*. New York: Charles Scribner's Sons.
Hall, S. (1986) "Gramsci's Relevance for the Study of Race and Ethnicity," *Journal of Communication Inquiry*, 10(2), pp. 5–27.
Hamilton, D., Austin, A., and Darity, W. A., Jr. (2011) *Whiter Jobs, Higher Wages: Occupational Segregation and the Lower Wages of Black Men* (Briefing Paper #268). Washington, DC: Economic Policy Institute (EPI).
Hamilton, D. and Darity, W. A., Jr. (2010) "Can 'Baby Bonds' Eliminate the Racial Wealth Gap in Putative Post-Racial America?" *Review of Black Political Economy*, 37(3–4), pp. 207–16.
Hamilton, D. and Darity, W. A., Jr. (2012) "Crowded Out? The Racial Composition of American Occupations," in J. S. Jackson, C. Howard Caldwell, and S. L. Sellers (eds.), *Researching Black Communities: A Methodological Guide*. Ann Arbor: University of Michigan Press, pp. 60–78, available at: www.jstor.org/stable/10.3998/mpub.1050883.5.
Hamilton, D. and Darity, W. A., Jr. (2017) "The Political Economy of Education, Financial Literacy, and the Racial Wealth Gap," *Federal Reserve Bank of St. Louis Review*, 99(1): 59–76.
Hannah-Jones, N. (2021a) "Democracy," in N. Hannah-Jones, I. Silverman, and J. Silverstein (eds.), *The 1619 Project*. New York: One World, pp. 7–38.
Hannah-Jones, N. (2021b) "Preface: Origins", in N. Hannah-Jones, C. Roper, I. Silverman, and J. Silverstein (eds.), *The 1619 Project*. New York: One World, pp. xvi–xl.
Harris, C. (1993) "Whiteness as Property," *Harvard Law Review*, 106(8), pp. 1707–97.
Hart, J. (2003) *Comparing Empires – European Colonialism from Portuguese Expansion to the Spanish–American War*. New York: Palgrave Macmillan.
Hart Research Associates (2023) "Hart Research Associates – *NBC News* Survey (Study #230102): Public Opinion Strategies." *NBC News*, available at: www.documentcloud.org/documents/23789655-full-nbc-news-april-2023-poll%20Accessed%20April%2023.
Haslanger, S. (2012) "Oppressions: Racial and Other," in S. Haslanger (ed.), *Resisting Reality: Social Construction and Social Critique*. Oxford University Press, pp. 311–38, available at: https://doi.org/10.1093/acprof:oso/9780199892631.003.0011.
Heckman, J. (1998) "Detecting Discrimination," *Journal of Economic Perspectives*, 12(2), pp. 101–16.
Hegewisch, A. and Tesfaselassie, A. (2019) "The Gender Wage Gap by Occupation 2018," Fact Sheet #C480, Institute for Women's Policy Research, Washington., DC, p. 3, available at: https://iwpr.org/wp-content/uploads/2020/08/C480_The-Gender-Wage-Gap-by-Occupation-2018-1.pdf.

Helms, J. (2008) "Implications for social policy of variability in racial groups' test scores: How cut scores on tests of cognitive abilities, knowledge, or skills matter," *American Psychologist*, 63, pp. 721–39.

Hernandez, M., Avery, D. R., Volpone, S. D., and Kaiser, C. R. (2019) "Bargaining while Black: The Role of Race in Salary Negotiations," *Journal of Applied Psychology*, 104(4), pp. 581–92.

Hernstein, R. and Murray, C. (1994) *The Bell Curve: Intelligence and Class Structure in American Life*. New York: Free Press.

Hill, H. (1988) "Myth-Making as Labor History: Herbert Gutman and the United States Mine Workers of America," *International Journal of Politics, Culture, and Society*, 2(2), pp. 132–200.

Hill, H. (1989) "Black Labor and Affirmative Action: An Historical Perspective," in S. Shulman and W. Darity Jr. (eds.), *The Question of Discrimination*. Middletown, CT: Wesleyan University Press, pp. 190–267.

Hinds, O., Lu, O., Wallace-Lee, J., and Kang-Brown, J. (2017) *Reconstructing How Counties Contribute to State Prisons*. Github: The Vera Institute of Justice, available at: https://github.com/vera-institute/incarceration_trends/blob/master/Workingpaper_Reconstructing-How-Counties-Contribute-to-State-Prisons.pdf?raw=true.

Hinton, E. (2016) *From the War on Poverty to the War on Crime: The Making of Mass Incarceration in America*. Cambridge, MA: Harvard University Press.

Hochschild, A. and Machung, A. (1989) *The Second Shift: Working Parents and the Revolution at Home*. New York: Viking.

Hoffman, F. L. (1892) "Vital Statistics of the Negro," *Arena*, 5(29), pp. 529–42, available at: https://archive.org/details/ArenaMagazine-Volume05/mode/2up.

Hoffman, F. L. (1896) *Race Traits and Tendencies of the American Negro (XI)*, (3 vols). New York: Publications of the American Economic Association and The Macmillan Company.

Hoffman, T. J. (2015) "The Civil Rights Realignment: How Race Dominates Presidential Elections," *Political Analysis*, 17(Article 1), pp. 1–23, available at: https://scholarship.shu.edu/cgi/viewcontent.cgi?article=1006&context=pa.

Holder, M. (2017) *African American Men and the Labor Market during the Great Recession*. New York: Palgrave Macmillan.

Holder, M. (2018) "Revisiting Bergmann's Occupational Crowding Model," *Review of Radical Political Economics*, 50(4), pp. 683–90.

Holder, M. (2020) *The Double Gap and the Bottom Line: African American Women's Wage Gap and Corporate Profits*. New York: The Roosevelt Institute, available at: https://rooseveltinstitute.org/publications/the-double-gap-and-the-bottom-line-african-american-womens-wage-gap-and-corporate-profits.

Holder, M. and Aja, A. (2021) *Afro-Latinos in the US Economy*. Lanham, MD: Lexington Books.

Holder, M., Jones, J., and Masterson, T. (2020) *The Early Impact of COVID-19 on Job Losses Among Black Women in the US* (Levy Institute Working Paper 963), available at: www.levyinstitute.org/pubs/wp_963.pdf.

Holder, M., Jones, J., and Masterson, T. (2021) "The Early Impact of COVID-19 on Job Losses Among Black Women in the US," *Feminist Economics*, 27(1–2), pp. 103–16.

Holzer, H. J. (1987) "Informal Job Search and Black Youth Unemployment," *American Economic Review*, 77, pp. 446–52.

Holzer, H. J. and Neumark, D. (2000) "Assessing Affirmative Action," *Journal of Economic Literature*, 38(3 [September]), pp. 483–568.

hooks, b. (1992) *Black Looks: Race and Representation*. Boston, MA: South End Press.

Hossein, C. S. (2019) "A Black Epistemology for Social and Solidarity Economy: The Black Social Economy," *Review of Black Political Economy*, 46(3), pp. 209–29.

Howell, C. and Turner, S. E. (2004) "Legacies in Black and White: The Racial Composition of the Legacy Pool," *Research in Higher Education*, 45(4), pp. 325–51.

Hull, A. G., Bell-Scott, P., and Smith, B. (1982) *All the Women Are White, All the Blacks Are Men, but Some of Us Are Brave: Black Women's Studies*. Old Westbury, NY: The Feminist Press.

Humes, K., and Hogan, H. (2009) "Measurement of Race and Ethnicity in a Changing, Multicultural America," *Race and Social Problems*, 1, pp. 111–31.

Hunt, E. K. (2011) *History of Economic Thought: A Critical Perspective*. 2nd edition. New York: Routledge.

Ignatiev, N. (1995) *How the Irish Became White*. London: Routledge.

Jackson, C. (2021) "What Is Redlining?," *New York Times*, August 17, available at: www.nytimes.com/2021/08/17/realestate/what-is-redlining.html.

Jones, J. (1985) *Labor of Love, Labor of Sorrow: Black Women, Work, and the Family from Slavery to the Present*. New York: Basic Books.

Jones, J. (1998) *American Work: Four Centuries of Black and White Labor*. New York: W. W. Norton.

Jorge, A. (2010) "The Black Puerto Rican Woman in Contemporary American Society," in M. J. Román and J. Flores (eds.), *The Afro-Latin@ Reader: History and Culture in the United States*. Durham, NC: Duke University Press, pp. 269–75.

Journal of Blacks in Higher Education (1999) "Why few Blacks apply for early admission," *Journal of Blacks in Higher Education*, 24(Summer), pp. 66–8.

Kajstura, A. (2023) "States to the Census Bureau: You created prison gerrymandering, you need to end it," Prison Gerrymandering Project, available at: www.prisonersofthecensus.org/news/2023/05/02/ncsl_report2023.

Kang-Brown, J., Hinds, O., Olive, L., Wallace-Lee, J., and Schattner-Elmaleh, E. (2018) "Incarceration Trends Project Data." Available at: https://github.com/vera-institute/incarceration-trends.

Kang-Brown, J., Hinds, O., Schattner-Elmaleh, E., and Wallace-Lee, J. (2020) "Data and Methods for Historical Jail Populations in US Counties, 1970–2018." The Vera Institute Incarceration Trends Project (Github), available at: https://github.com/vera-institute/incarceration_trends/blob/master/Methodology-for-Incarceration-Trends-Project.pdf?raw=true.

Katznelson, I. (2005) *When Affirmative Action Was White: An Untold History of Racial Inequality in Twentieth-Century America.* New York: W. W. Norton.

Keynes, J. M. (1946) "The Galton Lecture, 1946: Presentation of the Society's Gold Medal," *Eugenics Review*, 38(1), pp. 39–41, available at: www.ncbi.nlm.nih.gov/pmc/articles/PMC2986310/pdf/eugenrev00247-0048.pdf.

Kim, C. J. (1999) "The Racial Triangulation of Asian Americans," *Politics and Society*, 27(1), pp. 105–38.

Kim, C. J. (2018) "Are Asians the New Blacks? Affirmative Action, Anti-Blackness, and the 'Sociometry' of Race," *Du Bois Review: Social Science Research on Race*, 15(2), pp. 217–44.

Kim, M. (2015) "Pay Secrecy and the Gender Wage Gap in the United States," *Industrial Relations: A Journal of Economy and Society*, 54(4), pp. 648–67.

Kirby, J. B. (1980) *Black Americans in the Roosevelt Era: Liberalism and Race.* Knoxville: University of Tennessee Press.

Kline, P. M., Rose, E. K., and Walters, C. R. (2022) "Systemic Discrimination among Large US Employers," *Quarterly Journal of Economics*, 137(4), pp. 1963–2036.

Koch, J. V. and Swinton, O. H. (2023) "Colleges and Upward Economic Mobility: The Distinctive Contribution of HBCUs," *American Economic Review Papers and Proceedings*, 113(May), pp. 446–50.

Kolchin, P. (2009) "Whiteness Studies," *Journal de la Société des américanistes*, 95(1), pp. 117–63.

Krysan, M. and Moberg, S. (2021) "Tracking Trends in Racial Attitudes," Report, Institute of Government and Public Affairs, University of Illinois System, available at: https://igpa.uillinois.edu/programs/racial-attitudes-2021.

Kuhn, M., Schularick, M., and Steins, U.I. (2020) "Income and Wealth Inequality in America, 1949–2016," *Journal of Political Economy*, 128(9), pp. 3469–519.

Leonard, J. S. (1990) "The impact of affirmative action regulation and equal employment law on black employment," *Journal of Economic Perspectives*, 4(4), pp. 47–63.

Leonard, T. C. (2003) "'More Merciful and Not Less Effective': Eugenics and American Economics in the Progressive Era," *History of Political Economy*, 35(4), pp. 687–712.

Leonard, T. C. (2005) "Retrospectives: Eugenics and Economics in the Progressive Era," *Journal of Economic Perspectives*, 19(4), pp. 207–24.

Liu, J. M. (1992) "The Contours of Asian Professional, Technical and Kindred Work Immigration, 1965–1988," *Sociological Perspectives*, 35(4), pp. 673–704.

Loewen, J. (1971). *The Mississippi Chinese: Between Black and White.* Cambridge, MA: Harvard University Press.

Lofgren, Z. and Davis, R. (2023) "Black Americans in Congress 1870–2022." Washington, DC: US Government Publishing Office (online), available at: www.govinfo.gov/content/pkg/GPO-CDOC-118hdoc16/pdf/GPO-CDOC-118hdoc16.pdf.

López, G. and Gonzalez-Barrera, A. (2016) *Afro-Latino: A Deeply Rooted Identity among US Hispanics*. New York: Pew Research Center, available at: www.pewresearch.org/short-reads/2016/03/01/afro-latino-a-deeply-rooted-identity-among-u-s-hispanics.

López, N., Vargas, E., Juárez, M., Cacari-Stone, L. and Bettez, S. (2017) "What's Your 'Street Race?' Leveraging Multidimensional Measures of Race and Intersectionality for Examining Physical and Mental Health Status among Latinxs," *Sociology of Race and Ethnicity*, 4(1), pp. 49–66.

Loury, G. (2021) *The Anatomy of Racial Inequality: With a New Preface*. Cambridge, MA: Harvard University Press.

Loury, G. C. and McWhorter, J. (2022) "Why I Don't Capitalize 'Black,'" glennloury.substack.com, available at: https://glennloury.substack.com/p/why-i-dont-capitalize-black.

Magness, P. W. (2020) "Racism and the Early History of the American Economic Association," Economic History, available at: www.aier.org/article/racism-and-the-early-history-of-the-american-economic-association.

Manduca, R. (2018) "Income Inequality and the Persistence of Racial Economic Disparities," *Sociological Science*, 5(8), pp. 182–205.

Mansoor, S. and Carlisle, M. (2021) "When Your Body Counts but Your Vote Does Not: How Prison Gerrymandering Distorts Political Representation," *TIME*, July 1, 2021, available at: https://time.com/6077245/prison-gerrymandering-political-representation.

Mason, P. L. (1997) "Race, Culture, and Skill: Interracial Wage Differences among African Americans, Latinos, and Whites," *Review of Black Political Economy*, 25(3), pp. 5–39.

Mason, P. L. (1999) "Male Interracial Wage Differentials: Competing Explanations," *Cambridge Journal of Economics*, 23, pp. 261–99.

Mason, P. L. (2000) "Understanding Recent Empirical Evidence on Race and Labor Market Outcomes in the USA," *Review of Social Economy*, 58(3), pp. 319–38.

Mason, P. L. (2004) "Annual income, hourly wages, and identity among Mexican Americans and other Latinos," *Industrial Relations: A Journal of Economy and Society*, 43(4), pp. 817–34.

Mason, P. L. (2023) *The Economics of Structural Racism: Stratification Economics and US Labor Markets*. Cambridge University Press.

Mason, P. L., Myers, S. L., Jr., and Simms, M. (2022) "Racial Isolation and Marginalization of Economic Research on Race and Crime," *Journal of Economic Literature*, 60(2 [June]), pp. 494–526.

Medina, D. (2017) "Wealth Poverty at Social Intersections: Differential Access and Accumulation," MS Economic Policy and Theory thesis, available at: https://digitalcommons.bard.edu/levy_ms/7.

Menchik, P. L. and Jianakoplos, N. A. (1997) "Black–White Wealth Inequality: Is Inheritance the Reason?" *Economic Inquiry*, 35(April), pp. 428–42.

Merriam-Webster Dictionary (2024) Merriam-Webster.com (online), available at: www.merriam-webster.com/dictionary/asset.

Mincer, J. A. (1970) "The Distribution of Labor Incomes: A Survey with Special

Reference to the Human Capital Approach," *Journal of Economic Literature*, 8(1), pp. 1–26.

Mincer, J. A. (1974) *Schooling, Experience, and Earnings*. Cambridge, MA: National Bureau of Economic Research (NBER).

Morris, E. W. and Perry, B. L. (2016) "The Punishment Gap: School Suspension and Racial Disparities in Achievement," *Social Problems*, 63(1), pp. 68–86.

Morrison, T. (1993) "Women's History Month: Novelist Toni Morrison looks back on her youth and family and presents her newest book, 'Jazz.'" Interview by Charlie Rose, May 7, available at: https://charlierose.com/episodes/18778#.

Morrison, T. (1998) "Toni Morrison gives insight into her works 'Paradise' and 'The Bluest Eye,' criticizes sloppy criticism, and explains the challenge of writing about race for African-American writers." Interview by Charlie Rose, January 19, available at: https://charlierose.com/videos/17664.

Myers, S. L., Jr. (2017) "What have we learned about incarceration and race? Lessons from 30 years of research," in J. D. Ward (ed.), *Policing and Race in America: Economic, Political, and Social Dynamics*. Lanham, MD: Lexington Books.

Myers, S. L., Jr. (2021) "Bringing Research on Race and Crime into the 21st Century: Reflections from over the Years," *Review of Black Political Economy*, 48(1), pp. 123–7.

Myers, S. L., Jr. (2023) "Race, Racism and the Foundations of American Economic Thought," presentation at the Freedom and Justice 7th Annual Summer Conference, August 10–12. Haskell Indian Nations University, Lawrence, KS.

Myers, S. L., Jr. and Sabol, W. J. (1987) "Unemployment and Racial Differences in Imprisonment," *Review of Black Political Economy*, 16(1–2), pp. 189–209.

National Constitution Center (n.d.) "Constitution 101 Resources 13.5 Info Brief: The Women's Suffrage Movement." Available at: https://constitutioncenter.org/education/classroom-resource-library/classroom/13.5-info-brief-the-womens-suffrage-movement.

National Opinion Research Center (2021) "About the GSS." Available at: https://gss.norc.org/us/en/gss/about-the-gss.html.

National Partnership for Women and Families (2023) *The Paycheck Fairness Act*. Washington, DC: National Partnership for Women and Families, available at: https://nationalpartnership.org/wp-content/uploads/2023/02/the-paycheck-fairness-act.pdf.

National Women's Law Center (2020) *Promoting Pay Transparency to Fight the Gender Wage Gap: Creative International Models*. Washington, DC: National Women's Law Center (NWLC).

Neal, L. (1968) "The Black Arts Movement," *Drama Review*, 3(Summer), pp. 29–39.

Neal, L. (2024) *Any Day Now: Toward a Black Aesthetic*. New York: David Zwirner Books.

Neckerman, K. M. and Kirschenman, J. (1991) "Hiring Strategies, Racial Bias, and Inner-City Workers," *Social Problems*, 38(4), pp. 433–47.

New York Times (1908) "FUTURE AMERICANS WILL BE SWARTHY; Prof. Ripley Thinks Race Intermixture May Reproduce Remote Ancestral Type.

TO INUNDATE ANGLO-SAXON His Burden, Though Physically Thus Engulfed, Will Be to Bear Torch of Civilization," November 29, available at: www.nytimes.com/1908/11/29/archives/future-americans-will-be-swarthy-prof-ripley-thinks-race.html.

Nguyen, A. T. and Pendleton, M. (2020) "Recognizing Race in Language: Why We Capitalize 'Black' and 'White.'" Available at: https://cssp.org/2020/03/recognizing-race-in-language-why-we-capitalize-black-and-white.

Oliver, M. L. and Shapiro, T. M. (1995) *Black Wealth / White Wealth: A New Perspective on Racial Inequality*. New York: Routledge.

Orfield, G., Frankenberg, E., Ee, J., and Kuscera, J. (2014) *Brown at 60: Great Progress, a Long Retreat and an Uncertain Future*. Los Angeles: The Civil Rights Project, available at: www.civilrightsproject.ucla.edu/research/k-12-education/integration-and-diversity/brown-at-60-great-progress-a-long-retreat-and-an-uncertain-future/Brown-at-60-051814.pdf.

Orfield, G. and Jarvie, D. (2020) *Black Segregation Matters: School Resegregation and Black Educational Opportunity*. Los Angeles, CA: The Civil Rights Project at the University of California, available at: https://civilrightsproject.ucla.edu/research/k-12-education/integration-and-diversity/black-segregation-matters-school-resegregation-and-black-educational-opportunity.

Pager, D. and Western, B. (2005) *Race at Work: Realities of Race and Criminal Record in the NYC Job Market*. Published report presented at NYC Commission on Human Rights Conference "Race at Work: Realities of Race and Criminal Record in the NYC Job Market," December 9, Schomburg Center for Research in Black Culture.

Parenti, C. (2000) *The Lockdown: Police and Prisons in the Age of Crisis*. London and New York: Verso Books.

Pepin, J. R. and Cotter, D. A. (2018) "Separating Spheres? Diverging Trends in Youth's Gender Attitudes about Work and Family," *Journal of Marriage and Family*, 80(1), pp. 7–24.

Perea, J. F. (2011) "The Echoes of Slavery: Recognizing the Racist Origins of the Agricultural and Domestic Worker Exclusion from the National Labor Relations Act," *Ohio State Law Journal*, 72(1), pp. 95–138.

Petersen, N. and Omori, M. (2018) *Unequal Treatment: Racial and Ethnic Disparities in Miami-Dade Criminal Justice*. Miami: ACLU of Florida, available at: www.aclufl.org/en/publications/unequal-treatment-racial-and-ethnic-disparities-miami-dade-criminal-justice.

Pew Research Center (2018) "For Most Trump Voters, 'Very Warm' Feelings for Him Endured." Pew Research Center, available at: www.pewresearch.org/politics/2018/08/09/an-examination-of-the-2016-electorate-based-on-validated-voters.

Phelps, M. S. and Pager, D. (2016) "Inequality and Punishment: A Turning Point for Mass Incarceration," *Annals of the American Academy of Political and Social Science*, 663(1), pp. 183–203.

Pierson, E., Simoiu, C., Overgoor, J., et al. (2020) "A large-scale analysis of racial disparities in police stops across the United States," *Nature Human Behaviour*, 4(7), pp. 736–45.

Price, A. (2019) "Spell it with a Capital 'B,'" *Medium*, available at: https://insightcced.medium.com/spell-it-with-a-capital-b-9eab112d759a.

Price, G. N., Spriggs, W., and Swinton, O. H. (2011) "The Relative Returns to Graduating from a Historically Black College/University: Propensity Score Matching Estimates from the National Survey of Black Americans," *Review of Black Political Economy*, 38(2), pp. 103–30.

Price, G. N. and Viceisza, A. (2023) "What Can Historically Black Colleges and Universities Teach about Improving Higher Education Outcomes for Black Students?" *Journal of Economic Perspectives* 37(3): pp. 213–32.

Public Broadcasting Service (PBS) (2003a) "Race – The Power of an Illusion," Background Readings, Race Timeline – Go Deeper. Available at: www.pbs.org/race/000_About/002_04-background-02-12.htm.

Public Broadcasting Service (PBS) (2003b) "Race – The Power of an Illusion," Race Timeline – Go Deeper, available at: www.pbs.org/race/000_About/002_03_c-godeeper.htm.

Purnell, B. and Theoharis, J. (2019) "Introduction. Histories of Racism and Resistance, Seen and Unseen: How and Why to Think about the Jim Crow North," in B. Purnell, J. Theoharis, and K. Woodard (eds.), *The Strange Careers of the Jim Crow North: Segregation and Struggle Outside of the South*. NYU Press, pp. 1–42.

Qian, Z., Lichter, D. T., and Tumin, D. (2017) "Divergent Pathways to Assimilation? Local Marriage Markets and Intermarriage among US Hispanics," *Journal of Marriage and Family*, 80(1), pp. 271–88.

Quillian, L., Pager, D., Hexel, O., and Midtboen, A. H. (2017) "Meta-analysis of field experiments shows no change in racial discrimination in hiring over time," *Proceedings of the National Academy of Sciences*, 114(41), pp. 10870–5.

Quiñones Rivera, M. (2006) "From Trigueñita to Afro-Puerto Rican: Intersections of the Racialized, Gendered, and Sexualized Body in Puerto Rico and the US Mainland," *Meridians*, 7(1), pp. 162–82.

Ray, R. and Gibbons, A. (2021) "Why are states banning critical race theory?" The Brookings Institute Blog, available at: www.brookings.edu/blog/fixgov/2021/07/02/why-are-states-banning-critical-race-theory.

Reardon, S. F., Grewal, E. T., Kalogrides, D., and Greenberg, E. (2012) "Brown Fades: The End of Court-Ordered School Desegregation and the Resegregation of American Public Schools," *Journal of Policy Analysis and Management*, 31(4), pp. 876–904.

Reiman, J. and Leighton, P. (2016) *The Rich Get Richer and the Poor Get Prison: Ideology, Class, and Criminal Justice*. 10th edition. London: Routledge.

Remster, B. and Kramer, R. (2018) "SHIFTING POWER: The Impact of Incarceration on Political Representation," *Du Bois Review: Social Science Research on Race*, 15(2), pp. 417–39.

Reskin, B. F. (1999) "Occupational Segregation by Race and Ethnicity among Women Workers," in I. Browne (ed.), *Latinas and African American Women at Work: Race, Gender, and Economic Inequality*. New York: Russell Sage, pp. 183–204.

Rhee, J. (1994) "In Black and White: Chinese in the Mississippi Delta," *Journal of Supreme Court History*, 19(1), pp. 117–32.

Rice, A. (2021) "Political Economy and the Tradition of Radical Black Study," *Souls: A Critical Journal of Black Politics, Culture, and Society*, 22(1: Inheriting Black Studies), pp. 44–55.

Ripley, W. Z. (1899) *The Races of Europe: A Sociological Study*. New York: D. Appleton and Co.

Ripley, W. Z. (1908) "Races in the United States," *Atlantic Monthly* (December), pp. 745–59, available at: www.theatlantic.com/past/unbound/flashbks/immigr/rip.htm.

Roberts, D. E. (2004) "The Social and Moral Cost of Mass Incarceration in African American Communities," All Faculty Scholarship at the University of Pennsylvania Carey Law School (583), available at: https://scholarship.law.upenn.edu/faculty_scholarship/583.

Roberts, D. E. (2021) "Race," in N. Hannah-Jones, I. Silverman, and J. Silverstein (eds.), *The 1619 Project*. New York: One World, pp. 45–61.

Rodgers, W. M. and Spriggs, W. E. (1996) "What Does the AFQT Really Measure: Race, Wages, Schooling and the AFQT Score," *Review of Black Political Economy*, 24(4), pp. 13–46.

Rodriguez, C. E. (2020) *Puerto Ricans: Born in the USA*. Taylor and Francis [ProQuest Ebook Central].

Rodriguez-Knutsen, A. (2023) "Types of Racism: Internal, Interpersonal, Institutional, and Structural." Available at: www.ywcaworks.org/blogs/ywca/types-racism.

Roediger, D. R. (1991) *The Wages of Whiteness: Race and the Making of the American Working Class*. London: Verso Books.

Román, M. J. (2010) "Check Both! Afro-Latin@s and the Census," North American Congress on Latin America (NACLA), available at: https://nacla.org/article/check-both-afro-latins-and-census.

Rose, C. (2015) "Toni Morrison Beautifully Answers an 'Illegitimate' Question on Race (Jan. 19, 1998) / Charlie Rose" (online). Available at: www.youtube.com/watch?v=-Kgq3F8wbYA.

Ross, E. A. (1901) *Social Control: A Survey of the Foundations of Order*. New York: Macmillan Company.

Rothstein, R. (2017) *The Color of Law: A Forgotten History of How Our Government Segregated America*. New York and London: Liveright Publishing Corporation, a division of W.W. Norton.

Rousseau, N. (2013) "Social Rhetoric and the Construction of Black Motherhood," *Journal of Black Studies*, 11(5), pp. 451–71.

Ruggles, S. (2022) "Race, class, and marriage: Components of race differences in men's first marriage rates, United States, 1960–2019," *Demographic Research*, 46, pp. 1163–86.

Saad, L. (2019) "Fewer See Equal Opportunity for Blacks in Jobs, Housing," Gallup News, available at: https://news.gallup.com/opinion/gallup/246137/fewer-equal-opportunity-blacks-jobs-housing.aspx.

Sabin, J., Nosek, B. A., Greenwald, A. G., and Rivara, F. P. (2009) "Physicians' Implicit and Explicit Attitudes about Race by MD Race, Ethnicity, and Gender," *Journal of Health Care for the Poor and Underserved*, 20(3), pp. 896–913.
Schlosser, E. (2003) *Reefer Madness: Sex, Drugs and Cheap Labor in the American Black Market*. Boston: Houghton Mifflin Company.
Schuman, H., Steeh, C., Bobo, L., and Krysan, M. (1997) *Racial Attitudes in America: Trends and Interpretations*. Cambridge, MA: Harvard University Press.
Schwarz, K. (2022) *Reparations for Slavery in International Law: Transatlantic Enslavement, the Maangamizi, and the Making of International Law*. Oxford University Press, available at: https://doi.org/10.1093/oso/9780197636398.001.0001.
Scott-Clayton, J. (2018) *The Looming Student Loan Default Crisis Is Worse Than We Thought*. Washington, DC: The Brookings Institution, available at: www.brookings.edu/articles/the-looming-student-loan-default-crisis-is-worse-than-we-thought.
Shapiro, T. M. (2006) "Race, Homeownership, and Wealth," *Washington University Journal of Law and Policy*, 20(53), pp. 53–74.
Shapiro, T. M. and Kenty-Drane, J. L. (2005) "The Racial Wealth Gap," in C. Conrad, J. Whitehead, P. L. Mason, and J. B. Stewart (eds.), *African Americans in the US Economy*. Lanham, MD: Rowman and Littlefield, pp. 175–81.
Sharpe, R. V. (2019) "Disaggregating Data by Race Allows for More Accurate Research," *Nature Human Behavior*, 3(1240), available at: https://doi.org/10.1038/s41562-019-0696-1.
Shaw, E., Mason, C. N., Lacarte, V., and Jaregui, E. (2020) *Holding Up Half the Sky: Mothers as Workers, Primary Caregivers, and Breadwinners During COVID-19*. Washington, DC: Institute for Women's Policy Research, available at: https://iwpr.org/wp-content/uploads/2020/07/Holding-Up-Half-the-Sky-Mothers-as-Breadwinners.pdf.
Shulman, S. (1991) "Why Is the Black Unemployment Rate Always Twice as High as the White Unemployment Rate?" in R. Cornwall and P. V. Wunnava (eds.), *New Approaches to Economic and Social Analyses of Discrimination*. New York: Praeger Publishers, pp. 5–38.
Spriggs, W. E. (2020) "Is Now a Teachable Moment for Economists? An Open Letter to Economists from Bill Spriggs," Howard University Department of Economics, available at: web.archive.org/web/20201010090239/https://www.minneapolisfed.org/~/media/assets/people/william-spriggs/spriggs-letter_0609_b.pdf?la=en.
Spriggs, W. E. and Williams, R. (1996) "A Logit Decomposition Analysis of Occupational Segregation: Results for the 1970s and 1980s," *Review of Economics and Statistics*, 78(2), pp. 348–55.
Stainback, K. (2008) "Social Contacts and Race/Ethnic Job Matching," *Social Forces*, 87(2), pp. 857–86.
Stanton, E. C., Anthony, S. B., and Gage, M. J. (1881) *The History of Woman Suffrage, 1848–1920* (6 vols.). New York: Arno Press and the *New York Times*.
Steinberg, S. and Darity, W., Jr. (1985) "Human Capital: A Critique," *Review of*

Black Political Economy, 14(1), pp. 67–74, available at: https://doi.org/10.1007/bf02902610.
Stewart, J. B. and Coleman, M. (2005) "The Black Political Economy Paradigm and the Dynamics of Racial Economic Inequality," in C. Conrad, J. Whitehead, P. Mason, and J. Stewart (eds.), *African Americans in the US Economy*. Lanham, MD: Rowman and Littlefield Publishers, pp. 118–25.
Stone, A. H. (1906) *Studies in the American Race Problem*, ed. W. F. Willcox. New York: Doubleday, Page and Co.
Taibbi, M. (2014) *The Divide: American Injustice in the Age of the Wealth Gap*. New York: Spiegel and Grau.
Takaki, R. T. (1998) *Strangers from a Different Shore: A History of Asian Americans*. Updated and revised edition, 1st Back Bay edition. Boston: Little, Brown.
Tatum, B. D. (2017) *"Why Are All the Black Kids Sitting Together in the Cafeteria?" And Other Conversations about Race*. Revised edition. New York: Basic Books.
Tauheed, L. F. (2008) "Black Political Economy in the 21st Century: Exploring the Interface of Economics and Black Studies – Addressing the Challenge of Harold Cruse," *Journal of Black Studies*, 38(5), pp. 692–730.
Teixeira, P. N. (2000) "A Portrait of the Economics of Education, 1960–1997," *History of Political Economy*, 32(1), pp. 257–88.
Terborg-Penn, R. (1998) *African American Women in the Struggle for the Vote, 1850–1920*. Bloomington: Indiana University Press, available at: https://hdl.handle.net/2027/heb01762.0001.001.
Tharp, L. (2014) "I refuse to Remain in the Lower Case," Black in the World, Lori's Story, June 2, available at: https://myamericanmeltingpot.com/2014/06/02/i-refuse-to-remain-in-the-lower-case.
Tillinghast, J. A. (1902) "The Negro in Africa and America," *Publications of the American Economic Association*, 3rd series, 3(2 [May]), pp. 1–231.
Tracey, L. (2022) "The Combahee River Collective Statement: Annotated," JSTOR Daily, Annotations, available at: https://daily.jstor.org/annotations-the-combahee-river-collective-statement.
United States Department of Justice (1992) "National Drug Control Strategy: A Nation Responds to Drug Use." Washington, DC: Office of National Drug Control Policy (online), available at: www.ojp.gov/pdffiles1/ondcp/134372.pdf.
United States House of Representatives (n.d.a) "Black-American Members by Congress." History, Art, and Archives. Available at: https://history.house.gov/Exhibitions-and-Publications/BAIC/Historical-Data/Black-American-Representatives-and-Senators-by-Congress.
United States House of Representatives (n.d.b) "Historical Highlights: Immigration and Nationality Act of 1965." Available at: https://history.house.gov/Historical-Highlights/1951-2000/Immigration-and-Nationality-Act-of-1965.
United States National Archives and Records Administration (2021) "Educator Resources: Woman Suffrage and the 19th Amendment." Available at: www.archives.gov/education/lessons/woman-suffrage#background.
United States National Archives and Records Administration (2024) "14th Amendment to the US Constitution: Civil Rights (1868)." National Archives

(online), available at: www.archives.gov/milestone-documents/14th-amendment#:~:text=Passed%20by%20Congress%20June%2013,Rights%20to%20formerly%20enslaved%20people.

United States Senate Historical Office (n.d.) "Landmark Legislation: The Fourteenth Amendment." Available at: www.senate.gov/about/origins-foundations/senate-and-constitution/14th-amendment.htm.

United States Sentencing Commission (2023) "Demographic Differences in Federal Sentencing." United States Sentencing Commission, available at: www.ussc.gov/research/research-reports/2023-demographic-differences-federal-sentencing.

Valentino, L. and Yadon, N. (2023) "Intersectional Wealth Gaps: Contemporary and Historical Trends in Wealth Stratification among Single Households by Race and Gender," *Social Currents*, 10(1), pp. 3–16.

Viceisza, A. (2022) *Black Women's Retirement Preparedness and Wealth*. Washington, DC: Urban Institute, available at: www.urban.org/research/publication/black-womens-retirement-preparedness-and-wealth.

Wade, P. (2010) *Race and Ethnicity in Latin America*. 2nd edition. London: Pluto Press.

Walker, F. A. (1899) *Discussions in Economics and Statistics*. Statistics, National Growth, and Social Economics, 2. New York: Henry Holt and Company.

Walker, P. (2022) "Historical Terms and Why They Matter," Mission US News, available at: www.mission-us.org/2022/11/08/historical-terms-and-why-they-matter.

Wallace, J. M. and Goodkind, S. (2008) "Racial, Ethnic, and Gender Differences in School Discipline among US High School Students: 1991–2005," *Negro Educational Review*, 59(1–2), pp. 47–62.

Wang, W., Parker, K., and Taylor, P. (2013) *Breadwinner Moms: Mothers Are the Sole or Primary Provider in Four-in-Ten Households with Children; Public Conflicted about the Growing Trend*. Washington, DC: Pew Research Center, available at: www.pewresearch.org/social-trends/2013/05/29/breadwinner-moms.

Weaver, V. (2007) "Frontlash: Race and the Development of Punitive Crime Policy," *Studies in American Political Development*, 21(2), pp. 230–65.

Western, B. (2002) "The Impact of Incarceration on Wage Mobility and Inequality," *American Sociological Review*, 67(4), pp. 526–46.

Western, B., Kling, J. R., and Weiman, D. F. (2001) "The Labor Market Consequences of Incarceration," *Crime and Delinquency*, 47(3), pp. 410–27.

Whitten, N. and Torres, A. (1998) *Blackness in Latin America and the Caribbean: Social Dynamics and Cultural Transformations*. Bloomington: Indiana University Press.

Wicks-Lim, J. (2013) "A Stimulus for Affirmative Action? The Impact of the American Recovery and Reinvestment Act on Women and Minority Workers in Construction," in J. Wicks-Lim and R. Pollin (eds.), *Capitalism on Trial: Explorations in the Tradition of Thomas E. Weisskopf*. Cheltenham, UK and Northampton, MA: Edward Elgar, pp. 242–60.

Wicks-Lim, J. (2023) "Revising the Racial Wage Gap among Men in the United States: The Role of Nonemployment, Underemployment, and Incarceration," *Review of Black Political Economy*, 51(3), pp. 362–400.

Wicks-Lim, J. (2025) "The Persistence of Racial Inequality: The Earnings Gap among Women from 1979–2018," *Review of Black Political Economy* (online February 12), available at: https://doi.org/10.1177/00346446241301677.

Wiese, A. (2004) *Places of Their Own: African American Suburbanization in the Twentieth Century*. University of Chicago Press.

Willcox, W. F. (1899) *Negro Criminality: An Address Delivered Before the American Social Science Association at Saratoga, September 6, 1899*. Boston, MA: GEO H. Ellis, Printer, available at: https://www.loc.gov/item/06031900.

Wilkerson, I. (1989) "'African-American' Favored by Many of America's Blacks," *New York Times*, January 31, p. 1, available at: www.nytimes.com/1989/01/31/us/african-american-favored-by-many-of-america-s-blacks.html.

Wilkerson, I. (2016) "The Long-Lasting Legacy of the Great Migration," *Smithsonian Magazine* (September), available at: www.smithsonianmag.com/history/long-lasting-legacy-great-migration-180960118.

Williams, B. (2023) *Inmate Data Reallocation in the 2020 Redistricting Cycle*. National Conference of State Legislatures (NCSL), available at: www.ncsl.org/redistricting-and-census/inmate-data-reallocation-in-the-2020-redistricting-cycle.

Williams, E. (2021[1944]) *Capitalism and Slavery*. 3rd edition. Chapel Hill: University of North Carolina Press.

Williamson, V. (2020) "Closing the Racial Wealth Gap Requires Heavy, Progressive Taxation of Wealth". Washington, DC, Brookings Institution, available at: www.brookings.edu/articles/closing-the-racial-wealth-gap-requires-heavy-progressive-taxation-of-wealth.

Wilson, V. and Darity, W. A., Jr. (2022) *Understanding Black–White Disparities in Labor Market Outcomes Requires Models that Account for Persistent Discrimination and Unequal Bargaining Power*. Washington, DC: Economic Policy Institute (EPI), available at: www.epi.org/unequalpower/publications/understanding-black-white-disparities-in-labor-market-outcomes.

Wilson, V. and Jones, J. (2018) *Working Harder or Finding It Harder to Work: Demographic Trends in Annual Work Hours Show an Increasingly Fractured Workforce*. Washington, DC: Economic Policy Institute, available at: www.epi.org/publication/trends-in-work-hours-and-labor-market-disconnection.

Wilson, V. and Rodgers, W. M. (2016) *Black–White Wage Gaps Expand with Rising Inequality*. Washington, DC: Economic Policy Institute (EPI), available at: www.epi.org/files/pdf/101972.pdf.

Winlow, H. (2006) "Mapping Moral Geographies: W. Z. Ripley's Races of Europe and the United States," *Annals of the Association of American Geographers*, 96(1), pp. 119–41.

Winter, H. (2019) *The Economics of Crime: An Introduction to Rational Crime Analysis*. 2nd edition. London and New York: Routledge.

Wolff, R. D. and Resnick, S. A. (2012) *Contending Economic Theories: Neoclassical, Keynesian, and Marxian*. Cambridge, MA: MIT Press.

Wood, E. L. (2014) *Implementing Reform: How Maryland and New York Ended Prison Gerrymandering*. New York: Demos, available at:

www.demos.org/policy-briefs/implementing-reform-how-maryland-new-york-ended-prison-gerrymandering. .

Woodrum, E., Rhodes, C., and Feagin, J. R. (1980) "Japanese American Economic Behavior: Its Types, Determinants, and Consequences," *Social Forces*, 58(4), pp. 1235–54.

Wynter, S. (2006) "On How We Mistook the Map for the Territory and Re-imprisoned Ourselves in Our Unbearable Wrongness of Being, of Désêtre: Black Studies Toward the Human Project," in L. R. Gordon and J. A. Gordon (eds.), *Not Only the Master's Tools: African-American Studies in Theory and Practice*. London: Routledge, pp. 107–69.

Yi, Y. (2023) "Racial Inequality in the Prevalence, Degree, Extension, and Permeation of Incarceration in Family Life," *Demography*, 60(1), pp. 15–40.

York, E. and Hartt, M. (2023) "Sources of Personal Income, Tax Year 2020." Washington, DC: Tax Foundation. Available at: https://taxfoundation.org/data/all/federal/personal-income-tax-returns-pi-data.

Zandi, M., DeAntonio, D., Donaldson, K., and Colyar, M. (2021) "The Macroeconomic Benefits of Racial Integration," Moody's Analytics, October 6.

Index

abolitionism, 81, 98–9, 100, 149, 150, 151, 155, 258, 275-6 n.17
affirmative action, 54, 56, 57, 63–4, 168–9, 172–3, 174, 195, 246, 252, 271 n.48, 272 n. 65
AFL–CIO (American Federation of Labor and Congress of Industrial Organizations), 269 n.28
AFQT scores, 279 n.5
African American / Africana Studies / Black Studies, *see* Black Studies movement
Afro-Latinx people, 23, 65, 66–78, 79
Afro-Panamanians, 77–8
Aid to Families with Dependent Children (AFDC), 96
Alexander, Michelle, 44, 230, 244–6, 252
alliances, *see* coalitions
Amendments, Constitutional, *see* Fifteenth Amendment; Fourteenth Amendment; Nineteenth Amendment; Thirteenth Amendment
American Economic Association, 8, 123–6, 280 n.16
  Willcox School at, *see under* Willcox, Walter
American Equal Rights Association (AERA), 101–2
American Freedmen's Aid Commission (1865), 144
American Woman Suffrage Association (AWSA), 102, 104–5, 106, 259

Anderson, James, 142–3, 144, 146–7, 281 n.8
Anthony, Susan B., 100, 101
anti-Black racism
  among Latinx people, *see* Latinx community, anti-Blackness in
  definition of, 7–9, 265 n.7
  externally experienced, 66, 67–70
  forms of, 9
  and gender norms, 96
  Jim Crow, 49
  laissez-faire, 9, 39, 48–50, 51, 53, 54, 64, 186, 280 n.14
  stereotypes, *see* stereotypes, anti-Black
antidiscrimination laws, 8, 19, 40, 156, 214–15, 258
Anti-Drug Abuse Act (1986), 251, 296 n.66
Appeal to the Coloured Citizens of the World (1829), 142
Arthur, Chester A., 271 n.54
Asians, 58–62, 63, 271 n. 54
Asiatic Barred Zone Act (1917), 59
"Ask for More," 215–16
assets, 18, 197, 198, 199, 200, 201, 205, 209, 215, *see also* wealth
audit studies, 51-2, 176, 179, 181, 185, 192, 208

baby bonds, 215
Back to Africa movement, 18, 259
Bacon's Rebellion (1676), 73
Baldwin, James, 118, 169
"ban-the-box" policies, 195, 259

Banks, Nina, 96, 240, 275 n.12, 293 n. 30
Becker, Gary, 119, 126, 178
Bed-Stuy (Bedford-Stuyvesant, Brooklyn), 76
beliefs, social, 5
Belize, 77
Bell-Scott, Patricia, 20
Benjamin Roberts v. The Boston School Committee (1845), 151
Biden, Joe, 108, 216
Black Arts and Aesthetic movement, 169–72, 287 n.71
Black Codes, the (1865–7), 40, 276 n.21, 283 n.30
Black Disappearance Hypothesis, 125–6, 129
Black inferiority, myth of, 8, 11, 38, 123, 126, 129, 130, 144, 149, 168, 179
Black Lives Matter (BLM) movement, 21, 57, 259
Black Panthers, 81, 246, 259
Black Power movement, 25, 81, 169
Black Student Alliance (BSA), 170–1
Black Studies movement, 4, 25, 169–72
Blumer, Herbert, 270 n.43
Board of Education v. Dowell (1991), 285 n.59
Bobo, Lawrence, 30, 49, 50, 56, 64, 280 n.14
Brazil, 70, 76
Brooke, Edward William, 294 n.42
Brown v. Board of Education (1954), 6, 8, 156, 158, 268 n.26
Bush, George H., 250, 251

C.R.O.W.N. Act (Creating a Respectful and Open World for Natural Hair), 8
Cabral, Pedro Álvares, 70–1
capitalism, 17, 18, 20, 41, 82, 256
  capitalist competition, Marxist theory of, 41, 43, 268 n.20, 268 n.22
  definition of, 268 n.19
  industrial, 131
  laissez-faire, 21, 270 n.44, 279 n.14
capitalization, Black and White, 23–9, 266 n.30
care, communal, 275 n.11
Caribbean (including Afro-Caribbean), 25, 69, 70, 72, 76–8

Carter, Jimmy, 250, 295 n.61
Catt, Carrie, 105
Census, US, 15, 58, 68, 90, 124, 125, 199, 201, 232–4, 259
  of 1790, 73
  of 1860, 271 n.52, 291 n.2
  of 1870, 271 n.52
  of 1890, 271 n.52
  of 1940, 95
  of 1970, 73
  of 1980, 75
  of 1990, 75, 293 n.22
  of 2010, 229
  of 2020, 73
childcare costs, 208, 211–12, 218
  assistance with, 216
Chinese Exclusion Act (1882), 59, 61, 271 n.54
Chisholm, Shirley, 245
Civil Rights Act (1875), 102–3
Civil Rights Act (1964), 6, 8, 21, 41, 44, 45, 158, 159–60, 173, 177, 178, 203, 206, 224, 245, 246, 258
Civil Rights Act (1965), *see* Voting Rights Act
Civil Rights Act (1968), *see* Fair Housing Act
Civil Rights Movement, 39, 41, 44, 96, 109, 156, 158, 174, 177, 220, 246–7, 249, 254–5
  achievements of, 45, 49, 245, 248, 250, 258
  influence of, 81, 169
  integrationist phase of, 170
  intergenerational conflict in, 25
  post-Reconstruction, 103
Civil War, American, 33, 81, 98–100, 141, 142, 145, 146, 147, 149, 152, 188, 202, 220, 224
Clarke, Cheryl, 81
class struggle, 16, 18
Clinton, Bill, 250, 251
Clinton, Hillary, 107–8
coalitions, 21, 97, 106, 107–8, 109, 145, 146, 241, 259
  inter-gender, 101, 105, 260
  interracial, 98, 104, 121, 146
  intra-gender, 105
  intra-racial, 100–1, 104–5, 107, 121, 146, 241, 247, 249

Coates, Ta-Nehisi, 27
collective action, 4, 17, 21, 31, 35, 45, 79, 113, 257, 258
collective community work, unpaid, 240
colleges, public, 173, 216
Collins, Patricia Hill, 80
colonial America, Africans in, 26, 31, 32, 35, 36, 39, 64, 73, 220, 221, 257
  invention of an "exceptional race," 31–2, 38
colonization, 11, 70, 34, 35, 70–1, 266 n.2, 267 n.7
Columbus, Christopher, 71
Coman, Katherine, 280 n.21
Combahee River Collective, 19, 80–2, 274 n.1
Combahee River Raid, 81
Common School movement (1830–65), 146, 148–51, 154–5, 291 n.12
Commons, John R., 125, 130
Comprehensive Crime Control Act (1984), 250
concentration ratio, five-firm (CR5), 93, 95
Convention of 1869, 101
cooperatives, Black, 17
Costa Rica, 77
credit checks, employment, 186, 194–5
Crenshaw, Kimberlé, 19, 27, 81, 274 n.2
crime control, hypothesis of demand for, 243, 244, 247–50
criminal behavior, neoclassical economic theories of, 126–7
criminal justice system, 6, 123–32, 219–55
  stratifying function of, 220–5
criminal legal system, *see* criminal justice system
critical feminist theory, 20
critical race theory (CRT), 19–20
Crummel, Alexander, 149
Cuba (including Cubans), 68–9, 73, 77
culture
  African American (Black American, Black) 25, 69, 70, 170
  Afro-Latinx, 78
  economic theories using, 5, 8, 43, 179, 273 n.16
  efforts to eradicate Indigenous, 291 n. 5

and Eurocentrism, 10, 287 n. 71, *see also* elitism, western
  "of poverty," 8, 9, 22, 23, 29
  racism and, 9–11, 13, 26, 31–2, 38, 43
  West African, 69, 78

Darity, William A., Jr., 4, 6, 41, 43, 62, 75, 120, 142, 178, 215, 258, 224, 266 n.2
Davis, Angela, 92, 221, 259
Davis, Kathy, 80
decolonization, 10
Democratic Party, 61, 101, 102–3, 107, 143, 146–7, 156, 247, 249, 250, 275–6 n.17
discrimination theories
  neoclassical economic theories of, 3, 18, 113, 119, 127, 176
  statistical theory of, 182–3
  taste for discrimination theory, 113, 119, 126, 178, 242
discriminatory practices
  education, 286 n. 61
  employers, *see* employers, role in anti-Black practices
  employment, *see* employment, anti-Black practices; employment, discrimination in
  ex-felons, 178, 180, 230–1, 292 n.21
  hairstyles, 8
  housing, 12, 41, 50, 53, 152, 157, 248, 283–4 n. 39
  life insurance, 280, n.22
  mortgages, 12, 14, 117, 157, 203, 283–4 n. 39, *see also* mortgage lending, predatory; redlining
  see also racism
disenfranchisement, 7, 15, 16, 183, 193, 225, 233, 241
  of Black men, 40, 103
  of Black women, 40, 103, 105–6
division of labor, sexual, 188–9
domination, matrix of, 80
Dominican Republic (including Dominicans), 68–9, 74, 76–7
"double gap" in earnings/wages, 204–5, 208–9, 213, 215
"Double V" campaign, 284 n.49
Douglas, Davison, 148, 149, 151, 153, 157, 282 n.22

Douglass, Frederick, 282 n.24
Du Bois, W. E. B., 33, 102, 103, 130, 142, 143, 144, 146–7, 149, 161, 173, 276 n.32, 277 n.46, 281 n.8

early decisions (ED), college application, 167
earnings, weekly, 136, 137–8, 140, 207, 236
earnings ratio, Black–White, 45–7, 83–5, 178
economic theory, stratification, 4–7, 17, 23, 67, 113–14, 117–19, 120–1, 176–7, 178, 179, 198, 241–2, 254, 255, 256, 258
  intersectional approach to, 79–109
economics, 3, 6, 7, 15–16, 129, 131
  laissez-faire economics, 279 n.14
  mainstream, 43, 115, 116, 119, 240, 254, 256, 293 n.29
  neoclassical, 114, 115, 120, 122, 123, 126–7, 137, 176, 179, 254
economies, market-based, 4, 179
education, 114–19, 133–75
  access to, 14, 44, 115, 118, 119, 121, 133, 139, 141–74, 175
  as "great differentiator," 133
  as "great equalizer," 115, 133
  as source of economic power, 143–4
  as source of political power, 141–3
  as source of social power, 141, 144, 174
  attainment in, 6, 7, 16, 66, 115, 117–20, 133, 134–8, 139–41, 176, 178, 179, 181, 186, 189, 190, 193, 197, 205, 206, 212
  disciplinary practices, unequal, 163–4
  economics of, 114–19
  "educational clause," in labor contracts, 145
  laws prohibiting, 141–4, 281 n.9, 281 n.10, 281 n. 12
  "native schools," 145, 258
  political economy of, 141–55
  postsecondary, 164–74, 216, 282 n.21, 286 n.64, see also higher education
  postsecondary admissions criteria, racist, 166–9
  primary, 162–4
  public, development in North, 148–51, 153–5, 282 n.23, see also Common School movement
  public, development in South, 145–8, 151–2, 155
  resources, 6, 14, 44, 141, 147, 150, 154, 155, 158, 162, 164, 165, 168, 169, 172, 173, 174
  returns to (rewards from), 114–16, 136–41
  secondary, 162–4
Eisenhower, Dwight D., 295 n.54
Elementary and Secondary Education Act (ESEA) (1965), 158, 246
elitism, western, 81, see also culture, and Eurocentrism
Ely, Richard, 123, 124–5, 131, 280 n.16
emancipation, 16, 73, 125, 188, 189, 198, 202–3, 210, 215, 222
Emmet Till Antilynching Act (HR 55), 224
employers, role in anti-Black practices, 180–2, 185, 208
employment, 4, 151, 153, 199, 246
  affirmative action in, 56, 246
  anti-Black practices, 51, 92, 152, 154, 193–4, 269 n. 28, see also employers, role in anti-Black practices
  Asian, patterns of, 59–62
  discrimination in, 54–6, 160, 177, 181–2, 185–6, 203, 206, 213, 230–1, see also audit studies
  education attainment, role of, 6, 15, 115, 136–9, 154, 160, 181–2
  gender disparities in, 86–9
  networks, role of, 184
  policy solutions to anti-Black practices, 41, 177, 194–6, 206
  racial disparities in, 7, 45–8, 64, 86, 89–96, 138–9, 154, 186–7, 238
  racism in, 44–8, 64, 89–96, 160, 186 see also unemployment
Enforcement Acts (1870–1), 102
enfranchisement, 103, 155
  Black, 41
  Black men, 40, 102–3, 277 n.41
  Black women, 40, 106, 277 n. 45
  White men, 275 n. 16
  women, 105
Equal Pay Act (1963), 214
eugenics, 27, 73, 124, 125, 130, 131, 280 n.15

Evers, Medgar, 285 n.55
Executive Order 11246 (1965), 246
ex-felons, discrimination against, *see* discriminatory practices, ex-felons
expenditure, 197, 199, 205, 211–12, 218, 243, 252
exploitation, labor, 13, 17, 38, 60, 143, 266 n.2
externalities, 17–18

Fair Housing Act (1968), 41, 44, 45, 158, 245, 258
Fair Labor Standards Act (FLSA) (1938), 92–3
false consciousness, 16
Fanon, Frantz, 11, 267 n.7
Federal Housing Administration (FHA), 12, 157
feminism, 6, 19, 80, 96, 99, 101
  Black, 19–20, 27, 79, 81–2
  economic theory, 20, 240
  racism in, 104, 240
  second wave, 260
  see also critical feminist theory
Ferreira Da Silva, Denise, 70–1
Fifteenth Amendment, 40, 102, 103–4, 151, 258
"flight toward Whiteness,"75
Floyd, George, 21
Ford, Gerald, 295 n.61
"forty acres and a mule," 198
Fourteenth Amendment, 40, 99, 100–1, 102, 103, 151, 258, 275 n.16, 276 n.27, 277 n.41
Franklin, Benjamin, 33
Frazier, Demita, 81
Freedman's Bureau (Bureau of Refugees, Freedmen and Abandoned Lands), 144–5, 276 n.21, 282 n. 16
Freedom Riders, 245, 259
freedpeople, 143, 144, 145, 146, 147, 222, 258
Freeman v. Pitts (1992), 285 n.59

game theory, 269 n.29
Garvey, Marcus, 18, 259
GDP (Gross Domestic Product), 187, 256
gender, 30, 51, 177, 179, 184, 187, 189, 198, 199, 209, 213, 259
  and mass incarceration, *see* incarceration, mass, gendered impact of
  and sexual oppression, 81
  inter-gender coalitions, 101, 105, 107–8, 260
  occupational segregation by, 89–91
  oppression, *see* sexism
  racist norms of, 96
  social construction of, 20
  "street race-gender," 75
  unemployment by, 88–9, 139
  wage differences by, 83–5
gender differences, intra-racial, 204
"gender gap," 85–6, 192–3, 194, 197, 201, 203, 205, 206, 208, 214
gender studies, 4
gender-only analysis, 85, 89–90, 97
"Gentleman's Agreement," the (1907), 59
Goldwater, Barry, 247, 248
Gordon Nembhard, Jessica, 17, 216
Grant, Madison, 26, 33
Great Migration, the (1910–40, first wave; 1940–70, second wave), 153, 155–6, 193, 243, 245, 246, 255, 284 n.45
GSS (General Social Survey), 270 n.42

hair and African ancestry, 8, 76
Hall, Stuart, 10
Hamer, Fannie Lou, 21, 259
Hamilton, Darrick, 75, 215, 273
Hammond, Matthew Brown, 280 n.21
Hannah-Jones, Nikole, 27, 36, 267 n.2
Harper, Frances E. W., 82, 101
Harris, Cheryl, 34
Harris, Kamala, 108
Hawkins, Yusef, 9
Hayes Act (Hayes Compromise) (1877), 103, 146
healthcare, 12, 49, 95, 128, 149, 206, 244, 275 n.7
  mental, 217
hierarchy, racial, 49, 51, 128, 155, 224, 242, 243, 245, 246, 247, 250, 254–5, 261
  antebellum, 146
  durability (persistence) of, 39–41, 257–8
  privilege in, 44

restructuring of, 102, 103, 223, 244
role in social hierarchy, 57, 64, 148, 161, 219
higher education, 14, 63, 168, 171, 173
hiring practices, 183–4
historical womanist theory (HWT), 20–1
Historically Black Colleges and Universities (HBCUs), 171, 173–4, 259, 282 n.21, 287 n.73
Hoffman, Frederick, 125, 129–30
homeownership, rates of, 7, 12, 16, 21, 70, 157, 200, 209–10, 214, 256
hooks, bell, 10
Horton, Willie, 250
Hossein, Caroline, 18
household work, private
  as focus of White women, 240
  concentration of Black women in, 90–2, 177, 206
households, 3, 48, 62, 96, 122, 139, 141, 157, 189, 197, 201, 202, 203, 205, 209–10, 212, 235, 237, 239
  lower income, 215
  two-parent, 238
  with children, 211
housing discrimination, 12, 41, 50, 53, 152
HR 6963 (antilynching bill), 223
Hull, Akasha, 20, 81
human capital theory (HCT), 6, 115, 116, 120, 178, 179

ideologies, racist, 10, 31, 38, 79
Immigration Act (1924), 59, 61
Immigration Act (Hart–Cellar Act) (1965), 59–60, 61
imperfect (insufficient, inaccurate) information, 5, 183, 242
incarceration, mass, 13, 41, 122, 132, 219, 220, 226–9, 245, 251, 252, 254, 260, 291 n.14
  gendered impact of, 234–41
  impact on civil rights, 230–4, 292 n.21
  racial disparities in, 228–34, 236, 237, 254
  rates of, 67, 180, 222, 225–6, 233, 244, 256
income, 17, 43, 48, 64, 67, 83, 114, 121–2, 197, 198, 199, 215, 216, 238, 256, 260

disparities in, 44, 53, 205, 209
earnings and, 45–7
household, 66, 165, 211
median, 62
mobility, 244
role in college admissions, 14, 166–7
and wealth, 200–1, 202, 208
indentured servitude, 35–6, 37, 73
Indigenous Americans, 287 n.77, 291 n.5
inequality, economic, 3, 5, 41, 44, 54, 85
  blamed on Black people's choices, 50
integrated schools, 151, 153, 154, 161, 162, 282 n.25
  abuse of Black students, 283 n.25, 284 n. 43
intelligence agencies, 287 n.73
intersectional analysis, 19–20, 23, 79–80, 81, 82, 83–108, 109, 113, 198, 204, 256, 259, 260, 275 n.2

Jackson, Jesse, 25, 295 n.50
Jackson, Ketanji Brown, 173
Jet magazine, 171
Jim Crow era (1877–1964), 16, 23, 28, 40, 41, 45, 49, 50, 64, 73, 103–5, 122, 153, 156, 203, 220, 224, 245, 246
Jiménez Román, Miriam, 72
Johnson, Andrew, 99, 276 n.22
Johnson, Lyndon B., 32, 158, 168, 245–6, 275 n.17
Jones, Jacqueline, 31, 34, 36, 38, 92, 267 n.2

Kansas election (1867), 100–2
Kennedy, John F., 158, 247, 275 n.17, 285 n.55
Keynes, John Maynard, 280 n.15
Kim, Jean Claire, 60–1, 62–3
King, Martin Luther, Jr., 170, 246
Knights of White Camelia, 102
Ku Klux Klan, 102, 153

labor
  bonded, 35–7
  enslaved, *see* slavery
  forced, 146, 229, 230
  Indigenous, 35–36
  "reserve army of," 17, 268 n.22
  shortages, 62, 145

labor force participation rate (LFPR), 45, 46, 85, 95–7, 109, 187–9, 275 n.11
labor market, 13, 23, 47, 50, 67, 88, 116, 119–21, 126, 128, 138, 154, 214, 236, 256
  competition, 43, 114
  discrimination in, 50, 176–82, 197, 195–6, 208
  earnings, 174
  inequality in, 4, 117, 122, 155, 259
  racial disparities in, 125, 184–93, 213
Labor Quality theory, 120, 179
land theft, 122, 203
language, role of, 24–5
Latinas, Black or Afro-, 75–6, 204, 209
Latinx community, anti-Blackness in, 66–78
law enforcement response hypothesis, 243, 244, 250–2
laws, anti-Black, 15, 37, 64, 105, 150, 203, *see also* Jim Crow era
Lee, Sheila Jackson, 217
legacy preferences, college admissions, 14, 166
lesbians, 19, 81, 274 n.1
liberation movements, Black, 81–2, 169, *see also* Civil Rights Movement
literacy, 104, 142, 143, 209, 282 n.9, 282 n.10
living standards, 4, 54
Lorde, Audre, 81, 169
Loury, Glenn, 27, 266 n.30, 270 n.47
lynchings, 40, 103, 105, 152, 223, *see also* Emmet Till Antilynching Act

McCray, Chirlane, 81
McWhorter, John, 266 n.30
Mann, Horace, 278 n.3
March on Washington for Jobs and Economic Freedom (1963), 158, 245
Martin, Trayvon, 21
Marxist theory, 16–17, 20, 41, 43
Mason, Patrick, 75, 123, 128–9, 278 n.1
Mexico (including Mexicans), 68, 69, 73, 74
mestizaje, 72–3
migration, Black, 46, 69, 77, 153, 157, 258, *see also* Great Migration

military, federal, 156, 171, 282 n.19
minimum wage, federal, 93
Missouri v. *Jenkins* (1995), 285 n.59
"model" minorities, 62, 63
monopolies, 41, 56, 63, 64, 98, 141, 268 n.20
  in labor markets, 43–4
Montgomery, James, 81
Moreno Vega, Marta, 76
Morrison, Toni, 29, 32
mortgage lending, predatory, 12, 14, 203
multiracial analysis, 57–64
mutually constitutive, racial groups as, 28, 62–4
Myers Jr., Samuel, 17, 123, 128–9, 225–8, 254
"Mystic Years" (1867–73), 102

NAACP (National Association for the Advancement of Colored People), 156, 277 n.46, 284 n.49
Nadir, the (1873–1930), 40, 46, 98, 102–8, 152
Nat Turner rebellion, 142
National Action Network, 9, 259
National American Women's Suffrage Association (NAWSA), 104–6, 259
National Association of Colored Women (NACW), 92, 105
National Black Feminist Organization (NBFO), 82
National Socialist Feminist Conference (1975), 82
National Women's Party (NWP), 106
National Women's Suffrage Association (NWSA), 102, 103, 259
Nationalism, Black, 18, 81
Nationality Act (1790), 272 n.58
"Negro suffrage," *see* suffrage movement, "Negro suffrage"
New Deal, 12, 93, 193, 284 n.47
Nineteenth Amendment, 6, 40, 98, 105, 106
Nixon, Richard, 160, 248–9, 285 n.58, 295 n.54, 295 n.61

Obama, Barack, 22, 107, 108, 259
occupational crowding, 6, 179, 180, 181, 197
  Black women and, 192–3

cause of "double gap," 205
  and wage differentials, 189–92
"octoroon," 73
Okazawa-Rey, Margo, 81
Omnibus Anti-Drug Abuse Act (1988), 251
"one-drop" rule, 73
"opportunity hoarding," 191

Panama, 77–8
Panic of 1873, 102
parental rights, 221, 235
pay transparency, 213–14
Percent minority effect hypothesis, 245–7
phenotypical attributes, 3, 67, 70, 75
"pink-collar" work, 205
Plessy v. Ferguson (1896), 283 n.33
police, 13, 14, 57, 103, 123, 128, 219, 246, 247
policies, anti-Black, 6, 7–8, 23, 50, 66, 70, 73, 150, 179, 197
policing and corrections expenditure, trends in, 243, 244, 251, 252
policy intervention, 4, 9, 22, 23, 39, 50, 64, 78, 179, 195, 198
political agency, role of education in, 117–18, 221
political economy, 4, 6, 7, 16
  Black, 17–18
  simultaneity, 81
political organizing, urban, 241, 246
Poor People's Movement, 246
Portugal (including Portuguese), 70–1
"post-racial" environment, 73
poverty, 7, 15, 16, 66, 67, 70, 76, 92, 124, 126, 160, 162, 200, 221, 238
  "culture of," *see* culture, "of poverty"
  student, 285 n.60
  "War on", *see* "War on Poverty"
Powell, James, 246
prejudice, 9, 11, 14, 33, 63, 186, 242
"pre-market," 115, 179
presidential elections
  1920, 106
  1964, 247, 248
  1968, 248
  1972, 249, 250
  1976, 250
  1980, 249
  1984, 249

  1988, 249, 250
  1992, 250
  1996, 250
  2016, 57, 107
  2020, 108
prison gerrymandering, 232–4
prison labor, 230, 292 n.19
  contract systems, 230
  convict lease system, 105, 230
private household work, *see* household work, private
Progressive era, American (1896–1917), 124, 131
Progressivist German Historical School, 124
property, race as a produced form of, 17
property owners, Southern, 143, 146
psychology, social, 4, 5
public policy remedies, resistance to, 50–1, 54–7
public school system, 41, 103, 164, 246, 258
  see also education, public, development in North; education, public, development in South; school desegregation; school segregation
Puerto Rico (including Puerto Ricans), 68–9, 74, 76–7
Pullman Porters, the, 21, 259
punishment, 40, 99, 189, 219, 221, 222, 223, 224, 229, 252
  racialized patterns of, 220, 225

Quakers, 150, 155

race, as biological classification, 3, 30, 49, 64, 73, 126, 131
race, construction of, 30–65
  endogeneity of, 120, 257
race, social significance of, 31–9, 44–5, 220–1
  maintenance of, 39–57
race and ethnicity, intersection of, *see* intersectional analysis
Race Suicide Theory, 124–5, 129, 130–1
racial integration in education, limits to, 162–74
racial superiority, internalized belief in, 9, 10

racial threat theory, 241–5, 254
racism
  anti-Black, *see* anti-Black racism
  institutional, 6, 9, 11–14, 15, 180, 185–6, 257, 265 n.11
  internalized, 9–11, 12, 74, 75, 265 n.10
  interpersonal, 9, 11, 12, 13, 14, 15
  legalized forms of, 37, 166–9
  structural, 13, 14–15, 179, 180, 186, 257
  typology of, 9–13
Rainbow Coalition, 246, 259
"rainbow people," 72, 75
rational choice, individual, 113, 123, 126
rationality, 5, 15, 18, 30, 44, 71, 80, 113, 128, 132, 183–4, 242, 257, *see also* self-interest
Reagan, Ronald, 63, 249, 250, 260, 285 n.58
Reconstruction Act (1867), 99
Reconstruction era (1865–77), 16, 33, 40, 61, 92, 99, 103, 141, 147, 220, 222, 245, 260
  Second, 246
Red Shirts, 102
Red Summer, 106, 223
redlining, 12, 122, 203
reparations, 122, 198, 217, 259, 261
  HR 40, 217
representation, political, 99, 233, 234, 245, 259
  Black members of Congress, 103, 105, 223, 269 n.27
reproductive capacities, exploitation of, 20, 189, 217
Republican Party, 101, 102, 103–4, 107, 151, 152, 154, 156, 247, 248–9, 250, 275-6 n.17
"reserve army of labor," *see* labor, "reserve army of"
residential discrimination, *see* discriminatory practices, housing
resource hoarding, 6, 44, 67, 103, 118, 150, 153, 154, 158, 162, 164–5, 168, 242, 255
retirement, 199, 200, 205, 208, 209, 214, 215
"richer pool" theory, 183, 184
Ripley, William Z., 131
Rizo v. *Yovino*, 194, 213–14

Roberts, Dorothy, 37, 44, 238–9, 241, 267 n.2
Roediger, David, 33, 34
Roosevelt, Franklin D., 12, 93, 193, 284 n.47
Roosevelt, Theodore, 59, 131
Ross, Edward A., 125, 131
Ruffin, Josephine St Pierre, 277 n.43

salary histories, requesting, 186, 194, 213, 214
Santería, practice of, 78
school desegregation, 160, 260, 282 n.24, 282 n.25, 285 n.58, 285 n.59, 268–9 n.26
  see also integrated schools
school segregation, 150, 151, 174, 252, 283 n.31, 283 n.33
  de facto, 155, 159
  de jure, 155–6, 168, 173, 284 n.51
  21st-century, 155–56
segregation, 8, 23, 103, 125, 148, 149, 153–5, 175, 177, 184, 241, 242, 243, 248
  de facto, 50, 51, 248
  de jure, 50
  hotels, 283 n.39
  occupational, 89–95, 190, 203, 252, 268 n.25, 275 n.7
  residential (housing), 12, 14, 40, 50, 116–17, 152, 153, 174, 284 n.39, 284 n.40
  see also Jim Crow
self-determination, Black, 10, 18, 25, 71, 143
self-identification, racial, 67, 73, 74, 78
self-interest, 5, 130, 279 n.14
  collective, 4, 30, 79, 98, 113
  individual, 113
Seneca Falls Convention (1848), 98
sexism, 4, 6, 19, 20, 76, 80–1, 96, 105, 108, 181, 189, 240, 293 n.31
sexual abuse, 92
sexual violence, racialized, 92, 189, 293 n.31
Sharpe, Rhonda, 83, 274 n.3
Sharpton, Al, 9, 259
skin color, 10, 30, 31–2, 33, 40, 131
  and legal status, 37–8
skin tone, 30, 31, 75, 76

slave codes, 37–8, 221
slavery, African, 8, 36–9, 60, 61, 73, 96, 122, 144, 189, 198, 217, 221
 abolition of, 41, 98–9, 142, 149, 197, 222
 Black culture under, 31
 labor supply, 37, 61, 31
 legality of, 40, 99, 229, 292 n.16
 political infrastructure of, 31–9
 rationalizations of, 38, 49, 130, 149, 257, 260 n.2
 trade, 37, 38, 74, 77, 78, 267 n.10
Smith, Adam, 7
Smith, Barbara, 19–20, 81
Social and Solidarity Economy (SSE), 18
Social Darwinism, 124
social economy, Black, 18
social group
 as unit of analysis, 4, 5, 18, 57, 67, 120–1, 132, 179, 242, 257
 identity formation, 5, 24–7, 29, 32–4, 69, 120, 148, 154, 240, 257
socialism, 82
sociology, 4, 5, 7, 15, 30
Sojourner Truth, 82, 188, 259
Sowell, Thomas, 270 n.47
Special Field Order 15, 99
Spriggs, William, 116, 220, 280 n.20, *see also* "Two-bus theory"
Stanton, Elizabeth Cady, 100, 101, 104
stereotypes, anti-Black, 11, 12, 39, 50, 51, 52, 53, 76
Stewart, James, 4, 269 n.29
Stone, Alfred Holt, 130
"stop and frisk," 14
stratification, social, 4, 31, 36, 89, 132
stratification economics, *see* economic theory, stratification
structure, occupational, 93, 120
student loan debt, 165, 212
 forgiveness of, 216
suffrage movement
 "educated suffrage," 104
 "Negro suffrage," 100–2
 universal (1848–77), 98–102
 White woman, 102–8
 woman, 97–8
 "woman-suffrage-first,", 100–1
supply and demand, laws of, 119
Supreme Court, US, 6, 8, 103, 156, 160, 167, 173, 194, 214, 245, 272 n.65, 283 n.33, 285 n.59

Terborg-Penn, Rosalyn, 104–5, 275 n.14, 276 n.30, 277 n.43
Terrell, Mary Church, 82
terrorism, White, 102, 122, 152, 153, 224, 239, 277 n.38, 285 n.55, *see also* Red Summer; Tulsa massacre
Thirteenth Amendment, 6, 40, 99, 221, 229, 258, 276 n.21, 292 n.16
Thompson, Edgar T., 267 n.8
Tillinghast, Joseph, 125
Title VII (of 1964 Civil Rights Act), 177, 206
"tracking" in education, 153, 162, 164, 173
triangulation, racial, 60, 63
Trump, Donald, 57, 107–8, 271 n.49, 278 n.51
Tubman, Harriet, 19, 81, 82
Tulsa massacre (1921), 277 n.50
Tupinambá people, 70, 71
"Two-bus theory," 116–17, 280 n.20

Underground Railroad, 81, 259
unemployment, 6, 7, 8, 21, 45, 66, 67, 70, 176, 177, 181–2, 197, 200, 236, 252
 Black, 16, 22, 54, 221
 definition of, 281 n.3
 disparities in, 85–9, 109
 rate differentials, 136–7, 139, 184–7
 White, 22, 54
 see also employment
urban ghetto, 241, 246–7, 293 n.31
utility, 15, 113, 119, 178

violence, White supremacist, 27, 40, 102, 103, 146, 152, 171, 282 n.25, 285 n.55, *see also* terrorism, White
Violent Crime Control and Law Enforcement Bill (1994), 251–2
Virginia Slave Codes, 221
voting patterns, 107, 248
Voting Rights Act (1965), 41, 44, 45, 106, 158, 245, 258, 269 n.27

wage
 differentials, 176, 178–9, 181, 189–92, 193, 208
 disadvantage, 83–5

wage (cont.)
  "double gap" in, 192–3, 198–9, 204–9
  hierarchical, 120
  inequality, 6, 109, 83–5, 197
  "psychological," 33
  trend, relative 83–5
Walker, David, 142
Walker, Frances Amasa, 123, 124
Wallace, George, 243, 248
"War on Crime," 252
"War on Drugs," 249, 250, 251
"War on Poverty," 245
wealth
  accumulation, 12, 14, 114, 199, 204–5, 208, 209–10
  definition, 281 n.4
  gender inequality and, 203–4
  inequality, 48, 122, 160, 201, 202, 203, 259, 260
  intergenerational, 5, 210
  lack of, 165–6
  measuring, 199
  racial inequality and, 201–3
welfare programs, 96, 231, 235, 246
Wells, Ida B., 82
West African culture, see culture, West African

White supremacy, 24, 26, 40, 49, 98, 102, 103, 105, 122, 143, 145, 146, 149, 152, 171
  institutions of, 104
  internalized, 10
  preservation of, 13, 106
  violence of, see violence, White supremacist
whiteness, 10, 26–7, 28, 63, 72, 221
  as monopoly on social advantages, 41–4
  "becoming White," 34
  construction of, 32–4
  flight toward, 75
Willcox, Walter, 123, 124, 125–6, 130
  Willcox School, 125–6, 129
Williams, Eric, 37, 38, 266 n.2
Williams, John Bell, 248
Williams, Rhonda, 4, 41, 43
Williams, Walter, 270 n.47
womanhood, cult of, 188, 189
work ethic, 70
working conditions, 4, 21, 35, 61, 90, 92, 230, 272 n.56
World War II, 47, 156, 203, 224

X, Malcolm, 169